Producer Power | at the Bargaining Table

Producer Power | at the Bargaining Table

A Case Study of the
Legislative Life of S. 109

Randall E. Torgerson

University of Missouri Press
Columbia, Missouri

Standard Book Number 8262–0091–5
Library of Congress Card Number 76–113817
Printed and bound in the
United States of America
Copyright © 1970 by
The Curators of the University of Missouri

To my parents
Truman and Ruth Torgerson
Who taught me the virtues
of perseverance

Preface

Producer Power at the Bargaining Table is a case study of the legislative life of Senate Bill S. 109 and the changing power structure surrounding farm legislation in Washington. The study has three dimensions. First, it examines the issue of farm bargaining and the considerations given to this new idea by various segments of the agricultural industry. These include the issues associated with farm marketing and bargaining, and particularly the structural and functional relations of various farm organizations as they adapt to a rapidly changing economic environment. Secondly, the study traces a recent piece of farm sponsored legislation through the arena of lobby group coalitions, Administration deliberations, governmental agency interaction, and congressional committees. Thirdly, it casts some light on the changing balance of farm power on Capitol Hill and the lessons to be learned from it.

The study follows a pattern employed only infrequently in the past by political economists such as Charles M. Hardin in his book *The Politics of Agriculture*. Yet, economics carries a rich tradition of studies of changing working rules and institutional arrangements. A good share of these focus on case histories derived from court litigation proceedings.

One way to examine the issues is through the axes of orientation of pressure groups. Unlike the solely geographical structure on which the legislative bodies are organized and the professional nature of appointed members of the Executive Branch, the economic pressure groups represent special interests along occupational lines. John R. Commons, past leader of the institutional approach to the discipline of economics, regarded the economic pressure groups of America as comprising an occupational parliament that was more truly representative than the Congress elected by territorial divisions. Commons suggested that such groups, especially labor unions, general farm interest organizations, and farm cooperatives, were the most vital institutions in our society. He saw them as the lifeblood of democracy.

Maintenance of a climate in which the economic pressure groups can thrive in our contemporary environment may be looked upon as one means of maintaining a viable democracy. Thirty years ago Commons expressed this idea in *Institutional Economics II* (pp. 902–903).

> The rights of man are now his rights of free association . . . the civil liberties that make possible the voluntary association of labor unions, farmers' unions, business cooperatives, and political parties. It is these associations rather than the older individualism of free individual action, that are the refuge of modern Liberalism and Democracy from Communism, Fascism, or Banker Capitalism.

That the freedom to associate in interest groups or pressure groups constitutes one of our most basic freedoms has been recently noted by Harold F. Breimyer in *Individual Freedom and the Economic Organization of Agriculture.*

The idea that group interests are fundamental determinants of economic and political behavior has been espoused most recently by political scientists. Such writers as Arthur Bently, Earl Latham and David Truman have carried forth these ideas in their treatment of group behavior and pressure group theories. The parallel with the older institutional approach is striking. Recent studies by political scientists which incorporate these theories include Hadwiger and Talbot's *Pressures and Protests*, a case analysis of the Kennedy farm programs, Lester W. Milbrath's *The Washington Lobbyists*, a study of lobbyists and their groups presently active in Washington and Donald R. Hall's *Cooperative Lobbying — The Power of Pressure.*

Like other organizations in our society, the economic pressure groups must adapt to the changing social, political and economic environment of which they are a part. At times the legislatures are called upon to give protection to such organizations so that they may adapt to change and function in a new environment. The interdependence is mutual. While various interest groups are responsible for helping to improve the legislative process, the Congress is also responsible for fostering an environment for the development and growth of representative associations.

The story of S. 109 is best examined from such a viewpoint. It focuses on the first attempts by farm organizations to provide by legislation protection and institutional arrangements to enable farm bargaining to become established as a working part of the pricing mechanism. Much of the debate over this new process took place among pressure groups on an informal basis and off the record. The official positions of each organization were then presented in public hearings before congressional committees.

S. 109 traversed three such hearings in the Senate and one in the House of Representatives. Much of the information for this study is derived from the public record of the hearings, where much of the formal sparring took place, by tracing official organization positions on various issues. Congressional hearings are designed to permit all legitimate groups to express their views. Witnesses on both sides of questions have an opportunity to be heard, and their testimony is recorded and later published. Commenting on his observations of testimony presented by various interest groups at the June, 1966, Senate hearing on S. 109, Mr. Payanides, a member of the Cyprus legislature and agriculture committee, said, "Mr Chairman, if I may, this is not democracy in words but in action."

The study of S. 109 as the bill was conceived and guided through the legislative arena offers an exciting look at the conflicts engendered by pet philosophies and at the exercise of coordinated action in the legislative process. From the blow by blow account, the student of legislative process and farm policy should gain valuable insights into the interworking of economic pressure groups.

The book is written with several intents in mind.

First, I hope it will provide a stimulus that is both instructive and informative to farm leaders and students of farm organization development and legislative process in general.

Secondly, the reader should gain some insights into issues basic to the problem of farm bargaining. The struggle over S. 109 among farm organizations, some defensive and some divisive, should offer many lessons for future bargaining proposals.

Finally, as any case study must, the story of S. 109 will document a point in time. It is one that cannot be repeated.

Columbia, Missouri   R.E.T.
September, 1969

Acknowledgments

This book was written while I was conducting research under a Post Doctoral Fellowship at the University of Missouri. Initial probings into the legislative life of S. 109 revealed issues that were familiar to me based upon past research in Europe and at the University of Wisconsin. These issues served as a stimulus to dig further.

Early in my investigation, Robert Heiney, Legislative Director of the National Canners Association, suggested that S. 109 should be analyzed in terms of the broad issue of farm bargaining and not in terms of an isolated piece of farm legislation. I acknowledged his suggestion in subsequent work.

Sources of information for this study included personal interviews with lobbyists of numerous farm and non-farm groups, key legislators, legislative assistants, congressional committee staff, government personnel and other leaders involved in the bill; hearing records; news organs, and file materials. I am especially indebted to leaders in the American Farm Bureau Federation, the National Council of Farmer Cooperatives, the National Canners Association, the Ohio Farm Bureau and the Farmer Cooperative Service of the USDA for supplying source material. William Haffert's running commentary on S. 109 in the *Broiler Industry* magazine, beginning in 1966, was also most helpful in piecing together the story behind the measure.

I owe a special debt of gratitude to Harold F. Breimyer, a friend and colleague, for his meticulous reading of several drafts of this manuscript and for his critical and constructive comments. Other colleagues who offered their timely comments were Professors Jerry West, Dale Colyer and V. James Rhodes of the Department of Agricultural Economics, University of Missouri. David Leuthold, a Professor of Political Science and Director of the Public Opinion Survey Unit at the University of Missouri, was most helpful as a consultant during preparation of this manuscript and later as a reader.

Finally, I would thank my dear wife, Susan, for her patience and forbearance. Family harmony, through many long weekends and nights of burning the midnight oil, was only possible through her diligent efforts — efforts that were truly remarkable, given her pursuit of a Master of Music Degree even while this book was being written.

Errors in fact or judgment are, of course, my responsibility.

Contents

Abbreviations xiv

Glossary xv

1. The Problem 1

2. Initial Drafting 19

3. A Rocky Road: Early Promoting and Positioning 35

4. A Bitter Fight Looms 53

5. The Agricultural Producers Marketing Act: A New Bill 74

6. 1967: Year of Debate, Compromise and Fallout 94

7. 1967 Senate Hearing: All Hands on Deck 114

8. Compromise and Fallout 131

9. Amend or Kill 153

10. Horsetrading in Fresno, Horseplay on the House Floor 184

11. An Idea Takes Hold: The Meaning and Significance of S. 109 . . 205

Appendixes
A. Agricultural Bargaining Laws of California, Ohio and Oregon . . 235

B. Forms of S. 109 — 1964–1968 240

C. Substitute Versions of S. 109 Proposed by National
Council of Farmer Cooperatives and National
Milk Producers Federation 309

D. The Agricultural Marketing and Bargaining Act of 1969 319

Abbreviations

Farm pressure groups active in lobbying on S. 109.

AFB   American Farm Bureau Federation

AAMA   American Agricultural Marketing Association

NCFC   National Council of Farmer Cooperatives

NMPF   National Milk Producers Federation

NFU   National Farmers Union

NFO   National Farmers Organization

Trade groups active in lobbying on S. 109.

NCA   National Canners Association

NBC   National Broiler Council

NTEA   National Tax Equality Association

AFMA   American Feed Manufacturers Association

Departments or agencies of the United States Government.

USDA   United States Department of Agriculture

FCS   Farmer Cooperative Service

C&MS   Consumer and Marketing Service

ASCS   Agricultural Stabilization and Conservation Service

P&S   Packers and Stockyards Administration

FTC   Federal Trade Commission

Glossary

Farm organizations.   Any form of group action through which farm operators represent their economic and related interests. This general term
refers to cooperatives and bargaining associations as well as to general
farm groups.

General farm interest organization.   An organization through which farm
operators represent their professional interests along economic, social
and political lines. Generally, such organizations represent a mere horizontal combination of producers on a cross-commodity basis and do
not handle physical product flows.

Bargaining association.   A combination of farm operators, often organized
along commodity lines, for purposes of negotiating farm prices. Such
associations' activities are often synonymous with those of general farm
interest organizations.

Cooperative.   A business organization owned and controlled by farm
operators and operated for them on a cost basis. Such an organization
may handle the product flow from farmers to consumers, or it may
handle only one or more steps in the product flow.

Handler.   Anyone, other than an association of farmers, who purchases
raw farm products for purposes of selling them again in their marketing
area. A handler may be a conglomerate, corporate subsidiary, or privately owned processor or dealership.

Congressional Movement of S. 109	Legislative Highlights	External Events Having an Impact on S. 109
1950-1960		Cannery Growers, Inc. organized in 1950 (Ohio tomato case) NFO organized, Nov., 1955 AAMA organized, 1959 & incorporated, Jan., 1960
1961-1963 Bargaining bill drafted by AFB	Aggressive push by Ohio FB for bargaining legislation	Broiler grower blacklist generates widespread publicity (Arkansas broiler case) Freeman-Cochrane supply control measures defeated
1964 88th Congress 2d session	Several unsuccessful attempts to get bill introduced	NFO activities "hottest conversation piece around"
H.R. 11146 introduced by Rep. Secrest, May 5	Form of bill: Amendment to Capper-Volstead Act	
S. 2846 introduced as companion bill by Sen. Aiken & Sen. Lausche, May 15	AFB-NCFC-NMPF coalition discussions No hearings held on bill in 88th Congress	
1965 89th Congress 1st session		
Reintroduced in House by Rep. Secrest as H.R. 898, Jan. 4	Form of bill: Amendment to Capper-Volstead Act Canners and NBC protest bitterly	Ohio bargaining law passed, June 29
Bill reintroduced as S. 109 by Aiken, McCarthy & Young, Jan. 6	Field work by farm groups to build bargaining idea	
1966 89th Congress 2d session		Report of National Commission on Food Marketing P&S hearings Arkansas broiler case
Senate Agr. Subcommittee hearing on S. 109, June 14	USDA cool to AFB bill Farm groups cool to C-V amendment route	

Congressional Movement of S. 109	Legislative Highlights	External Events Having an Impact on S. 109
Senator Aiken reintroduced S. 109 as an amendment in form of a substitute, Sept. 21		
Senate Agr. Subcommittee hearing on substitute version, Sept. 28	Lively debate over provisions of S. 109	Raisin Bargaining Association organized Dec. 9
1967 90th Congress 1st session	AFB catches bargaining bug	
S. 109 reintroduced by Aiken, Lauche & Young, Jan. 11	Coalition forms in opposition	NFO milk stop
	Press debate	"Food group" debate between Robert Heiney & John Datt
	Bill gains many House sponsors	
Senate Agr. Subcommittee hearing, May 2	United farm front	Freeman's Press Club speech, May 16
Jordan Subcommittee rewrite to fair practices bill	Farm fallout	President Johnson's press conference on farm bargaining needs, Aug. 18
House Agriculture Committee hearing, Sept. 21	Bill bottled up in House Rules Committee by Sisk	
1968 90th Congress 2d session		P&S issues decision and cease-and-desist order in Arkansas broiler case, Jan. 23
	Fresno meeting, Jan. 5	Mondale bill introduced, Feb. 15, S. 2973
House Floor debate, March 25	Veto effort by farm groups	
Signed into law by President Johnson, April 16	Administration of act assigned to FCS-USDA, Aug. 27	Bargaining idea gains wide acceptance among farm operators
1969 91st Congress 1st session		Mondale bill reintroduced, Feb., S. 2973
Farm Bureau bill to amend S. 109 introduced by Rep. May, April 3, H.R. 9950		
Companion bill introduced by Aiken, S. 2225		
Senate Agr. Subcommittee hearing on amendment, Nov. 20	Lack of consensus concerning to whom bill should apply	

Survival in the coming world of monopolies will not be easy, but evidence already suggests what is necessary for survival. If cooperatives are going to be around to serve farmers in the future, they must fight to enhance their market power by every economic, organizational, and legislative device available.[1]

Robert L. Clodius

Chapter 1
The Problem

Farm operators are restless. Strong undercurrents of change in traditional farm markets have upset established marketing patterns and caused anxiety and apprehension about the future. The result has been a re-evaluation of farm organization efforts and a reassessment of existing farm programs. Some farm leaders have concluded that to survive and compete in the agriculture of tomorrow farmers must organize to exert greater bargaining strength.

In the main, farm unrest among the United States' 2.9 million producers has been caused by dissatisfaction with low farm price and income levels. While farm firms have become larger and fewer, they still number in the millions, and the individual farm operator remains powerless in his dealings with food processors and distributors. Advancing technology in this country, the widespread adoption of similar technology in foreign countries and unhappiness with farm programs initiated in the 1930's have each made farm operators interested in finding better ways to manage their industry and thus to enjoy better returns.

Farm unrest also stems from two fundamental changes that have occurred in farm markets. The first has been the displacement of conventional open assembly markets by direct marketing, formula pricing, contract production on specification and vertical integration. Some of these changes reflect an attempt to "industrialize" the farm production process. They are also indicative of the struggle for market power within the agri-business complex.

The second fundamental change in farm markets has been the shift of market power into the hands of fewer and larger marketing firms. In particular, food chains and food processors with strong national brands have replaced the once-prevalent small market outlets for farm products. The enormous disparity in the size of firms has been characterized by Willard F.

1. Robert L. Clodius, "The Role of Cooperatives in Bargaining," *Journal of Farm Economics,* 39 (December, 1957), 1271.

Mueller, Director of the Bureau of Economics for the Federal Trade Commission, who describes the largest food manufacturer as having "assets about equal to the *combined* assets of the nearly 1,300 dairy cooperatives operating in the United States. The seven largest manufacturing corporations — each with assets of $500 million or more — had [in 1967] combined assets equal to those of the over 8,000 agricultural marketing and supply cooperatives." [2] The imbalance in economic power is not only readily apparent; it is awesome. As farm operators have organized in an attempt to hold their place in this rapidly changing structure of farm markets, they have generated one of the major controversies in modern American agricultural affairs.

This controversy centers upon the organization of producers for bargaining purposes. As farm political power has diminished and farm programs have come increasingly under the scrutiny of consumer-oriented legislators, farm operators have sought new, nonpolitical, ways to influence the level of farm prices through group pressure activities. The tactics have included organization of local bargaining units to negotiate with processors over terms of sale, including price, for specialty crops; negotiation of premiums over and above minimum prices established in connection with federal milk marketing orders and agreements; bargaining attempts on a national scale and on a cross-commodity basis by the National Farmers Organization (NFO) and the American Farm Bureau Federation's (AFB) American Agricultural Marketing Association (AAMA). In addition to such bargaining efforts, producers have continued to market their products through farmer-owned cooperative business organizations in an attempt to share in the more profitable sector of the marketing cycle.

These organizing experiences of farmers have involved encounters with processors and other handlers of farm products. Many instances have been documented in which farm organizations have met with strong resistance and discriminatory activity by food marketing firms, which prefer by-and-large to procure farm food and fiber directly from individual producers at the lowest possible prices. Inevitably, questions have been raised about the legal rights of producers to organize for bargaining purposes.

As a consequence, legislation to provide a more definitive legislative base for bargaining activities and to protect farm operators and their associations from discrimination by large processors was introduced before the U.S. Congress in 1964. This book is a study of the legislative life of this bill and the issues surrounding it. Both have lessons for farmers as they prepare for a new era in farm organization, and both are instructive with respect to the changing balance of farm influence in Congress.

2. Willard F. Mueller, speech, "Cooperatives' Contributions to Effective Competition," Washington, D.C., October 9, 1967. In September, 1969, Mueller returned to his professorship in Agricultural Economics at the University of Wisconsin, from which he was on leave.

Three Case Experiences

S. J. Buck's *The Granger Movement* describes some of the opposition to that movement by commission men in 1872, an early example of opposition to farm organization efforts.[3] Established and organized economic power manifested its opposition in the form of discriminatory practices then, and it has continued to do so, often during an organization's formative stages, the time in which an organization is exceptionally vulnerable. Three modern instances in which processors took action to penalize individual farmers seeking to organize for bargaining purposes had a particular bearing upon the legislative life of Senate Bill S. 109. One of them can be said to have fathered it. Certainly, each influenced the progress of the bill at a different stage in its development, and for this reason each will be reviewed individually.

The Ohio Tomato Case. Bargaining efforts on behalf of Ohio tomato growers began in early 1949 when a group of local growers around Toledo formed a bargaining association. They charged themselves 1 per cent of their gross income as dues and also utilized a binding membership agreement. When the growers organized to bargain over contract terms, they were met with strong resistance from the processors, who had previously contracted with growers on an individual basis.

The efforts by growers continued, however, and resulted in the formation of Cannery Growers, Inc., in 1950. The purpose of this association was to help grower-members negotiate more favorable tomato contracts with processors, not only in terms of the prices paid, but with the grading program as well. Their organized efforts continued to be met with substantial processor resistance in 1951.

Appeals were made to the Justice Department for preventive relief. On May 21, 1952, the Federal Trade Commission issued a complaint under section 5 of the FTC act, charging certain processors with conspiring and engaging in a planned common course of action to boycott certain tomato growers. This charge of collusion was first supported by an initial decision issued by the hearing examiner on February 3, 1954. However, the examiner dismissed the complaint in a second such decision, issued on August 8, 1954, and in 1955 the FTC officially dismissed without prejudice the complaint against H. J. Heinz, Hunt Foods, Campbell Soup, Stokely-Van Camp and ten other canners of tomato products. The commission reported that while three of the companies did engage in a common boycott in the spring of 1951, they did not thereafter. Since growers had strengthened their organizations, it was

3. Solon Justus Buck, Ph.D., *The Granger Movement: A Study of Agricultural Organization and Its Political, Economic and Social Manifestations, 1870–1880* (Cambridge: Harvard University Press, 1913), 16–19, 55.

concluded that "it would not be in the public interest for the Commission to issue an order to cease and desist at this time." [4]

On appeal, the FTC ruled that "the record substantially supported the hearing examiner's first finding regarding the existence in 1951 of an agreement to boycott the cooperative." An order was subsequently issued on June 29, 1956, directing the processors involved to cease and desist

> from entering into, continuing, cooperating in, or carrying out any planned course of action, understanding, agreement, combination, or conspiracy, to do or perform any of the following acts or things:
>
> (a) Refusing to grant recognition of, or to negotiate or deal with, Cannery Growers, Inc., an association of tomato growers, as a bargaining agent for its grower members;
> (b) Refusing to purchase, or to contract to purchase tomatoes from growers who are members of Cannery Growers, Inc.[5]

This cease-and-desist order was set aside on July 17, 1959, however, by the U.S. Court of Appeals. The court relied on the hearing examiner's finding that the practices complained of had been discontinued and that the bargaining association had gained a strong position in the industry. In addition, the court said that "early in 1952 all the respondent processors with the exception of Campbell freely negotiated with the co-op." [6]

By 1960, Cannery Growers, Inc., was again seeking the assistance of the FTC. As one farmer recalled the events that transpired in the 1958 growing season, the association "attempted to negotiate with Heinz for a decent price and there was a real hassle. The association was literally destroyed by the processors. I got a pretty small contract. . . . After that year, I dropped out of the association. And right away, I got big increases in acreage." [7]

Such discriminatory activity was not uncommon in Ohio, and it was also reported in other states where vegetable growers were organizing. One document filed by Cannery Growers, Inc., with the FTC was an affidavit by a former fieldman of a large processing company reporting the following instructions given him regarding the 1960 crop season.

> My instructions were to contract all the acreage I could among the nonmembers of Cannery Growers, Inc. and in addition thereto I was to indicate to member growers that if they decided to grow for (processor) during the 1960 season, it would be to their advantage for them to resign from Cannery Growers, Inc. I was supplied with a form letter of resignation that could be modified in three ways so that it would not look like they all came from the same source and possibly be traced

4. Federal Trade Commission, press release, August 22, 1955.
5. Allen A. Lauterbach (General Counsel, American Farm Bureau Federation), testimony in U.S. Senate, Subcommittee of the Committee on Agriculture and Forestry, *Hearings on S. 109*, 89th Cong., 2d sess., 1966, 35.
6. *Ibid.*
7. Robert Summer, testimony in *Hearings on S. 109*, 17.

back to (processor). . . . We were to advise the growers that if they wanted to grow the same acreage as they had last year, they would have to resign from the Cannery Growers Association. If they did not care to resign, the acreage would be cut to approximately one-half.[8]

According to the fieldman, the company proposed spending up to $100,000 to discourage the effort by farmers to organize for bargaining purposes.

The FTC was also supplied with a copy of a memorandum dated September 22, 1959, from the fieldman's supervisor advising as follows.

As I understand it, some of your growers have asked questions about our position regarding our relations with the association in the future. I am sure you know that we intend to do business with others wherever possible, even at the additional expense that might be involved.

We cannot request any grower to resign from the association but to let them know via propaganda what we intend to do is another thing, and you should proceed to let it be known in your area. This is a program that we will pursue until completed.[9]

In spite of evidence of these practices, the FTC was unwilling to hold another hearing unless the Cannery Growers, Inc., could give satisfactory proof of the existence of a combination or conspiracy of two or more processors to carry on coercive tactics against the association or its members. In fact, FTC officials admitted to Farm Bureau representatives in a 1964 meeting that the FTC was powerless to help growers secure immediate relief against coercive tactics of processors.[10] Collusion among big processors fell within the jurisdiction of the FTC, but individual acts by these same processors against growers or their association did not.

This course of events irritated Ohio tomato growers. To their way of thinking, tomatoes could get awfully ripe in the five to six years the FTC consumed in arriving at a final decision. It was lost time. In addition, it was difficult to agree with the statement that Cannery Growers, Inc., "occupied a strong position in the industry" when the largest soup manufacturer in the country refused even to recognize them. In the words of one bargaining association official:

Our experience made it very clear that without some legislative control of fair practices, processing firms could make it very unpleasant for a farmer who wanted to become a member of a cooperative marketing association. These unpleasantries took the form of harassment, acreage cuts, unnecessary delays in contracting, poor grading, and a variety of treatment that made it clear that the buying company was not pleased at the farmer's action.[11]

8. Lauterbach, testimony in *ibid.*, 35.
9. *Ibid.*, 36.
10. *Ibid.*
11. C. William Swank (Assistant Executive Vice-President, Ohio Farm Bureau), letter to author, April 16, 1968.

Dissatisfied with the lack of prompt legal relief through the FTC and the continual harassment by processors, Ohio growers decided to seek state and national legislation that would outlaw such discriminatory practices.

Coinciding with this desire for bargaining legislation was the merger in 1962 of the Cannery Growers, Inc., with the Ohio Agricultural Marketing Association, a member of the American Agricultural Marketing Association affiliated with AFB. This action added strength to the bargaining position of growers and also gave them access to a knowledgeable legislative lobby in Ohio and Washington, D.C.

In 1963, the Ohio Farm Bureau was instrumental in introducing a bill in the Ohio General Assembly that — as finally passed — was known as Senate Bill 60. The Farm Bureau received strong support from Ohio dairy cooperatives in introducing this measure, which included in its initial wording language about fair trade practices and also a bit of "Wagner Act" language. This latter part proposed that when an association represented 60 per cent of the producers of a given processor, the processor would be required to bargain in good faith.

Both ideas generated strong opposition from processors and were rather coolly received by some members of the state legislature. As a result, the "Wagner Act" language was dropped from the bill early in the session. Hearings were then held at which the H. J. Heinz Company led the fight for the processors.[12]

The bill did not pass in the 1963 legislative session, but it was reintroduced in 1965. Despite the open opposition of processors involved chiefly in processing milk and tomatoes, the bill passed and was signed into law. The language of the bill was fairly mild, but it established two points. First, it defined a procedure for receiving complaints by the director of agriculture about discriminatory practices against growers, for hearing these complaints, and for taking appropriate court action if the complaint appeared justified. The redress feature gave growers more confidence because they knew they had some protection. Secondly, the measure forbade processors boycotting or "shutting-off" a producer because of his membership in a bargaining association. Significantly, the price gains achieved in negotiations with processors coincident with the passage of the bill represented, at that time, the biggest gains in the entire history of tomato bargaining activity in Ohio.[13]

In summary, Ohio tomato growers found that new legislation was necessary to handle successful negotiations and to check the harassment by processors. As will be shown later, this case provided a lesson not lost by advocates of national protective legislation. In fact, the Ohio Farm Bureau provided the main push for new national bargaining legislation.

12. C. William Swank, personal interview, April 30, 1968.
13. *Ibid.*

The Arkansas Broiler Case.   Ellis Hale raised broilers for a living. With his wife and four children, Hale lived on a farm in Scott County, south of Fort Smith, Arkansas. Like 4,000 of the state's other 4,400 broiler growers, he contracted with a broiler company under terms of a "growout" contract or agreement. Hale furnished the labor, land, facilities, litter and other equipment necessary for raising the birds. The integrating company furnished the chickens, feed, medication and field services. In some cases, the company provided these items to growers on a credit basis, while in others they were supplied as company-owned resources, with the grower paid on the basis of a straight fee per marketed bird.

Mr. Hale was equipped to raise about 50,000 broilers at a time. Allowing time for the eight week growout period and cleanup, he generally averaged about 225,000 broilers a year. His investment in land, buildings and equipment was in excess of $40,000. Mr. Hale's gross income was roughly $15,000 a year, out of which he paid monthly installments on his mortgages, plus other fixed expenses that amounted to approximately $700 per month. After these expenses were deducted, he had returns of only $6,600 to labor, management and equity capital — a minimal living standard for a family of six. Hale was recognized as an above-average grower, and he maintained membership in the Arkansas Farmers Union.[14]

Mr. Hale isn't growing broilers today. He hasn't grown any since October of 1962, when his contract or agreement was terminated by the local company, a wholly owned subsidiary of Arkansas Valley Industries (AVI), a large, integrated company. The reasons for termination of his contract were Hale's membership in the Northwest Poultry Growers Association and his efforts to organize other growers.

The Northwest Poultry Growers Association (NWPGA) was formed in the latter part of 1961 as an association of independent broiler growers interested in furthering their mutual economic interests. In 1962, the association conducted numerous meetings in northwest Arkansas. At about this same time, Mr. Hale, his father and brother, and other poultry growers in the area south of Fort Smith became concerned about the problems being encountered increasingly by broiler growers and "by irregularities in our business transactions with the local poultry company." [15] These concerns led to an investigation of possibilities for forming a broiler growers' organization. The group found that growers in northwest Arkansas, Kansas, Missouri and Oklahoma had already organized and were holding regular meetings. After attending meetings in each other's respective areas, the Scott County growers joined with the Northwest group in April of 1962 and started to organize

14. Ellis Hale, testimony in *Hearings on S. 109*, 88. The foregoing description of Mr. Hale's operations is based upon his testimony and evidence found in USDA, Packers and Stockyards Division, Consumer and Marketing Service, Docket No. 3497, January 23, 1968. Hereafter cited as P&S Docket 3497.

15. Hale, testimony in *Hearings on S. 109*, 84.

growers in Scott County under the name of the Northwest Poultry Growers Association. Local meetings of the association were generally well publicized and well attended by interested broiler growers. Membership in the NWPGA in 1962 rose to 313 — compared with only a few incorporating members in 1961 — dues-paying broiler growers who raised approximately 21 million broilers annually and had about 12,700 laying hens. The association became acquainted with the Southwest Arkansas Poultry Growers Association and affiliated with the U.S. Poultry and Egg Producers Association.

Riding on the tide of the Kennedy Administration's New Frontier farm program, the NWPGA sought as a principal objective federal legislation authorizing marketing orders covering the production of broilers and eggs. NWPGA argued that the production of broilers should be limited by a self-supporting supply management program that would improve market prices and the level of income received by broiler growers. A petition to this effect, addressed to the Secretary of Agriculture, was circulated among growers in July of 1962. The response was very good, and over 90 per cent of the growers contacted are reported to have signed the petition.[16] These efforts by the association generated intense local interest and conversation.

The organizing and petitioning activity of the growers association did not please members of the Arkansas Poultry Federation, an organization of poultry integrators. Three of its principal members — Arkansas Valley Industries, Ralston Purina, and Tyson's — did not favor marketing orders and were critical of the objectives of the NWPGA. As a consequence of their attitude, these large integrators in the fall of 1962 refused to enter into or to continue growout contracts or agreements with broiler growers who were active members of the association, and through concert of action, the integrators combined or arranged to boycott them.[17] As a result of this active opposition, independent broiler growers became afraid to join the NWPGA or to remain active in it. By 1963, membership in the association had dropped to 23 broiler growers.

The events that led to the demise of the growers' association were exposed by Leland DuVall, farm editor of the *Arkansas Gazette*.[18] In a Sunday farm review entitled "Broiler Growers Report 'Blacklist' by Feed Dealers," DuVall reported that growers were reaching a point at which they were being forced to choose between putting chicks in their houses or belonging to the Northwest Poultry Growers Association. Based in part on an interview with R. J. Tryon, a broiler grower from Noel, Missouri, the article described the practice of blacklisting by integrators and the producers' plight. According to

16. *Ibid.*, 86.
17. P&S Docket 3497, 18.
18. Leland DuVall, "Broiler Growers Report 'Blacklist' by Feed Dealers," *Arkansas Gazette* (Little Rock), August 26, 1962, 10. Since 1960, Mr. DuVall has reported changes in economic organization of the Arkansas poultry industry. His first article on the subject was "Poultry Efficiency Still Can't Insure Profit to Operator," *Arkansas Gazette*, June 26, 1960, 12.

Tryon, broiler growers were finding " 'that they have been living off the depreciation of their investment and have been earning nothing'." [19] This article drew the attention of major farm organizations and is blamed, according to DuVall, for subsequent investigations by the Packers and Stockyards Division (P&S) of the United States Department of Agriculture (USDA).

The experiences of the Hales between May and August of 1962 show the progressive disintegration of the growers' association. Ellis Hale's leadership in organizing Scott County growers resulted in his being elected chairman of his local organization and his father's being appointed as a director of the Northwest Poultry Growers Association. Both Mr. Hale and his father and brother had growout contracts or agreements with AVI's Scott County Feed Company. In May of 1962, the Hales undertook to organize membership meetings in and around Waldron, the county seat of Scott County. The first meeting was held at the Courthouse in Waldron during the middle of May. The meeting was well publicized and was attended by more than 50 growers.

> As the farmers arrived at the appointed time, we found that the local poultry company had cars and trucks parked strategically on the square around the courthouse. The Poultry company officials were situated in the different approaches to the courthouse so that each farmer attending knew that he was being watched and it was clearly evident that the poultry company was trying to discourage attendance. During the course of the meeting a poultry company truck with a loud or no muffler gunned or raced its motor near the courthouse for quite some time, drowning out the speaker's words.[20]

The presence of Scott County Feed Company President W. H. Clements and other company employees caused much concern among several of the growers arriving to attend the meeting. Nevertheless, the three Hales and several other growers joined the NWPGA at the close of the meeting.

In August of 1962, Ellis Hale learned that he was going to be cut off from feeding broilers. Upon inquiring of Mr. Clements why this should be so, Clements indicated that he understood that Jimmy Hoffa was behind the organization.

> He said, "We don't want that do we?" Clement then told Hale that "this organization is causing us a lot of trouble here." He said, "Every time you have a meeting I spend a half a day the next day on the telephone on calls from different parts of the state." Clements stated further, "They want to know who attends the meeting, what was discussed there, how many people attended it, what the growers' attitudes was, and what he was going to do about it." Clements said to Hale, "They put the monkey on my back and I have to try to stop the organization." [21]

19. *Ibid.*
20. Hale, testimony in *Hearings on S. 109*, 86.
21. P&S Docket 3497, 15.

Roy Hale and R. J. Hale also found their agreements terminated, and they have not grown broilers since October of 1962. With their contracts terminated, the Hales tried to contract with other companies, but to no avail. As one avenue of redress, the Hales filed a civil suit against the poultry companies in hopes of recovering losses in income. However, attorneys in the case estimated that the cost of preparing the suit and presenting it would be in excess of $10,000. Because the Hales were unable to provide these funds, the attorneys withdrew from the case.

Operation of Three Integrated Broiler Processing Firms, 1962

	Integrators		
	Arkansas Valley Industries	Ralston Purina	Tyson's Foods
Broilers Processed in 1962	36,456,000	17,250,000	12,019,000
Percentage Processed Broilers Grown under "Growout" Contract or Agreement	85%	84%	100%*
Number of Growers under Contract or Agreement	765	295	335
Number of Growers who Belonged to Northwest Poultry Growers Association	21	45	52

Source: USDA, Packers and Stockyards Division, Consumer and Marketing Service, Docket No. 3497, January 23, 1968.

* Tyson's obtained almost twice the number of broilers from its contracted growers as it was able to process in 1962.

After acknowledging a complaint issued to them, investigators of the Packers and Stockyards Division of the Consumer and Marketing Service of the USDA initiated an investigation in December of 1962. Investigators interviewed Mr. Clements on December 4, 1962, and determined — upon reviewing with him an affidavit filed by Ellis Hale on August 24, 1962 — that Clements acknowledged the affidavit as being true and correct with one exception. The exception concerned the portion that read ". . . that W. H. (Sonny) Clements stated that he was in no position to say since he was being told to do this by his superiors, but did not divulge who his superiors were; . . ." Mr. Clements said the word "superiors" should be changed to "associates" and then said that the word "associates" referred to members of the Arkansas Poultry Federation.[22] In the findings of fact, the Packers and Stockyards judicial officer ruled that AVI's purpose in cutting off the growers involved, and the effect of such action, was to intimidate other growers and destroy the NWPGA operations in and around the Scott County area of Arkansas.[23]

In the spring of 1962, as the organizational efforts of the NWPGA became well known in the northwest area of Arkansas, many growers operating

22. *Ibid.*, 16.   23. *Ibid.*, 17.

under growout contracts or agreements with Purina's Gold Bond Poultry Company were questioning their Purina dealers about the firm's attitude regarding growers' associations. At a regular dealers meeting, Thomas Hagan, Purina's district salesman and flock coordinator, told dealers that he would explore the company's attitude and report later. At a subsequent meeting in midsummer of 1962, Hagan told the dealers that Purina did not want to deal with any grower who was a member of the NWPGA. Curtis Markham, a Purina dealer, stated that Hagan told the dealers "that he didn't want any of us dealers feeding any growers that belonged to this organization . . . he said that he'd get a list and that he didn't want to see any of these reports coming in with these growers' names on them." [24]

Purina was not alone. About the first of May, 1962, Roy Grimsley, a vice-president of Tyson's, telephoned A. L. Hollingsworth, the general manager of the Farmers Cooperative in Cave Springs, Arkansas. Grimsley told Hollingsworth that the NWPGA was controlled by unions and "should be stopped." Grimsley stated that the only way to stop the association was to blacklist the grower-members of the NWPGA and quoted the names of seven local growers to Hollingsworth. Mr. Hollingsworth gathered from the conversation that the names of the seven growers "had been pretty well circulated to other feed dealers." [25]

Such activities by the large integrating companies resulted in another complaint being filed with the Packers and Stockyards Division of the USDA on March 31, 1965. In part it charged that the integrating companies "through concert of action and known similar conduct among them, did combine or arrange with one another to boycott, 'blacklist,' and refrain from entering into or continuing growout contracts or agreements with, broiler growers who were known to be, or who were suspected of being, active members of an association organized by, and to further the mutual interests of, broiler growers who operated under growout contracts or agreements." [26]

Extensive hearings on the complaint were held between June 23, 1965, and May 26, 1966, at Fort Smith and Fayetteville, Arkansas, and received wide press coverage. In an article in the *Tulsa Daily World* on April 21, 1966, the Hale case was explicitly noted:

> During the defense testimony presented at Fayetteville in January, AVI officials testified that they discontinued service to Ellis Hale, a Waldron area grower because of his inefficiency.
> However, Hale said a government audit of AVI books indicated that each of the firm's broiler growers fell into an inefficient bracket. . . .
> He said each of the growers fell below the average efficiency rating quoted by AVI during the January hearing, which would be an impossibility.
> Haller introduced another document showing that broilers produced

24. *Ibid.*, 13.   25. *Ibid.*, 10.   26. *Ibid.*, 21.

by W. H. (Sonny) Clements, AVI official, were among the most inefficient in the group.[27]

From the hearing transcript, which totaled 3,146 pages of testimony, the hearing examiner filed his findings on June 19, 1967. He recommended that the respondents be found to have violated the act as charged and that the respondents be ordered to cease and desist from such violation. Further, they were, in effect, to reinstate any producer whose growout contract was terminated.

Following several efforts by the corporate integrators to reopen the hearing and questioning regarding the Secretary of Agriculture's jurisdiction in the poultry field, the Packers and Stockyards Division issued a Decision and Order known as P&S Docket No. 3497 on January 23, 1968 — six years after initial complaints of discrimination had been stated. It ordered the respondent corporations Arkansas Valley Industries, Inc., Ralston Purina Company and Tyson's Foods, Inc., to cease and desist from:

> (1) refusing to deal with a poultry farmer because of his affiliation or connection with any association or organization formed to further the mutual interests of poultry producers; (2) harrassing, intimidating, coercing or threatening to refuse to enter into contracts or agreements with poultry farmers because of their affiliation with any association; (3) refusing to reinstate, upon the basis of current terms, any poultry producer whose contracts or agreements were terminated for reasons of his association; (4) entering into, continuing, cooperating in or carrying out any agreement or combination to boycott, blacklist, harass, intimidate, or coerce any poultry producer or farmer for any reason whatsoever.[28]

The Arkansas broiler case was generally regarded as presenting clearcut evidence of discriminatory activities undertaken by giant agri-business firms. It demonstrated the helplessness of the individual farmer in dealing with the corporation. Like the Ohio tomato case, the experience of Arkansas broiler growers was destined to have a major impact on the process of enacting national bargaining legislation.

The California Raisin Case. In terms of experience, bargaining associations in California offer years of firsthand knowledge and expertise. Many of these groups developed in conjunction with the establishment of state and federal marketing orders in the 1930's. The marketing order mechanism seemed inadequate, however, and a need was felt to exist for additional bargaining legislation. In 1961, a state law was enacted based upon experiences of California bargaining groups. Under the provisions of this law, new bargaining efforts — typified by the Raisin Bargaining Association — have been initi-

27. Dallas K. Ferry (Executive Director, United States Poultry and Egg Producers Association), testimony in *Hearings on S. 109*, 76.
28. P&S Docket 3497, 26.

ated in a more favorable legal and organizational climate. A brief review of events leading to enactment of the bargaining law will provide a format to the development of the raisin association. In a manner more subtle than the tomato and broiler cases, the experience of raisin growers played an important role late in the life of the federal bargaining bill.

Group bargaining activities in California have been accepted since the end of World War I, when the peach growers organized the California Peach Growers Association. Following reorganization in 1936 as the California Canning Peach Association, the group engaged in price negotiations with canners of cling peaches. It is thus one of the oldest commodity bargaining associations in the United States. The changing market structure faced by CCPA is probably typical of other bargaining groups in the fruit and vegetables industry during the past two decades.

In 1950, there were over 45 canning companies processing cling peaches in California. Today, there are approximately 20.[29] In prior years, growers enjoyed a personal acquaintance with the chief officer or owner of the canning company where they sold their peaches. In contrast, there are now only 5 proprietary companies and 2 cooperative canning associations of basically local orientation. The remainder are nationally owned companies, some of which are conglomerates engaged in other business activities unrelated to processing fruits and vegetables.

The change most noticeable to the grower involves his personal relations with the company. Today's grower must deal with the company fieldman, and policy makers are far removed from the individual growers. Producers no longer enjoy the personal contact with their buyers and the chance to discuss growing problems.

This impersonalization of business is relatively new to agriculture, and in many cases, it has led to abuses that farmers have found hard to overcome. While few canning companies have policies that specifically encourage discriminatory and intimidating practices by fieldmen, the latter operate on a commission basis and are not controlled by the parent companies. Fieldmen often have taken advantage of the peach farmer, who has production costs of over $700–$800 per acre invested in his orchard [30] and who deals with perishables. His is a precarious situation. As suggested by Ralph Bunje, nineteen-year veteran manager of the California Canning Peach Association, canning companies often resist grower organization efforts.

> Our experience is that processors will, as a matter of good business, resist and undertake to destroy the opportunities for growers to create organizations that will come between them and their grower suppliers with respect to their purchase of fruits and vegetables. The same arguments

29. Ralph Bunje (General Manager, California Canning Peach Association), testimony in *Hearings on S. 109*, 157.
30. Ralph Bunje, testimony in U.S. House of Representatives, Committee on Agriculture, *Hearings on S. 109*, 90th Cong., 1st sess., 1967, 107.

and same objections would prevail here and, in fact, do prevail here that prevailed in opposition to the development of organized labor unions. Nevertheless, if farmers are to take their rightful place in today's society, they must be given protection with respect to the opportunity to organize in order to bargain for the sale of their production under the circumstances that exist today.[31]

Faced with processor resistance, fruit and vegetable bargaining groups in California sought legislation that would provide a legal climate for bargaining and thus protect farmers in their right to act through their own associations.

Initial drafting of the bill was undertaken in the belief that the discriminatory practices by fieldmen would continue until legislation was enacted to impose penalties upon processors severe enough to make them enforce adherence by all employees to company policies and the law. In a redrafting of the original proposal by the California Agricultural Council, a state group composed of bargaining associations and marketing cooperatives, two significant changes were made.[32] First, the language of the bill was changed to make clear that the prohibitory practices applied specifically to relationships with bargaining associations, that is, the marketing cooperatives were excluded from such legislation.[33] Also, such unfair trade practices as they related to bargaining associations were placed in a separate chapter of the Agricultural Code rather than being included in the chapter authorizing the creation and operation of nonprofit cooperative business organizations. While these changes were hammered out by the Agricultural Council, the bill itself was carried by the State Department of Agriculture in spite of opposition from the California Farm Bureau.

This "bill of rights" for bargaining associations — known as Senate Bill No. 127 — was signed into law on May 27, 1961. According to Robert D. Williams, coauthor of the bill, the measure "declares that it is the public policy of the State of California to establish and support the right of any farmer to join voluntarily and belong to cooperative bargaining associations." [34]

Another bill signed into law in 1965 established a check-off procedure as a method for collecting dues for the bargaining association. Assembly Bill No. 1191 requires the dealer or processor of farm products to deduct and pay a farmer's dues to the farmer's association whenever the farmer gives written

31. Bunje, statement in U.S. Senate, Subcommittee of the Committee on Agriculture and Forestry, *Hearings on S. 109*, 89th Cong., 2d sess., 1966, 160.

32. Allen F. Mather (General Counsel, Sunkist Growers, Inc.), memo, "Proposed Capper-Volstead Act Amendment Relating to Unfair Practices," to F. R. Wilcox (General Manager, Sunkist Growers, Inc.), May 19, 1964.

33. Cooperatives were exempted because they, like the bargaining associations, were working toward the same economic goals for farm operators. Since the legislation required was for bargaining associations only, it was determined that the unlawful practices should apply, not to farmer-owned cooperative businesses, but to noncooperative enterprises that engaged in discriminatory practices.

34. Robert D. Williams (California State Senator), testimony in *Hearings on S. 109*, 153.

notice of the assignment of such dues. This deduction may never, however, exceed 2 per cent of the total value of the product delivered.

Senate Bill No. 127 and Assembly Bill No. 1191 have enabled California bargaining associations to organize and perform in an improved legal climate. With respect to such organizations, the history of the formation of the Raisin Bargaining Association is instructive.

A number of raisin growers in the rich San Joaquin Valley considered forming a bargaining association with encouragement from the California branch of the Farm Bureau's agricultural marketing association. However, leaders recognized two obstructions in the path of organizing such an association: [35] Several associations had come and gone in the past, and growers felt a reluctance to join a new organization that might offer no more than "promises" with no action in improving economic returns. Also, many of the processors materially influenced individual growers' enthusiasm by telling them that "the market could not stand an increase in price or that he, as an individual packer, was willing to pay a higher price if others would do so." Given these circumstances, organizers had to wait for an opportune time to initiate organizing activity.

The opportunity came in October of 1966, when a major packer announced a price of $20 per ton less than had been paid growers during each of the three previous years. Many growers who had earlier been persuaded by packers to deliver their raisins on an "open-price contract" were incensed. They felt they had been betrayed. The opportunity to organize raisin growers into a bargaining association was at hand.

At a meeting during the third week of October of a few key independent growers, agreement was reached on an outline for a course of action and a program that would provide a basis for gaining the confidence of growers. The first well-publicized organization meeting on October 31, 1966, drew about 300 growers. The group discussed and agreed to two proposals: (1) a grower who signed a membership agreement with the association would not be bound to the association until a minimum of 50,000 tons of raisins were signed up, and (2) membership fees would not be charged until the 50,000 ton goal was realized and the association had become operative. The growers elected Ernest A. Bedrosian — one of their own growers — Chairman and empowered him to appoint steering and finance committees. In so doing, they made the decision not to use a professional organizer to lead the new organizing effort.

Mr. Bedrosian sought the counsel of such seasoned bargaining experts as Ralph Bunje of the Canning Peach Association and Richard Black of the California Freestone Peach Association. He also drew upon the advice of Mr. Frank Bennett, Deputy Director of the State Department of Agriculture, and

---

35. Ernest A. Bedrosian, speech, "Strengthening Cooperative Bargaining Through Improved Organizing Methods," Los Angeles, California, January 7, 1968.

officers of the Sun-Maid Raisin cooperative. On the advice of such experts —
and with encouragement from the California Farm Bureau — Mr. Bedrosian appointed a large steering committee from among the most outstanding
growers in the area. This group of 52 member growers from 21 producing
districts became the incorporating Board of Directors for the new association
when the Articles of Incorporation were signed on December 9, 1966.[36] The
large membership of the board provided a broad base from which the message of the association could be personally conveyed to large numbers of
growers. If each board member would sign up just ten new members, the association would have a membership of over 500 growers.

The new association employed brochures, newspaper advertisements
and appropriately timed press releases to aid in its organizing efforts. For six
weeks during November and December, "picketing" procedures at packing
plants were initiated to demonstrate to the public that growers were in trouble and that the farmer's interests were in the best interests of the community
as a whole.[37] Despite packer opposition to organizing efforts, the demonstra-
tions were followed by 13 district meetings attended by 2,000 raisin growers.
The aims and activities of the bargaining association were explained at these
meetings, and information packets were distributed. However, only 10 per
cent or slightly over 200 growers, representing about 13,000 tons of raisins,
signed membership agreements following these meetings. Directors in each
district followed up the meetings by visits with the growers who had attended,
and within two months and five days, the association had signed up 50,967
tons of raisins. It thus became operative on February 16, 1967, as the Raisin
Bargaining Association.

Immediately, negotiations with the raisin packers over content and form
of contracts began. The packers made some 43 suggested changes, of which
the association's Board of Directors incorporated 90 per cent in the final contract.[38] At the same time, the association continued its membership drives.
By June 1, 1967, 1,024 growers, representing over 70,000 tons of raisins,
had signed membership agreements with the association. During the summer
of 1967, further negotiation with raisin packers resulted in eleven packers
signing a two-year Contract of Sale with the association by September 14,
1967. At this point the association began price discussions for that portion of
the crop sold directly by growers to packers, that is, free tonnage.

The influence that the association had upon raisin prices during its first
year of operation is indicated by an accounting for the total tonnage produced in the 1967 crop year. The total tonnage of raisins produced in 1967
was estimated to be 170,000 tons — about 90,000 tons less than the 1966

36. Raisin Bargaining Association, historical sketch in program for first anniversary banquet, December 7, 1967.
37. Bedrosian, speech.
38. Murray Norris, "Organized Raisin Growers Get Higher Prices," *California
Farmer* (December 2, 1967), in files of American Farm Bureau Federation.

crop year and 22,000 tons short of domestic market needs. When the 40 per cent share of the Sun-Maid Raisin Growers Cooperative was accounted for, roughly 100,000 tons were available as free tonnage. Of this amount, the RBA represented about two thirds, in contrast to normal crop years when it would have represented about one third of the free tonnage. The cooperation of the Sun-Maid cooperative in holding the line made the RBA's position even stronger. During negotiations, packers offered $260 per ton, about $30 per ton higher than the amount paid in 1966. The association, however, insisted on $325 per ton. The RBA eventually compromised at $305 per ton, which represented a 30 per cent increase over the price paid in 1966.[39]

The packers, much to their surprise, were able to market the 19½-to-20-cent raisins to the trade without much difficulty, despite their earlier protests and the fact that the largest corporations, such as Del Monte and Cal-Pack, were slow to recognize the efforts of the Raisin Bargaining Association.

The over-all effect of the association from the growers' viewpoint has been very stabilizing. Allen Mather, General Manager of the Sun-Maid cooperative, credits the RBA with rounding out the raisin growers' "farm team." According to Mather, "It was and is our belief that the RBA can be of substantial assistance in helping to stabilize raisin marketing in the domestic and Canadian markets, *i.e.*, the markets into which the free tonnage is shipped." [40]

In contrast to the experiences of Arkansas broiler growers, the successful formation of the Raisin Bargaining Association, in spite of the odds, serves as a recent example of growers' organizing for purposes of bargaining with processors. Clearly, this type of organizing effort could take place with some protective legislation on the books and if farm leaders capitalized upon an opportune time to organize.

The Raisin Bargaining Association was an associate member of the Fresno County Farm Bureau, and 85 per cent of its members were also members of the Farm Bureau.[41] This linkage served to stimulate support for a national bargaining bill, making the success of this bargaining effort highly relevant to the history of S. 109, the focus of this study.

Implications for Organization and Legislation

The experiences of farmers in Ohio, Arkansas and California recounted in this chapter are typical of a problem that farm operators have confronted

39. *Ibid.*
40. Allen F. Mather (General Manager, Sun-Maid Raisin Growers Association), letter to Kenneth D. Naden (Executive Vice-President, National Council of Farmer Cooperatives), December 8, 1967.
41. Paul H. Huber (General Manager, Raisin Bargaining Association), letter to author, July 25, 1968.

in the 1960's. The five-year vacillation of the Federal Trade Commission on the Ohio tomato case proved highly unsatisfactory to Buckeye growers. As a result, they sought relief through state legislation and succeeded in enacting a "mild" protective bill.

In Arkansas, broiler growers' complaints were not heeded for a long period of time, due in part to a question of the jurisdictional rights of the Packers and Stockyards Division in integrated poultry situations. Almost six years passed before a cease-and-desist order was issued to the three large poultry integrators.[42] Costs of civil action were prohibitive to individual growers, and many suffered from loss of income, foreclosure and family hardships during the interim.

California farmers likewise claimed that company fieldmen were often second-rate men in their own organizations who were looking for big commissions, not for future years' crops.[43] As a consequence, legislation applying to bargaining associations was sought in the state legislature. Under the act passed, such organizations as the Raisin Bargaining Association have been able to develop without fear of reprisal from processors.

In a country as large as the United States, however, large food manufacturers and chain stores tend to procure their needed supplies in several states. What affects the tomato grower in Ohio may well affect the market available to growers in New Jersey. Similarly, the fact that many farm products are substitutes for one another affects the economic climate of the farming industry as price levels are successfully negotiated in one sector and not the other. These considerations were closely scrutinized by corporation executives and farm leaders alike. Farm leaders concluded that state laws were not a sufficient antidote to challenges of the changing economic organization in agriculture.

42. On July 30, 1969, the U.S. Court of Appeals for the Eighth Circuit ruled, on a technical point, that the law did not give P&S authority to issue a cease-and-desist order. In the future, P&S would have to control poultry dealers and handlers, the court ruled, either through having the Justice Department present the case of P&S in court or by using P&S authority to license poultry dealers. In effect, this decision restricted P&S administrative proceedings in such cases as the Arkansas broiler case that involve poultry integrators.
43. Ralph Bunje, personal interview, June 13, 1968.

S. 109 is a Farm Bureau Bill. It was originated, pushed and inspired all the way by the American Farm Bureau. It is a concept to enhance bargaining power and group action, and by it to remove obstacles in farmers' mind to joining the bargaining branch of the American Farm Bureau Federation — The American Agricultural Marketing Association.

Kenneth Naden[1]

Chapter 2

Initial Drafting

On April 16, 1968, while on a Viet Nam strategy planning mission in Honolulu, President Lyndon B. Johnson signed into law, without comment, the Agricultural Fair Practices Act of 1967. This event culminated four years of action on what has been described as "one of the best examples that has recently been available of the innumerable economic and political influences that come to bear on a piece of so-called 'farm legislation'." [2] The bill that led to this act — variously known as the "Secrest bill," "S. 109," "Aiken bill," "bargaining bill," "little Wagner Act," "marketing rights bill," and the "Bunje bill" — traveled a rocky road from the time it first appeared as a resolution of the American Farm Bureau Federation (AFB) until the last requests for a veto as it awaited President Johnson's signature. It brought into play all brands of lobby forces as it was batted between farm pressure groups, legislators, opposing processor and integrator groups, governmental agencies, congressional committees and both houses of Congress. In the process it tested the tenacity of the farm front and the patience and fortitude of many. When it ultimately became law, frustrated legislators breathed a deep sigh of relief.

The Agricultural Fair Practices Act of 1967 represents a landmark piece of legislation. Not only is it the first piece of general agricultural marketing legislation to be enacted in recent decades, but it is also the first reaffirmation by Congress of its long-standing, fifty-year policy in support of group action by farm operators. A piece of farm bargaining legislation that originated from grass-roots America, it precipitated the most hotly contested confrontation between producers and processors in recent legislative history. Having survived at least nine burial attempts, the final form of the measure represented a rewritten version that reflected considerable compromise and a more limited objective than the original.

As drafted by the AFB and introduced in Congress in May of 1964, the bill was designed to provide protection for bargaining associations from discriminatory activities by processors and other handlers. It was also designed,

---

1. Kenneth D. Naden (Executive Vice-President, National Council of Farmer Cooperatives), personal interview, April 1, 1968.
2. Kenneth D. Naden, letter to author, May 9, 1968.

by virtue of an amendment to the Capper-Volstead Act, to give farm bargaining efforts by general farm interest organizations and other associations protection from antitrust policy. To achieve adherence to its purposes, the bill included rigid enforcement procedures.

As passed in April of 1968, the bill did *not* extend to bargaining associations any latitude under antitrust laws and was confined only to protection from discriminatory activities. Moreover, the acts outlawed by the bill applied not only to handlers, but to bargaining associations and farmer cooperatives as well. Furthermore, the enforcement section was watered down to a mere injunctive relief provision through the courts or the Secretary of Agriculture. While it thus fell substantially short of its original mark, the new law can nevertheless be viewed as public sanction for farm bargaining efforts and as a prologue to future legislation.

Farm Pressure Groups in a Pressure Group Society

Pressure groups, and the legislators with whom they interact, are often considered the chief actors in today's legislative process. With an assist from the executive branch or any one of a number of governmental agencies, a legislative proposal's chances for passage are enhanced, although not assured. Much depends upon the strength of opposing pressure groups and the measure's general acceptance. The legislative life of the Farm Bureau's bargaining bill marked the emergence of the farm bargaining idea and featured a toe-to-toe battle between economic pressure groups representing processors and producers.

Farm pressure groups in Washington are characterized by three types of organizations: general farm interest organizations, commodity and service organizations and councils representing cooperative business organizations. Of these, the best known are such general farm interest groups as the National Grange, National Farmers Union, American Farm Bureau and the National Farmers Organization. Such organizations purport to harmonize and represent the economic interests of all types of producers and often speak for rural America as well. Each, except for the NFO, has had a long history of involvement in political pressure group activities. Despite this long history, a new channel for democratic action was promoted by the Kennedy Administration, according to a study by Hadwiger and Talbot, because the farm organizations had bogged down to wheel track rather than representative behavior.

An early farm proposal of the Kennedy Administration — a 1933 program revitalized by Economist Willard Cochrane — would have raised the status of the USDA-affiliated Agricultural Stabilization and Conservation Services (ASCS) at the expense of existing farm groups.

One could not assume that existing organizations in 1961 were neutral mechanisms to mirror farmer views. These organizations often seemed less interested in learning what grass roots farmers wanted than they were in strengthening certain rural attitudes which would generate support for their own long-established policies, and then in capitalizing on this support in their lobbying activities. Some farm organizations seemed to give highest priority to an effort to weaken or destroy competitor groups.[3]

This stiff indictment against farm groups by Hadwiger and Talbot helped to activate them from their complacency. To many a neutral observer, the trite expressions of "farm prices are made in Washington," and "get the government out of agriculture" developed a hollow ring the third time around. Many more important issues were at stake.

By far the largest of the general farm interest organizations in 1961 was the American Farm Bureau Federation. The organization represented 1.7 million member families and was younger than the Grange and the NFU but older than the NFO. The predominantly Midwest organization was headquartered in Chicago but maintained a sizable Washington office. It developed out of a close link with the federal and state extension services in the early 1920's into one of the most articulate spokesmen for the farm front during the "farm bloc" era of the 1920's and 1930's. Once a major supporter of cooperative business organizations, the AFB has in recent years frequently expressed its feelings of futility toward cooperative activities because of a lack of pay-off from them. Coincidentally it has voiced a conservative ideology that places it in company with such lobbies as the National Association of Manufacturers, the U.S. Chamber of Commerce and other business groups. Ties with these groups extend even to political education activities. Since the early 1960's, the AFB has turned to an action program designed to give members greater bargaining power.

One of the prime movers in getting the AFB involved in bargaining activities was the rise of the youngest of the general farm interest organizations — the NFO. Perhaps because of its militant approach to the farm price problem, the NFO has attracted more public attention in the 1960's than has any other farm group. Born of disgruntled farm operators in the Midwest in the mid-1950's, the NFO differs in organizational structure from other general farm interest organizations. Unlike them, it is highly centralized, with action units at the local, county and national levels. Farm delivery stops, implemented by the organization to build its membership and to teach members the disciplines of a bargaining unit, have attracted widespread attention and criticism. To the surprise of many critics however, the NFO has passed the amorphous "farmer movement" stage and is a viable, though secretive, organization.

The oldest general farm interest group — the National Grange — has

3. Don F. Hadwiger and Ross B. Talbot, *Pressures and Protests: The Kennedy Farm Program and the Wheat Referendum of 1963* (San Francisco: Chandler Publishing Company, 1965), 55–56.

served agriculture for more than 100 years. Still a fraternal organization, it has experienced some rebirth through concentration upon youth education programs. However, its membership is small and its political influence has waned accordingly. Policy positions of the Grange have been closely correlated with those taken by the USDA. The membership strength of the Grange is found in the Northeast, Pacific Northwest, and the Middle Atlantic states. Frequent mention of merger with the NFO has raised eyebrows of many farm leaders. Nevertheless, the courtship continues.

The National Farmers Union — the fourth general farm interest organization — is smaller than the Grange. Its membership strength is in the Plains area, and to a lesser extent in the Midwest and South. In terms of philosophical orientation, the NFU was regarded in 1961 by standards of the agri-business community as radical and at the opposite polar extreme of the AFB. It has maintained close linkages with cooperative grain terminals and for many years was governed by the same board of directors. The NFU has traditionally carried the banner for government involvement in farm policy and has maintained close partisan connections with the Democratic party. During the Kennedy Administration, it was responsible for gathering a coalition of farm groups, still in existence, which served as a backstop for the Administration's farm proposals. More recently, it has maintained support for further institutionalization of the ASCS committee system.

Commodity and service organizations comprise the second — and most numerous — type of farm pressure group operating in Washington. Commodity organizations such as the National Milk Producers Federation represent various dairy groups throughout the country. Similarly, the National Association of Wheat Growers, National Livestock Producers Association and others represent a variety of production interests through individual or group membership. It has become fashionable in some quarters to suggest that these specialized groups are among the most influential spokesmen for farm operators.[4] However, the effectiveness of individual commodity groups is limited by conflicts between commodities and by the existence of "bargaining" and "operating" factions within these organizations. In addition to the strictly commodity groups, some pressure groups within this category — such as the National Rural Electric Cooperative Association — represent special service interests.

Cooperative business organizations constitute a third type of farm pressure group. Such organizations are represented through an apex organization known as the National Council of Farmer Cooperatives. Cooperatives have generally shunned any articulated involvement in politics as a "principle" of operation, although the NCFC was established by E. G. Nourse and others in

---

4. For example, USDA's former Director of Economics Walter Wilcox, during a guest lecture to an Agricultural Policy class at the University of Wisconsin in the spring of 1965, cited the commodity lobby groups' influence on farm legislative matters in Washington.

1928 in part to involve cooperatives more actively in the affairs of government and to give them a more active voice in Washington. Composed of a mixed membership of state cooperative councils and individual "bargaining" and "operating" associations, the NCFC represents a variety of commodity interests. To a much lesser extent, the Cooperative League of the USA, which is headquartered in Chicago, also represents farmer cooperative interests. Many legislators have encouraged cooperatives to beef up their Washington lobby activity in recent years, taking note of the rather low-key support by cooperative business organizations throughout the country.[5]

Farm legislative proposals such as S. 109 normally originate with the pressure groups and are promoted by them through receptive legislators. Representatives of the pressure groups work with officials of the legislative, executive and judiciary branches of government in an effort to influence their decisions and to promote their bills.[6] By this means, the farm pressure groups represent a communications link between farm operators throughout the country and the governmental decision makers.

The work of the pressure groups notwithstanding, some of the most influential lobbying takes place outside of this framework. Because of differing agency interests or philosophies some of the most powerful attempts to influence decisions are directed by some government officials against other government officials.[7] In addition, very effective lobbying activity is carried out by "built-in" lobbyists who have seats in Congress and who are spokesmen for certain interests. Their involvement in decision making gives them a strategic position to influence the outcome of pending legislation. Finally, lobbying frequently takes place between the executive and legislative branches of government. Most executive departments maintain a full-time congressional liaison staff to protect department appropriations and facilitate communications. In this role, governmental agencies such as the USDA may be looked upon, in one sense, as just another type of pressure group.[8]

To secure support sufficient to passage, a farm bill must fulfill a need and represent a consensus among a few or all of the farm pressure groups and the USDA. Support from nonfarm allies such as business, labor or consumer groups is also solicited. In view of the decreasing numbers of congressmen from rural areas and the growing influence of off-farm segments upon farm

5. Among others, Walter Mondale (Senator, Minnesota) recently encouraged the NCFC to strengthen its lobby activity in Washington.

6. Lester W. Milbrath, *The Washington Lobbyists* (Chicago: Rand McNally & Company, 1963), 8. According to Milbrath, lobbying is "the stimulation and transmission of a communication, by someone other than a citizen acting in his own behalf, directed to a government decisionmaker with the hope of influencing his decision."

7. *Ibid.*, 9.

8. According to Kenneth Parsons, a student of John R. Commons, Commons suggested that the State should be looked upon not only as an umpire, but also as an active participant in the economy. For further reference, see Kenneth H. Parsons, "Social Conflicts and Agricultural Programs," *Journal of Farm Economics*, 43 (August, 1941), 743–64.

legislation in recent years, it has become important for farm groups to achieve broad-based support for their proposals in order to rate any consideration in Congress.

The Legislative Route

Once a bill has been drafted and cleared with other pressure groups, the sponsoring organization must find legislators in both houses of Congress to introduce it. The more legislative cosponsors of a bill, the more likely it is to attract public attention and catch the eye of the chairman of the standing committee to whom it is referred. Occasionally, a major bill is acted upon initially by the full committee; however, most bills are referred first to subcommittees. The significance of committee handling of a bill is clear: It is here that the most crucial action of the legislative process takes place.[9] Pressure groups fighting to defeat a bill can take advantage of any one of several legislative hurdles to stop it at the committee level. Furthermore, key legislators can exercise their influence more readily in the committee process than in a floor action. In the past decade, the agricultural committees of both houses of Congress have been dominated by conservative Southern Democratic leadership.

It has been pointed out that the congressional subcommittees carry the real work load in Congress and that they are of "single prominence in the legislative process." [10] Not only do the subcommittees hold public hearings in which opposing views about a bill may be aired, but they also hold closed executive sessions in which special interest groups and legislators may compromise their positions and arrive at a final proposal through give-and-take. Since a pending measure may favor one group at the expense of another, the battles between groups frequently focus on writing the provisions within this committee sphere of action. The legislators' logic, suggestions by the committee's staff, the influence from various interest groups and the analysis and recommendations of the USDA and other governmental agencies — a farm bill is subject to all as it traverses a winding and hazardous course before it is finally reported out from the committee.

But while a bill is pending action before the full House or Senate, various tactics can be used in delaying its scheduling for floor action. Further, it can be modified on the floor of either house, depending upon the rule granted to it and the format used for debate. And once passed by the Congress, it can be either signed into law or vetoed by the President.

Thus, although originating from public and private interest groups, a piece of farm legislation is carefully scrutinized by many other interests that

9. Ross B. Talbot, "Farm Legislation in the 86th Congress," *Journal of Farm Economics*, 43 (August, 1961), 582.
10. *Ibid.*

Organization Chart of the American Farm Bureau Federation
Showing Main Divisions and Positions of Personnel Playing Key Roles in S. 109

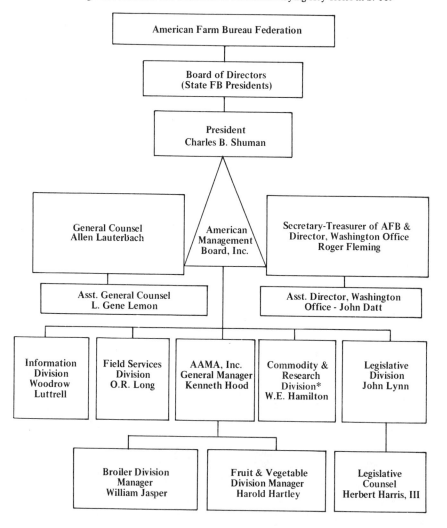

*   This organization chart shows the main divisions and positions of people who were involved in
the four-year legislative life of S. 109. Subsequent changes that have occurred from time to time
are not taken into account.

AMERICAN FARM BUREAU FEDERATION AND PERSONNEL PLAYING KEY ROLES IN S. 109

Charles B. Shuman helped establish farm bargaining as an on-going function of the AFB through formation of the AAMA in 1960. However, it was the AFB's General Counsel, Allen Lauterbach, who saw the need for new legislation and who was the initiator and key coordinator of efforts to legislate S. 109 throughout its four year life. In this pivotal role, Lauterbach relied heavily upon his assistant Gene Lemon for legal research and legwork.

With Lauterbach acting as the chief coordinator in Chicago, the key legislative strategists in lobby group coalitions and on Capitol Hill were John Datt, Assistant Director of the Washington Office, and Herbert Harris, III, Legislative Counsel. John Lynn served as the key contact man with Senator Jordan and the Bureau of the Budget.

When the chips were down and the AFB was racked with internal quibbling over provisions in S. 109, it was the AAMA grower committees that played an instrumental role in promoting basic bargaining legislation. Co-ordinator of this effort was AAMA General Manager Kenneth Hood who was assisted by William Jasper, the AAMA's energetic Broiler Division Manager.

Photographs courtesy of the American Farm Bureau Federation.

John Datt

Jack Lynn

Herb Harris III

Charles B. Shuman
President

Al Lauterbach
General Counsel

Dr. Kenneth Hood
General Manager, AAMA

Gene Lemon
Assistant General Counsel

Dr. William Jasper
Assistant General Manager

can help mold it or scrap it. All of these influences were evident throughout the legislative life of S. 109 as it was guided through Congress.

Farm Bureau Experiences a Need

The legislative life of S. 109 had its origin in the Ohio Farm Bureau as a result of the case, described previously, in which Ohio tomato growers were subjected to a lengthy Federal Trade Commission litigation proceeding. Many growers had been members of both the Ohio Farm Bureau and Cannery Growers, Inc., the latter of which had been attempting to bargain with processors since 1949. Further impetus for the proposed bargaining bill was provided by the successful national organizing experiences of the AFB in establishing the American Agricultural Marketing Association (AAMA).

Late in 1959, a decision was reached by the AFB to make its debut in the bargaining field. The idea of putting the Farm Bureau into the role of a coordinator for existing bargaining associations had been debated within the organization's policy-making network during 1958 and 1959. President Charles B. Shuman believed that too much attention had been devoted to technical aspects of farm production and not enough to marketing problems. Besides, Farm Bureau policy makers could not accept the idea that they should stick to legislative activities and let the NFO do the bargaining.[11] If there was anything to the whole bargaining idea, the AFB wanted to be a part of it.

AFB-sponsored organizational meetings for the AAMA were held in the fall of 1959 on the premise that the AFB needed to be involved in bargaining as well as legislative activities. As originally conceived, membership in the AAMA was to be composed of bargaining associations that were nominated for membership by the state Farm Bureaus.[12] The AAMA, in turn, was designed to be a national bargaining affiliate of the AFB. The major push for organizing a national association came from the fruit and vegetable commodity people within the AFB and from bargaining associations in New York, New Jersey, Ohio and Wisconsin with whom they were working. The fruit and vegetable branch had frequently called these groups together for information meetings and for purposes of discussing their mutual problems.

At one of the first meetings for purposes of organizing the bargaining association, Mr. Shuman made four distinct points: (1) the AFB was going to form the AAMA; (2) the AFB was going to make the AAMA succeed; (3) if possible, the AAMA was going to organize without any further legislation; (4) the AFB was going to control the AAMA.[13] The reason for this last

11. Farm Bureau staff members, confidential interviews. Information for this section came from extensive interviews with Farm Bureau staff members at the state and national levels. To encourage candor, the author agreed to protect the confidentiality of such sources.
12. *Ibid.*   13. *Ibid.*

point lay in the history of the Farm Bureau. Many state Farm Bureaus had been responsible for providing seed capital and for organizing many earlier cooperatives. However, these organizations eventually were able to stand on their own feet and subsequently detached themselves from Farm Bureau without repaying the seed money. This left many AFB organization people from state to national levels smarting because they supposedly retained nothing of benefit to their organization from their efforts in starting the cooperatives.[14]

The AAMA was formally organized in January of 1960 and incorporated under Illinois cooperative law as an affiliate of the AFB. Membership in the AAMA was comprised of producers organized through bargaining associations. The affiliate was first managed by Allen Lauterbach, General Counsel of the AFB who had come to the AFB in 1945 as an administrative assistant. A graduate of George Washington University Law School and the Wharton School of Finance, Lauterbach was the son of a well-respected general manager of a Chicago-based dairy cooperative, and he knew both the cooperative business and general farm interest organization sides of the issues. As a former employee of the USDA, he also knew the inner workings of various governmental agencies in Washington and understood the dynamics of the nation's capital. During the first several years of AAMA's operation, Lauterbach served as the key decision maker of the program, and Harold Hartley served as the key staff coordinator. Possibly because of the Ohio case the first AAMA bargaining efforts involved processing tomatoes, but in 1962 the organization launched another pilot project for processing apples.

In both of these efforts, the bargaining associations encountered the full treatment of discrimination from processors.[15] The biggest problem in organizing was to eliminate fears on the part of producers that they were doing something illegal or that they could not overcome obstacles through the bargaining approach. Such fears were often instilled and nurtured by processors. In particular, farm operators feared that reprisals from processors would follow if they became active in the bargaining associations.

These frustrations precipated some of the first AFB discussions about a possible bargaining proposal for national legislative action.[16] Although proposals such as Congressman Robert Poage's "Family Farm Income act of 1960" — which extended federal market orders and national stabilization programs to all commodities — were much in evidence as part of the Ken-

14. The author has been consistently confronted with this feeling on the part of organization staff in several state Farm Bureaus and among line staff people in the American Farm Bureau Federation. General farm organizations are characteristically the protectors and promoters of cooperative business activity. This feeling implies confusion about the roles of the general farm groups.

15. John Datt (Legislative Director and Assistant Director, Washington Office, American Farm Bureau Federation), personal interview, June 11, 1968.

16. Allen A. Lauterbach (General Counsel, American Farm Bureau Federation), personal interview, September 13, 1968.

nedy Administration's New Frontier program, the AFB feared "government control" and wanted to promote strong growers' associations. Lauterbach pulled together the suggestions of organizers in the field and gradually developed the first ideas about what an AFB proposal should contain.

A major change occurred in the AAMA program in 1962, when the affiliate began to emphasize itself as a marketing agency in common and began to organize from within the Farm Bureau. Instead of continuing to emphasize working through existing bargaining associations such as Cannery Growers, Inc., and California Canning Peach Association, the AFB set out to involve itself directly in bargaining along with its traditional legislative and service activities. State "marketing" associations were organized to provide a running gear for the AAMA program. Under the legal umbrella of the AAMA, state associations could coordinate and strengthen their bargaining activities. In particular, the AAMA could furnish the member association with information about the economic factors relating to its bargaining program, intelligence on processor operations and contract analysis.

Many observers close to the AFB suggest that its entry into the bargaining field would never have occurred had it not been for the opportunity created by the activities of the newly formed NFO. Some state Farm Bureaus capitalized on fear of the NFO to sell themselves to processors as "a responsible organization, based on sound economic logic." [17] At the same time, however, the AFB entry into bargaining was indeed spurred by the Ohio and other experiences. Furthermore, it was consistent with a long-standing plank in the Farm Bureau's policy platform: to enable farmers to do for themselves what the government would be or is now doing.[18] Despite the consistency of the bargaining approach with Farm Bureau philosophy, many state leaders and some staff people within the Farm Bureau were cool to the whole idea.

This coolness to the bargaining idea was not appreciated by organizers at the grass roots. In particular, the 1,200 grower members of the Cannery Growers, Inc., in Ohio had since 1960 experienced renewed discrimination from four major canners in their area. Representatives of Hunt Foods, Inc., H. J. Heinz, Campbell Soup Company and Mirzel Canning Company were alleged to have been contacting growers and advising them to stay out of Cannery Growers, Inc., or suffer the consequences of no contract or one greatly reduced.[19] Acting as spokesman for the bargaining association, the Ohio Farm Bureau in 1960 requested the AFB to take action in behalf of the group. Later, when the battle-scarred Cannery Growers, Inc., merged with the Ohio Agricultural Marketing Association in 1962, Douglas R. Stanfield

17. C. William Swank (General Manager, Ohio Agricultural Marketing Association), letter to Luke F. Beckman (President, Minster Canning Company), April 11, 1962.

18. Herbert Harris, III (Legislative Counsel, American Farm Bureau Federation), personal interview, June 10, 1968.

19. Robert Cousino (President, Cannery Growers, Inc.), letter to Federal Trade Commission, January 26, 1960.

and his staff of the Ohio Farm Bureau inherited the responsibility of dealing with these large processors. The state group wasted no time in again encouraging the AFB to fulfill its desire to assist bargaining associations.

In January, 1960, Mr. Stanfield asked the AFB to contact the FTC and other agencies in Washington to secure preventive relief, and to pursue national bargaining legislation. Also, other state Farm Bureaus involved in organizing tomato growers in the East and apple growers in the East and West pleaded for greater involvement of the AFB. Like the Ohio organizations, these bargaining associations had experienced resistance from processors and knew that existing legislation provided an inadequate legal base for farm bargaining activities. By the end of 1962, farm bargaining was the most talked-about subject at farm organization and trade association conferences.

In a digression from a prepared manuscript before a marketing institute in Princeton, New Jersey, on November 5, 1962, AFB President Charles B. Shuman talked directly to fruit and vegetable canners and suggested that if producer bargaining failed because of processor opposition, it would become necessary for his organization to seek legislative assistance and to actively work for marketing order programs.[20] This threat did not go unnoticed by processor groups.

The going was a bit difficult within the AFB, however, for a variety of reasons. State leaders from areas that had not undertaken any bargaining activity, in particular the leadership of the Illinois, Indiana and Iowa Farm Bureaus — the power bloc group within the AFB at that time — looked askance at the whole process. Their attitudes became clear when they were cornered into the dilemma of asking themselves about what purpose and role they and the AFB were originally designed to fulfill.[21] Their skepticism about bargaining had developed from the powerful insurance and supply businesses with which they were associated and from their long association with the livestock marketing groups; they tended to look down their noses at growers of tomatoes, cucumbers and other cash crops. Opposition to bargaining activity also came from some Farm Bureaus in the South and West who thought such activity appeared too much like "labor unionism."

The momentum of the bargaining proposal was also daunted within the AFB staff. The Field Services Division, which was charged with the responsibilities of seeing that the county and state Farm Bureaus followed organization guidelines, particularly wanted to preserve its decision-making structure.[22] In addition, the Commodity Division, which maintained a liaison with commodity marketing cooperatives, didn't like the bargaining idea. Even the

20. National Canners Association, "Government-Industry Report," December 14, 1962. In his speech, Mr. Shuman also argued against the Kennedy farm program by announcing, "Government supply-management rejects the market price system as a means of guiding production and substitutes the dictates of government planners who of necessity base their decisions on political expediency."

21. Farm Bureau staff members, confidential interviews.

22. *Ibid.*

Washington Legislative Office and the Information Division had not become knowledgeable about the bargaining idea and were slow in warming up to it. Besides the resistance it met within the line staff, the bargaining involvement encountered less than enthusiastic support from some rather conservative elements within the AFB hierarchy.

The AFB management team, constituted as the American Management Board, Inc., was formulated as a three-man committee consisting of President Shuman, Chief Executive Officer Roger Fleming and Chief Counsel Allen Lauterbach. This arrangement made the three men officers of the total scope of AFB and affiliated activities and forced cooperation between the president, a farmer and the chief staff officer. While the AFB operated under the guidance of policy resolutions that presumably originated at the local county Farm Bureau level and were passed on through the district, state and national levels, the management committee was not without its influence over the general posture of the organization. For these reasons, some of the first battles in the life of S. 109 were fought within the AFB itself.

Despite the internal barriers, bargaining proponents within the AFB succeeded in organizing about twenty state marketing associations by the end of 1963. Even though relatively few of the state Farm Bureaus had become actively involved in a bargaining program, progressive elements in the Ohio, New York, New Jersey, Pennsylvania, Michigan and Colorado Farm Bureaus actively supported their counterparts in other states. Within the AFB staff, Allen Lauterbach, Harold Hartley, Herbert Harris, III, and John Datt actively pushed for legislative proposals that would satisfy the demands of the activist state groups. Allen Lauterbach assumed responsibility within the management committee for drafting the bill and seeing it through.

The 1964 policy resolutions of the organization, formulated in December of 1963, did not provide a strong plank for bargaining legislation.

> Farmers should not be denied the right to market their products because of voluntary membership in a marketing association.
> In some areas various unfair trade practices have been used in order to discourage farmers from participating in marketing and bargaining programs. We support national and state legislation to prohibit discriminatory practices.[23]

The plank pointed out, further, that guidelines for drafting a national bargaining bill could be found in the proposals enacted and pending enactment in several state legislatures.

Even though it was not strong, the bargaining plank had been forced to survive an attack from the President of the Illinois Agricultural Association, Bill Kuhfuss, to kill it in the resolutions committee.[24]

23. American Farm Bureau Federation, *Policy Resolutions for 1964* (Washington: American Farm Bureau Federation, 1963).
24. Farm Bureau staff members, confidential interviews.

State Legislation as a Forerunner to Drafting a
National Bargaining Bill

Just as labor unions were not motivated to lobby for bargaining legislation until employers attempted to curb their organizing efforts, so farm operators were not concerned with bargaining legislation until processors questioned and resisted their right to organize for bargaining purposes. Such resistance in 1960 had caused officials of Cannery Growers, Inc., and the Ohio Farm Bureau to call upon the AFB for help in seeking relief from discrimination by processors. In response, a bill was drafted by Allen Lauterbach and confidentially circulated for review within the Office of the General Counsel of the USDA.[25] However, it wasn't until 1962, when the AAMA organizers themselves began to run into the same difficulties, that serious consideration was given to pursuing new legislation.

Coinciding with the AFB decision to pursue the matter was the announcement by processors of their intention to make wider use of advance producer-processor contracts. According to Allen Lauterbach, the 1963 Annual Report of the Campbell Soup Company referred to the expected use of forward contracting.[26] In addition, many processors, such as the Musselman Division of the Pet Milk Company, sent letters to growers that raised questions about the legality of negotiated prices between producers and processors under antitrust laws.[27] Such operating changes and the emphasis of questions of legality impressed bargaining association organizers with the need for a new look at the legal status of farm bargaining. In studying the matter, they examined existing federal legislation that related to organized farm activity and bargaining statutes enacted in the states of California and Oregon (see Appendix A).

One federal law, more than any other, was seen by the AFB as a foundation statute that gave farm operators the right to organize for purposes of cooperative marketing. The Capper-Volstead Act of 1922 clearly endorsed as a matter of national policy the right of farmers to organize for purposes of conducting cooperative business activity. The act, often referred to as the "Magna Carta" of agricultural marketing cooperatives, gave cooperatives immunity from antitrust laws, provided that their operations did not unduly increase prices and provided that they met certain specifications set forth in the act.

Although the Capper-Volstead Act authorized cooperative business ac-

25. R. J. Mischler (General Counsel, USDA), letter to Roger Fleming (Secretary-Treasurer and Director, Washington Office, American Farm Bureau Federation), September 8, 1960.
26. Allen A. Lauterbach, speech, "Building Marketing and Bargaining Strength of Farmers," Annual Meeting of the Michigan Agricultural Cooperative Marketing Association, April 21, 1964, 3.
27. Pet Milk Company, Musselman Division, Biglerville, Pennsylvania, letter to growers, March 11, 1963.

tivity, it did not refer to the general farm interest organizations, the other type of organization structure through which farm operators typically associated. The absence of such mention was a source of discomfort to legal advisors of the American Farm Bureau and other general farm interest organizations. No federal legislation, including the Capper-Volstead Act, specifically referred to farm bargaining activity. The Capper-Volstead Act was generally interpreted as referring in a precise sense to the activities of cooperative business organizations instead of as blanket endorsement of the act of working together in pursuit of common goals. As general farm interest organizations like the AFB reoriented themselves to add farm bargaining to their organizational activities, the need for a clarifying federal statute to spell out the right of farmers to organize through professional interest organizations was clear. In this respect a precedent had been established by bargaining association laws enacted in several states.

As predecessors to what would be faced in passage of national bargaining legislation, the legislative experiences in Ohio and California provided instructive lessons for the proponents of national legislation. The Ohio Farm Bureau, in particular, had learned much from its work to secure bargaining legislation at the state level following the Ohio tomato case. The legislation was modified substantially from a "little Wagner Act" before being enacted in 1965, when processors — led by the H. J. Heinz Company — had openly challenged it.[28] During the hearings the Farm Bureau had a look at a young attorney, Edward Dunkelberger, who testified against the Ohio Farm Bureau and argued that canners had rights, too. Dunkelberger would later represent the National Canners Association in the congressional hearings on S.109.

Despite the Ohio processors' claims that they would be harassed and could not run their companies under the provisions of the Farm Bureau bill, the measure cleared the Statehouse.[29] The problem had then been to get a rule in the Ohio Senate, where a bottleneck in the Senate Rules Committee had materialized. The Ohio Farm Bureau found it necessary to convince Governor James Rhodes to send a special message to the Senate urging passage of the bill. With this executive push, Ohio Senate Bill 60 cleared the Rules Committee and was passed by the full Senate on June 29, 1965 (see Appendix A).

In developing the legislation, Ohio Farm Bureau officials had for guidance and precedents bargaining bills already enacted in the states of California and Oregon. As cited earlier, the California law, enacted in 1961 as Senate Bill No. 127, specifically authorized the establishment of bargaining associations as distinct from cooperative business organizations engaged in marketing. Similarly, the Oregon statute enacted in 1963 gave producers the "right to join voluntarily and belong to" a bargaining association.[30] Each of

28. Douglas R. Stanfield (Executive Vice-President, Ohio Farm Bureau), telephone interview, September 30, 1968.
29. C. William Swank, personal interview, April 30, 1968.
30. Oregon, *Revised Statutes* (1963), c. 646, secs. 515–45.

the laws spelled out types of discriminatory practices and provided penalties for violation of them.

The Ohio, New York, California and Oregon statutes — all enacted in the past decade — suggest how recently interest in farm bargaining has peaked and how slow in coming legislation recognizing the legal rights of farm operators to organize for bargaining purposes has been.[31] Importantly, the state laws provided limited avenues of relief in the absence of federal legislation. As successfully enacted bargaining bills, the state laws served as forerunners to early drafts of the national proposal and offered encouragement to the enthusiasts for national legislation.

Fresh from winning several preliminary skirmishes within the AFB, proponents of national bargaining legislation set out late in 1963 to develop a proposal that would build upon the experiences and needs of the state Agricultural Marketing Associations. AFB leadership at this point was more concerned with organizing the AAMA than in securing legislation to assist in the producer-organizing efforts. However, the confrontations with the H. J. Heinz and Campbell Soup companies accelerated concern, and Allen Lauterbach capitalized on the opportunity to draft the initial versions of a bill to be introduced in the second session of the Eighty-eighth Congress.[32] The California statute, and to a lesser extent the Oregon and Ohio measures, served as blueprints for the proposal. The fact that the AFB was drafting a bill became public through a talk delivered by Lauterbach to a bargaining association conference in Houston, Texas, on January 11, 1964. Lauterbach stressed that the federal antitrust laws did not effectively deal with unfair trade practices carried on by some processors and that new legislation was needed to prohibit them.[33] He also called for new interpretation of the effect of antitrust laws on farm bargaining activities.

The Lauterbach draft legislation was discussed with the AFB Washington legislative team of Herbert Harris, III, Legislative Counsel, and John Datt and John Lynn, Legislative Directors. Copies of the first draft were also mailed to the state Farm Bureaus with expectations that the bill would be introduced early in the congressional session. In a letter accompanying the draft to county Farm Bureaus in Ohio, Douglas Stanfield said that the bill

---

31. The Farm Bureau claims to have been involved in bargaining since 1921, when an association was formed in Utah for processing vegetables. Many dairy groups organized independently for "bargaining" purposes in the early 1900's. In many instances, however, the distinction between developing cooperative business organizations and bargaining associations has not always been clear.

32. According to Farm Bureau sources, the H. J. Heinz Company, as late as 1964, offered a grower contract in New York that contained a provision stating that a grower could not join a bargaining association. Efforts by the author to confirm or deny this information have been unsuccessful.

33. Allen A. Lauterbach, speech, "Some Legal Developments of Interest to Bargaining Cooperatives," *Proceedings of the Eighth National Conference on Fruit and Vegetable Bargaining Cooperatives* (Washington: Farmer Cooperative Service, USDA, 1964), 49.

was "absolutely essential as a first step" if any progress was going to be made in their bargaining efforts.[34] As drafted, the measure was in the form of an amendment to the Capper-Volstead Act and contained only two sections: The first defined four unlawful practices; the second stipulated criminal penalties and treble damages for violating the act. The language of the bill referred vaguely to "association of producers" without defining the term "bargaining association." It was simply antidiscriminatory in nature. A copy of the draft as circulated follows.

AN ACT

To amend Chapter 12 of Title 7 of the United States Code with respect to the control of unlawful practices affecting associations of producers of agricultural products and members thereof.

Be it enacted by the Senate and House of Representatives of the United States of America in Congress Assembled, that the Act to authorize associations of producers of agricultural products, approved February 18, 1922 (42 Stat. 388, 7 U.S.C. s291-2) be amended by the addition of new Sections 3 and 4, reading as follows:

Section 3.   Unlawful practices — It shall be unlawful for any processor, handler, distributor, or agent thereof, or for any other person, doing business in interstate or foreign commerce, who purchases or contracts to purchase an agricultural commodity from a producer engaged in the production of agricultural products, to do any of the following:

(a) Interfere with, restrain, coerce or boycott any agricultural producer in the exercise of his rights to join and belong to an association of producers of agricultural products;

(b) Discriminate against any agricultural producer with respect to price, quantity, quality or other terms of purchase of raw agricultural commodities by reason of his membership in, or contract with, such association;

(c) Pay of loan money, or give any other thing of value, to a producer as an inducement or reward for refusing to or ceasing to belong to such association;

(d) Knowingly make false reports about the finances, management or activities of such associations, or knowingly interfere in any way with the efforts of such associations in carrying out the legitimate objects thereof.

Section 4.   Criminal penalty — Damages —

(a) Any person who violates, or combines or conspires with any other person to violate, any provision of Section 3 of this Act is guilty of a misdemeanor, and, on conviction thereof, shall be punished by a fine not exceeding $1,000, or imprisonment not exceeding one year, or both, in the discretion of the court.

(b) Any person injured in his business or property by reason of any

34. Douglas R. Stanfield, letter to county Farm Bureau presidents, February 6, 1964.

violation of, or combination or conspiracy to violate, any provision of Section 3 of this Act may sue therefor in the district court of the United States for the district in which the defendant resides or is found or has an agent, without respect to the amount in controversy, and shall recover threefold the damages sustained, and the cost of the suit, including a reasonable attorney's fee.

(c) The foregoing provisions shall not be construed to deprive the proper State courts of jurisdiction in actions for damages thereunder.

In his attempts to discuss the bill with certain members of Congress, John Datt of the AFB's office in Washington encountered skepticism about the proposal.[35] Consequently, a second draft was developed essentially in the same form as the first, but broadened by the defining of an additional unlawful practice regarding grower contracting. A new section, entitled "Affiliation of Associations," was also added. It declared that "nothing in this Act shall be construed to forbid the affiliation of an association . . . with other associations having similar objectives." In a background statement designed to accompany the second draft, the AFB stated that there was nothing in existing law that prohibited such an affiliation but that the new section would further clarify the matter.[36]

Efforts to get the bill introduced were expanded by soliciting the help of other farm organizations. The possibility remained open that the second draft would be amended further if it was decided not to tie the proposed language to the Capper-Volstead Act. The demands of bargaining associations for new protective legislation had finally resulted in a proposal drafted by one of the major farm interest organizations.

35. Allen A. Lauterbach, letter to Douglas R. Stanfield, February 12, 1964.
36. American Farm Bureau Federation, draft of "Background Statement in Support of Legislation Making Illegal Certain Unfair Trade Practices," February 12, 1964.

President Shuman of the American Farm Bureau Federation asked the NCA Board . . . to support his effort to establish bargaining associations. . . . The NCA Board listened carefully and politely took no action. . . . Canners showed no disposition to give voluntary recognition to bargaining associations. Carrying out a threat he had made, President Shuman and the AFBF drafted and obtained Congressional sponsors of S. 109.[1]

Robert B. Heiney

Chapter 3

A Rocky Road: Early Promoting and Positioning

Perhaps because of the predominance of Democratic congresses in the past twenty years or because of its philosophical belief that the government should be the referee and not the playmaker, the AFB has often found itself opposing much prospective farm legislation. In this position, it has argued for less, and not more, government involvement in handling farm surpluses, regulating the market and disposing of food and fiber through domestic and foreign programs. The AFB's traditional plea has been for a return to the free market where price would be the regulator, a posture that set it apart from other general farm interest and commodity groups in Washington. Politicians, who typically consider involvement in any farm legislation hazardous, have especially avoided AFB proposals, most of which have automatically sparked controversy. Thus, while the bargaining proposal represented a departure from past AFB "free market" pleas, politicians nevertheless saw in it a head-on contest between producers and processors.

Among farm pressure groups in Washington, the AFB was a loner, finding its best allies among business groups. One astute Washington observer clearly recognized the dilemma of the farm group; it had acquired a peculiar posture in Washington, as with its members, because it hadn't passed any legislation of its own creation for a long period of time.[2] At the same time, it had been dubbed a spoiler for beating down other legislation, including the Freeman-Cochrane supply control program and the 1963 Kennedy wheat referendum.[3] Legislative strategists for groups that might have allied

1. Robert B. Heiney (Director, Government-Industry Relations, National Canners Association), letter to a constituent, November 8, 1967.
2. A respected lobbyist for another farm organization offered this observation in a confidential interview.
3. Don F. Hadwiger and Ross B. Talbot, *Pressures and Protests: The Kennedy Farm Program and the Wheat Referendum of 1963* (San Francisco: Chandler Publishing Company, 1965), documents the history of these proposals.

themselves with the AFB wanted to avoid identification with such a posture; too many opposing groups and legislators, not to mention the USDA, were out to work against the antagonist organization for its past "sins." According to Charles B. Shuman, the AFB was fully cognizant that it was going against a hostile Congress with its bargaining proposal.[4] Finding congressional sponsors would not be easy; the AFB needed allies.

To bolster its legislative strength and to involve other farm organizations in the bill, the AFB counseled with the National Milk Producers Federation (NMPF) and the National Council of Farmer Cooperatives (NCFC). Philosophically, the NMPF was fairly close to the AFB, having promoted numerous "self-help" measures that would transfer surplus handling functions from the government to the dairy cooperatives. The NCFC was drawn into the inner circle because of its vocal and influential Midwest and West Coast bargaining association contingent. Together, these three organizations comprised a coalition that became involved in drafting and sponsoring the bargaining proposal.

The Coalition: AFB-NCFC-NMPF

A great deal of preliminary work was put into the AFB draft by Mike Norton, Secretary of the NMPF, Ken Naden, Executive Vice-President of the NCFC, and the AFB Washington office team. Early assumptions that the Capper-Volstead Act, Federal Trade Commission Act and the Packers and Stockyards acts included all the law that was needed for bargaining purposes had been demolished by experiences with the FTC in the Ohio tomato case. In addition, there was the unresolved experience of broiler growers in Arkansas. The initial work of the coalition accordingly focused on the form that the bill should take.

In terms of form, the California bargaining bill was looked upon as a model in drafting efforts, but the AFB looked as well to amendment of the Capper-Volstead Act because of its legal stature as a foundation antitrust statute. Amending the act would have two advantages. First, amending was regarded as an easier legislative route than attempting to legislate a new law for bargaining that would likewise provide some antitrust immunity.[5] Second, clarification of the affiliations aspect through amendment would lend legitimacy to the AFB's involvement in bargaining, since the AFB could not qualify as a Capper-Volstead cooperative business organization, and the AAMA was an affiliate of the AFB. The AFB is organized under Illinois not-for-profit organization law, with membership comprised of the state Farm Bureaus. It was thought that the Capper-Volstead Act and the Cooperative

4. Charles B. Shuman (President, American Farm Bureau Federation), personal interview, September 25, 1968.
5. Farm Bureau staff members, confidential interviews.

Marketing Act should be amended to cover this arrangement. Furthermore, the AFB felt that combinations put together for purposes of bargaining necessarily exist under varied conditions depending on the requirements of state law. The Missouri and Illinois Farm Bureaus are organized under state not-for-profit laws. In contrast, the Wisconsin and Indiana Farm Bureaus are organized under state cooperative laws. Yet to bargain successfully, it seemed necessary to have a coordinating device for all the state bargaining associations, regardless of the variations in organization.

For example, the AFB must be sure that the New Jersey Farm Bureau does not accept negotiated bargaining terms that are not acceptable to members of the New York and Ohio Farm Bureaus. The Capper-Volstead and Cooperative Marketing acts do not explicitly cover such relationships or the exchange of information between cooperatives and not-for-profit groups. The AFB thought the acts should be amended to protect such activities.

Finally, the term "bargaining" was not mentioned in the language of the Capper-Volstead Act, with the resulting assumption that the act did not apply to bargaining activity.[6] The original goal of the AFB, then, was an amendment that would spell out the legal authority of bargaining associations more clearly. While agreeing with the over-all objectives of new legislation, other members of the alliance were not keen on this amendment emphasis.

The National Council of Farmer Cooperatives from the outset was in support of a bargaining bill that would strengthen farmers' group efforts. Strong impetus for this action came from NCFC bargaining association members, particularly those in California. Historically, the council addressed itself to generalized support for the cooperative principle — working together toward a common goal — and did not distinguish sharply, possibly for internal political reasons, between operating cooperative business organizations and "bargaining" cooperatives. Nevertheless, it had a mandate through long-standing policy resolutions to support bargaining legislation. Specifically, one resolution adopted in 1940 and revised in 1964 read:

Bargaining Activities of Cooperatives — The Council supports legislation designed:
1. To authorize associations of producers of agricultural products to bargain singly and jointly for price and other terms of trade involved in the more effective marketing of their products.
2. To authorize cooperative associations to become members of bargaining agencies and to initiate and utilize federal or state marketing order agreements and to employ common marketing agencies.
3. To protect cooperatives from actions by distributors, handlers or buyers of farm products which in any way may hinder, obstruct or interfere with the formation and operation of farmer-controlled cooperative associations.

6. *Ibid.*

Another resolution adopted in 1958 and reaffirmed in 1964 supported legislation in behalf of bargaining efforts.

> *Bargaining Associations* — The National Council of Farmer Cooperatives favors the adoption of federal and state legislation to create a more favorable climate in which cooperative bargaining associations can develop more effective bargaining power for the sale of their commodities.

Based upon these resolutions, the council worked closely with the AFB in developing a legislative proposal. However, it did not concur with the idea of amending the Capper-Volstead Act. It felt that the anti-cooperative elements in Washington that had shown considerable strength during the tax hearings in the 1950's and early 1960's might attempt to engineer a wholesale revision of the act if an amendment were undertaken, and opening the act to amendments was therefore considered dangerous by the council.[7] But despite its reservations, the council went along with amendment proposed by the AFB in hope that the action would stimulate interest and debate for bargaining legislation.

Like the NCFC, the National Milk Producers Federation reluctantly supported the amendment approach. It felt that sufficient case history had already been built within the framework of the Capper-Volstead law by dairy cooperatives. Amendment might make it difficult for these dairy groups if the case history were subject to new questions in terms of an amendment.[8] However, the NMPF agreed that some type of bargaining legislation would be good and that it was something they wished dairy groups could have had thirty years ago.

The NMPF was first introduced to the new proposal in its usual winter meeting with AFB legislative officials in January of 1964.[9] Although the NMPF President Glenn Lake was pushing for bargaining legislation that went far beyond the AFB measure, the NMPF Board of Directors received the Farm Bureau bill with the idea that any legislation strengthening farm organization efforts would be beneficial.[10] Importantly, the NMPF recognized also that the AFB was looking for a piece of legislation that was not highly controversial.[11] The organization's leaders felt that this proposal by the AFB was constructive even though it did not regard it as an important piece of leg-

7. Kenneth D. Naden (Executive Vice-President, National Council of Farmer Cooperatives), personal interview, April 1, 1968.

8. Patrick Healy (Assistant Secretary, National Milk Producers Federation), personal interview, June 13, 1968.

9. According to E. M. Norton (Secretary, National Milk Producers Federation), Allen A. Lauterbach (General Counsel, American Farm Bureau Federation) initiated discussions about the bargaining proposal in 1963, and they continued on an informal basis until the proposal was introduced in May, 1964.

10. The National Milk Producers Federation, as well as the NCFC, was experiencing a strong pressure from its dairy bargaining contingent. Mr. Norton felt that the bargaining proponents were making a strategic mistake by demanding an all-encompassing piece of legislation.

11. Healy, interview.

islation insofar as dairy producers were concerned. Their goal was simply to protect dairy interests.

The positions of the three groups centered upon two points. The AFB camp felt that the Capper-Volstead Act was broad enough and sufficient to cover bargaining efforts if it was properly amended. The NCFC and the NMPF supported a bargaining bill, but they were not enthusiastic about amending the Capper-Volstead Act. They had a tremendous fear that opening the act to amendment would jeopardize the series of legal decisions that had been passed down since enactment of the bill. This possibility was especially imminent should anything short of a united farm front support the proposal.

The alliance found unanimity on one point, however; it did not want to pass a bill that would give the NFO a better lease on life. The NFO was viewed by all three organizations as a threat, symbolized by a just-completed NFO holding action that had upset local milk markets and caused considerable friction with cooperatives.[12] Cooperative business organization leaders maintained that the NFO action was a malicious attempt to tear down institutions that had taken years to build. The issue of whether all types of farm organizations would be considered cooperatives was a perpetual source of problems to the life of S. 109. Indeed, beneath the clouds of political courting and clandestine maneuvering, it was, perhaps, the central issue.

Are All Farm Organizations Cooperatives?

The discussions surrounding S. 109, beginning at this point, brought into the open a question that had been kept buried for some time: are *all* farm organizations cooperatives? Some were innocently unaware of the divisive power of the question, and others deliberately kept it hidden. The entry of the AFB into bargaining helped to force attention to the issue, but the existence and activity of NFO was a more potent influence. Open discussion of the issue caused new wounds and left old scars festering. Seldom viewed in the panorama of basic changes that were shaking farm markets, and seldom examined for the structural and functional relations of complementary organizational forms, the issue unfortunately intruded itself on an emotional basis.

The entry of the NFO and AFB into bargaining was looked upon in some quarters with remembrances of the Farm Holiday movement and the Wisconsin milk pool in the 1930's. Yet, this entry was never viewed in historical context for lessons to learn. As a point of debate among the AFB-NCFC-NMPF coalition, the issue of whether all farm groups are cooperatives was also the basis for plotting against the NFO. Ultimately, it was to result in such vague language that it would serve as a major setback to the bill at a later point in the life of S. 109.

12. *Ibid.*

Introduction of the Bill

With a proposed draft of the bargaining bill in hand and the support of the coalition secure, the AFB set out once again to find congressional sponsors. This task proved to be more difficult than had been anticipated. With the AFB's reputation for defeating legislation, not making it, legislators viewed the organization with caution. Furthermore, the whole idea of bargaining in agriculture — except in such areas as California — was new and not widely accepted. Many congressmen were apprehensive about it.

The responsibility for finding sponsors for the AFB bill fell upon John Datt. As an early organizer of bargaining associations in the AFB's fruit and vegetable commodity branch, Datt knew the difficulties facing bargaining associations and what legislation was needed to help them.[13] He faced several problems, however. His immediate superior, Roger Fleming, Director of the Washington office and responsible for AFB's legislative committee structure, was something less than enthusiastic about the idea of bargaining and didn't want to push any provision in legislation for which there wasn't a clear-cut statement in the AFB's policy resolutions. In addition, Datt had to find congressmen who would introduce the bill, a search that went on for months. Finally, Congressman Robert T. Ashmore of South Carolina was asked to introduce the bill, but he refused. As a result of this reception, Datt got cold feet and admitted that he couldn't find anyone.[14]

The job of finding a congressman to sponsor the bill then moved to the Ohio Farm Bureau. The Ohio organization was constrained in talking up the bargaining bill by the lingering AFB resentment over the manner in which the Ohio group promoted its chain store purchase idea among other state Farm Bureaus in 1963.[15] Despite this limitation, Douglas Stanfield and other Ohio officials accepted the challenge and pursued it vigorously. Their first contact was Congressman Delbert Latta, a Republican representing a cash-crop district in Ohio heavily populated by Farm Bureau members. Congressman Latta was asked to speak at the Ohio Farm Bureau's annual meeting on the condition that he would later introduce the bill. Latta, who is regarded as speaking for canners' interests better than the canners do themselves, accepted the speaking engagement but later refused to introduce the bill.[16] His role in the life of S. 109 did not end with this refusal.

The Ohio Farm Bureau turned next to another of its Republican congressmen, William McCulloch, ranking member of the House Judiciary Committee. As a senior member of the committee to which the bargaining bill would likely be referred, McCulloch was considered a prime sponsor for

13. John Datt (Legislative Director and Assistant Director, Washington Office, American Farm Bureau Federation), personal interview, June 11, 1968.
14. Douglas R. Stanfield (Executive Vice-President, Ohio Farm Bureau), telephone interview, September 10, 1968.
15. *Ibid.*   16. *Ibid.*

the measure. However, he also had his reasons for not wanting to introduce such a bill. Finally, Stanfield succeeded in getting Congressman Robert Secrest from the 15th District of Ohio to introduce the bill. Secrest, a Democrat and former official of the FTC, shared strong feelings about the rightness of the proposal, and it was introduced in the House of Representatives late in the session on May 5, 1964, as H.R. 11146 (see Appendix B). As expected, it was referred to the House Judiciary Committee, which sent copies to the FTC and USDA for reports.

Securing sponsorship in the Senate proved much easier. The AFB called upon a long-time friend of the farmer, Senator George Aiken of Vermont, the ranking minority member of the Senate Committee on Agriculture and Forestry. Senator Aiken considered himself a protector of farm interests and had long served as a-catalyst in getting the farm groups to work together. The companion bill to H.R. 11146 was introduced in the Senate on May 15, 1964, as S. 2849 under the cosponsorship of Senator Aiken, a Republican, and Senator Frank Lausche of Ohio, a Democrat. By its success in having the bill introduced in the Congress, the Ohio Farm Bureau had scored a major victory for farm operators over conservative elements in the AFB who had a distaste for any bargaining legislation.

The measure as introduced was in questionable form from the viewpoint of some coalition members, but it had nevertheless survived another crisis in its struggle for life. As introduced, the Secrest bill was in an elementary form that sought to amend the Capper-Volstead Act of 1922 by adding three sections. The first section defined practices that would be in violation of the law if they were "knowingly" committed. These included interfering with, resisting, coercing or boycotting farm operators in the exercise of their right to join an association of producers; discriminating against any person with respect to price, quantity or quality of his product; encouraging a producer to breach or cancel his membership agreement in a producer association; providing financial inducement for not joining; and making false reports about the association of producers.

Section two of the amendment contained the enforcement provision. Specifically, it provided for criminal penalties for those guilty of violating the act, and the opportunity for those damaged by it to sue in district court for treble damages.

The third part of the amendment was designed by the AFB to condone legislatively the affiliation of an association of producers with other associations having similar objectives or with "bona fide agricultural or horticultural organizations whose primary objectives are to promote, protect, and represent the business and economic interests of farmers and ranchers." As such, it had specific reference to the affiliation relationship between the AFB and the AAMA.

The bill did not get much play after its introduction late in the second session of the Eighty-eighth Congress. Even though some major hurdles had been cleared in getting the bill that far along, the general attitude was not enthusiastic. NFO activities were the hottest conversation piece around, and even some state Farm Bureau people raised the question, "Why are we for this kind of bill when it would help NFO?" [17] Furthermore, representatives from farm districts, already few in number, faced further depletion in their ranks after the 1964 reapportionment ruling. Legislators were certainly not going to act upon such a controversial issue until they received pressure and support from their constituents; thus, the bill did not receive a push even from the legislators who had introduced it.

At the executive session meeting of the National Canners Association's Board of Directors on May 29th, Charles B. Shuman explained the bargaining program of the AFB. To the surprise of NCA officials, Mr. Shuman reiterated his idea, first expressed in meetings in the fall of 1962, that the AFB was *not* thinking of collective bargaining as practiced by organized labor.[18] However, he suggested that there was a growing belief that marketing orders were not a substitute for collective bargaining. Shuman posed as the alternative to the AFB program the NFO's approach of force in which the role of "market price" was misunderstood. According to him, the AFB's problem was that "9 times out of 10 it seems the processor slams the door in our face." [19] He suggested that somebody was going to organize farmers and that the canners' resistance to AFB bargaining efforts was "childish." In answer to the continued resistance, he said, the AFB had introduced H.R. 11146, which, however, would not require anyone to deal with the AAMA or require anyone to belong. In short, the AFB President said that his organization resented the "big brother" attitude on the part of canners.

After careful study, the NCA concluded in a stormy reaction that the bill represented an unprecedented intrusion of the Federal Government into the commercial negotiations and dealings between processors and growers.[20] Furthermore, the NCA argued that the bill would destroy the processors long-recognized right to deal or refuse to deal with whom they pleased. Further, the NCA regarded the measure as imposing severe criminal penalties for entirely legitimate conduct. Although H.R. 11146 was not essentially an antitrust measure and was not concerned with cooperative business organizations, the NCA recognized that it was an amendment to the Capper-Volstead Act that would grant partial antitrust immunity to bargaining associations. This NCA position in opposition was a standoff to the AFB's proposal.

17. William Anderson (Assistant Legislative Director, American Farm Bureau Federation), personal interview, April 2, 1968.
18. National Canners Association, "Synopsis of Remarks of Charles B. Shuman," NCA Board of Directors Meeting, May 29, 1964, in files of Luke F. Beckman (President, Minster Canning Company).
19. *Ibid.*
20. National Canners Association, Memorandum Re: "Analysis of H.R. 11146," June 3, 1964, in files of Luke F. Beckman.

At this critical stage in the life of the bill, the AFB had not yet fully caught the "bargaining bug." [21] Many local and national leaders preferred to continue the AAMA efforts without additional legislation, although they did not actively oppose the bill outside of AFB confines. But full-fledged support was not forthcoming, either; a group of influential AFB leaders still looked upon AFB as a Capper-Volstead cooperative and shared strong feelings that the organization was covered adequately by the Capper-Volstead Act. Obviously, AFB proponents of national bargaining legislation had a major internal education job to do, if grass-roots support for the bill was to be forthcoming.

Transmitting The Bargaining Idea. Conveying the idea that a general farm organization such as the American Farm Bureau needed additional legislation to engage in bargaining activities proved to be difficult. After all, the general interest organizations had preceded most regional cooperatives and had, in fact, given birth to some. A further handicap was the apathy with which many state groups viewed bargaining activity. Most were content with limiting their activities to "grass-roots" policy formulation. Livestock farmers in the Midwest were still oriented to traditional farm markets and not to direct confrontations with processors and other handlers through direct selling, contracting and other means. In addition, many state Farm Bureaus had let their insurance and supply business activities become primary and seemed unaware of the basic structural and functional changes taking place within the farm organizations and among farm groups. The role of bargaining in price discovery appeared foreign.

Given these perceptions, several state leaders of Farm Bureaus were antagonistic to the bargaining proposal. This was particularly true of those states that were active in supply businesses and those that were opposed to involvement in any kind of marketing activity. Officials of these organizations disliked bargaining associations and viewed them as a threat. Farm Bureaus in Minnesota, Indiana, Tennessee, Missouri, Wisconsin and Texas expressed much concern. They protested.

In addition to opponents in AFB ranks, many legislators in Washington had to be convinced of the need for such legislation and the place of farm bargaining in the future. Congressional action can be encouraged in several ways; campaign contributions by proponents are, of course, effective, but a proposal containing well-thought-out provisions can often get action on its own merits. The bargaining proponents within the AFB thought that they had a bill that merited consideration on the latter count.[22] To secure critical grass-roots support for the bill, the Ohio Farm Bureau and similar organizations vigorously talked up the need for bargaining legislation.

21. C. William Swank (Assistant Executive Vice-President, Ohio Farm Bureau), personal interview, April 30, 1968.
22. Shuman, interview.

Should the Capper-Volstead Act Be Amended?

As proponents of the bargaining bill continued to develop their ideas and win converts to the need for legislation, controversy heightened over whether the Capper-Volstead Act indeed provided sufficient protection, and whether the best tactic was to amend that act. The questions had been raised at an earlier point in discussions between the AFB-NCFC-NMPF coalition. Now the matter was opened to further debate as these groups sent the bill out to their members across the country for legal review and interpretation.

In a May 15, 1964, issue of a member newsletter known as the "Washington Councilor," the National Council of Farmer Cooperatives called attention to the newly introduced bill with the following statement.

> The stimulus for this bill comes from the persistent refusal of processors to recognize producers' associations for bargaining purposes. Such refusal to recognize, and intimidation of prospective cooperative members have become more apparent as organization of bargaining associations was accelerated in recent years.

The NCFC circulated copies of the bill to its membership, asked their opinion about the bill's content and suggested two possible amendments. One would have inserted the phrase, "other than associations of producers as defined under the Capper-Volstead Act," in the prohibitions section of the bill, thus exempting cooperative business organization from the prohibitions of the act. The second suggested amendment applied to the same section and added to it, "provided that 'association' as used hereafter in this section, shall pertain to any association of agricultural producers which, in bargaining for its members, assumes product ownership, or otherwise incurs financial responsibility to each producer for sale of the product." [23] The purpose of the first amendment was to assure that cooperative business organizations, as voluntary farm organizations working toward the same goals as the bargaining associations, were not subjected to the bill's restrictions. The second amendment represented an effort to avoid offering any protection to the NFO.

These amendments reflected some of the objections raised by the NCFC Board of Directors when the Secrest bill was discussed during its June meeting. The board had raised three fundamental concerns about the draft bill: (1) the legislation should not apply to cooperatives; (2) it did not want to do anything in any way, shape or form that could be of benefit to NFO; (3) the NFO should be excluded by defining a bargaining association as an organization that assumed some kind of responsibility for marketing members' crops.[24] This last concern, expressed by Ralph Bunje of the California Can-

23. National Council of Farmer Cooperatives, "Washington Councilor," May 15, 1964.
24. John Datt, memo to Charles B. Shuman, Roger Fleming (Secretary-Treasurer

ning Peach Association, implied that the NFO did not assume any responsibility. Bunje believed that failure to make such a distinction would "tend to create labor union type of organization and could very well provide a real boon for groups like the N.F.O." [25]

Several members of the NCFC gave the bill immediate attention in response to the NCFC's request for a reading and interpretation. In Wisconsin, Mr. Milo Swanton, widely respected Executive Secretary of the Wisconsin Council of Agricultural Cooperatives, called a luncheon meeting of farm officials and cooperative attorneys in Madison. Joining Swanton at the meeting were Frank Wing and Attorney Dale Thompson, representing the Wisconsin Farm Bureau; and Vernon Stuck and Attorney Walter Ela, representing the Wisconsin Council of Agricultural Cooperatives. Following the Madison discussion, the Wisconsin cooperative group was advised to exercise great care "lest inadvertently greater damage be done to co-ops generally than the benefits to a relatively small group of organizations would warrant." [26] Furthermore, the state cooperative council was cautioned by its attorney that cooperative business organizations, defined as handlers in the Secrest bill, could not refuse to accept NFO members as producers without being accused of boycotting them.

The results of the meeting were reported in a letter to Kenneth Naden of the National Council of Farmer Cooperatives.

> The general need for such legislation was expressed by Frank Wing of the State Farm Bureau. Individual growers of cash crops in Wisconsin have, in years past, experienced pressures similar to those defined in the state of Ohio.
>
> It was generally agreed, that, if at all possible, it would be better to try to solve the problems by some other approach, such as through the federal anti-trust section, rather than attempt to amend so basic an act as Capper-Volstead.
>
> It was generally agreed that if the bill were to pass, cooperatives should be exempted. However, there were a few mental reservations as to what effect such exemption for cooperatives in this matter might have upon the general cooperative image. [27]

In stating these views, Swanton cited three points that would receive much attention in subsequent handling of the bill: (1) the need for legislation to alleviate pressures upon farmers and their bargaining groups, (2) the question-

and Director, Washington Office, American Farm Bureau Federation) and Allen A. Lauterbach, June 19, 1964.

25. Ralph Bunje (General Manager, California Canning Peach Association), letter to Harold Hartley (Manager, Fruit and Vegetable Division, American Agricultural Marketing Association), July 1, 1964.

26. Walter Ela (Attorney), letter to Milo Swanton (Executive Secretary, Wisconsin Council of Agricultural Cooperatives), July 7, 1964.

27. Milo Swanton, letter to Kenneth D. Naden, July 6, 1964.

able wisdom of amending the Capper-Volstead Act and (3) concern for the cooperatives' image.

Mr. Swanton expressed the group's opinion that the first suggested amendment — exemption for cooperatives — would be agreeable. The Wisconsin people felt, however, that the second amendment appeared to be an attack on collective bargaining associations. More precisely, Swanton wrote that the group would like to see the amendment apply "to a vicious group such as NFO but it's a ticklish task to apply this to NFO without adversely affecting bargaining groups doing a constructive job." [28] Swanton also expressed fear that the third portion of the bill might be misconstrued by NFO leaders to give their organization a free rein to continue forcing dairy cooperatives to enter into contracts with it. Since farm leaders in Wisconsin and Washington, D.C., did not consider the NFO a cooperative under terms of the Capper-Volstead Act, the affiliations section of the bill was looked upon as legitimizing the NFO plant contracts and as helping them as much as the AFB. At the end of his letter, Swanton summed up his feelings with the comment, "Generally speaking, there was hope that action on H.R. 11146 might be cut off by reason of congressional adjournment."

Many congressmen also sent copies of the bill to farm organizations and trade groups in their home districts for review. Congressman Charles Teague of California used a somewhat different tack. He had introduced a bill identical to H.R. 11146 in the Eighty-eighth Congress, and in a letter to F. R. Wilcox, General Manager of the Sunkist Growers, on May 11, 1964, Congressman Teague requested an appraisal of his bill H.R. 11331 by officials of the orange growers' cooperative.

In reviewing the Teague proposal, Allen Mather, then legal counsel for the Sunkist organization, noted that the language of the bill closely paralleled the provisions of the California bargaining association law.

> At the time the legislation was being considered in California we saw the same thing that is occurring in connection with this national legislation, namely the lumping together of marketing with bargaining associations. As we analyzed the factual circumstances, there was no need for this type of legislation in connection with marketing cooperatives. As we know them here, the grower who chooses to market through a cooperative sends all of his produce to that cooperative. Hence he is not in a position of having reprisals taken against him by outside processors. This situation, of course, can be completely different with respect to a bargaining cooperative that does not actually market the commodities to the consumer. In any event, in California we redrafted the language of the original proposal so that the prohibitions apply specifically to bargaining associations. [29]

---

28. *Ibid.*
29. Allen F. Mather (General Counsel, Sunkist Growers, Inc.), memo to F. R. Wilcox (General Manager, Sunkist Growers, Inc.), May 19, 1964.

In analyzing the proposed national legislation, Mather made a clear-cut case for differentiation between marketing cooperatives and bargaining associations. Based upon these differences, he advocated excluding marketing cooperatives from operation of the national legislation.

Mather also shared his views on the advisability of amending the Capper-Volstead Act:

> At the Federal level I would feel very strongly that the proposal should not arise as an amendment to the Capper-Volstead Act. The Capper-Volstead, imperfect as it may be, is the Magna Carta for cooperatives. We are aware that anti-cooperative groups have raised questions about the Capper-Volstead Act whenever the opportunity has presented itself. It appears to me that this proposal for amending that Act would provide another opportunity for general attacks on the Capper-Volstead Act.[30]

Regarding the third section of the bill, Mather pointed out that the purpose of this section was directed to the relationship of the AAMA to the AFB. However, Mather was concerned with its implications in respect to the broader question of cooperative development through a federated system of merger or acquisition rather than as a limited matter of legitimatizing bargaining activity. The Sunkist attorney therefore dismissed this section as being premature and not of sufficient value to include in the proposal.

Such close scrutiny of the bill by farm groups and legislators raised many questions and uncertainties and made forward progress difficult in the Eighty-eighth Congress. While Congressman Secrest was working hard for a committee hearing before Congress adjourned on August 22nd, the bill was tied up in committee over a constitutional question regarding state legislatures.[31] Another Ohio Congressman, Republican William McCulloch, was reported to have been very much involved with this delay. John Lynn, the AFB lobbyist who worked closely with the bill, suggested that state Farm Bureaus write to members of the House Judiciary Committee and request at least a one-day hearing on the bill even though possibilities of passage were considered remote.[32] However, Shuman discouraged a one-day hearing and suggested that "if this is all we can do — nothing would be better." [33]

In early anticipation that the bill might come to hearing before the House Judiciary Committee, several organizations had drafted testimony, but their preparation went for naught when momentum for a hearing was not generated. Also anticipating a hearing, Congressman Latta of Ohio called a meeting of various parties in his Washington office on August 17. Attending were Messrs. Reeder and Connaly of the H. J. Heinz Company, Page of the

---

30. *Ibid.*

31. John C. Lynn (Legislative Director, American Farm Bureau Federation), memo to Allen A. Lauterbach, July 22, 1964.

32. *Ibid.*

33. Charles B. Shuman, memo to Allen A. Lauterbach, in files of American Farm Bureau Federation.

Campbell Soup Company, Robert Heiney of the National Canners Association; Allen Lauterbach, Herbert Harris and John Datt represented the American Farm Bureau, and Vice-President Robert Summer, Wendell Weller, George Morrison and Morris Allton represented the Ohio Farm Bureau. Although Latta had called the meeting on the basis of information he had received that the canners could live with the bill if changes were made in the penalty clause, the canning company officials announced at the meeting that they were opposed to the bill in its entirety.[34] Latta displayed his primary sympathy to the canners by then suggesting that the AFB should reduce its efforts in promoting the bill.[35] Despite the vain efforts of Lauterbach and Harris to establish the necessity of such legislation, the unsuccessful conference had one benefit: It pinpointed the processors' stand on the bill.

The proponents also learned some lessons from the confrontation with the processors. To succeed in getting congressional action on the bill, other states would have to show interest and get behind it. Importantly, the Ohio Farm Bureau officials also recognized that if the Secrest bill were to come to a public hearing, they would have to produce witnesses who could testify that they had been discriminated against. These conclusions were spelled out in a meeting of the AFB-NCFC-NMPF coalition in the fall of 1964. For the first time each organization presented its formal views on the bill based upon feedback from its member organizations.[36] The National Milk Producers Federation assumed a position similar to its earlier stand on the bill. According to Pat Healy, Assistant Secretary, the dairy groups said, "Look, we have weathered this storm already. We're sympathetic, but don't do anything that will wreck us now." [37]

In a similar fashion, the National Council of Farmer Cooperatives, represented by Ken Naden and its new Director of Marketing and International Trade, Robert Hampton, expressed fear of amending the Capper-Volstead Act. The council, which is composed of bargaining associations as well as marketing and supply cooperative business organizations, had experienced some intramural fighting within its own ranks about whether to support bargaining legislation at all.[38] The principal opposition came from dairy and other cooperatives that had fresh and bitter memories of the NFO attempt to overrun them. Generally, the NMPF and NCFC insisted upon approach through new agricultural legislation rather than through the Capper-Volstead amendment.

The AFB, represented by Allen Lauterbach of the Chicago headquarters and John Datt, Jack Lynn and Herbert Harris of the Washington office,

34. Morris E. Allton (Staff member, Ohio Farm Bureau), memo to Douglas R. Stanfield, August 24, 1964.
35. Allen A. Lauterbach, personal interview, June 19, 1968.
36. L. Gene Lemon (Assistant General Counsel, American Farm Bureau Federation), personal interview, June 19, 1968.
37. Healy, interview.
38. Naden, interview.

still maintained that the Capper-Volstead Act, if clarified, was broad enough and sufficient to cover their bargaining efforts. This position was based, in part, on a meeting Allen Lauterbach held with officials of the FTC in October. The officials indicated that the farm proposal could expect a boost from investigations of the National Commission on Food Marketing.

With these three rather irreconcilable positions, some alternative solution or middle ground had to be reached. The three organizations agreed with the general objectives of the bill. The disagreement focused on what means should be used to attain them, and it was suggested that a new approach would be desirable. Nonetheless, the organizations agreed to introduce the bill again in the Eighty-ninth Congress to keep the momentum alive.

When Congress adjourned in 1964, it left H.R. 11146 in the same state as it had been introduced. It never moved beyond the Judiciary Committee and died with the Eighty-eighth Congress.

1965: Year of Education and Discussion

As the new year was rung in, and with it the first session of the Eighty-ninth Congress, the AFB bargaining bill was reintroduced in the House by Congressman Secrest on January 4, 1965, as H.R. 898 and referred to the Judiciary Committee. On the Senate side, the bill was reintroduced on January 6, 1965, by Senator George Aiken under the bipartisan cosponsorship of Senators Frank Lausche of Ohio, Eugene McCarthy of Minnesota and Milton Young of North Dakota. The bill carried a number that it would retain to its final stage of enactment — S. 109 — and was referred to the Senate Committee on Agriculture and Forestry.

In form, the measure was exactly the same as the 1964 bill in proposing to amend the Capper-Volstead Act, though division continued among the farm organizations with respect to this feature of the bill. Nevertheless, the National Farmers Union (NFU), which for the moment seemed to forget its rivalry with the AFB, called it a "stiff Federal criminal antitrust weapon." [39] S. 109 was still viewed coolly by many state Farm Bureaus, however, and did not receive support from the AFB press. However, other groups did not delay in discussing the proposal.

At its annual meeting in Seattle, the National Council of Farmer Cooperatives devoted considerable discussion to the form the bill should take. In the main, these discussions were limited to informal meetings with the bargaining association members of the council. These meetings confirmed that the opinions expressed earlier by the council's Washington officials, that it would be unwise to open the Capper-Volstead Act to amendment, were widely held within the NCFC. However, the members remained fully behind

39. National Farmers Union, "Bill to Bolster Farmer Bargaining Power, Protect Him from Coercion, Introduced," *Washington Newsletter*, January 15, 1965.

the intent of the bill. It was mutually agreed that another course of action had to be found that could achieve the objective without involving the Capper-Volstead Act in any way.

The alternative offered by the NCFC was a "Capper-Volstead type" act for bargaining associations only. A draft of this proposal was submitted to members of the coalition in the form of a letter from Naden to Allen Lauterbach of the AFB dated March 30, 1965. Copies of the letter were mailed to Mike Norton of the NMPF, John Datt of the AFB's Washington office and Douglas Stanfield of the Ohio Farm Bureau. In this letter, Naden indicated NCFC's feeling that a differentiation between marketing cooperatives and bargaining associations had to be made.

> As we agreed last fall we have given some thought to the form of language which might be used in H.R. 898 or a similar bill which would achieve the objective without involving Capper-Volstead in any way. The best way seems to be to write a bill as a separate Capper-Volstead type act for bargaining associations only. Then its meaning and intent and applicability will be clear.
>
> The enclosed draft can serve as a starting point for further discussion of the exact wording which might be used. The suggested wording does not pin down the exact dividing line between "bargaining" and "operating" cooperatives but indicated that no coverage is intended here for the cooperatives which warehouse, grade, pack, and process farm products. One dividing line between the bargaining associations covered by this proposed wording and cooperatives now under the Capper-Volstead Act would be whether they have capital investment in fixed facilities for handling products of the members.[40]

In presenting the NCFC view, Mr. Naden advocated a simple and bold approach to the problem at hand instead of the backdoor strategy suggested by the AFB. Though the approach went directly to the heart of the problem, it was clearly somewhat ahead of its time; the membership in few, if any, of the farm organizations were ready to accept this type of legislation.[41] The draft transmitted by Naden's letter was as follows.

PROPOSED LANGUAGE TO AMEND SECREST-AIKEN BILL
H.R. 898
A BILL
To control unfair practices affecting associations of producers of agricultural products and members thereof engaged in bargaining.

---

40. Kenneth D. Naden, letter to Allen A. Lauterbach, March 30, 1965.

41. Naden's proposal would have provided enabling legislation for an association organized for the *exclusive* purpose of bargaining for terms of sale. Associations that had no capital investment in fixed facilities for handling members' products would be so defined. This proposal was not acceptable to AFB personnel, however, because Farm Bureaus in some states were handling products. Furthermore, the proposal required that the association take title to the product. Many bargaining associations, Farm Bureaus included, were not organized to do so.

Be it enacted by the Senate and House of Representatives of the United States of America in Congress assembled:

SECTION 1: That persons, such as farmers, fruit growers, ranchers, dairymen, and others engaged in the production of agricultural products may act together in associations, corporate or otherwise, with or without capital stock for the exclusive purpose of bargaining for desirable terms of sale in interstate and foreign markets for the raw products of the persons so engaged. Such associations may conduct joint promotion activities and may conduct their marketing through a common sales agency; and such associations and their members may make the necessary contracts and agreements to effect such purposes; provided, however, that such associations are operated for the mutual benefit of the members thereof as producers and conform to all of the following requirements:

(1) That no member of the association is allowed more than one vote because of the amount of stock or membership capital he may own therein; or that the Association does not pay dividends on stock or membership capital in excess of eight percent per annum; and

(2) That the association shall not deal in the products of nonmembers to an amount in greater value than such as are handled by it for members; and

(3) That the association takes title to products of its members for which it acts as bargaining agent for such products.

SECTION 2: Unlawful Practices. It should be unlawful for any processor, handler, distributor, dealer, or agent thereof, doing business in interstate or foreign commerce who purchases or contracts to purchase an agricultural commodity from a producer engaged in production of agricultural products, who belongs to or seeks to belong to any association defined in SECTION 1, knowingly to do any of the following:

REMAINDER OF H.R. 898 REMAINS SAME

The American Farm Bureau was typical. Despite the energetic efforts of Ohio's Douglas Stanfield — who was the strongest spokesman for the bill in 1964–1965 — many of the state Farm Bureaus maintained a passive attitude toward S. 109.[42] The passivity made clear to proponents of the bill within the AFB that their public relations work in Washington would have to be supported by a major member relations effort.[43] To circumvent antagonistic state hierarchies, bargaining proponents sponsored farm-operator tours for producers of similar crops in different states; the tours provided the opportunity to mingle and to exchange ideas. Heavy emphasis was also placed on enacting state bargaining laws.[44]

The activities of the AFB's Washington office with respect to S. 109 were characterized by foot dragging throughout 1965, with no great effort made to have hearings or any other action taken. The AFB Washington con-

42. Datt, interview.
43. Anderson, interview.
44. A bargaining bill was even introduced in the Illinois Legislature in 1965, but it did not receive a warm reception from the state's Republicans.

tingent appeared to be content to have S. 109 sitting before the Senate and House as proof of the intention to clobber the canners and other processors if they continued to fight farm bargaining efforts.[45] They seemed to be relying on the Washington truism that the threat of legislation sometimes achieves the same effect, without actually having it enacted into law.

Toward the end of 1965, the purpose of the S. 109 proposal was finally being promoted into national policy by the state Farm Bureaus active in bargaining. Simultaneously, some AFB officials, finally recognizing the problems of bargaining associations, began to think that there might be something worth while in this type of legislation after all. The idea began to catch fire.

45. Robert B. Heiney, personal interview, April 3, 1968.

We want to emphasize that Farm Bureau does not seek, and will not support, legislation . . . to force processors to negotiate with marketing associations. We seek only legislation which sets forth rules of fairplay on the part of the processor and others in their business relationships with farmers and ranchers.[1]

Charles B. Shuman

It's getting late. We move now or maybe, never.[2]

Dr. Kenneth Hood

Chapter 4

A Bitter Fight Looms

While 1965 passed without legislative action of any kind on the bargaining measure, 1966 proved to be highly volatile. Senator Aiken's increasing interest in the bill led to his maintaining close contact with the AFB. He informed them of the possibilities of bringing the bill to hearing and played an instrumental role by insisting that all farm groups would have to support the bill or it wouldn't get to first base.[3] As a result of Aiken's interest, the Senate Agriculture Committee became the critical arena for S. 109, providing a stimulus for further discussion among the farm organizations.

Informal meetings among coalition members and state groups took place throughout the first three months of 1966. In March, Douglas Stanfield of the Ohio Farm Bureau led a delegation of legislative committeemen to promote S. 109 on Capitol Hill. During his visit, he charged that some processors were showing a reluctance to bargain with farmers' associations and were threatening to contract in other states.[4] Stanfield also conferred at this time with officials of the AFB and the NCFC, who were trying to determine productive alternative approaches to the bargaining proposal from a wide range of suggestions.

Legal analysis within the AFB had resulted in a continued focus on devising an amendment to the Capper-Volstead Act that would protect bargaining groups while exempting cooperative business organizations from the provisions directed at processors. The AFB legal staff was also giving consideration to an entirely new proposal that would stand alone and contain in-

1. Charles B. Shuman (President, American Farm Bureau Federation), testimony in U.S. Senate, Subcommittee of the Committee on Agriculture and Forestry, *Hearings on S. 109*, 89th Cong., 2d sess., 1966, 15.
2. Kenneth Hood (General Manager, American Agricultural Marketing Association), speech, "Challenges in Marketing," Norman, Oklahoma, May 1, 1968.
3. Charles Weaver (Legislative Assistant to Senator George Aiken), personal interview, April 5, 1968.
4. Ohio Farm Bureau, press release, March 14, 1966.

junctive relief in the enforcement provisions. The National Council of Farmer Cooperatives' bargaining proposal drafted in 1965, however, had been found unacceptable to the Farm Bureau.[5] Support for this approach would have constituted recognition that the AFB was a different type of organization than cooperative business organizations. Most AFB people were not prepared to say this. Such an approach, it was felt, could have also jeopardized the existing bargaining associations and would have been disastrous if the legislative attempt failed. The AFB's rejection of the cooperative council's proposal and the possibility of a hearing prompted an intensive study by Kenneth Naden and Robert Hampton of the NCFC.

The NCFC consulted with USDA officials in exploring various possibilities, a liaison of considerable irritation to the AFB.[6] However, the NCFC had run into flak from its marketing cooperatives concerning the proposed "Capper-Volstead type" of bargaining bill. The term "bargaining" was still unpopular among cooperative managers who had been shaken to their heels by the NFO challenge. Yet, the bargaining association membership within the council continued vigorously to advocate some type of national legislation. A compromise had to be found, and the NCFC selected three possible approaches: (1) a producers' "Wagner Act," (2) a collective bargaining amendment to the federal marketing orders act and (3) an antidiscrimination bill modeled after the Packers and Stockyards Act.[7]

Of the three alternatives, the "Wagner Act" type of proposal with a closed-shop, or compulsory recognition, feature was considered by NCFC to be the most desirable approach to bargaining legislation. However, since this approach departed from the voluntary principle, it would not be acceptable to the AFB. The federal-order approach, in contrast, had a voluntary aspect in that it required a two-thirds majority vote to be instituted but still forced handlers to recognize farm organizations. The third choice was a new trade bill that would include direct penalties and private prosecution provisions, and/or cease-and-desist provisions with USDA prosecution as a second-stage penalty. The cooperative council had decided that the most important purposes of any legislation should be the creation of uniform conditions for negotiations and the prevention of discrimination by processors. These considerations were expressed to coalition members during a meeting on March 30th.

The results of this meeting were reflected by the NCFC in its April 8 report to members. It announced that three alternative approaches to new legislation were being given consideration: (1) strengthening federal market

5. Allen A. Lauterbach (General Counsel, American Farm Bureau Federation), personal interview, September 19, 1968.
6. Charles B. Shuman, personal interview, September 25, 1968.
7. American Farm Bureau Federation, file notes, March 30, 1966.

order authority, (2) amending other antitrust statutes such as the Packers and Stockyards Act and the Federal Trade Commission Act and (3) developoping a new piece of agricultural legislation.[8] Of the three alternatives, the NCFC favored the Packers and Stockyards Act as a model for a new approach to drafting the bargaining bill. The NCFC move away from the AFB draft strained relations within the coalition.

Like the NCFC, the National Milk Producers Federation attempted to draft a proposal that would fulfill the objectives of the AFB bill, but that would not utilize the Capper-Volstead amendment route. It fervently wanted to avoid giving the NFO any opening and, in fact, desired a bill that would enable its member cooperatives to expel NFO farmers whom they regarded as degrading their own cooperative organizations.[9] The NMPF also sought to accomplish another objective that was dear to the hearts of some members: legislation to enable them to negotiate with more than one processor at a time in connection with "super-pool" negotiations on federal order markets. With these purposes in mind, the dairy group drew up a proposal of its own in preparation for the June hearing on S. 109.

USDA Role: Support or Opposition?

In developing an alternative proposal, Kenneth Naden of the NCFC consulted with USDA officials, and Attorneys John Bagwell and Charles Bucy of the USDA's General Counsel's office worked closely with the cooperative council in shaping suitable language for the bill.[10] In these deliberations it was decided that livestock and poultry were already covered by the Packers and Stockyards Act and that grains and other commodities were covered by other types of programs. The new proposal would be limited exclusively to the fruit and vegetable industry, where most of the trouble had occurred.

Through such deliberations, the USDA gradually became involved in the S. 109 legislation, and the department's interest in S. 109 increased gradually as the bill gained momentum. In pre-S. 109 days, USDA-AFB relations could have best been described as lacking cogency. Secretary of Agriculture Orville Freeman and the USDA had been verbally castigated by AFB officials on many occasions, and some Washington observers considered that it would be inhuman for Freeman to turn his other cheek. Expectably, then, the first USDA reaction to the AFB proposal was to view it with suspicion

8. National Council of Farmer Cooperatives, "Washington Councilor," April 8, 1966.
9. Patrick Healy (Assistant Secretary, National Milk Producers Federation), personal interview, June 13, 1968.
10. Robert N. Hampton (Director of Marketing and International Trade, National Council of Farmer Cooperatives), telephone interview, June 29, 1968.

and to scrutinize it carefully.[11] To its surprise, it found no trickery or antigovernment schemes. The measure seemed aimed at solving an immediate problem and was constructive in nature.

Under Secretary of Agriculture John Baker, a former official of the National Farmers Union, took note of the bill and followed it closely. He brought S. 109 to the attention of members of the National Advisory Committee on Cooperatives, chaired by him, for the first time on March 16th.[12] Federal order specialists Herbert Forest of the Dairy Division and Floyd Hedlund of the Fruit and Vegetable Division of Consumer and Marketing Service (C&MS) of the USDA were assigned to make special studies of the bill. As this attention developed, USDA officials of the highest echelon were faced with the decision of whether to support the Farm Bureau bill as embodied in S. 109 or whether to support an alternative proposal as contemplated by the NCFC and NMPF.[13]

Meanwhile, the Farm Bureau's AAMA had initiated a project to organize broiler growers beginning in February, 1966, and had concentrated its efforts in nine Southern states. This project, which followed on the heels of the Farm Bureau's pilot projects in processing tomatoes and apples, was destined to influence the decisions of Southern legislators at a later point in the life of S. 109. The Farm Bureau's efforts sparked open criticism from the National Broiler Council (NBC), a trade group dominated by broiler integrators, that the promises of the AAMA would not be fulfilled. In response, AAMA officials adhered publicly to their concept of "bargaining" by stating that they were opposed to withholding products from the market and had no intention of striking their growers in a dispute.[14] They were going to rely instead on publicizing the results of negotiations if the integrators and contract growers couldn't agree to contract terms.

The response of the National Broiler Council to farm organizing efforts indicated that interest in the bargaining idea and related farm legislation was not limited to the farm sector. Other trade groups were giving S. 109 equally intensive study. In a widely circulated legal analysis by its attorney, James F. Rill, the NBC argued that while S. 109 was not an antitrust statute, its provi-

11. David Angevine (Administrator, Farmer Cooperative Service, USDA), personal interview, June 15, 1968.
12. David Angevine, letter to author, November 27, 1968. Members of the committee were representatives from the American Institute of Cooperation, National Council of Farmer Cooperatives, Cooperative League of the USA, National Rural Electric Cooperative Association, National Milk Producers Federation and the National Federation of Grain Cooperatives.
13. According to Harold F. Breimyer (Professor of Agricultural Economics, University of Missouri), who was then staff economist of C&MS, USDA, the bill lost its Farm Bureau tag quickly in C&MS and was more closely identified with Kenneth D. Naden (Executive Vice-President, National Council of Farmer Cooperatives). However, officials of the FCS admit that there were reservations within the USDA about supporting a Farm Bureau bill.
14. "Bitter Fight Looms Over Farmer 'Bargaining Bill'," *Broiler Industry*, 29, 6 (June, 1966), 24.

sions closely paralleled those of the Sherman and Clayton acts and other state laws.[15] The analysis also criticized the language of the bill as vague and uncertain and claimed that its passage would jeopardize ordinary commercial activity. It argued further that the major activities prohibited by S. 109 were already prohibited by existing laws. NBC's attack on the Farm Bureau bill generated considerable publicity and interest.

Other factors added suspense in the prelude to the June, 1966, hearing. Hearings on the Arkansas broiler case drew much publicity, especially the testimony of Ellis Hale and other growers that they had been blacklisted and were faced with empty broiler houses. Concurrently, publicity on rising food prices threw the spotlight on Secretary Freeman, who found himself under Administration pressure to curb prices of food and farm products, while farm groups were adamant in insisting that any such action would be, in the mildest terms used, a breach of faith. In this uncomfortable setting, Secretary Freeman launched a publicity campaign that reverted to one of his older lines that the farmers were in fact subsidizing consumers.[16]

As preparations for the hearing continued, the NCFC circulated drafts of its new substitute proposal.[17] While the cooperative council and dairy federation's drafts merely frustrated Senator Aiken, who wanted to see a united farm front in support of the bill, they infuriated AFB officials, who suggested that "Naden was carrying water for the USDA." [18] But the reality of NCFC opposition to the Capper-Volstead amendment route forced AFB officials to consider some alternatives of their own and to plan for hearing strategy. Internally, the AFB was receiving static from some of its state groups on the inclusion of criminal penalties and treble damages; external opposition to the penalties and damages features on the part of processors, of course, continued. Consequently, the organization had drafted some supplementary revisions to the enforcement section of the bill providing for injunctive relief.

AFB prehearing strategy called for convincing the Senate subcommittee of the need for bargaining legislation, while at the same time leaving the impression that the AFB was not "wedded" to the specific language of S. 109.[19] The AFB continued to promote, throughout the country, President Shuman's "opponent gain" concept of "bargaining," which stressed the advantages of

15. James F. Rill (Attorney), memorandum, "Possible Effect And Summary Section-By-Section Analysis of S. 109 (Aiken Bill to Prohibit Interference With Agricultural Bargaining Associations)," to R. Frank Frazier (Executive Vice-President, National Broiler Council), May 19, 1966. This analysis was reported in the trade press; see *The Poultryman*, June 10, 1966, 11.

16. "Administration does About-face on Farm Pricing Policies," *Dairy Record*, 66 (May 11, 1966), in files of American Farm Bureau Federation.

17. National Council of Farmer Cooperatives, draft of a bill to "control unfair trade practices affecting producers of fruits and vegetables and associations of such producers," April 25, 1966.

18. Farm Bureau staff members, confidential interviews.

19. Herbert Harris, III (Legislative Counsel, American Farm Bureau Federation), memo to Allen Lauterbach, June 2, 1966.

marketing efficiency gained through production to specification, advance contracting and long-range planning for best utilization of productive resources, plant capacity and other factors. The AFB's coalition partners agreed to testify for "the principles of the bill" in a June meeting called by the Farm Bureau.

The essence of the contest shaping up between farm groups and processors was well expressed by William Haffert, Jr., editor of *Broiler Industry* magazine:

> A sort of "cloak and dagger" aura has begun to pervade the efforts of the American Farm Bureau Federation to organize the broiler growers into bargaining associations, and the movement may reach the proportions of a drama later this month. . . .
>
> In effect, the issue for the first time will be joined between the contract farmer, as a collective bargainer, and the buyer in much the same connotation that the union in industry deals with the employer. At stake is a potentially historic piece of agricultural legislation.[20]

June, 1966, Hearing: Positions And Issues

S. 109 finally reached the hearing stage on June 14, 1966, when it came before the Senate Agriculture Subcommittee after two years before Congress. Early in the public hearing on the virtues and deficiencies of the proposed legislation, it became apparent that the bill was not taken lightly. In fact, for a measure designed to be uncontroversial, it generated considerable heated testimony.

The hearing got off to a deliberately cautious and low-key start when George Aiken, its Senate author, testified that "this bill does not in any way grant special privileges to farmers, to farmer cooperatives or to agricultural associations of any kind. It undertakes to give them the same rights and protection as are now enjoyed by the people they have to deal with . . . S. 109 is nothing more or less than a fairplay bill." [21] Cosponsor Lausche reinforced this approach by suggesting that the bill simply attempted "to create 'rules of the road' and prevent improper conduct." The tone Aiken and Lausche attempted to give to the hearing suggested that the express purpose of S. 109 was to establish working rules by which farm operators could organize to represent their mutual interests. It was a bargaining bill.

Testimony from the cosponsors was followed by a statement presented in behalf of the USDA by Martin Abrahamsen, Deputy Administrator of the Farmer Cooperative Service. The department had not been able to reach a decision on whether or not to support a Farm Bureau-sponsored bill.[22]

20. "Bitter Fight Looms Over Farmer 'Bargaining Bill'," 24.
21. George Aiken (Senator, Vermont), testimony in *Hearings on S. 109*, 2–3.
22. Reports vary about the reasons that the USDA did not take a more firm stand in behalf of S. 109. While animosity against the Farm Bureau did exist, Harold Brei-

Strong sentiments for supporting such needed legislation were offset by bitter memories of Farm Bureau attacks upon the department and the Secretary. In addition, Joseph Knapp, Administrator of the FCS, maintained loyalty to the NCFC on the cooperative exemption issue. In this situation, Abrahamsen could testify only that the bill was "receiving thorough study" within the department — an embarrassing admission. His statement brought a rejoinder from Aiken.

> *Senator Aiken.* Yes. I note that the Department is in sympathy with the general objectives of the bill. What do you understand the general objectives to be?
> *Mr. Abrahamsen.* To improve the farmers' bargaining position.
> *Senator Aiken.* And I am also interested and a bit surprised to see the Department shying away from proposed legislation which is considered complex. What is complex about this proposed legislation?[23]

Later, Senator Aiken added, "It [the USDA] has had a long history of supporting cooperative efforts, and, as I say, it is too bad it just did not continue." He also chastised the USDA for following orders "to hold down consumers prices one way or another."

After these preliminaries, the hearing settled down to three days of testimony by lobby groups representing assorted interest groups within and without agriculture. Farm groups displayed impressive cohesion by testifying for the need for bargaining legislation even though many recommended that an alternative form would be desirable. Lobby groups representing assorted processors, conglomerates and anti-cooperative contingents in Washington protested.

Initial testimony on behalf of the farm groups came from sponsors of the bill — the American Farm Bureau — headed by Charles B. Shuman and an impressive entourage of AFB legal experts and farm operators. As a *pro forma* matter, Shuman cited a 1965 policy resolution of the AFB regarding the organization's belief in the free market. In part, this resolution stated that the "Farm Bureau marketing programs should be founded on the belief that market power of farmers can be achieved by the use of the market price system." Shuman then observed that the wider use and acceptance of contract

---

myer claims that many in the USDA felt that the testimony of Martin Abrahamsen (Deputy Administrator, Farmer Cooperative Service, USDA) did not reflect the degree of support within the USDA for the bill. One can speculate upon several motives. Joseph Knapp (Administrator, Farmer Cooperative Service, USDA) felt that cooperatives should be exempted. Also, there may have been a bit of strategy with the NCFC and NMPF, both members of the USDA's Cooperative Advisory Committee, for not making the Capper-Volstead amendment look good before the Senate committee. Finally, there may have been some reluctance to support the measure because of NFO activity and the unpopularity of the bargaining issue among cooperative business advocates. As suggested in Chapter 11, the decision was made at high levels within the USDA and was not Abrahamsen's responsibility.

23. *Hearings on S. 109,* 9.

marketing in agriculture had created an opportunity for the bargaining type association to negotiate favorable contracts on behalf of its members. He pointed out that the success of such an association was dependent on the number of producers who would voluntarily join. While earlier laws "granted farmers the right to market cooperatively through their own marketing associations," Shuman repeated the AFB contention that "this right is not completely protected, and the scales of bargaining power are today weighted heavily in favor of buyers." [24]

Two reasons were cited by Shuman for the imbalance in bargaining power: (1) processors had grown to huge proportions through acquisitions, mergers and diversification and (2) farmers had been discouraged from exercising their right to act cooperatively by reprisals and fears of reprisals from some processors.

As evidence of the corporate growth trend, Shuman noted the acquisition and diversification activities of such companies as Home Food Products Corporation, Campbell Soup Company, Libby, McNeill & Libby and the Ralston Purina Company. To illustrate the inherent difficulties involved in dealing with these large firms, Shuman placed in the record an exchange of telegrams between himself and William B. Murphy, President of the Campbell Soup Company, regarding the bargaining efforts by AAMA in behalf of growers. Murphy's reply, in a telegram dated March 14, 1966, explicitly denied recognition to the bargaining efforts by AAMA in behalf of growers:

> There are so many considerations of a processing and final products marketing nature that influence the contract terms we offer farmers that negotiations with you would be detrimental to our business, and, in the long run, not beneficial to farmers. For this reason we do not consider it practical for us to carry on formal negotiations with your organization on the matter of the contract terms that we would expect to offer to farmers with whom we would hope to contract tomatoes. We shall continue our method of conferring with farmers with whom we have contracts or with whom we would like to have contracts.[25]

To the Farm Bureau, Murphy's response characterized the rigid intention of a company not to recognize any organization that attempted to stand between the company and the grower. It has been reported widely that Murphy on one occasion declared, "No one is going to come between me and my producers." [26] More explicitly, the response, the AFB felt, was an obvious side step by a company attempting to avoid confrontation with a national bargaining organization.

Shuman's case for the need for bargaining legislation in dealing with

24. Charles B. Shuman, testimony in *ibid.*, 10.
25. *Ibid.*, 16.
26. Harold Hartley (Manager, Fruit and Vegetable Division, American Agricultural Marketing Association), personal interview, October 13, 1969. This widely reported quote referred to a telegram received earlier by the AFB from Murphy.

large-scale businesses was convincing. However, he ended his testimony with a statement that would prove to be disastrous:

> We want to emphasize that Farm Bureau does not seek, and will not support, legislation . . . to force processors to negotiate with marketing associations. We seek only legislation which sets forth rules of fairplay on the part of processor and others in their business relationships with farmers and ranchers.[27]

This statement was to prove unsettling and destructive at a later point in the life of S. 109. Its imprecise and simplistic definition of bargaining and the purposes of the legislation contributed to many of the difficulties throughout the history of the S. 109 legislation.

The AFB planned dramatic illustration of the effect of reprisals upon the imbalance of bargaining power. Six farm operators, each carefully selected, were to provide testimony based upon the relevance of his individual experiences to the situations that S. 109 was designed to correct.[28] Their appearance made an impressive showing to the senators. They included growers of tomatoes, cabbage, apples and broilers from Ohio, New York, Virginia, New Jersey and Mississippi. Each testified about such discriminatory activities as acreage cutbacks, down-grading, or contract refusals based upon their membership in local or state bargaining associations.

Testimony by the AFB was wrapped up by Allen Lauterbach, General Counsel of the AFB and chief architect of S. 109. He reviewed the record of various statutes and administrative proceedings, emphasizing the Ohio tomato case.

> Our purpose in reviewing this Ohio FTC case is to point out that present legal processes under the FTC Act are inadequate where immediate relief is needed by farmers to restrain unfair trade practices by processors.[29]

Lauterbach also called attention to the problems that marketing cooperatives might experience under S. 109. In reference to the differences between bargaining associations and marketing cooperatives, Lauterbach suggested that "we do not believe that S. 109 should apply, directly or indirectly, to agricultural co-operatives which perform their legitimate purpose under law." [30] His statement represented a concession to demands of the marketing cooperative members of the NCFC and NMPF. In a capstone appeal, Lauterbach de-

---

27. Shuman, testimony in *Hearings on S. 109*, 15.

28. Farm operators presenting testimony on behalf of the AFB were Robert Summer, Tiffin, Ohio; Francis Kirby, Albion, New York; Garland Lewis, Laurel, Mississippi; Alfred Snapp, Winchester, Virginia; John Pew, Camden, New Jersey; and Ralph Gillmor, Fremont, Ohio.

29. Allen A. Lauterbach, testimony in *Hearings on S. 109*, 36.

30. *Ibid.*, 38. Mr. Lauterbach personally felt that cooperatives should have been exempted from the unlawful practices set forth in the act. However, other AFB officials did not share his feelings.

manded legislation that would provide prompt legal relief for farm operators and suggested the addition of an injunctive relief provision in the enforcement section of S. 109.

From the initial statements by the Senate sponsors of the bill and the testimony of originating farm groups and the USDA, three basic intents of the bill became clear. The first was to provide a legal foundation for bargaining activity on behalf of farm operators. This intention was hinted at in the term "association of producers" and again in the third section of the bill, which sought to establish the legality of affiliation of a bargaining association with a general farm organization. Its vagueness was intentional. The second intent of the bill — much more explicit — was to provide relief for farm operators and their associations from discriminatory activities by processors. Thirdly, as an amendment to the Capper-Volstead Act, S. 109 also carried some overtones of antitrust legislation.

Opponents of S. 109. Those testifying in opposition to the bill were many, and their objections seemed to find no end. In all, representatives of ten different agri-business — roughly divided into three groups according to the issues that ran through their testimony — or anti-cooperative associations testified against S. 109. The most vocal group was concerned about the antitrust overtones of the bill and the possibility that bargaining might "curb competition." A second group was disturbed about the one-sidedness of the bill and for strategic reasons stressed protection for the farmer's right not to join an association. The third group consisted of "fence riders" who would not take a firm position on the bill but nevertheless implied an attitude of opposition to it.

Of those who were most adamant against the elementary form of S. 109, the National Canners Association's position, represented by Edward Dunkelberger, stands out as a carefully studied and prepared piece of work. The calculated strategy of this association was spelled out in a later interview with the Director of Government-Industry Relations of the NCA, Robert Heiney,[31] According to Heiney, the NCA at the outset concluded that S. 109 was a disguised basic antitrust proposal and the first in a potential series of legislative proposals that would enable farmers to bargain collectively. The NCA's subsequent actions were governed by this perception.

In the hearing, the NCA used strong language to establish the canners' position against any government involvement. Dunkelberger testified that "it would be totally inequitable for the Federal Government to inject itself into the canner-grower, or canner-bargaining association business relationship by imposing unprecedented criminal penalties for activities that are either vaguely defined or adequately covered by existing State and Federal laws." [32]

31. Robert B. Heiney (Director, Government-Industry Relations, National Canners Association), personal interview, April 3, 1968.
32. Edward Dunkelberger (Attorney), testimony in *Hearings on S. 109*, 122.

His argument was climaxed with the following statement.

In summary, S. 109 would make impossible any meaningful negotiation between a processor and individual growers, and would expose processors to innumerable lawsuits and criminal prosecutions for virtually every operating decision. Its provisions would grossly discriminate against purchasers of agricultural commodities, and some of its vague and ambiguous language raises serious constitutional questions. Existing Federal and State laws provide wholly adequate protection for all parties concerned. Accordingly, we strongly urge this subcommittee to recommend against enactment of S. 109.[33]

A letter from William B. Murphy, President of the Campbell Soup Company, supported Dunkelberger's statement. In part, the letter cited earlier testimony by AFB President Charles Shuman that the Farm Bureau "does not seek and will not support legislation to force processors to negotiate with bargaining associations." According to Mr. Murphy, Shuman's statement was in direct conflict with "the practical effect of S. 109."

The canners were joined by a strong anti-cooperative contingent that testified against "granting any more special privileges to farmers." The National Tax Equality Association (NTEA), the National Association of Wholesalers and the National Independent Meat Packers Association all were heard. The NTEA was known to the farm groups through its vigorous testimony against cooperatives in earlier tax hearings. Although it had as its historic purpose the curbing of "inequalities of Federal income taxation between cooperative and non-cooperative forms of business organization,"[34] the NTEA was in 1966 opposing cooperatives in the interest of fostering "competitive" equality. According to the NTEA, it also sought to "prevent legislation that would give further special advantages to cooperatives under the antitrust laws."

Former Federal Trade Commission Chairman Earl W. Kintner, speaking for the NTEA, charged that S. 109 was "fundamentally inconsistent with the body of federal antitrust laws" in its use of the term "boycott" to deny the individual processor the "right unilaterally to deal with a customer."[35] He also charged that the due process clause of the Fifth Amendment "requires that criminal statutes contain a clarity of expression and sufficiency of guidelines such that one can assess, before acting, whether his contemplated actions are unlawful." The strong objections of the NTEA to S. 109 can be summarized as follows. First, they maintained that the proposed legislation was already covered by existing federal trade regulation laws or was inconsistent with federal antitrust laws such as the Sherman Act, the FTC Act and the

33. *Ibid.*, 126.
34. Jack L. Lahr (Attorney), testimony in *Hearings on S. 109*, 48.
35. Earl W. Kintner (Attorney, National Tax Equality Association), statement in *ibid.*, 48.

Clayton Act as amended by the Robinson-Patman Act. Secondly, it was argued that S. 109 contained constitutional defects as a criminal statute.

Finally, the NTEA questioned whether the legislation was necessary even if it was "prompted by the existence of the proscribed tortious acts against cooperatives in the United States." The National Association of Wholesalers joined in this criticism, expressing its concern about the "special privileges accorded cooperatives under the various tax, antitrust and trade laws of the Nation." Similarly, the National Independent Meatpackers Association testified that such actions were already covered by existing legislation.

Associations representing livestock and cotton interests also joined the pleas against S. 109. By and large, these groups represented the independent merchants, dealers and ginners. Much of the livestock dealers' testimony was clearly influenced by NFO withholding activity and emphasized the farm operators' right "not to join" an association. The testimony submitted by the Independent Livestock Marketing Association of Columbus, Ohio — suggesting that S. 109 would offer the NFO shelter for its activities — is typical.

> We oppose this bill because there is utterly no justification for it in the livestock industry; because it is being sought by those who don't need it with motives to say the least suspect: Farm Bureau; and because it would be a measure of protection for NFO whose avowed purpose is to destroy the open, competitive marketing system which exists today, and who has engaged in known acts of coercion and discrimination in the livestock marketing industry in recent years. We suggest that this is simply a bad bill and should be defeated, but at the very least, it should be worded as not to apply to the livestock industry.[36]

The Certified Livestock Markets Association of Kansas City said that the bill did not aim at maintaining a fully competitive price economy but appeared to contemplate some form of "collective bargaining, contract marketing, and so-called fair share of the food dollar." [37]

Like the livestock interests, representatives of cotton ginners and warehousemen found the language of S. 109 quite unpalatable. Texas merchants, who were spearheading an anti-cooperative public relations campaign, in particular found the definition of cooperatives as "associations of producers" to be too broad. They suggested that cooperatives do not always serve the best interests of their members and that, if S. 109 were passed, "all cotton farmers will constitute a captive market for cooperative gins." The cotton shippers also testified that the bill was "entirely onesided," and that, because its prohibitions were so general and vague, it would "threaten any marketing agency daring to compete in a legitimate but vigorous manner with a cooper-

36. Charles E. Connor (Counsel, Independent Livestock Marketing Association), testimony in *ibid.*, 105.
37. C. T. Sanders (General Manager, Certified Livestock Markets Association), testimony in *ibid.*, 132.

ative." The shippers also opposed the "ambiguous extension of antitrust exemption" in the third section of the bill.

Of the "fence riders" on S. 109, the position of the National Broiler Council (NBC) was most conspicuous. The NBC testified via a letter that it had taken no position on the bill. Its reticence was perhaps based on the fact that several of its prominent members were under investigation by the Packers and Stockyards Division of the USDA in the Arkansas broiler case. Rather than replying to the charges of Ellis Hale and other representatives of broiler growers made in the Senate hearing, Frank Frazier of the NBC suggested that "a better forum for determining the truth of these charges" would be the P&S Division of the USDA.

The National Livestock Feeders Association was also noncommittal. Perhaps reflecting its traditional conservative attitude as well as concern about NFO activities, this association of livestock feeders restricted its testimony solely to the issue of providing protection for those producers who choose not to join an association.

Obviously, S. 109 as an amendment to the Capper-Volstead Act raised a variety of issues. The major points articulated in opposition to the bill may be summarized as follows: (1) the provisions of S. 109 were general and vague, (2) farm organizations already had too much protection under the antitrust laws, (3) existing legislation already covered the types of discriminatory activities listed, (4) the bill was one-sided in that it protected only farm organizations, (5) it should protect those producers who did not want to join a farm organization and (6) it would force processors to deal with a farm organization instead of allowing a company to select its own suppliers. While some of the arguments were legitimate, others were speculative overstatements designed to prevent further movement of the bill. Despite their objections, each organization testified that it was not opposed to the farmers' right to engage in group action.

Proponents of S. 109. About fifteen different organizations testified to the need for new farm legislation in the bargaining area. Senator George Aiken saw the numbers showing support of S. 109 as a valid measure of the need for this type of legislation. If the appeals presented by some farm groups came as disappointments to the AFB, the support of others must have been a pleasant surprise. The National Farmers Union, the Cooperative League of the USA, the California Farmer-Consumer Information Committee, the National Catholic Rural Life Conference, the Eastern Milk Producers Association and the Big Ten Milk Producers Association all gave their wholehearted support to the bill as written.

A close look at the groups supporting S. 109 as written indicates that the traditional foes of AFB philosophy on other fronts rallied to support this effort to establish farm bargaining legislation. Farm legislative history is filled with tangles between the National Farmers Union and the AFB, yet NFU stood with the Farm Bureau. Support also came from groups with a consumer or labor orientation such as the Cooperative League, the California Farmer-Consumer group and the Catholic farm lobby group.

Interestingly, two of the three partners in the AFB-NCFC-NMPF coalition did not give undivided support to the bill. In testifying before the subcommittee, Patrick Healy, Assistant Secretary of the National Milk Producers Federation, argued that passage of a bill like S. 109 "would be another important step in encouraging farmers to make self-help efforts to improve their own position in the market through cooperative organization." However, he did not recommend enactment of the bill as written.

> Although the National Milk Producers Federation is in agreement with the purposes and objectives of S. 109, we would like to see this legislation set up as an independent act with enforcement in the Department of Agriculture, if that can be worked out, and, if not, then in the Federal Trade Commission, under procedures which would be relatively more flexible and which could operate more quickly to provide relief.[38]

The NMPF then presented the subcommittee chairman, Senator Everett Jordan of North Carolina, with a copy of a bill that would stand on its own feet and which pertained only to cooperatives. Known as the "Cooperative Marketing Interference Act," the bill cited and defined the same unlawful practices as did S. 109 but rested all enforcement procedures with the Federal Trade Commission. The NMPF version also was restricted to antidiscriminatory activity only and did not relate to other bargaining issues.

If the NMPF testimony smacked a little of contact with USDA officials, the case presented by the National Council of Farmer Cooperatives left no doubt of the department's influence. Kenneth Naden, Executive Director of the NCFC, endorsed the idea of a USDA regulatory approach rather than attacking the problem through the Capper-Volstead amendment. He suggested that S. 109 was "an expression of a growing awareness that farmers need further protection in their rights to form cooperative associations in order to gain an equitable and fully competitive position in the marketplace." [39] While he recognized that certain laws had provided that farmers could organize without violating antitrust laws, "no clear provisions have been set forth to protect farmers fully in the exercise of such rights."

The NCFC expressed in the hearing its feelings that the amendment of the Capper-Volstead Act involved undesirable risks. It also suggested that the language of certain prohibitions could be strengthened. Instead of supporting the AFB version of the bill, the NCFC proposed to enact a separate fair trade act modeled after the Packers and Stockyards Act. In proposing this bill, Mr. Naden suggested that it be looked upon as an antitrust statute and be limited to fruits and vegetables only. This "Fruit and Vegetable Pro-

38. Patrick Healy, testimony in *ibid.*, 108.
39. Kenneth D. Naden, testimony in *ibid.*, 110.

ducers Fair Trade Act of 1966" would utilize the "extensive experience" of the USDA by having the Secretary of Agriculture handle the complaints, investigations and hearings, and the issuance of cease-and-desist orders. By charging the Secretary with responsibility for investigations, the NCFC official declared, the legislation would relieve "small farmers or cooperatives with limited resources of an impractical responsibility for establishing proof of violation." In presenting these substitute bills, the NCFC and NMPF made clear that their apprehensions about opening the Capper-Volstead Act to amendment had crystallized to the decision not to support the form of S. 109.

Following the NCFC presentation, Senator Aiken engaged Naden in a discussion about the antitrust nature of the problems S. 109 was designed to rectify.

> *Senator Aiken.* . . . I am just wondering . . . whether the proposed legislation can be classified as an antitrust statute. S. 109 is aimed at a single company which may be discriminating and there would be no collusion involved in those cases at all. If several companies get together, and say we agree on the price we are going to pay these fellows, we agree on the method we are going to use against them, that would be, I would assume, an antitrust violation. However, we are glad to have the proposal because after all, it may help solve the entire problem.
> *Mr. Naden.* It needs attention.
> *Senator Aiken.* And correct some of the abuses which according to the witnesses have taken place.
> *Mr. Naden.* Yes; it needs attention badly.[40]

The Packers and Stockyards approach to the discrimination problem was also promoted by the United States Poultry & Egg Producers Association, which highlighted events of the Arkansas broiler case in its testimony, including an appearance of broiler grower Ellis Hale. Dal Ferry, Executive Director of the association, testified that his close study of the Arkansas case had convinced him that ". . . it would be better to strengthen the Packers and Stockyards Act where it is now deficient, make the act apply to any commodity and amend the act to eliminate jurisdictional problems." [41] Mr. Ferry also said he would like to see the P&S Division of USDA receive adequate financing to do the job that he felt needed to be done.

The Poultry and Egg Association also suggested that the committee should give attention to the possibilities that legislation, such as the Automobile Dealers Franchise Act, might serve as a model for similar farm legislation to develop countervailing power for farmers in an integrated agriculture. According to Ferry, Senator Herman Talmadge of Georgia had recommended such an approach in a speech to the association in June of 1962.

40. *Hearings on S. 109*, 117.
41. Dallas K. Ferry (Executive Director, United States Poultry and Egg Producers Association), testimony in *ibid.*, 79.

Considerable discussion followed the testimony by Mr. Hale and Mr. Ferry. One exchange focused on a problem central to vertical integration in the broiler industry: market concentration and local monopolies. Cosponsor of the bill, Senator Milton Young of North Dakota, zeroed in on this point.

> *Senator Young.* I would like to ask a question. Is there any open market at all where a broiler producer can go and market his product, say, if he does not have a contract?
>
> *Mr. Ferry.* I am not aware of any except some very small operations that have a kind of a personalized business or they might be operating with some small stores or have personal customers or something like that.
>
> *Senator Young.* The cattle feeding industry, as you know, is going in that direction. There is still an open market but much of the fed cattle are being bought by packers directly from the farmers and the more they do this, the more they are destroying, of course, the open market that they could depend on for a bargaining position. I can see where the broiler producers are in a rather weak position. They no longer have an open market. There no longer is any real competition. The only thing you can do is to organize and bargain with the integrators. You have to have an organization, and I think some Government protection is in order for the producers to get a fair break.[42]

Testimony about the broiler case and the need for improved financing of the Packers and Stockyards Division came from yet another source. Harry Graham, Legislative Representative for the National Grange, testified that in the Grange view, "the legislation seems to us to be more related to antitrust activities" and therefore should be an amendment to the Packers and Stockyards Act.[43] The National Grange supported additional legislation to accomplish its ultimate objectives: (1) to preserve the farmer's right to associate freely, (2) to bargain collectively and (3) to conduct referendums without interference from those who have vested interests in the acceptance or rejection of programs under consideration.

While most testimony at this stage focused on the protective aspect of the bill — and not on the establishment of bargaining privileges for farm operators — some testimony did direct itself to the bargaining question. John Handy, President of the Great Lakes Cherry Producers Marketing Cooperative, concluded his prepared statement in support of S. 109 or similar legislation with a paraphrase, "If it is good for the United Automobile Workers and AFL-CIO, why couldn't it be good for farmers?" [44]

Senator Aiken replied, "That is a good question. It is surprising that you get different answers to that question." Some of the different answers had

42. *Hearings on S. 109*, 82.
43. Harry Graham (Legislative Representative, National Grange), statement in *ibid.*, 42.
44. John Handy (President, Great Lakes Cherry Producers Marketing Cooperative), testimony in *ibid.*, 99.

emerged earlier, when Senator Aiken pursued the question with the representative of the National Canners Association and at the same time sparred with and chided his fellow Senator from North Carolina, Senator Everett Jordan.

> *Senator Aiken.* But you, in principle, opposed to marketing orders?
> *Mr. Dunkelberger.* Yes, sir.
> *Senator Aiken.* And you are in principle, opposed to the cotton bill which passed the Senate yesterday whereby, when two-thirds of the cotton producers vote to market assessments on the producers that the other third has to come across with a dollar a bale?
> *Senator Jordan.* This bill also provides he gets it back if he doesn't want to participate.
> *Senator Aiken.* If he can go up to those big 6-foot fellows and say, I want my dollar back.
> *Senator Jordan.* That sounds a lot different from what the — actual — all he has to do is apply.
> *Senator Aiken.* I didn't say that yesterday.
> *Mr. Dunkelberger.* We have no position on that cotton bill.
> *Senator Jordan.* This is an entirely different situation because this is a producer bill that was passed yesterday which they want themselves. They have to vote on it.
> *Senator Aiken.* Now, do you have a position on collective bargaining or union shop?
> *Mr. Dunkelberger.* No sir; we do not. Our association has no position on what you might call labor relations.[45]

Representatives of the California fruit industry wrapped up the testimony in support of a bargaining bill. Ralph Bunje, General Manager of the California Canning Peach Association, testified that the California bargaining bill of 1961 "has not been too effective for a number of reasons, the principal one being that the penalty provisions of the bill are not adequate to actually arrest some of the activities that we know are going on." [46] Bunje gave full support to the NCFC proposal.

Perhaps the clearest testimony in behalf of a bargaining bill was offered by Richard L. Black, Manager of the California Freestone Peach Association. Mr. Black testified that a federal statute was needed to create a more favorable legal climate for bargaining associations.[47] Such a statute, according to Black, should contain the following: (1) a clear statement that existence of member-owned and -controlled bargaining and marketing associations are in the national interest and that they should be encouraged until such time as member growers, through their cooperatives, are as strong in price bargain-

45. *Hearings on S. 109*, 128.
46. Ralph Bunje (General Manager, California Canning Peach Association), statement in *ibid.*, 158.
47. Richard L. Black (Manager, California Canning Peach Association), statement in *ibid.*, 156.

ing as their processor customers and (2) a statement of unfair and discriminatory trade practices on the part of processors. Mr. Black also advocated clarifying and modifying the federal antitrust laws with respect to their application to bargaining associations and a continuing policy of education among personnel of the USDA about bargaining associations.

In sum, the proponents of new farm legislation rested their case, having made the following points: (1) testimony by farm operators clearly attested to the fact that they had been discriminated against; (2) there was a need for a federal statute which would clarify the rights of farmers to engage in bargaining activity; (3) prompt relief was needed in discriminatory cases; (4) farm operators could take a lesson from labor legislation and (5) Congress had long supported self-help efforts on the part of farm operators. Two farm groups that were conspicuously absent from testimony on these issues were the Missouri-based Midcontinent Farmers Association and the National Farmers Organization.

The Issues

In the privacy of their own councils and in the cloakroom, two problems never explicitly stated in the hearing occupied the minds and discussions of farm leaders. The first concerned critical definitions of "cooperative" and "general farm interest organization." The second issue was, "How do we enact a favorable piece of legislation and still not give NFO a free rein?" The two were interrelated.

The latter issue had an impact upon the former in a negative sense: How could the NFO be written out of the bill without writing the AFB out? It was argued, without great success, that all organizations involved in bargaining activity other than the NFO were cooperatives. While this argument had some legal base, in the functional economic and social sense it did not stand up. Furthermore, the issue was fogged by the growing number of contractual producers who supplied their land and labor in the production process but allowed integrators to supply the variable inputs such as livestock, feeds, medicines and equipment. Their position was thus not dissimilar to that of a wage worker. In addition, many bargaining associations preferred to label themselves "cooperatives," in the cooperative business organization sense, although in many cases they never took title to the goods or handled them.

Obviously, the definitional issue was not clear-cut even without the bogeyman existence of the NFO. Yet it was the nervous concern with the NFO and the debate among the bargaining proponents about how best to shut out NFO that succeeded in wiping out all but the faintest hope for a bargaining bill. The testimony drafted by AFB staff for presentation by President Shuman had laid the groundwork for the predicament. The web had become further entangled when Allen Lauterbach, General Counsel of the AFB, called attention to the fact that some marketing cooperatives might experience difficulties under the second section of the amendment because they did handle farm products. In an attempt to delineate this issue, Lauterbach had made the following comment.

> As you know, many agricultural cooperatives operate as a "processor" or as a "handler" in the marketing of agricultural commodities. Such cooperatives purchase their members' products and then sell the products in the name of the association. Any income realized by the cooperative in the sale of such commodities is later returned to members as patronage dividends or refunds. Other cooperatives are organized by producers for the purpose of selling their products through negotiations with buyers. They are not handlers. The handling and bargaining cooperatives represent two different approaches to the objective of improving marketing through cooperative action. At times these two approaches are competitive in that they seek the opportunity to serve the same growers.[48]

In his dissection of the problem, Lauterbach had overlooked a fact, basic to farm organization development, that farm operators have characteristically used two complementary organization forms — cooperatives and professional interest groups — in representing the economic interests of their farm firms.

Having suggested that these two types of organizational structures were at odds with one another, Lauterbach had then proceeded to give a soft sell for the bill's third section, which would allow "the affiliation of an association of farmers with other associations of farmers having similar objectives, *or with general farm organizations.*" The effort to legitimize the affiliation of the AAMA with the American Farm Bureau was implicit, but the backdoor attempt at securing bargaining legislation proved ineffective. The AFB people had earlier thought that the legislation could be accomplished under the "association of producers" language of the Capper-Volstead Act. In other words, the AFB did not want to force a distinction between a cooperative and a general farm interest organization. Some staff members viewed them as essentially the same.

Taking issue with this conceptualization of a general farm interest organization as a cooperative, Kenneth Naden of the NCFC had argued in the hearing that a structural dichotomy does exist between cooperatives and general farm organizations. Accordingly, "unless general farm organizations give cooperatives attention they cannot advance." [49] To this he added, "if they don't give cooperatives verbal support it creates divisiveness and impotence, and creates a need for the so-called national commodity association." In recognizing this functional attribute of general farm interest organizations, Mr.

48. Allen A. Lauterbach, testimony in *ibid.*, 37–38.
49. Kenneth D. Naden, personal interview, April 1, 1968.

Naden faulted them for not protecting cooperatives. "The simple matter is that general farm organizations are not doing their duty," he said.

In spite of Naden's view, the position of the NCFC in the June hearings reflected an obvious internal compromise between the bargaining association advocates of national legislation and the marketing cooperatives who were seeing NFO ghosts. The scope of the NCFC proposal was limited to fruits and vegetables despite clear-cut testimony of the need for such legislation in the poultry industry. In attempting to differentiate between the California bargaining associations and the NFO, Mr. Ralph Bunje had stated:

> We also believe that it is important to delineate what an association of producers is because we feel that it is important that it should apply only to farmer-owned and controlled cooperative fruit and vegetable bargaining and marketing associations. I say this because we do not believe that it would be wise to enable any group of growers that do not have marketing responsibilities to form bargaining associations and then be entitled to the benefits of this type of legislation.[50]

The emphasis here was given to responsible as opposed to irresponsible action, not to what is required to accomplish a successful bargaining effort. It also appears that Mr. Bunje had been speaking for an approach to bargaining based on local autonomy as contrasted to a national organization effort.

In a similar vein, the NMPF's Pat Healy had testified that the bill was "aimed specifically at cooperatives because in the last analysis, we believe that the cooperative is the best tool that the farmers can have working for him in the marketplace and that if farmers would organize themselves cooperatively, they would have more bargaining power." [51] This reaffirmation of the cooperative way of doing business was another expression of concern by dairy cooperatives to the NFO "threat" while simultaneously covering a conflict between internal "bargaining" and cooperative business organizations.[52]

The hopscotching testimony makes clear the vacillation of the AFB-NCFC-NMPF coalition between the two issues. The preoccupation with the NFO bargaining idea and the NFO as a threat to established organizations overshadowed the structural and function relations of the two basic organization forms and foreshadowed internal transitions taking place in the functional roles of general farm interest organizations. In the process, what was intended and halfheartedly supported as an initial piece of bargaining legislation became lost in the shuffle to preserve propriety and face.

The objections to S. 109 as drafted by the AFB and introduced in 1965

50. Ralph Bunje, statement in *Hearings on S. 109*, 159.
51. Healy, testimony in *ibid.*, 109.
52. E. M. Norton, who was then Secretary of the National Milk Producers Federation, is credited with handling this situation within the federation to the benefit of cooperative business organizations even though he was ridiculed by the dairy bargaining associations.

by Aiken, Lausche, McCarthy and Young were that it risked opening the Capper-Volstead Act to amendment and that it didn't approach the bargaining issue squarely. An overriding fear that it might help the NFO was also present. Nevertheless, the farm organizations had turned out in general support for the principles of S.109 and made a strong case for more legislation. In particular, the pleas for preventive relief from discrimination by processors and other handlers were impressive enough to encourage pursuit of the bill. S. 109 had passed its first test.

We believe that specific legislation should be enacted providing that all processors, shippers, and buyers of farm products, engaging in or affecting interstate trade, are prohibited from obstructing the formation or operation of a producer's bargaining association or cooperative, and from influencing producers' understanding of or voting on marketing orders or similar programs.[1]

National Commission on Food Marketing

Chapter 5

The Agricultural Producers Marketing Act: A New Bill

The objective of AFB's initial proposal, the Secrest bill, was to provide an opening wedge for bargaining activity. Its introduction was intended as a "Magna Carta" that would stir up interest and create an atmosphere for bargaining. Yet it was looked upon as a mere first step in creating bargaining legislation. The Capper-Volstead amendment approach offered the advantage of working through amendment to an existing foundation antitrust statute to establish protection for bargaining coupled with enforcement provisions. While treble damages would be automatic under such a statute, criminal penalties were also typical in antitrust legislation and were viewed as necessary to put teeth in the bill. However, the amendment appproach had given rise to strong protests from the processing community in the June hearings. The strength of the opposition was cause for a serious appraisal of the bill's chances in Congress.

A Pause For Re-evaluation

In a meeting called in late June to discuss the hearing on S. 109, AFB officials decided to press for favorable committee action on the bill. An "Action Requested" letter sent by Jack Lynn to the state Farm Bureaus on June 17th had encouraged them to effect immediate contact with Senate Agriculture Committee members. To promote further acceptance of its concept of bargaining legislation, the AFB strategists encouraged state groups to work for state bargaining legislation similar to that which had been successfully adopted in Ohio, New Jersey, New York, California and Oregon, with the Ohio law pointed to as a model. AFB planners also suggested that the findings of the National Commission on Food Marketing be publicized for purposes of creating wider understanding of the issues and that the AFB consider a "little Wagner Act" as a future policy development issue. The officials

1. National Commission on Food Marketing, *Food: From Farm to Consumer* (Washington: U.S. Government Printing Office, 1966), 111.

resolved to push for legislation consistent with the two-pronged philosophy: "No one will look after the interests of farmers but farmers themselves. The primary role of the Federal Government in the marketing field is to enforce rules of fair play and not be the play maker." [2]

Concurrent with AFB's deliberations, S. 109 was being carefully weighed by Senator George Aiken. A great believer in the food industry and the ability of the industry to police itself, Senator Aiken sympathized with the processors' objections to the criminal provisions.[3] He also recognized that the canners and anti-cooperative people meant business in their opposition to the bill. Upon encouragement from Senator Aiken and amid reports that the "controversial and politically sensitive" bill would be defeated, the AFB finally concurred with the idea that it would be dangerous to amend the Capper-Volstead Act.[4]

The alternatives were to let the bill die or to develop a new proposal that would improve upon the language of the initial bill but stand on its own base. Already, two proposals had been submitted in the hearing as alternatives to the Capper-Volstead amendment, one by the National Council of Farmer Cooperatives and the other by the National Milk Producers Federation. The NCFC wanted to turn the responsibility over to the USDA and go the P&S procedural route. The dairy people, however, wanted a Cooperative Marketing Interference act that would extend provisions of the Federal Trade Commission Act and the enforcement authority of the FTC to protect the rights of agricultural producers to belong to cooperative associations.

The AFB decided early that it could not live with the P&S type of administrative procedures. According to traditional AFB "get the Government out of agriculture" philosophy, such a course would unnecessarily involve the governmental bureaucracy.[5] Similarly, the FTC route involved long and entangled procedures that had proved unsatisfying in the Ohio tomato case. Coupled with the procedural maze was the FTC's reputation of being unsympathetic to farm organization efforts. The AFB was looking for legislation that would not only force the handler to stop his discriminatory activities,[6] but guarantee as well the right of the individual producer to get immediate relief.[7]

The search for a new approach to the bill led the AFB to evaluate labor

2. American Farm Bureau, files on S. 109, 1966.

3. Charles Weaver (Legislative Assistant to Senator George Aiken), personal interview, April 5, 1968.

4. "FB Bill Defeat Seen; Controversy Flares," *The Poultryman*, June 24, 1966, in files of American Farm Bureau Federation.

5. William Anderson (Assistant Legislative Director, American Farm Bureau Federation), personal interview, April 2, 1968.

6. Allen A. Lauterbach (General Counsel, American Farm Bureau Federation), personal interview, June 19, 1968.

7. John Datt (Legislative Director and Assistant Director, Washington Office, American Farm Bureau Federation), personal interview, June 11, 1968.

legislation for possible approaches to the problem.[8] Organized labor had been granted an antitrust exemption through section b of the Clayton Act. In addition to this basic statute, the Norris-LaGuardia Act and others not anti-trust in themselves had built upon and bolstered the initial exemption in the Clayton Act. AFB strategists felt that farm groups could proceed legislatively in a similar step-by-step fashion once they established that farm operators could rightfully engage in bargaining activity and not fear being charged with violation of antitrust laws.

Having drawn parallels with labor legislation, the AFB determined, based on the Ohio tomato case, that any changes needed in a bill had to include immediacy — justice should be swift. It was decided late in 1965 that the remedy needed in addition to strong penalties was the opportunity to go to the courts for an injunction to prohibit interference. Because the earlier version of the bill had not included this feature, in the June hearing Allen Lauterbach of the AFB had advocated injunctive relief measures.[9]

Despite considerable opposition to S. 109, Senator Aiken remained optimistic about getting Senate action on the bill during 1966. But he also forecast some changes as the bill moved along the congressional route. One of the veteran Senator's major concerns was what the House Judiciary Committee would do to the bill if it passed the Senate.[10] The climate in the House committee was not regarded as favorable.

If Senator Aiken's concerns for revisions were not enough to change the minds of AFB officials, attitudes expressed by the FTC, Department of Agriculture and Department of Justice served as arm-twisters.

In particular, a letter from Paul Rand Dixon, Chairman of the FTC, written in response to a request by House Judiciary Chairman Emanuel Celler on August 13, 1965, for an FTC opinion on H.R. 898 and H.R. 5951 — bills similar to S. 109 — supported the processors' contentions that the measures were unnecessary.

Dixon's letter, which included a dissenting view by Commissioner MacIntyre, suggested that the unlawful practices cited in the bills were already covered by sections 1–3 of the Sherman Act and by section 5 of the FTC Act. Furthermore, Dixon viewed the treble-damage actions in the enforcement provision as unnecessary. He pointed out that section 4 of the Clayton Act provided for treble-damage actions for persons injured by reason of anything forbidden in the antitrust laws. On the basis of his observations about the House bills introduced by Congressmen Secrest and Quie, the FTC Chairman concluded that "it does not appear to the Commission that

8. L. Gene Lemon (Assistant General Counsel, American Farm Bureau Federation), personal interview, June 19, 1968.
9. Lauterbach, interview.
10. "S. 109 Action Still Possible in '66: Aiken," *Poultry & Egg Weekly* (July 2, 1966), in files of American Farm Bureau Federation.

there is any necessity for the enactment of H.R. 898 or H.R. 5951." [11] Farm groups, presumably, had all the protection they required.

Commissioner Everett MacIntyre dissented from the Dixon opinion, citing the experience of tomato growers in Ohio.

> I do not concur in the report of the Commission on H.R. 898 and H.R. 5951 that there is no necessity for the proposed legislation. In making this report it appears that the Commission turned its head away from results such as were experienced in the *Tomato* case, FTC Docket 5994 (52 FTC 1607–1658). [12]

This view by one of the FTC's own commissioners showed clearly that the frustrating experiences of the "small" farm operators were not passing by unnoticed.

As if spurred by the FTC action, the USDA finally replied to the request from Senate Agriculture Committee Chairman Allen J. Ellender — after a full year and a half delay. In the letter dated July 19, 1966, from Under Secretary John A. Schnittker, the department took a position favoring the general objectives of the bill but not recommending enactment in its present form. Schnittker indicated that amendment of the Capper-Volstead Act might cause confusion with respect to the meaning and intent of that "basic" legislation. In addition, he suggested that the section applying to the affiliation of agricultural associations "could be construed as to weaken present antitrust policy." [13]

To the opposition of the FTC and USDA, the Department of Justice added its voice. Ramsey Clark indicated to House Judiciary Chairman Celler that Justice opposed the Secrest bill on the basis that it might be interpreted as having the effect of forcing purchasers to buy from cooperatives and their members. [14]

Since each of these letters had been cleared by the Bureau of the Budget from the standpoint of the Administration's program and could thus be read as Administration attitudes, the AFB was prompted to reconsider full revision of its bargaining proposal.

In redrafting the bill, the AFB decided to include an injunctive relief measure similar to the right to injunction found in the Norris-LaGuardia Act. For the penalty provisions, the AFB directly adopted phrasing used in the 1964 Civil Rights Act, which was also similar to that in Title 15, section 68, of the Wool Labeling Act. [15] The AFB decided to maintain the criminal pen-

11. Paul Rand Dixon (Chairman, Federal Trade Commission), letter to Emanuel Celler (Chairman, House Committee on the Judiciary), July 15, 1966.

12. *Ibid.*

13. John A. Schnittker (Under Secretary, USDA), letter to Allen J. Ellender (Chairman, Senate Committee on Agriculture and Forestry), July 19, 1966.

14. Ramsey Clark (Deputy Attorney General), letter to Emanuel Celler, July 25, 1966.

15. Lemon, interview.

alty provisions in the redrafted version of the bill, with full knowledge that the whole processing community had become aroused and strenuously objected to them. AFB's recollection of experiences during the 1965–1966 period when the AAMA was attempting to bargain with the Campbell Soup and Mott apple-processing companies and broiler integrators had convinced the Farm Bureau of the necessity of the provisions. By identifying discriminatory activity through proposed legislation, the AFB felt it was "really tearing the scab off of a situation which had existed a long time." [16]

Throughout the deliberations over the form a new bill should take, Senator Aiken repeatedly reminded the AFB that it would have to muster the support of all farm groups and the USDA to be successful in securing passage of the bill. Following a meeting with AFB officials during the first week of August, Senator Aiken contacted leaders of the National Council of Farmer Cooperatives and the National Milk Producers Federation and urged them to get together with the AFB to resolve their differences.

The NCFC-AFB-NMPF coalition met soon after and discussed a new draft that had been worked out by Allen Lauterbach and Gene Lemon of the AFB's General Counsel's office and Herbert Harris, III, of the AFB Washington office. During the discussions, Mike Norton, Secretary of the NMPF, made a strong case for going after bargaining legislation a piece at a time rather than attempting to achieve everything at once.[17] The veteran Washington lobbyist felt that the Congress and many farm groups were not prepared to support the sweeping piece of legislation that was anticipated in the original Capper-Volstead amendment. As a result of these deliberations, the coalition supported the AFB's redrafted version, which had gradually acquired a "fair play" rather than a "bargaining" theme.

The revised version was sent to Senator Aiken by the AFB, with a cover letter explaining the intended effects of each section. Senator Aiken was satisfied with the package and circulated the bill to members of the Senate Agriculture and Forestry Committee. In a letter to Harker Stanton, Counsel of that committee, AFB Secretary-Treasurer Roger Fleming stated that the organization was supporting a separate act to meet the criticisms of the first bill raised by Under Secretary of Agriculture Schnittker.[18] Mr. Fleming reiterated the AFB position, first presented in the June hearing, that the coverage of S. 109 should be broadened to include the "threat" to discriminate against producers and should authorize civil action for preventive relief. Each of these proposals added new dimensions to the draft.

In addition to these changes, the AFB draft advocated authorization for

16. Herbert Harris, III (Legislative Counsel, American Farm Bureau Federation), personal interview, June 11, 1968.
17. E. M. Norton (Secretary, National Milk Producers Federation), personal interview, November 11, 1968.
18. Roger Fleming (Secretary-Treasurer and Director, Washington Office, American Farm Bureau Federation), letter to Harker Stanton (Counsel, Senate Committee on Agriculture and Forestry), August 8, 1966.

the Secretary of Agriculture to bring civil action for preventive relief. The inclusion of this feature represented a concession on the part of the AFB to the USDA and other prospective supporters of the measure. The AFB also asked for inclusion of a "severability clause" that would allow other provisions of the act to stand in case one portion was found invalid. Conspicuously absent in the letter was any mention of support for section 5 of the previous bill, the affiliation of associations section. In fact, the AFB recommended that this section should be eliminated, as suggested by the Under Secretary.

The behind-the-scenes work on amendments continued in the form of closed meetings with Senator Aiken and the Senate Agriculture Committee staff. As it did, many farm organizations and trade groups in Washington continued to think that S. 109 stood little chance of getting beyond the Senate Agriculture and Forestry Committee because of the controversy it generated in the June hearing. The bill had been so strongly criticized by trade and farm associations alike that most political observers thought it was dead. Nevertheless, a few trade associations such as the National Broiler Council speculated that "the current airing may serve to bolster, through the publicity attached to the hearings, the long-run cause of the proponents of the bill." [19] The revitalized efforts of the AFB, of course, provided ready evidence that the bill was not dead, and indeed the AFB political machine was being greased and cranked up for the run of its life.

The Aiken Amendment

The scurrying by the AFB and its allies following the June hearing on S. 109 had its payoff when Senator Aiken took command and engineered a major overhaul of the original bill in the Senate Agriculture and Forestry Committee. In several executive sessions held in late July and early August, the newly redrafted bill was further reworked in a manner that enabled it to stand on its own merits. In a major tactical maneuver by Senator Aiken, the new version of the bill was introduced as an amendment in the form of a substitute for the original version of the bill. An explanation of the substitute version accompanied the bill on August 9th.[20] The bill carried the title "Agricultural Producers Marketing Act of 1966."

Importantly, Senator Aiken had assessed the general climate and the political currents that prevailed and had decided that he did not want a bill of specific advantage to farm groups.[21] What he now sought in S. 109 was a fair-play bill, an approach that would have a good chance of getting through both houses. He recognized that the real problem was to guide the bill

19. National Broiler Council, "National Broiler Council News," June 16, 1966, 4.
20. "Explanation of Proposed Substitute for Text of S. 109," in U.S. Senate, Subcommittee of the Committee on Agriculture and Forestry, *Hearings on a Substitute Amendment to S. 109*, 89th Cong., 2d sess., 1966, 177–78.
21. Weaver, interview.

through a Senate Agriculture Committee dominated by Southern senators of conservative business leanings. Consequently, the substitute version of the bill offered by Aiken did not emphasize bargaining, although it did reaffirm the farmers' rights to organize for their mutual interests.

The substitute version contained six sections instead of the original three (see Appendix B) and differed in other significant respects from its earlier counterpart. Instead of being an amendment to the Capper-Volstead Act, the bill now stood on its own base as a separate act. Its purpose was explicitly stated as being "to establish standards of fair practice required of handlers in their dealings with producers of agricultural products and their cooperative associations." Terms such as handler, producer, association of producers and persons were again defined, but the substitute bill specifically excluded cooperative associations in the definition of handler.[22]

Associations of producers were defined as "any farmer-owned and controlled cooperative marketing, bargaining, shipping, or processing organization as defined in the Agricultural Marketing Act of 1929 or the Capper-Volstead Act of 1922."

The substitute version also provided an additional means of enforcement through injunction proceedings to be instituted by the aggrieved party or the Secretary of Agriculture. The district courts were given jurisdiction without regard to whether the aggrieved party had exhausted his administrative remedies. Finally, the substitute contained legislative findings relating to interstate commerce, defined terms and included threatened as well as actual interference or discrimination. The redrafted bill omitted the section in the original bill that referred to the affiliation of special-purpose farm groups with general farm organizations.

The short explanation accompanying the proposed substitute for the text of S. 109 pointed out these differences in the bill but failed to distinguish between the two types of organizations through which farm operators have characteristically organized: cooperative businesses and professional interest organizations.[23]

As amended by the substitute, the bill would prohibit handlers of agricultural products from performing specified acts injurious *to producer cooperatives* (i.e. interference with producers joining or continuing as members, and false reports about the cooperatives or interference with

22. This meant that the AFB strategists pursued a similar course of action as proponents of California bargaining legislation in 1961. Because cooperatives organized by and for farmers were not the source of discriminatory practices, no need was seen for making the unlawful practices applicable to them.

23. As has been stated previously, farm operators have characteristically organized through two types of organizations. Almost all marketing legislation preceding S. 109 pertains to cooperative business organizations. The legal standing of professional interest organizations, such as the AFB and other general farm interest organizations, has never been explicitly clarified by an Act of Congress. As drafted in 1964, the AFB bill intended to do this.

their operations). Violations would constitute misdemeanors punishable by fine and imprisonment, and subject violators to civil suits for treble damages. Injunctive relief on petition of the aggrieved party or the Secretary of Agriculture is also provided for.[24]

In other words, the explanation attempted to lump all types of farm organizations together and call them "producer cooperatives." The text of the bill, however, gives a slight hint of an attempt to distinguish between the forms by using the generic term "farmer-owned and controlled" in section 3c. Despite the weak attempt, the application of protection to such professional interest organizations as the AFB — as intended originally — appears to have been partially lost in the redrafted version.

Other than the deletion of the affiliations section, the addition of the injunctive relief provisions, the exemption of farmer cooperatives and a few other lesser changes, no major new provisions were included in the substitute bill. Study and evaluation of the bill's provisions occupied the attention of various groups preceding and following the September hearing.

Should Marketing Cooperatives Be Exempt? Many followers of S. 109 outside the coalition were surprised by the introduction of an amendment in the form of a substitute. But the provisions of the substitute were soon being openly discussed within the USDA, among farm organizations and among trade groups. Of the changes that commanded attention, one stood out as a basis for considerable debate and divergence among farm groups.[25] It concerned the exemption of marketing cooperatives from the unlawful practices section of the bill.

This issue was not new to the life of S. 109. Such an exemption had been strongly advocated by the NCFC since the introduction of H.R. 11146 by Congressman Secrest in 1964, but the original bill had made no distinction between farm organizations. As a result, the NCFC had drafted a "Capper-Volstead type" act for bargaining associations only, specifically omitting marketing cooperatives. A later version presented in the June hearings applied to bargaining associations representing growers of fruits and vegetables.

This same issue had been carefully weighed earlier, when the California legislature handled its bargaining association bill in 1961. Those deliberations were settled by writing a state law that applied exclusively to bargaining associations and the processors with whom they dealt. The California statute had just been used on August 16, 1966, in a suit filed by the California Canning Pear Association against California Packing Corporation and eight

24. My italics.
25. The reader is cautioned to observe the distinction between issues debated among farm groups and those debated between producers and processors. As clearly discerned in the June hearings, the major issue between producers and processors focused on use of criminal penalties. However, the co-op exemption debated among farm groups was hidden.

other canners for failure to establish pear prices in negotiation with the bargaining association.[26]

Few marketing cooperatives felt that their member relations programs should be upset by the necessity of formal negotiations with their own members; the whole idea was most distasteful. More substantially, the reasoning of the NCFC for not wanting to have the prohibitions of the bill apply directly to its marketing cooperative members was straightforward.[27] First, the council suggested that marketing cooperatives did not represent a threat against other farmers who wanted to exercise group action through bargaining cooperatives. Second, cooperatives usually had specific contracts of performance with their members. The contractual relationship established a legal obligation to operate in their members' best interests, and the cooperative could not thus be equated to a corporate processor. The council argued further that the marketing cooperative and its members were not in the same arena of action, since the cooperatives were involved in integrated operations as an extension of the farm firm. Unlike independent processors, cooperatives did not negotiate with members in the buying and selling of farm products.

As interpreted by the NMPF and the NCFC, the discrimination features of the bill applied specifically to independent processing companies, and the bargaining features applied only to bargaining associations. Marketing cooperatives were not involved. Inevitably, the NFO question entered the discussions. Was the NFO a cooperative?

The argument for cooperative exemption was convincing enough to the AFB that it went along with the NMPF and NCFC as one way of keeping the coalition together.[28] The AFB recognized that it did so at some risk, since it was a little vulnerable with respect to this position. Senator Aiken accepted the argument and introduced the phrase "other than association of producers" as an exemption for cooperatives from the term "handler" in the substitute version of the bill. However, the peace and quiet concerning this feature did not last for long.

Opposition to the exclusion of cooperatives from S. 109 originated in the Department of Agriculture's Consumer and Marketing Service.[29] Harold F. Breimyer, staff economist to the administrator of C&MS, took issue. In

26. Don Razee, "Pear Association Takes Canners to Court," *California Farmer* (September 2, 1966), in files of American Farm Bureau Federation.

27. Kenneth D. Naden (Executive Vice-President, National Council of Farmer Cooperatives), personal interview, April 1, 1968.

28. Datt, interview.

29. Harold F. Breimyer (Professor of Agricultural Economics, University of Missouri), personal interview, March 28, 1968. The intraservice discussions about S. 109 within the USDA began in March, 1966, and continued through the September, 1966, hearing. Because the Secretary's office was forced to assume a position on the bill following the successful June hearing, responsibility for handling S. 109 gradually shifted to the FCS.

his view, cooperatives couldn't legislate upon others something that they were not willing to accept themselves. Moreover, apart from the intrinsic issue, Breimyer saw the spotlighting of special treatment for co-ops as poor strategy. After achieving a consensus within C&MS on this issue, Breimyer confronted Joseph Knapp, Administrator of the Farmer Cooperative Service, with his observations and promptly drew fire. Knapp maintained that farmers did not need protection against themselves,[30] and an intraservice controversy of mild dimensions bubbled until Knapp retired in the spring of 1966.

When David Angevine, formerly Washington Public Relations Director for the Cooperative League of the USA, was appointed to replace Knapp, Breimyer again approached a group from FCS with his position. The general feeling among FCS officials was that Breimyer had concurrence from C&MS and all that was desired was FCS concurrence. The argument was accepted by Angevine over the opposition of one or two FCS people.[31]

At a later meeting, held in the office of Assistant Secretary John Baker, representatives from C&MS, FCS and the Office of the General Counsel were called upon for their advice to help shape a department position on S. 109. FCS Administrator Angevine said at the time that he would not support exempting cooperatives from the definition of handler because such an exemption, if enacted, would be tailor-made to support the opponents' claim that cooperatives receive "special treatment." [32] Others argued that such an exemption would make it difficult for the department to secure consensus within the Administration if such an exemption stayed in the bill.

With this advice, Mr. Baker called together supporters of the bill — including the AFB, NCFC, NMPF, National Grange, NFU and others — and told them that the department would support S. 109 but would ask the subcommittee to eliminate the cooperative exemption. Baker pointed out that with elimination of the exemption, the bill could gain Administration support. The department's position was discussed thoroughly and aroused some initial disagreement. Pat Healy of the NMPF maintained — with memories of the NFO encounters — that cooperatives had to get their members in line occasionally and that the exemption should be kept intact. However, Baker argued that cooperatives could perform discriminatory acts just like any other business. Kenneth Naden of the NCFC countered that discrimination had never become an issue with cooperatives, and the NCFC was enraged at the suggestion that it was. The AFB, NMPF and the NFU took positions similar to the council's. Angus McDonald, Research Director for the National Farmers Union, maintained that cooperatives should be exempted from the bill but that the NFU "didn't have the fears that what might happen would be

30. Homer Preston (Assistant Administrator, Farmer Cooperative Service, USDA), personal interview, June 18, 1968.

31. Farmer Cooperative Service officials, confidential interviews.

32. David Angevine (Administrator, Farmer Cooperative Service, USDA), letter to author, July 30, 1968.

as damaging as those who were dead set against having cooperatives coming under the provisions of the bill." [33]

Despite the heated discussions, Assistant Secretary Baker was adamant that the department would support only a bill that applied to any handler, including cooperatives. The USDA decision, according to Naden, proved that "there is a serious fundamental misunderstanding about cooperative processing as a basis for the deletion." [34] This skirmishing characterized preparation for the September hearing that the Agriculture and Forestry Committee, meeting in executive session in September 21, directed its subcommittee to hold on September 28th.[35]

The September, 1966, Hearing

Hearings on the substitute amendment to S. 109 began on September 28, 1966, when Subcommittee Chairman Jordan introduced Senator Aiken as "sort of the Father of this bill." Aiken, in turn, acknowledged the strenuous opposition to the bill in the June hearing and the fact that the farm organizations were not in full agreement on the bill. The Vermont Senator said that he had suggested that "the farm organizations get together and see what they could agree on and see what they could do to overcome the legitimate objections of the opposition." [36] Senate cosponsor Milton Young of North Dakota then stated his opinion that the substitute represented a reasonable compromise.

The hearing got off to a fast start when David Angevine, Administrator of the FCS, accompanied by D. Morrison Neely of the Office of the General Counsel and Kenneth Samuels, Director of the Marketing Division of the FCS, testified in behalf of the Department of Agriculture and gave qualified endorsement to the bill. Angevine called attention to the growing integration of production and marketing of agricultural products, the increased control of these functions by large, diversified corporations and the expanded use of contracting by such corporations to fulfill their needs.[37] He viewed these developments as weakening the marketing and bargaining position of individual farmers.

> It is essential to protect the rights of producers to join together in cooperatives to perform necessary marketing operations, including bargaining with processors and other buyers over the sale of the producers' farm products. Cooperative bargaining has come into prominence as the

33. Angus McDonald (Director of Research, National Farmers Union), personal interview, April 4, 1968.

34. Naden, interview.

35. National Canners Association, "Government-Industry Report," September 22, 1966.

36. George Aiken (Senator, Vermont), testimony in *Hearings on a Substitute Amendment to S. 109*, 178.

37. David Angevine, testimony in *ibid.*, 180.

old market system is being displaced by contractual arrangements in the production of agricultural products.[38]

In citing the need for such legislation, the department drew also upon the recently published report *Food: From Farmer to Consumer* released by the National Commission on Food Marketing. The report called for new legislation to prohibit processors or other buyers "from obstructing the formation of operations of a producers' bargaining association or cooperative."[39] While the Food Commission differentiated between the two types of organizations, the FCS did not, in its testimony, make this distinction.

After presenting the USDA position first communicated by Baker to supporters of the bill, Angevine proposed three amendments to the substitute. The first was to delete the phrase "other than an association of producers" so that the term "handler" would apply to all handlers and cooperatives.[40] Secondly, the department advocated a more specific definition of the term "producer" that would omit the confusing term "raw agricultural products." Finally, the change from "purchase" to "purchase or acquisition" in section 4d of the bill was advocated to clarify that contract production was included.

The deletion of the cooperative exemption, advocated by Angevine, was to cause considerable dissension among other supporters of the bill. Moreover, by suggesting that all cooperatives should be classified as handlers instead of just making the prohibitions applicable to farmer cooperatives or just leaving the "sleeping dog lie," the Administrator of the Farmer Cooperative Service lit a fuse leading to a major falling-out among supporters of the bill at a later stage.

Proponents of the Substitute Version. The strong, though qualified, support for the bill offered by the Department of Agriculture was bolstered by the testimony of the AFB-NCFC-NMPF alliance. Interestingly enough, Senator Jordan called upon John Lynn of the AFB, Patrick Healy of the NMPF and Kenneth Naden of the NCFC to testify all at the same time. Lynn led off for the trio by testifying that the substitute amendment improved upon the original version of the bill by standing on its own base and by meeting certain objections of Under Secretary of Agriculture Schnittker, already cited.[41] The AFB called for early enactment of the bill.

Healy of the NMPF followed the AFB and provided further support for the substitute version. In an appeal for protective legislation, the official statement of the NMPF drew a parallel with labor.

38. *Ibid.*
39. National Commission on Food Marketing, *Food: From Farmer to Consumer*, 111.
40. Angevine, testimony in *Hearings on a Substitute Amendment to S. 109*, 181.
41. John C. Lynn (Legislative Director, American Farm Bureau Federation), testimony in *ibid.*, 183.

Congress has provided extensive safeguards to prevent management from interfering with the right of labor to belong to unions. All that cooperatives are asking here is a modest and reasonable version of the same type of protection for farmers who wish to avail themselves of the right accorded them by Congress, to organize and belong to agricultural cooperatives.[42]

Like the NMPF, the NCFC, through Naden, stated its opinion that the substitute bill represented a distinct improvement over the original bill.

After presenting their official statements, the three officials engaged in a less formal dialogue with the committee, which focused on provisions of the bill and specifically on the amendments proposed by the Department of Agriculture. Although commending the department for taking a position on S. 109, Healy spoke for the coalition in registering opposition to the deletion of the cooperative exemption:

Mr. Healy. We do have strong objection to their first proposal that the cooperative exemption contained in the amendment which is before the committee be deleted, and we are of one accord, the American Farm Bureau Federation, the Cooperative Council, and the National Milk Producers Federation in this feeling, and we have met together and decided how we want to approach this thing, and I would ask at this time Mr. Naden to speak to this point.[43]

Later in the hearing the following exchange took place.

Mr. Naden. The reason for putting that exemption in there, Mr. Chairman, and our reason for opposition to the deletion is that the processing cooperative is a different kind of handler than that to which this bill is directed.

The processing cooperative represents another group of farmers, not an investor-owned kind of corporation. So, therefore, the processing cooperative is not in the arena of action to which this bill is directed. The arena of action is the bargaining activity between a group of farmers who want to form a cooperative and·those to whom they sell their products.

Therefore, the processing cooperative represents one group of farmers that have a cooperative and have an organization, and they are not in the arena of action. We are not even talking about them in terms of the bill. . . .

Now, we fear that the deletion of this exemption runs a grave risk of pitting one group of farmers against another, and we want to avoid that if we can. We believe the USDA reservation on this point is based on [a] false premise that opens the door for discrimination by cooperative processing organizations, and that they should be treated the same as other processors in this regard. . . .

42. Patrick Healy (Assistant Secretary, National Milk Producers Federation), testimony in *ibid.*, 184.
43. *Ibid.*

Mr. Lynn. Mr. Chairman, on behalf of the Farm Bureau we would like to concur in what Mr. Naden has said. . . .
Senator Jordan. You are talking about, I presume, a group of dairy farmers had a cheese manufacturing plant, and that would be a farmer-owned cooperative.
Mr. Naden. Yes, sir. . . .
Senator Jordan. You are opposed to striking this out as recommended by the Department?
Mr. Healy. Oh, yes.
Mr. Naden. Yes, strongly.
Senator Jordan. So are you, Mr. Lynn?
Mr. Lynn. Yes.[44]

The direct assault upon the department's position provided the first clear-cut example of the unanimity among the three farm organizations in the public hearings. However, the effect of the coalition's strong plea for maintaining the cooperative exemption was partially offset by the testimony of another farm organization official.

Harry Graham, Legislative Representative for the National Grange and onetime state legislator, went to great lengths to support the department's position for deleting the cooperative exemption, while at the same time supporting the general objectives of the bill. In a direct and carefully constructed appeal to Senator Jordan, Mr. Graham chose language that Senator Jordon, the son of a Methodist minister, was sure to understand.[45]

Is it to be held that a crime committed by a sinner is punishable under law and the same crime committed by a saint is forgivable under grace? Is extortion by a priest less a crime than extortion by a member of the Mafia? Are the proper and justifiable exemptions given to cooperatives under the Clayton Act to be used to justify economic aggression against groups and individuals? Is corporate crime more heinous than cooperative crime?[46]

After using this somewhat colorful language to dramatize his appeal, Graham proceeded to stress the difference between an exemption under an antitrust law as intended in the original version and the prohibitions discussed in S. 109 as amended. According to his analysis of the proposal, "exemptions under the antitrust law are hardly the same as exemptions which deal with activities which generally are conceded to be pretty well in the criminal area, such as extortion, blacklisting, and coercion."[47]

The testimony of proponents of the bill made clear that the major point of divergence was the cooperative exemption. In part, the difficulty stemmed

44. *Hearings on a Substitute Amendment to S. 109*, 186–87.
45. Harry Graham (Legislative Representative, National Grange), personal interview, April 4, 1968.
46. Harry Graham, testimony in *Hearings on a Substitute Amendment to S. 109*, 193.
47. *Ibid.*, 189.

from varying definitions of "cooperative" and the differences between operating cooperatives and bargaining associations. The AFB had inserted the language in the bill and supported it, along with the NCFC and the NMPF.

Support for the substitute bill also came from a host of other farmer-consumer organizations in the form of letters and telegrams. Testimony in this form was offered by Angus McDonald of the National Farmers Union; Charles Paul, Director of the California Department of Agriculture; Jerry Voorhis, Executive Director of the Cooperative League; Ralph Bunje, General Manager of the California Canning Peach Association; B. I. Freeman, Secretary-Manager of the Great Lakes Cherry Producers Association; Mrs. Grace McDonald, Executive Secretary of the California Farmer-Consumer Information Committee; Dallas Ferry, Executive Director of the U.S. Poultry and Egg Producers Association; John York, General Manager of the Eastern Milk Producers Cooperative; Clarence Gallenstein, President of the Big Ten Milk Producers Association; John W. Mitchell, President of the Merced-Stanislaus Family Farmers; and Right Reverend Edward O'Rourke, Executive Director of the National Catholic Rural Life Conference. While the farm organizations were more nearly of one mind than they had been during the earlier hearing, the opponents were equally of one mind in opposition.

Opponents to the Substitute Version. When it was time for the opponents of the bill to testify, they found that their objections to the bill had already been presented in part by certain proponents: the USDA and the National Grange. However, this fact had no effect on the length or spirit of their testimony in firm opposition to the bill. The opposition was led by the NCA and its attorney Edward Dunkelberger. Dunkelberger reiterated eight primary points raised by the NCA in the June hearing, the principal objection being that the bill would deny to processors the right to choose their suppliers. The changes that had been made in the bill were not regarded as changing the substantive prohibitions.

The fundamental objections of the canners to the new amendment fell into three broad categories.[48] First, the NCA maintained that the bill remained "grossly discriminatory" in that it applied to processors and handlers and not to bargaining associations or their producer members. This exemption was contrasted with the provisions of the Labor-Management Relations Act, which applied to the labor unions as well as to the management. Secondly, the language of the bill was objectionable to the NCA. Specifically, the canners objected to the problems that might result from additional pay or inducement to nonmembers of an association as opposed to members. The final NCA objection was that the right of a processor to refuse to deal with a particular supplier or customer was denied.

Mr. Dunkelberger concluded his remarks with crisp summarization.

48. Edward Dunkelberger (Attorney), testimony in *Hearings on a Substitute Amendment to S. 109*, 195.

The National Canners Association is opposed to the substitute, as it was to S. 109 because the bill: is one-sided and grossly discriminatory; authorizes harsh criminal penalties, treble-damage actions, and injunctions in Federal courts to be imposed against processors, but not against bargaining associations or their members; prohibits vaguely defined activity on the part of processors, and overlaps many provisions of existing statutory and common law; and revokes the right of the processor to choose his suppliers.[49]

This outright opposition to the bill, despite the claim that the NCA had no policy position with respect to collective bargaining, hit hard with the committee. Senator Aiken attempted to clarify the NCA's position.

Senator Aiken. I assume, Mr. Dunkelberger, the recommendations of the Department of Agriculture do not go very far toward meeting your objections. They go some distance but not very far, isn't that right?

Mr. Dunkelberger. Senator Aiken, with regard to the definition of "farmer," I do not believe we have any comments. With regard to making it clear that a processing cooperative will not be a handler, the National Canners Association has processing cooperatives as members, as well as independent companies. We would agree 100 percent that the provisions of this bill should not apply to any independent processor. Neither one is engaged in activities, as far as we know, that would justify such harsh legislation.[50]

For the first time in the public hearings, it appeared that certain cooperative canning companies that belonged to both the NCFC and the NCA were objecting to the S. 109 legislation in *sub rosa* fashion.

The lead-off processor testimony of the NCA was followed by that of representatives of two other categories of opponents to the bill: the anti-cooperative contingent, embodied in the National Tax Equality Association, and producers in certain commodity sectors such as cotton and livestock.

The NTEA had three basic objections to the substitute.[51] First, it argued that the substitute put independent companies at a competitive disadvantage with cooperatives with regard to certain services that might be offered. Second, certain traditional forms of business dealings, such as between proprietary processors and producers, were put in jeopardy as being criminal in nature. Finally, the NTEA argued that section 4b, which prohibited discrimination against a cooperative producer, was vague, unconstitutional and unenforceable.

The Texas cotton industry provided the most vocal opposition from the commodity sectors. The Texas Independent Ginners Association argued that the amendments were too broad and far reaching and that they were un-

49. *Ibid.,* 196.
50. *Ibid.,* 197.
51. George R. Kucik (Attorney), testimony in *Hearings on a Substitute Amendment to S. 109,* 198.

fair and discriminating against the right of the farmer not to join an association of producers. Moreover, the Texas group felt the bill would restrict competition among independent and cooperative ginners by limiting certain competitive practices. To the arguments of the Texans, W. C. Helmbrecht, Jr., of the Independent Cotton Industries Association added the charge that the revised wording of S. 109 was "tantamount to outlawing the noncooperatives in the cotton industry." [52]

Letters and telegrams supporting the opposition to the amended bill were received by the committee from Charles E. Connor, Counsel for the Independent Livestock Marketing Association; John Killick, Executive Secretary of the National Independent Meat Packers Association; Lex Killebrew, Executive Secretary of the Arkansas Poultry Federation; Don F. Magdanz of the National Livestock Feeders Association (a farm commodity association); and F. Y. Tiernan, Senior Vice-President of the H. J. Heinz Company.

The opponents to the proposal — the processors, the anti-cooperative people and some commodity groups — rested their case on basically the same arguments that were presented in the June hearing. However, they concentrated on the criminal penalties, the "unwarranted" restrictions on competitive activities and the fact that the legislation would not apply equally to cooperatives and producers as well as other handlers. In recognition of the conflicting positions in the testimony presented by the various interest groups, Senator Aiken commented at the close of the hearing, "We do have a real problem here, Mr. Chairman, and we do want to be fair to everybody in order to solve their problems." [53] S. 109 had survived another hearing, but the only real sign of progress was that its proponents, with exception of one provision, had solidified in their support for it.

Reintroduction of S. 109 in the 90th Congress

From the September hearing, it was evident that rigorous opposition still confronted the bill. Yet, it was also evident that the proponents felt that the rewriting of the bill as a new piece of legislation, with the exception of one provision, was a major accomplishment. Both the farm organizations and the Department of Agriculture now agreed generally that further legislation was desirable. Based on the reports of the National Commission on Food Marketing, these components of the farm sector also felt that it was necessary to foster more group action.

As the major architect of the bill, the AFB was faced with some key decisions. Politics, it is frequently said, is the art of compromise. Since World War II, the AFB had acquired a reputation for not playing the legislative game. The general farm group seemed determined to take all or nothing and

52. W. C. Helmbrecht, Jr. (Executive Vice-President, Independent Cotton Industries Association), testimony in *ibid.*, 209.
53. George Aiken, testimony in *ibid.*, 210.

as a consequence was often severely criticized for being too hard and uncompromising.[54] But if S. 109 was to survive in the legislative arena, it was necessary to find some grounds for compromise.

The most thorny issue following the September hearing concerned the exemption of "associations of producers" from the definition of "handler" and thus from the prohibitions of the proposal. In a memo to the AFB Chicago office, John Datt of the Washington office identified this issue as the most controversial part of the bill.[55] And it was upon this issue that the AFB decided to "roll with the punches so long as it preserved the major objectives of the legislation." [56] The decision on the cooperative exemption was not considered to be very significant at the time, since the NCFC had not indicated its inclusion was necessary for NCFC acceptance.[57] Moreover, many farm groups still felt that the bill had little chance of passing, and the AFB saw no need to make a major fight for the exemption, even though they were initially for it. However, a time was to come when they would have second thoughts.

Added incentive for the decision not to stand on the exemption issue grew out of discussions that took place during the December, 1966, annual meeting of the American Farm Bureau. At that meeting, members of the voting delegation from Texas raised questions about the cooperative exemption that indicated that they were receiving flak from cotton industry people in their home state.[58] Apparently, large grain companies operating in Texas were also involved in stirring up opposition to the S. 109 measure. At the same time, many Farm Bureau members from other states saw S. 109 as a frontal attack on cooperatives.[59] After a lengthy discussion, the issue was settled verbally with an unrecorded agreement that the AFB would support a definition of handler that included cooperatives.

AFB faced another key decision on whether the penalty provisions should be maintained in the bill. The NCA had found the criminal penalties objectionable in the extreme. And representatives of the cotton ginners felt that the provisions would outlaw the long-standing practice of going down the road and haggling over ginning rates. In spite of these arguments, the AFB regarded some type of penalty provisions and avenues of recourse for farm operators necessary and determined further that the injunctive relief measures were absolutely essential. The treble-damages provision was highly desirable as a means of assuring compliance, and inclusion of the criminal penalties in the bill had merit as a strategic maneuver, in spite of the strenuous objections it engendered from the processing community.

In stern opposition to having cooperatives covered by the bill's prohibitions, the NCFC continued to object to compromises offered by Senator

54. Anderson, interview.
55. John Datt, memo to Allen A. Lauterbach, September 29, 1966.
56. Anderson, interview.
57. Datt, interview.   58. *Ibid.*   59. *Ibid.*

Aiken and the USDA. Opinions on the issue differed. Based on their experience in the state legislature, California cooperative officials felt that cooperatives should be exempted. In part, their attitude accounted for the NCFC's position on the issue.

In contrast, Charles Brannan, former Secretary of Agriculture and currently General Counsel for the NFU, did not regard the classification of cooperatives as handlers as being too serious. He felt cooperatives should be viewed as extensions of the members' farm firms and therefore not as handlers in the sense for which the prohibitions were designed to apply.[60] Given Brannan's theoretical principle, cooperatives could not be construed as handlers in any case.

The most adamant resistance against allowing cooperative exemption came from Charles Connor, Counsel for the Independent Livestock Marketing Association. The controversy worsened.

As S. 109 was appraised for reintroduction into the Ninetieth Congress, Senator Aiken decided that removal of the cooperative exemption was necessary. Although he was somewhat reluctant to remove the cooperative exemption, Aiken felt, from a realistic point of view, that it was necessary to assure further movement of the bill.[61] Herb Harris of the AFB and Harker Stanton, counsel to the Senate Agriculture and Forestry Committee, spent long hours rephrasing key sections of the bill. Most of the suggested amendments offered in the September hearing by the USDA and others were incorporated into S. 109.

The dissension among farm groups generated by Aiken's decision was a source of considerable frustration to him. To meet the NCFC's objections, AFB officials sat down with Bob Hampton of the NCFC in an attempt to work out a compromise. The result was a new section (g) in the prohibition section that exempted producer associations that handled farm products. The earlier draft exempted cooperatives from the definition of "handler"; the new approach exempted cooperatives from the prohibitions. The draft including this section was sent to Senator Aiken; however, he refused to include section g on the basis that he wouldn't permit cooperatives to discriminate. Furthermore, he indicated that he wouldn't introduce the bill unless the NCFC would support the proposal without section g. S. 109 was in a state of crisis.

In response to the crisis, AFB officials met with Kenneth Naden of the NCFC late on January 9th in an effort to hold the original S. 109 coalition together. However, Mr. Naden refused to support the bill without section g. John Datt of the AFB pleaded to save the bill but finally indicated that the Farm Bureau would have no alternative but to let everyone know who had

60. Robert N. Hampton (Director of Marketing and International Trade, National Council of Farmer Cooperatives), personal interview, April 4, 1968; Graham, interview; McDonald, interview.
61. Weaver, interview.

killed it. This possibility led to a reassessment of NCFC's stand, and the meeting ended with Naden's permission to introduce the bill without the exemption. However, Naden's approval was conditional on an agreement that the organizations in the coalition would take one more look to see if something else could be worked out.

Amid reports that NCFC and USDA officials were cogitating over a whole new approach to the farm income problem, the AFB decided to initiate pressure on certain cooperative leaders in an effort to pull the NCFC back into line and to save the AFB bill. The crisis was heightened when Senator Aiken suddenly cooled off on the whole idea of an S. 109 type measure.[62] The main burden for resolving the issue rested upon the shoulders of Charles Shuman and Allen Lauterbach as they flew to New Orleans in mid-January for a crucial meeting with the NCFC Board of Directors. While the meeting was initially called to straighten out a rift that had developed between the AFB and certain supply cooperatives as represented by the NCFC over an AFB purchasing program, the S. 109 crisis gave added meaning to the meeting.

AFB officials seized upon the opportunity to discuss the S. 109 dilemma informally with bargaining association officials from the West Coast.[63] Despite somewhat strained Washington relations between the organizations, the New Orleans efforts proved successful. The NCFC's opposition was neutralized to a position of lukewarm support when S. 109 was termed a "useful first step" by one NCFC official.[64] As Senator Aiken prepared the bill for reintroduction, he sought and received concurrence from Naden.

The bill introduced to the Senate on January 11th retained its number, S. 109.

62. L. Gene Lemon, memo to Allen A. Lauterbach, January 10, 1967.
63. Charles B. Shuman (President, American Farm Bureau Federation), personal interview, September 25, 1968.
64. Robert N. Hampton, speech, "The 'Climate of Opportunity' for Bargaining in Today's Markets," *Proceedings of the 11th National Bargaining Conference* (Washington: Farmer Cooperative Service, USDA, 1967), 69.

Feelings are running high about the
agricultural producers' first formal
collective bargaining proposal, with
employer groups opposing Senate
Bill 109 and most farmer organizations supporting it. . . . However,
the arguments raised against S. 109
. . . appear to be calculated to provoke emotional response more than
thoughtful appraisal.[1]

William A. Haffert, Jr.

Chapter 6
1967: Year of Debate, Compromise and Fallout

S. 109 was the subject of widespread controversy and debate throughout 1967. As reintroduced in the first session of the Ninetieth Congress by
Senator Aiken, it reflected four significant changes. First, the title had been
changed to the "Agricultural Producers Marketing Act of 1967." Secondly,
the prohibitions of the proposed new law had been extended to apply to producers' associations. Next, the definition of "producer" had been clarified.
Finally, the words "or acquisition" had been inserted in section 4b to assure
that contract production was covered by provisions of the bill. The rewritten
bill thus embodied most of the modifications suggested by the USDA, including the controversial definition of a cooperative as a handler.

Changes in the atmosphere surrounding the life of the bill also became
evident. The reintroduced version picked up many new supporters in Congress and received vigorous coverage by the AFB press. Cosponsoring the
bill along with Senator Aiken were Senators Frank Lausche of Ohio and Milton Young of North Dakota. Sponsors on the House side included Congressmen Robert T. Stafford of Vermont (H.R. 4152), Mrs. Catherine May of
Washington (H.R. 4889) and John H. Kyl of Iowa (H.R. 5007).

By March 6, a total of seventeen members of the House of Representatives had introduced similar bills. House support came from such ranking
members of the Agriculture Committee as Representative E. C. Gathings of
Arkansas, vice-chairman of the committee, Representative John L. McMillan
of South Carolina, third-ranking member, and Congressman Charles Teague
of California and Mrs. May of Washington, who were the second and third
ranking minority members of the committee. The momentum generated by
these sponsors gave the bill a new lease on life for the Ninetieth Congress.

Fair Treatment or Fear Treatment

The fresh approach to S. 109 taken by the AFB following its March,
1967, board meeting undoubtedly added vitality to the new life of the bill.

1. "S. 109 and 'free enterprise'," *Broiler Industry*, 30, 4 (April, 1967), 8.

That strong congressional support was forthcoming was a tribute both to the growing support for some type of bargaining legislation in the congressional districts and to the homework of the legislative counsel and the press team. In a letter to state Farm Bureaus dated January 25th, John Lynn, Legislative Director of the AFB, had expressed hope "that the bill would be reported by the full committee and passed by the Senate early in this session." [2] With House action expected at a later date, he called upon the state organizations to communicate with their senators and to urge early consideration and passage of the bill.

To complement their correspondence action within the Bureau, the AFB also launched a publicity campaign early in the year in the official AFB "Newsletter." More articles about S. 109 appeared in the newsletter during the first three months of 1967 than during the preceding three years in which the bill was before Congress. The AFB's intention in this coverage was threefold. First, it hoped to draw members' attention to the legislative progress of the "marketing rights" bill. Also, the recognition given each legislative sponsor of the proposal by prominently displaying his picture in the newsletter was assumed to be welcome exposure for such supporters. Further, the AFB hoped the articles, by stressing the limited objective of the bill, would calm some of the internal opposition. Thus, President Shuman's testimony in June, 1966, which began, "Farm Bureau does not seek, and will not support, legislation which is designed to force processors to negotiate . . ." [3] was reprinted several times. The repeated emphasis upon this latter point was designed to tone down any interpretation of S .109 as "Wagner Act" legislation for farm bargaining purposes.

Despite AFB's overt attempt to convince those involved of its limited concept of the bill, opponents did not take long in questioning the AFB's purposes. Throughout 1966, the National Broiler Council had suggested its opposition to S. 109 by widely circulating a negative memo written by its attorney James Rill. Upon encouragement from John Datt and other AFB lobbyists to present their case in the open, the NBC announced formal opposition to the bill in January, 1967. [4] The National Canners Association, in a more subtle fashion, called its members' attention to the fact that the American Farm Bureau was "working hard and with significant success in obtaining supporters for the bargaining bill (S. 109) . . . ," [5] and the NCA Washington "Report" tabbed the bill as essentially the same as its predecessors and

2. John C. Lynn (Legislative Director, American Farm Bureau Federation), letter to state Farm Bureaus, January 25, 1967.

3. Charles B. Shuman (President, American Farm Bureau Federation), testimony in U.S. Senate, Subcommittee of the Committee on Agriculture and Forestry, *Hearings on S. 109*, 89th Cong., 2d sess., 1966, 15.

4. *The Poultryman* (January 20, 1967), in files of American Farm Bureau Federation.

5. National Canners Association, "Government-Industry Report," February 9, 1967.

therefore equally objectionable. The canners also singled out Mrs. May, a member of the President's Food and Fiber Commission and a member of the House, for supporting the proponents.

> Mrs. Catherine May, one of our favorite members of Congress, unfortunately has succumbed to the proponents. Her remarks on introducing the bill on February 6 demonstrate how the FAIRPLAY slogan will be used in seeking passage of the bill.[6]

Finally, the NCA urged its members to write their congressmen and senators and to give them their views regarding reintroduction of the "collective bargaining" bills.

The rewritten S. 109 quickly became different things to different people. While processor groups viewed it as a "collective bargaining" bill, the congressional sponsors of the bill such as Mrs. May considered it a much needed "fair play" measure. In contrast, the chief promoters of the bill preferred to promote it as the "marketing rights" bill. The constant attacks upon S. 109 by their trade association counterparts was particularly unsettling to Farm Bureau legislative personnel who were imbued with the "free market" and "get the Government out of agriculture" philosophy. Frequent jostling by the trade organizations rattled the Washington team and created fears that S. 109 conflicted with basic Farm Bureau philosophy. As weeks passed, it became clear to AFB personnel that if the battle over S. 109 was going to be won, it would be through unnatural channels within the organization.

Within the AFB, the bargaining people and grower committees, in contrast to the usual state and county Farm Bureau legislative committees, were carrying the bulk of the effort in promoting the bill. To many of the older rank-and-file members of Farm Bureau, the bargaining idea remained new and hard to digest. Compounding the problem was the view of some staff members of the legislative and commodity branches within the AFB who saw the AAMA activities as a threat to their own programs. Supply cooperatives sponsored by the Farm Bureau in several states even refused to promote S. 109 through the NCFC and other organizations, in fear that bargaining efforts would be used against them. Clearly, the AFB was handicapped by relative inaction on the part of some within its own ranks. At the same time, it had to promote the bill through rank amateurs on the bargaining and grower committees. Promotion efforts began to bog down.

The climax to the pulling and tugging was reached during the AAMA's annual meeting in Chicago on March 8, 1967. John Lynn of AFB's Washington office raised questions on the floor about the necessity of S. 109 and what he was going to tell legislators and traditionally strong AFB allies among processor groups.[7] In response, William Jasper of the AAMA staff declared that

6. *Ibid.*
7. Farm Bureau staff members, confidential interviews.

S. 109 was necessary for the AAMA program and made a plea for organization loyalty.

The AAMA's demands for legislating S. 109 into law were supported by AFB President Shuman, and through his leadership, the Board of Directors, in their March meeting, listed passage of S. 109 as their top priority item for 1967. The formal action of the board seemed to galvanize the organization, and much of the wavering was forgotten. With directive powers maintained in Chicago, the Washington team became invigorated with a sense of purpose seldom witnessed by observers in the nation's capital.

Hopes for congressional approval were brightened when Senator Aiken indicated early in February that hearings on the bill would soon be held. AFB's John Datt suggested in a February magazine article that the marketing rights bill was essential to AFB's goal of getting government out of the business of controlling farm supplies and prices.[8] Strong voluntary groups were considered a prerequisite to this transition. Datt argued that accordingly, S. 109 was fitting to AFB philosophy and could be looked upon as a natural vehicle for the recommendations of the National Commission on Food Marketing.

Senator Aiken's announcement raised expectations for a March hearing and set wheels in motion for collecting appropriate testimony. As the hearing approached, three groups could be identified on the farm front. The original AFB-NCFC-NMPF coalition maintained its working relationship at the insistence of Senator Aiken, but the broadening of prohibitions to apply to marketing cooperatives introduced a new strain on the alliance. Some regional cooperatives involved in contracting broilers became concerned about dealing with bargaining associations,[9] and voiced their opposition to S. 109 directly to the NCFC. Their opposition was later articulated through such trade associations as the NBC and the American Poultry Institute. Similar situations existed in the fruit and vegetable canning industry. This activity by a few operating cooperatives affiliated with NCFC placed the organization in a difficult position and was troublesome to the farm front.

The National Advisory Committee on Cooperatives of the U.S. Department of Agriculture, appointed by Secretary Freeman in 1961, was a second force.[10] The committee had first met to discuss S. 109 on March 16, 1966, in an attempt to arrive at a departmental position for the June hearing; it did not consider the bill again until it was taken up for discussion at a series of regular monthly meetings beginning February 2, 1967. Under the leadership of

8. "Marketing Rights Bill Has A Chance," *Feedstuffs*, 39 (February 11, 1967), in files of American Farm Bureau Federation.

9. Kenneth D. Naden (Executive Vice-President, National Council of Farmer Cooperatives), personal interview, June 10, 1968.

10. USDA, Farmer Cooperative Service, *News for Farmer Cooperatives,* December, 1961, 10. Readers should note that considerable overlap existed between membership in these various groupings. For instance, the NCFC participated in all three of the alliances.

Assistant Secretary John A. Baker, the committee served as a sounding board for discussion of department policies relating to cooperatives and as a clearinghouse for proposals such as S. 109. The advisory group met in February, March and April in preparation for the department's testimony before the Senate subcommittee.

The third grouping consisted of the Committee of "17," which represented — in the main — a carry-over from a coalition organized by the NFU in 1961 to support the new national Administration.[11] Since 1961, the coalition of farm groups had met informally on a regular basis at the Grange building in Washington to settle some of their differences and discuss pending legislation before hearings took place. Mr. Harry Graham, Legislative Director of the National Grange, had become heir to the group and served as spokesman. The original seventeen organizational participants included representatives of the National Farmers Organization, National Farmers Union, Midcontinent Farmers Association, National Council of Farmer Cooperatives, National Federation of Grain Cooperatives, National Corn Growers Association, Western Wheat Growers Association, National Wheat Growers Association, National Cattle Feeders Association, Grain Sorghum Producers Association, National Peanut Growers Association, Soybean Producers of America, National Egg Association, National Poultry Association, Dairymen's League and the National Rural Electric Cooperative Association. In addition to the original seventeen, representatives of Associated Dairymen and of the USDA also met with the group informally during 1967. The department was generally represented by Tom Hughes and Ed Jaenke.

While this combination of general farm interest and commodity organizations deemed the proposed antidiscriminatory legislation as highly desirable, based on experiences of farm operators in Ohio and broiler producing states, some resentment had been created when several of them were not consulted by the AFB in formulating the proposal as reintroduced in the Ninetieth Congress. In particular, the National Grange seemed troubled by the same professional jealousy of the AFB it had earlier publicly displayed before the Senate subcommittee in 1966. These feelings did not prevent the meetings between the NFU, Midcontinent Farmers Association, NCFC, National Grange and the USDA from serving as a vehicle for coalescing a force in support of S. 109 with minor changes.[12]

As the likelihood of early hearings increased, the three farm groups prepared hearing testimony and mapped strategy for achieving a legislative victory. The first step in the strategy was the redrafting of the bill by Herb Harris, Legislative Counsel of the AFB. His objective was to prepare a bill that

11. Don E. Hadwiger and Ross B. Talbot, *Pressures and Protests: The Kennedy Farm Program and the Wheat Referendum of 1963* (San Francisco: Chandler Publishing Company, 1965), 57.

12. Harry Graham (Legislative Representative, National Grange), personal interview, April 4, 1968.

would accommodate the interests of all proponents as expressed in the previous hearings. More importantly, the measure had to be in a form in which it would be referred to the House Agriculture Committee rather than the Judiciary Committee. To allow room for modification — and thus safeguard the survival of such critical provisions as the penalty elements — the terms of the bill were consciously overextended slightly.

Concurrently, efforts at securing as many congressional sponsors as possible for the legislation went forward. Success in this direction continued as Senators Frank Church of Idaho and Quentin Burdick of North Dakota announced their sponsorship of S. 109 on March 6th.

On a third front, the proponents of the bill set out to rally as much support among farm groups as possible. Given the history of competition among farm groups, an effort of this sort involved reconciling pet philosophies and healing old wounds. For the AFB, it also meant consultation and shoulder-to-shoulder work with the USDA.

In a further effort to smooth the way, the AFB sought to clear the draft with probable opponents. In part, they were successful. However, the reaction from others who were approached made clear that some very formidable opposition lay ahead.

As charges of one-sidedness and trickery mounted from the opposition to S. 109, proponents countered with an effective issue of their own — law and order. In a context of farm unrest, accentuated by the findings in the Arkansas broiler case, Claude Gifford, Economics Editor for the monthly *Farm Journal* magazine, coined a slogan for the proponents of S. 109: "Fair treatment instead of fear treatment." This attitude was echoed by Senator Aiken in an interview on "Inside Agriculture," a weekly radio service of Velsicol Chemical Corporation, on March 10th. According to Aiken, there was no reason why S. 109 should be opposed "unless these processors and handlers that are opposing it desire to be unfair to the producers."

On March 13th, this fair treatment plea was pursued by 91 Michigan Farm Bureau leaders who arrived in Washington for a three-day visit with their legislators. These county Farm Bureau legislative committeemen requested support for the bill that would "protect the rights of farmers to bargain with processors," and "outlaw processor retaliation or intimidation against farmers who join cooperatives or marketing associations." [13]

The impact of the Michigan group — the only mass effort by farm operators to contact personally senators and congressmen on Capitol Hill — and the efforts of Farm Bureau broiler bargaining associations in the South helped in getting additional sponsors for the bill in the House. In addition to Congressmen Stafford, May and Kyl, the following legislators had introduced their versions of the marketing rights bill by March 27: John M. Zwach of Minnesota (H.R. 5275), Watkins M. Abbitt of Virginia (H.R. 3505),

13. Michigan Farm Bureau, Information Division, press release, March 13, 1967.

Charles Teague of California (H.R. 5353), Thomas S. Kleppe of North Dakota (H.R. 5449), John R. Rarick of Louisiana (H.R. 5478), William Scott of Virginia (H.R. 5495), Mark Andrews of North Dakota (H.R. 5756), John L. McMillan of South Carolina (H.R. 5774), Charles Mathias, Jr., of Maryland (H.R. 5775), George Goodling of Pennsylvania (H.R. 5873), Fred Schwengel of Iowa (H.R. 5900), Paul Findley of Illinois (H.R. 6141), Frank Thompson of New Jersey (H.R. 6172), E. C. Gathings of Arkansas (H.R. 6262), Clarence Miller of Ohio (H.R. 6728), Irving Whalley of Pennsylvania (H.R. 6890), Harley Staggers of West Virginia (H.R. 7002), Albert Quie of Minnesota (H.R. 7247) and Kenneth Gray of Illinois (H.R. 7334). The Farm Bureau's "marketing rights" bandwagon was rolling and included the bipartisan support of more than ten members of the House Agriculture Committee.

Opponent Strategy: Fairplay or Foul Ball?

The apparent success of farm groups in securing legislative sponsors for S. 109 caused widespread concern among integrators and processors. In recognition of the proponents' determination and perseverance, opponents of S. 109 decided that it was time for more forceful mobilization. Political analysts were forecasting the ultimate passage of the bill. Farm writers suggested that the farm sector was gearing up for major action on it. By March, one prognosticator was actually suggesting that S. 109 would be hard to stop.[14] With congressional support mushrooming, the processing community was jolted into action.

On February 16th, representatives of several national food processing trade associations met to form an *ad hoc* committee to oppose S. 109. Robert B. Heiney of the National Canners Association led the group in drawing up plans for fighting the bill.[15] The main objections of the NCA to the proposal were its criminal penalty provisions and regulation of processors in the canner-grower bargaining association relationship.

> . . . the proposal has built into it a pressure which would distinctly give the bargaining association an advantage in its dealings with processors. It interjects the government into a private contractual relationship; it has a lever in it which would make it difficult for an individual canner to select individual growers with whom to do business.[16]

From all indications, the processing and trade organizations would henceforth pull no punches. S. 109 was now caught up in a fight for its life.

14. "S. 109 will be hard to stop," *Broiler Industry*, 30, 3 (March, 1967), 6.
15. "Processor Groups Unite in Opposition To Bargaining Bill," *Feedstuffs*, 39 (February 25, 1967), in files of American Farm Bureau Federation.
16. Robert B. Heiney (Director, Government-Industry Relations, National Canners Association), statements on "Inside Agriculture," radio broadcast, March 10, 1967.

Opponents to the bill, like their proponent counterparts, could be categorized in essentially three groups. The first was the well-financed processing community lobby led by the quiet and unassuming NCA. Initially, the *ad hoc* committee consisted only of representatives of the National Broiler Council and the canners group. Several weeks later, however, the U.S. Chamber of Commerce, the National Independent Meat Packers Association, the American Poultry Institute and the American Feed Manufacturers Association affiliated with the committee. The most vocal opposition was to come from the *ad hoc* committee.

The politically powerful cotton interests were also identifiable in opposition. To a great extent, the opposition of the cotton group was fostered by efforts of the Texas Independent Ginners Association, beginning late in 1966. The cotton industry was capable of marshaling substantial opposition to legislation it considered unfriendly and did so with S. 109. The American Cotton Shippers Association played a significant part in early opposition, with the American Cotton Compress and Warehouse Association later assuming a major role as an opponent of the AFB proposal.

Diversity and independence characterized the third grouping of opponents. Large food firms, handler associations and trade groups antagonistic to farm organization efforts — each undertook courses of opposition. The Campbell Soup Company publicly labeled the bill a "little Wagner Act." Ralston Purina lobbied directly against the bill through its Washington representative William Foster, and the Pet Milk Company through former Under Secretary of Agriculture, True Morse. Both Cargill and Del Monte companies appeared later on the scene. Typical of action by a handlers group was the work of the lobby of the Independent Livestock Dealers Association of Columbus, Ohio. The National Tax Equality Association, a group of arch-conservative, anti-cooperative businessmen, also made its appearance.

Taken together, these three broad groups in opposition to S. 109 were capable of an offensive the thought of which sent a chill into Capitol Hill, the Administration and the AFB legislative team.

The attention of the press seemed to focus primarily upon the maneuvering of the Broiler Council in the prehearing tussle. In assuming an open position against S. 109 in late January, Frank Frazier of the NBC had argued that the bill would extend certain immunities to farmers who bargain collectively with processors. He also labeled S. 109 a "bargaining" bill, a position involving some risks for the trade organization. By opposing the bill, as its integrator members wanted, the NBC ran the risk of alienating its farmer-grower committee at a time when the trade associations were in dire need of grass-roots support due to the Farm Bureau's organizing efforts in the Southern states.[17]

Following pleas for a write-in campaign against S. 109 to their constitu-

17. "Some S. 109 Issues," *Broiler Industry*, 30, 2 (February, 1967), 14.

ents in February, the *ad hoc* committee launched a big push in opposition to the bill in March. Processors and integrators at that time began a massive program at the grass-roots level to encourage contact with senators and congressmen. As part of this effort, the NBC organized a "Broilercade" of about 25 members who visited about 80 congressmen in their Capitol Hill offices, promoting the Broiler Council position and distributing a leaflet entitled "Fairplay or Foul Ball?" The NBC also hosted 31 House members and 12 or more congressional aides at an evening reception.[18] Only one Senator, Democrat Sam Ervin of North Carolina, attended the reception. Whether the sparse senatorial attendance indicated problems for the NBC on the Senate side was unclear. One commentator suggested that Senator Ervin's presence at the reception might have been a tip-off to the sentiments of his fellow North Carolina Democrat Everett Jordan.[19] As Chairman of the Senate Agriculture Subcommittee, Jordan was a key figure in the developing S. 109 controversy.

The "Fairplay or Foul Ball" leaflet accomplished its purpose in attracting publicity and was even read into the *Congressional Record* by Congressman Phil Landrum of Georgia.[20] The leaflet charged that S. 109 was "unfair . . . unreasonable . . . [and] unnecessary." Echoing a position taken in the earlier hearings, it maintained that the practices prohibited in S. 109 were already covered by existing law and that the structure already provided adequate protection for agricultural producers. The NBC also struck again the familiar theme that processors would be forced to deal with an association of contract growers.

The leaflet, widely distributed, was but one tack. The NBC also prepared tapes for broadcast on 700 radio stations in the broiler producing belt. To represent a geographical cross section of the industry, the program featured interviews with integrators from Tennessee, Georgia, Pennsylvania and Maryland. The broadcasts warned that the bill might drive a wedge between the time-honored relationships existing among many integrators and growers. Though the effects of NBC's publicity tactics could not be assessed by proponents, it was clear that reply was in order.

In response to President Shuman's directive following the March AFB Board meeting and the AAMA annual meeting, the AFB called a meeting of its coalition on March 27. The business at hand was the preparation of a rebuttal to the comments being circulated by food processors and the NBC. On the same day, Legislative Director John Lynn called upon the state Farm Bureaus for an "all-out effort" in order to counter the gains being made by the opponents. In a remark designed to spur state AAMA officials — who were bitterly complaining about the NBC propaganda campaign — to political activity, John Datt of the Washington office proclaimed: "They [bargain-

18. *Ibid.*
19. *Ibid.*
20. U.S. *Congressional Record*, 90th Cong., 1st sess., 1967, CXIII, Part 6, 7409.

ing proponents] can't just sit on their hind end and howl like dogs." In a supporting effort, the AFB prepared an explanation of the bill and made it available to proponents and opponents alike.

The word battle accelerated when the American Feed Manufacturers Association joined the chorus protesting the bill. The association's "Washington Feedline" of March 28 suggested that "on the surface it appears that, like motherhood, no one could oppose S. 109." [21] Nevertheless, the AFMA questioned the need for S. 109 and suggested that it was one-sided. The "Feedline" also suggested that the bill could cause problems for feed manufacturers.

According to the AFMA, the same practices that could put a handler in jail under the bill could be carried out by a producer with no penalties. Citing the events of the March milk delivery stop carried out by the NFO, the feed association claimed that farm operators and farm organizations had indeed carried out "unfair practices" against other producers, cooperatives and independent handlers. Accordingly, if any legislation was passed, "it should apply equally to all persons." [22]

Although the NFO milk action gave scare ammunition to opponents, it served proponents by attracting attention to the S. 109 proposal. Syndicated journalists Richard Wilson and Paul Hope wrote feature articles on the producers' plight.[23] Feeling the impact of these articles, the NCA reported to members that with the milk withholding effort of the NFO, "the Farm Bureau's collective bargaining proposal is getting a little more publicity than we feel it would otherwise merit." [24] Ignoring the fact that the Justice Department issued a complaint and a federal court granted a temporary injunction against the NFO, the canner organization made no attempt to analyze and evaluate this government and court action with regard to S. 109.[25] The unexpected assist also prompted retorts from other opponents of S. 109, including the U.S. Chamber of Commerce.

Like the broiler association, the American Cotton Compress and Warehouse Association brought members to town in April to lobby against S. 109. The cotton representatives started with the White House, then visited with Secretary Freeman, several under secretaries and Horace Godfrey, a North Carolina native who was Administrator of the politically powerful Agricul-

21. American Feed Manufacturers Association, "Washington Feedline," March 28, 1967.

22. *Ibid.*

23. Richard Wilson, "Farmers' Revolt of Important Proportions," *The Evening Star* (Washington, D.C.), March 27, 1967, in files of National Canners Association; Paul Hope, "Spilt Milk and Political Tears," *ibid.*

24. National Canners Association, "Government-Industry Report," March 31, 1967.

25. Until this time, the NCA and other trade groups had argued that S. 109 was one-sided and that processors needed protection from some militant farm groups. In the NFO case, the government did take action.

tural Stabilization and Conservation Service. The delegation also paid personal visits to agriculture committee members in both houses, arguing that the S. 109 proposal was unfair to independent cotton handlers.

However convincing, the arguments and propaganda by the processor groups were dismissed by at least one writer as nonsense and calculated to "provoke emotional response more than thoughtful appraisal." [26] Instead, he suggested that if these groups wanted government controls on agriculture abandoned, "then they should accept the bitter with the sweet in a 'free' society — the right for farmers to bargain voluntarily for a better position, and to seek in Congress legislation strong enough to make their efforts effective." [27]

The NCA, NBC, AFMA, U.S. Chamber of Commerce and the cotton interests were not prepared to accept the "bitter." They considered themselves powerful enough to kill S. 109 in isolation, without ramifications for other programs. So effective were these groups in registering grass-roots opposition to the bill that by the end of March and early April political analysts were suggesting that passage in the current session of Congress was questionable.

The Political Dilemma of S. 109

The objections of the NCA and NBC and their allies raised enough questions about the merits of S. 109 to jeopardize an early hearing on the bill. While the bill was designed to curb unfair trade practices affecting farm operators, opponents fought it as though it dealt with the deeper issue of farm bargaining. They were primarily concerned with what the bill "might" imply. Tactically, they proclaimed that they were not opposed to bargaining rights for producers but that the bill would regulate only one party to the bargaining process.

At the same time, the popularity of the idea of farm bargaining power inspired by the NFO milk action was reaching new heights throughout the countryside. The AFB was riding the crest of popularity of this issue with its legislative proposal. Simultaneously, the AAMA was proceeding under full steam with its efforts to organize bargaining units in the field. However, Farm Bureau organizers continually met stiff resistance from integrators and processors — especially in efforts to organize broiler growers in the South. The combination of these events — organizing efforts by the Farm Bureau, the NFO milk withholding action and the rising popularity of farm bargaining as a means of improving farm incomes — culminated in the political controversy that embroiled S. 109.

At the root of the debate was an even more fundamental question. It fo-

26. "S. 109 and 'free enterprise'," 8.
27. *Ibid.*

cused on growing unhappiness with farm programs, themselves products of the depression 1930's. Mr. William Haffert, Jr., captured the essence of this aspect of the S. 109 controversy in a *Broiler Industry* editorial entitled "S. 109 and 'free enterprise'." [28]

> Something terribly important is involved here . . . and it goes beyond the broiler industry. After receiving $60 billion or so in direct and indirect subsidies over the past 35 years, an important segment of our farmers is asking for freedom to run its own affairs.
>
> The Farm Bureau takes the position that if marketing of farm products is not organized by farmers themselves, this function will be taken over by labor unions, the business community or the federal government.
>
> There's a power vacuum here . . . and its going to be filled. Criticism of S. 109, without even accepting the principle that such legislation is justifiable is tantamount to inviting — tomorrow or the day after — a full scale Wagner Act for agriculture. What a Pandora's box that would open.

In addition, Haffert offered the processors and integrators a piece of advice. If the bill was as one-sided as they claimed, he suggested that they could do an "infinitely better service" by promoting modifications to Congress.

By singling out the crucial farm policy issue, Haffert put his finger on the central and most sticky agricultural issue of the decade: Who is going to control American agriculture? The economic organization of agriculture was at stake. If the processing community recommended constructive changes to the AFB proposal, it would solidify the farmer's continued role as an independent entrepreneur or contractee. Farmers could organize into viable bargaining units for purposes of negotiating terms of trade with processors and integrators. (Such action, of course, would result in increased costs to processors, which ultimately would be passed on to consumers in the form of higher prices.) More importantly, however, passage of S. 109 would enhance the possibility that the farm enterprise would remain in the hands of commercial farmers.

An economic organization of agriculture built around farmers was at odds with the organizational design envisioned by many corporate feed companies. They saw an "industrialized" agriculture run by 6 or 8 major integrators in which management, partial ownership and partial risk rested with the corporate entity. The farm operator assumed the role of a contractee who carried out directives of the corporation and exercised his managerial abilities with company-owned livestock or crops on his own farm. Another variation of this design was complete ownership of factors of production, including land, by the integrator. In this design the farmer became a wage earner and was bound by contractual arrangements to the corporate body. In practice,

28. *Ibid.*

this backward integration — as experienced in the production of eggs, broilers, turkeys, hogs and some specialty crops — had been dissatisfying to farmers involved and was the source of much farm unrest.

With the emergence of such basic issues underlying the debate surrounding S. 109, a political dilemma of far-reaching proportions was at hand. The issues were not taken lightly by either side. Up to this point, the processors and integrators had assumed a position of strong opposition to the bill on the simplistic grounds that its provisions were unnecessary and already covered by existing law. Now the deeper issue had surfaced.

The farm groups supporting the proposal pushed hard for enactment of a "basic" fair practices act that would provide immediate injunctive relief to

Critical underlying questions, issues such as "Who is going to control American agriculture," surfaced in the S. 109 debate preceding the May, 1967, Senate hearing. Reprinted by special permission from *Farm Journal*, October, 1967. Copyright 1967 by Farm Journal, Inc.

Sliding farm prices and rising costs in early 1967 caused widespread farm unrest and hit dairymen especially hard. NFO's milk withholding action drew public attention to the farmers' plight and coincidentally to S. 109.

An exclusive Herald cartoon by Jim Zilverberg. Printed with permission from the *Farmers Union Herald.*

the individual farm operator. Although congressional support of the farmer's right to organize and integrate forward in the market place dated from such well-known acts as the Clayton Act of 1914, the Capper-Volstead Act of 1922, the Cooperative Marketing Act of 1926 and the Agricultural Marketing Agreements Act of 1937, legislation of post-World War II vintage was nonexistent. With the rise of the new farm bargaining concept, farm operators and their farm organizations sought a bill that would outlaw discriminatory acts that were committed against them and also reaffirm long-standing congressional support for their right to organize.

Between these two opposing forces, the politicians preferred to straddle and seek an atmosphere for compromise. The task appeared awesome and politically hazardous. On the one side, there were organizations representing America's three million farm businessmen and the bulk of the nation's farm production. On the other were the politically influential trade associations representing processors and corporate integrators. Events leading to and following the May, 1967, hearing put S. 109 in a different perspective in contrast to the early flurry over the proposal.

Senate Hearing Preliminaries

With the political dilemma apparent, a major question arose: Was S. 109 too hot to handle? Congress, if it acted as it had occasionally with other controversial issues, could conveniently postpone action on the bill. The pending report of the President's Food and Fiber Commission was a ready excuse. At the same time, however, enough momentum had been gathered by the additional sponsors of the bill that Senate inaction would be dangerous on many counts. About March 15, however, the word spread that the White House had stepped into the picture and was gathering opinions on S. 109 from the Justice, Agriculture and Commerce departments and the Federal Trade Commission. All executive agencies were to make recommendations to the Bureau of the Budget by March 31st.

The USDA, which had just confronted the NFO milk delivery stop, was somewhat reluctant to handle another volatile bargaining question. Nevertheless, the department finally went to work on S. 109 during the last week of March and sent a two-page résumé to the White House in which it went on record as generally favoring the bill. The crucial question now facing backers of the bill concerned what position the Justice Department would assume. If Justice continued to oppose the bill as it had the 1965 version, the bill was given something less than a 50-50 chance of passing. However, if it conceded that its initial objections had been removed by subsequent modifications, chances of the bill moving through Congress were greatly enhanced.

The turn of events precipitated by White House interest sent the contestants scurrying. Far from being dead, S. 109 was revived and was certain to come to hearing. This likelihood signaled a change in strategy by the opponents, as evidenced in the May hearing.

Through the spring, the USDA continued to meet with its Cooperative Advisory Committee for purposes of making its views known. By and large, the department's attention focused on the enforcement section, which it thought should be enlarged to include administrative proceedings of the Packers and Stockyards type. The Committee of "17" farm groups also met and discussed alternative institutional arrangements that could provide a table around which bargaining efforts could commence.

Recognizing that Senate Agriculture Subcommittee Chairman Jordan of North Carolina held one of the keys to passage of S. 109, the AFB focused on him in pushing for a hearing on the bill. A crucial role in this endeavor was played by the North Carolina Farm Bureau, already active in developing a bargaining program in two commodities: apples and broilers. Mr. B. C. Mangum, President of the North Carolina Farm Bureau, stressed to Senator Jordan that S. 109 was needed to create confidence in the minds of producers and to provide them with a more secure feeling in bargaining programs.[29] In particular, North Carolina broiler growers had been afraid of losing their contracts if they joined a bargaining association. Senator Jordan was made aware of this situation and was encouraged to bring the bill to an early hearing. While Senator Aiken was in a position to force a hearing on S. 109 as ranking minority member of the Senate Agriculture and Forestry Committee, the AFB's Washington staff decided that it would be more effective in the long run to wait for Senator Jordan to make up his own mind to call the hearing. In the meantime, it sought additional sponsors for the bill.

AFB officials met in a strategy session on April 3rd in Chicago to review the bill's chances in Congress. Attending this meeting were Al Lauterbach and Gene Lemon of the general counsel's office, Dr. Ken Hood and Dr. Bill Jasper of the AAMA, John Datt of the Washington staff, Harold Hartley of the AAMA's fruit and vegetable marketing division, O. R. Long, head of AFB field services, and Creston Foster of the information department. In a candid assessment of the Washington situation, Mr. Datt reported that the NCA had widely distributed an article presenting its views on collective bargaining and that the NBC was active in bringing many people to town. In addition, he reported that the U.S. Chamber of Commerce and the AFMA had entered the struggle in opposition to S. 109. The opposition was saying, "If AFB can't pass the bill, it certainly can't bargain." In sizing up the situation, Datt suggested that the pace had quickened, the opposition was getting bolder and that the going would be rough.

The AFB was aware that it was fighting two battles: one in the country

29. B. C. Mangum (President, North Carolina Farm Bureau), personal interview, December 11, 1968.

and one in the halls of Congress. In the country, the AFB had to compete for the support of farmers with the independent and corporate handlers and the operating and farm supply cooperatives. The contest in Congress was between the AFB and its allies on the one side and the NCA, broiler integrators and other related groups on the other.

As a step in its congressional strategy, the AFB decided to concentrate on legislators whose votes on S. 109 would be "No" and to raise questions in their minds about the merits of the bill. Personal contact by members with legislators in their home districts was also to be encouraged, with the support of a full mobilization of AFB forces. In doing so, they encouraged state Farm Bureaus to contact sympathetic organizations in their states for purposes of developing a potent force to win votes in Congress.

The day after the strategy meeting, John Datt and Herb Harris of the Washington office paid a visit to the White House to acquaint Administration officials with the legislation and AFB's purpose in proposing it. Although the legislative strategists felt they made little impact upon their host, Presidential Assistant Devere Pearson, they did communicate the Farm Bureau's views on the bargaining issue.

The AFB held other meetings with USDA officials and with certain opponents to S. 109 in an unsuccessful effort to neutralize them. Among the latter were James Rill, attorney for the NBC, and Clinton Stokes of the U.S. Chamber of Commerce. The chamber, however, became increasingly vocal against S. 109, apparently as a result of the influence of certain corporations such as Campbell Soup and other large agri-business companies. Despite these vocal opponents, the AFB did succeed in achieving support for the measure from the National Livestock Producers Association and from Don Magdanz, Executive Secretary-Treasurer for the National Livestock Feeders Association.

A prehearing climax to the jostling for position occurred in a debate in mid-April before the "food" group, a monthly luncheon meeting of about 80 lobbyists representing all aspects of the food trade.[30] The debate featured John Datt of the AFB and Bob Heiney of the NCA, who presented their arguments, pro and con, on the merits of the proposed farm bill, with inconclusive results.

While an awareness of the bill's limited purpose was being communicated to other lobby groups and legislators on Capitol Hill, the grass-roots effort by the grower committees and state Farm Bureaus began to show results when Senator Jordan announced that hearings on S. 109 were scheduled for May 2 and 4.

Throughout April, more congressmen introduced versions of S. 109. The increasing legislative support was encouraging, although a few setbacks

30. Lee Campbell (Executive Director, American Poultry Institute), personal interview, June 13, 1968. Mr. Campbell served as chairman for the "food" group in 1967.

were also experienced. Within the AFB itself, old-line members felt the existing proposal was going too far and said so. Their statements that they would not support "Wagner Act" legislation or the use of force aroused the proponents of the measure. It was also reported that considerable agitation was developing in some segments of the fruit and vegetable industry for revision of S. 109. The work of the cotton industry became evident also when Congressman Robert Poage, Chairman of the House Agriculture Committee, backed off from a previous stand in which he was favorably disposed to the bill to a position of finding it unacceptable without certain revisions.[31]

Freeman Enters the Matter

The USDA had initiated studies of bargaining proposals independent of S. 109 early in 1967, in response to findings of the National Commission on Food Marketing and inquiries of farm groups such as the NCFC. No reference to these studies was made, however, until the slide in farm prices in the first three months of 1967 led to a three-day trip by Freeman, Secretary of Agriculture, through four Midwestern states. While the price-cost squeeze had caused some farm unrest and subsequent discussions about farm bargaining in 1966, the price breaks in 1967 were associated with the NFO milk delivery stop and other expressions of discontent. The purpose of Freeman's trip was to get a more precise reading on farm attitudes.

Meetings between the Secretary and farmers were billed as "shirtsleeve conferences." In each, Freeman expressed concern that farm prices had decreased 8 per cent from nine months earlier and that costs had increased 3 per cent. Following a meeting in Hutchinson, Kansas, Mr. Freeman flew to Ames, Iowa, where he suggested that government farm programs alone could not produce adequate farm incomes and hinted, for the first time, that the Administration was considering possible legislation that would give farmers the same rights of collective bargaining that were held by labor unions. During the trip, the Agriculture Secretary asked for advice from farmers and reportedly received plenty of it.[32] In fact, the shouting for more farm bargaining power caught him by surprise.

Freeman made further reference to the USDA studies in a press conference in Washington the following week and expanded upon the findings. In substance, he said that legislation to enable farmers to bargain in the marketplace without running afoul of antitrust laws should be considered. The National Industrial Recovery and Wagner acts were suggested as models for farm bargaining legislation. When asked whether S. 109 would help farm

31. "Poage Opposed To S. 109 in Its Present Form," *Poultry and Egg Weekly* (April 22, 1967), in files of American Farm Bureau Federation.
32. "Freeman Says Farmers May Get Law for Collective Bargaining," *Minneapolis Tribune,* April 20, 1967, in files of National Canners Association.

bargaining efforts, Secretary Freeman replied that it was "just a little step along the way." [33]

If the Aiken bill was just a "little step," as Mr. Freeman suggested, it was quite apparent that the opponents were taking it very seriously. One large chemical company with a small food processing subsidiary was so concerned about S. 109 that it reportedly pulled a man out of retirement to lobby against it. Similarly, the NCA acknowledged to members that the nine additional sponsors of S. 109 in the House, bringing the total to 31, was a fairly impressive list and encouraged its members to "re-educate" legislators. [34] The new sponsors included Congressmen Harsha of Ohio, Shipley of Illinois, Sisk of California, Morse of Massachusetts, Smith of Oklahoma, Springer of Illinois, Matsunaga of Hawaii, St. Germain of Rhode Island and King of New York.

As the date for the May hearing approached, S. 109 again became the subject of editorializing in trade journals and newspapers. Mr. Lex Killebrew, Executive Secretary of the integrator-dominated Arkansas Poultry Federation, suggested in the *Arkansas Poultry Times* that S. 109 was "another example of an outside group pushing for something of which it has no knowledge." [35] By his analysis, the language of the bill would eliminate the freedom of choice of both buyer and seller within the poultry industry. In a thoughtful appraisal of the bill, the editor of the *American Poultry and Hatchery News* suggested that questions of loyalty and efficiency might be at stake. The editorial took aim at the plight of the small producer in contrast to a huge governmental agency.

> Biggest problem with the Federal Trade Commission is that it is too slow, cumbersome or inadequate to act. The Federal Trade Commission has said of the original version of S. 109 that there isn't any reason for its enactment. FTC could do a great service to the nation by demonstrating that it can act. The experience of this writer with respect to FTC's ability to act in enforcing the Fair Trade Practice Rules for the Baby Chick Industry can not be described as encouraging. Perhaps, of course, our industry was too small to warrant the full attention of such a mighty agency. [36]

In an article in *Farmland*, a Washington observer suggested that S. 109 was not a final answer to the farmer's prayer for more bargaining power because it was essentially defensive in content. [37]

33. Farm Reports, "Washington Farm Letter," Letter No. 1232, April 28, 1967.
34. National Canners Association, "Government-Industry Report," April 26, 1967.
35. Lex Killebrew, "*H.R. 323-S. 109* Labelled Blunders—Industry Urged To Work Together For Realistic Answers," *Arkansas Poultry Times*, May 4, 1967, in files of American Farm Bureau Federation.
36. "S. 109: The Stakes Can Be High," *American Poultry and Hatchery News*, 44, 5 (May, 1967), in files of American Farm Bureau Federation.
37. "Unusual Farm Unity for Bargaining Bill," *Farmland*, 34, 10 (May 31, 1967), 1.

These appraisals typified the thorough treatment that all segments of the industry were giving the proposal. From farmer to consumer, an interest in the marketing rights measure was apparent. As the May 2nd hearing date approached, coalitions of both farm organizations and processors made last-minute preparations for the Senate subcommittee hearing.

Chapter 7

1967 Senate Hearing: All Hands on Deck

With a list of more than 30 witnesses waiting to testify before the Senate subcommittee, it was evident that the hearing on S. 109 was not going to be of the simple, one-day variety. Senator Everett Jordan opened the hearing by inserting into the record a letter from Agriculture Secretary Orville Freeman to Senator Allen Ellender, Chairman of the Senate Agriculture and Forestry Committee, a report on the bill from the Department of Agriculture and the Senate committee staff's explanation of the bill.

Freeman's letter gave powerful backing to the bill. In it, he suggested that the purpose of S. 109 was to establish necessary standards of fair practices required of handlers in dealing with producers.[2] Cooperative action in agricultural production and marketing was increasing, he said, in response to the need (1) to achieve more orderliness and efficiency in production and marketing and (2) to protect and improve bargaining relationships between producers and marketing firms in the face of changes taking place in the marketing system.

At the same time, Freeman noted three specific developments in agriculture that were weakening the marketing and bargaining position of individual producers. These were the growing integration of production and marketing, the increased control of these functions by large, diversified corporations and the expanded use of contracting by such corporations to meet their needs.

> If this bill were enacted, many producers who fear harassment or discrimination would feel free to join a cooperative association. It would help producers use cooperatives as a more effective tool in marketing their products.[3]

The strong endorsement of S. 109 by the USDA and the announced clearance by the Budget Bureau set the stage for a lively hearing.

In its report, the Department of Agriculture recommended several amendments to S. 109. These included (1) Deletion of the word "boycott" in

1. George Aiken (Senator, Vermont), testimony in U.S. Senate, Subcommittee of the Committee on Agriculture and Forestry, *Hearings on S. 109*, 90th Cong., 1st sess., 1967, 13.
2. Orville L. Freeman (Secretary, USDA), letter to Allen Ellender (Chairman, Senate Committee on Agriculture and Forestry), May 1, 1967.
3. *Ibid.*

section 4a of the bill and substitution of more precise language; (2) Providing for enforcement of the act through administrative procedures under the jurisdiction of the Secretary of Agriculture similar to procedures embodied in the Packers and Stockyards Act; (3) Giving the Secretary authority to request restraining orders to prevent irreparable harm to producers pending the implementation of such administrative proceedings. In contrast to this report, the staff explanation by the Agriculture and Forestry Committee gave a section-by-section explanation of the bill and a comparison of the 1967 proposal with the two earlier versions.

The first to present live testimony in behalf of S. 109 were three senators, of whom two were sponsors. Senator Aiken argued for the need of reasonable farm prices to assure satisfactory income levels. The Vermont Republican cited a drop in net farm income from 80 to 72 per cent of parity in the period from April, 1966, to April, 1967. This situation, he said, could not be allowed to continue without threatening the economy. He also felt that discrimination against producers who attempted to bargain collectively could not be tolerated. Importantly, the Senate author of S. 109 announced three additional sponsors of the bill: Senators Philip Hart of Michigan, Birch Bayh of Indiana and Bourke Hickenlooper of Iowa.[4]

Senator Aiken encouraged early enactment of the bill. His colleagues Senators John Williams of Delaware and Frank Lausche of Ohio — who followed him in testifying — took issue with certain provisions. Senator Williams, widely regarded as the Senate watchdog on trade regulation matters and as a close associate of the broiler and feed trade, urged the elimination of the criminal provisions in the bill on the grounds that they were unnecessary. Williams argued that injunctive relief measures and triple-damages provisions were adequate.

> It is my understanding that the bill is designed to protect the rights of the farmer to join cooperative farmer organizations without fear of discrimination or retaliation on the part of any dealer because he has done so. I feel that the bill is necessary from that standpoint. I think it does carry out this objective.[5]

Senator Williams also stressed the "basic" freedoms of any farmer to join or not to join an organization and the right of dealers to choose their own customers.

Like Senator Williams, Senator Lausche, a cosponsor of the bill, gave his strong but qualified endorsement. The Ohio Democrat saw S. 109 as designed to create rules of the road and to prevent improper conduct. The bill did not create marketing associations because the right to join or not to join was the right of farmers to carry out under their own volition. In a strategic move, Senator Lausche proceeded in a point-by-point discussion of the pro-

4. George Aiken, testimony in *Hearings on S. 109*, 9.
5. John Williams (Senator, Delaware), testimony in *ibid.*, 13.

hibitions. He challenged the bill's opponents to point out that these provisions actually would do what the opposition claimed in prehearing publicity. When it came to the enforcement section, however, the cosponsor of S. 109 stated that the triple-damages provisions were a "blood-letting" operation and that the criminal penalties were not needed.[6] This proposed gutting of the enforcement provisions by a cosponsor of the bill came as a severe blow to its backers.

If any one thing characterized the 1967 Senate hearing on S. 109, it became evident when Secretary of Agriculture Freeman took the stand to testify personally in behalf of the bill. The appearance of the top federal agricultural officer contrasted with the earlier hearings in 1966, when the USDA was represented by Martin Abrahamsen, Deputy Administrator of the Farmer Cooperative Service, in the June hearing and David Angevine, FCS Administrator, in the September hearing. At the 1967 hearing, as the Secretary's presence indicated, all officers were on deck.

Appearances by the department in earlier hearings clearly represented no stand by USDA and the Administration. Now, Secretary Freeman represented an Administration that had succeeded in aligning each of the agencies behind the bill — including the FTC and the Justice departments. For the first time, its ship was in order.

Secretary Freeman displayed his fighting form when he declared that enactment of S. 109 could be another bench mark, in contrast to his previous characterizing of the bill as a "little step along the way," for farmers in their fight for fairer prices. He argued that while the Capper-Volstead Act was a "Magna Carta" for farmers' cooperatives, it fell short of giving the farmer equal opportunity with other sectors of the economy.

> It is consistent with the American free enterprise system that farmers join together to build their strength to bargain in the marketing process.
> One way to do this is a bargaining association. Through cooperation, many farmers can act and speak as if they were a single producer. Such unity is the basis of bargaining power. Through group effort, farmers can hope to survive in today's increasingly large-volume market where many products are produced under contract arrangements between the processor and the producer.[7]

To his strong pitch for more bargaining activity, however, the Secretary added a recommendation for several amendments to S. 109, previously described in the Agriculture Department's report.

Under questioning, Secretary Freeman concurred with Senator Lausche's thoughts on the elimination of the criminal penalties and took the opportunity to promote the department's recommended enforcement proce-

6. Frank Lausche (Senator, Ohio), testimony in *ibid.*, 19.
7. Orville L. Freeman, testimony in *ibid.*, 19.

dure. The Secretary further suggested that a suitable substitute for the triple-damages provision would be wording calling for sequential issuance of a complaint, a hearing and potentially a cease-and-desist order.

A Strengthened Coalition

AFB President Shuman took strong issue with Freeman's position on enforcement procedures when he followed him in testimony. Claiming that S. 109 was one of the most important legislative matters to come before the Agriculture Committee in recent years, Shuman stressed that the penalties should be retained in the bill in order to avoid wholesale disobedience and violation of the law. Furthermore, the AFB President argued that it was very important to retain the injunctive relief measures so that producers would not be subjected to delays and red tape involved in "bureaucratic channels." [8]

Shuman concluded his testimony, largely devoted to defining what the proposed legislation did and did not do, by putting a question point-blank before the subcommittee.

> We believe that producers' marketing power must be strengthened through their organized but voluntary efforts to improve the efficiency of our marketing system. This is the basic philosophy that is involved in the farm bureau marketing activities. To be successful, such activities must be directed toward realistic goals. Producers want to work together to earn — I want to emphasize that — a higher net income in a market directed economy. To do so, they must be protected from unfair practices by purchasers as specified in this act. We believe that the issue before the committee is simply this: "Are you in favor of protecting the marketing rights of farmers and ranchers?" [9]

The testimony of the AFB was followed by that of a representative of another major, if sometimes inconspicuous, group of proponents of S. 109: the bargaining associations. Representing those on the Pacific Coast, Ralph Bunje, General Manager of the California Canning Peach Association, offered a two-part argument concerning the need for S. 109. He reported that his California experience had shown that field representatives and broker-buyers for large companies engaged in discriminatory practices that were unknown to top management and uncontrolled by them. [10] Bunje cited one case, settled out of court, in which a large canning company was charged under California law with discriminating against members of the California Canning Pear Association. Such activity would never have occurred, he said, if laws with severe penalties were on the books.

8. Charles B. Shuman (President, American Farm Bureau Federation), testimony in *ibid.*, 27.
9. *Ibid.*
10. Ralph Bunje (General Manager, California Canning Peach Association), testimony in *Hearings on S. 109*, 29.

The second point of Bunje's testimony was directed to the bargaining aspect of the legislation. In an argument on behalf of his vocal, if minority, contingent within the National Council of Farmer Cooperatives, Bunje submitted that S. 109 was necessary because it would "tend to equalize the bargaining strength of growers versus their processor customers." [11] He argued that the bill, rather than being one-sided as suggested by some opponents, would merely rectify and adjust what he saw as a presently one-sided arrangement benefiting processors. As evidence of the need to achieve a more balanced power, Bunje cited the very character of the opposition witnesses before the committee. His avenue of argument for increased bargaining power for farm operators was echoed by other backers of the bill.

In a statement closely paralleling Bunje's, Patrick Healy, Assistant Secretary of the National Milk Producers Federation, made a capsule argument for S. 109 and drew a simple picture of the struggle over the bill.

> Basically, cooperatives enable individual farmers by acting together as an organized group to improve their economic lot by bargaining more effectively for the sale of their commodities.
>
> It is, therefore, to be expected that proprietary processors, who would stand to benefit from cheap prices for raw commodities, would oppose any effort to organize farmers into an effective bargaining unit.
>
> In some cases, this opposition has taken the form of unfair practices, such as coercion, threats, and discrimination. The problem has been particularly bad when new cooperatives were being formed and when they were least able to resist this type of pressure.[12]

A representative of the NCFC, another member of the AFB coalition, also attempted in his testimony to put to rest arguments thrown up by the opposition. Mr. Robert Hampton, Director of Marketing Services, testified that S. 109 would not deprive handlers of their rights to choose their suppliers, based on economic realities.[13] He argued that it was illogical to assume that S. 109 would preclude handlers from providing "ordinary business services" to producers, as some opponents argued, unless the services were already prohibited under other price discrimination or antitrust laws.

Farm Unity

Perhaps the most impressive display of farm unity in post-World War II history followed, when long-time competitors and often philosophical enemies of the AFB testified in behalf of the bill. In lengthy appearances before the subcommittee, Harry Graham of the Grange, Angus McDonald of the

11. *Ibid.*, 32.
12. Patrick Healy (Assistant Secretary, National Milk Producers Federation), testimony in *Hearings on S. 109*, 67.
13. Robert N. Hampton (Director of Marketing and International Trade, National Council of Farmer Cooperatives), testimony in *ibid.*, 54.

National Farmers Union and Oren Lee Staley of the NFO voiced their approval of S. 109, but not without slaps at AFB for past sins.

In anticipation of the Mondale bill that would be introduced in Congress the following year, Graham outlined three alternative approaches to the bargaining legislation that were under consideration by the Grange but upon which final decision had not been made: (1) The creation of a board similar to the National Labor Relations Board; (2) Removal of the agricultural exemption from the Wagner Act; (3) Collective bargaining related to the federal farm programs and marketing orders. In a scathing attack on the AFB's failure to support federal farm programs, Mr. Graham suggested that this lack of support was calculated to encourage deterioration of the agricultural economy to a point at which farmers would join bargaining associations out of desperation. However, the Grange joined the other farm organizations in approving S. 109, subject to some recommended modifications.

Graham, who was leader of the *ad hoc* agricultural Committee of "17," saw S. 109 as meeting a basic need for immediate relief for the "little fellow." [14] Citing the problems of producers of perishable products, Mr. Graham stressed the need for rapid action through the individual's access to the courts and through the injunctive authority of the Secretary of Agriculture. To support his argument, he cited the case of *Hale* vs. *Tyson, Arkansas Industries and Ralston Purina* in which it took eight months to establish whether the P&S Division had the power of subpoena and eight weeks to conduct the preliminary hearings.

Graham also stressed the need for some provision that would require the processor to "bargain in good faith" with an association of producers. To make this point explicit, he drew a parallel from labor history.

> I think that we are deluding ourselves with the idea that once an association or a bargaining association is formed *per se* that they bargain with processors or that the processors will bargain with them. This is not necessarily so. The experience in labor legislation history proved that in earlier years. And one of the reasons for this provision being included in the Wagner labor relations bill was that they found out that labor unions could be organized, but that they still did not necessarily have any bargaining rights. And so into the Wagner Labor bill came the provision requiring that employers bargain in good faith. And when an organization, an association of famers or cooperative represents the majority, if not all of the production of the commodity in an area, and one processor upon whom they are dependent does not bargain with them, the association is empty handed, that is all. [15]

To these arguments, Graham added a strong plea for retention of the criminal penalties in the bill as written. He openly disagreed with Senator

14. Harry Graham (Legislative Representative, National Grange), testimony in *ibid.*, 54.
15. *Ibid.*, 57.

Lausche's comment that the triple damages were bloodletting. The Grange Legislative Director suggested the damage provisions were not that meaningful, because "large corporations pay their fines with relative ease since the courts have rules that these fines are deductible expenses." [16]

In a summarization of his argument for S. 109 — and also looking ahead to future legislative needs — Graham sounded a warning to farm operators of the need for national farm organizations.

> The time is long passed when the individual farmer or small association of farmers can effectively bargain with nationwide firms. The possibility and the probability of large firms continuing to play both ends against the middle simply precludes any kind of action which might improve the farmer's position in the marketplace.[17]

Graham's strong articulation of the case for additional farm legislation was supported by another member of the *ad hoc* agricultural committee and often times chief rival of the AFB — the National Farmers Union.

The testimony of Mr. Angus McDonald, Director of Research for the NFU, in complete support of S. 109, came as a surprise to many. McDonald regarded the bill as "just one more step to protect the free enterprise system." [18] He made extensive and effective use of the Arkansas broiler case to dramatize three points: (1) The "deplorable situation" disclosed by the USDA investigation was proof positive of the need for S. 109 legislation; (2) The Justice Department and the FTC should be condemned for their failure to respond to the case. (According to McDonald, the Justice Department had not responded to a letter written on November 10, 1964, in which the NFU supplied information about the conditions encountered by Arkansas broiler growers. Based on the failure of Justice to respond and to handle the case, the NFU was forced to conclude that the department was not sympathetic to cooperatives); (3) The seemingly interminable procedure with which the USDA handled the Arkansas case.

> However, some of these acts, these illegal acts, . . . were carried on in 1961. This is now 1967. And while the Department has moved against them after a long investigation and study, it seems obvious to us that a farmer, the poor farmers in the area, and in other areas of the United States, cannot wait 5 or 6 years to obtain relief. We endorse this bill as generally written to pass.[19]

In what was for NFU a rare display of agreement with the AFB and disagreement with the Secretary of Agriculture, McDonald dissented from the USDA's suggestion that enforcement should be the privilege of the Secretary

16. *Ibid.*, 60.
17. *Ibid.*
18. Angus McDonald (Research Director, National Farmers Union), testimony in *Hearings on S. 109*, 62.
19. *Ibid.*, 66.

through a P&S type of procedure. The NFU held that the injured producer or cooperative association "should be allowed to go to the courts, and if they win their case, to get triple damages." [20]

In concluding his remarks in support of S. 109, McDonald suggested that what was really being decided was which of three roads agriculture would traverse. He suggested that economic concentration in agriculture could well increase to a point at which a few large corporations would determine and control the economic life of the nation. He saw as a second possibility the complete control of agriculture, production and distribution by the government. McDonald's third route — and that favored by NFU — would allow farmers complete freedom in attaining an equality of bargaining power.

The testimony of the Grange and the NFU was supported by yet a third farm organization. Fresh from a news-catching milk delivery stop, Oren Lee Staley of the National Farmers Organization appeared before the committee in support of S. 109. NFO's appearance — encouraged by other members of the Committee of "17" of which it had been a member since 1961 — marked the gradual growth of the young militant group into a professional interest organization. Staley stated that NFO could support S. 109 because it would "help stop harassment, intimidation, and threats against farmers and their organization." [21] He reiterated the NFO's belief that the law of supply and demand would not present farm operators with fair prices unless equal strength existed between buyers and sellers. In a plea for industry-wide bargaining, Staley suggested that S. 109 would spell out more clearly the rights of farmers in their bargaining efforts. He also suggested, as an afterthought, that considerations should be given to a "Wagner Act" for farmers.

Those testifying in favor of the passage of S. 109 at this point made up a formidable farm front. AFB, the original sponsor of the bill, had been joined by the Secretary of Agriculture, senators from key agricultural states and the nation's largest and most influential cooperative federations and general farm interest organizations. Regional farm, labor and consumer organizations had rallied to the S. 109 cause as well. Organizations that submitted testimony in behalf of the bill included the California Farmer and Consumer Information Committee, Eastern Milk Producers Cooperative Association, The Cooperative League of the USA, Santa Clara County (Calif.) Central Labor Council, California Conference of Machinists and various other state and county farm organizations.

The closest analogy of the farmer's current quest for bargaining power to the earlier plight of labor workers was drawn by Michigan's Senator Philip Hart, a relatively new sponsor of the bill. The Michigan Democrat heard in the criticisms directed to the Aiken bill an echo, if not a playback, of a debate

20. *Ibid.*
21. Oren Lee Staley (President, National Farmers Organization), testimony in *Hearings on S. 109*, 126.

thirty years before. To make his point, Senator Hart used a paragraph from a telegram from the President of the Campbell Soup Company to the President of the AFB regarding S. 109. By substituting the words "workers" for "farmers," "work" for "grow," and "automobiles" for "tomatoes," the telegram could be made to read:

> We are always ready to meet with workers and especially those who wish to work for us, but we do not consider it desirable for anyone to stand between the workers and us. For this reason we do not consider it practical for us to carry on negotiations with your organization on the matter of the contract terms that we would expect to offer workers with whom we would hope to contract for automobiles.[22]

In a strong endorsement of the bill, Hart — a former member of the National Food Marketing Commission — testified that unanimous agreement existed on the commission concerning the necessity for legislation to protect the right of producers to organize. Furthermore, he stated: "We in Michigan certainly know that collective bargaining produces a more adequate income for the man who produces goods." [23]

As in earlier hearings, representatives from commodity groups that had experienced discrimination presented testimony. Idaho and Oregon potato bargaining associations presented their stories after being introduced by Co-sponsor Senator Church of Idaho. Representing the farm groups, attorney Lawrence Alioto of San Francisco presented testimony concerning an antitrust case that his law firm was prosecuting in behalf of the potato growers against the H. J. Heinz Company and the Simplto Companies on charges of price fixing. In a point-by-point dissection of S. 109, Mr. Alioto pointed out why, in his opinion, the antitrust laws were adequate to combat price fixing but not adequate to combat the practices that S. 109 sought to outlaw.[24] His argument centered on the fact that while the Sherman Act applies to contracts, combinations and conspiracies, it requires the action of two or more parties contracting, combining or conspiring with each other. In contrast, the proposed bill dealt with the conduct of single firms, whose actions in many cases had been sufficient to undermine farmers' associations.

Alioto argued further that section 2 of the Sherman Act required the plaintiff to prove actual or attempted monopolization of a part of interstate trade or commerce. The ability of individual farmers to bear the burden of proof in such litigation proceedings was entirely out of the question. In short, he argued that S. 109 and section 2 of the Sherman Act covered completely different areas of behavior.

Dal Ferry, former Executive Director of the U.S. Poultry and Egg Pro-

---

22. Philip A. Hart (Senator, Michigan), testimony in *ibid.*, 98. The telegram from the Campbell Soup Company was first introduced as evidence in the 1966 Senate hearings on S. 109.

23. *Ibid.*, 99.

24. Lawrence Alioto (Attorney), testimony in *Hearings on S. 109*, 41.

ducers Association represented the second commodity group. Ferry, who had appeared at earlier hearings along with Ellis Hale, testified that on December 31, 1966, his organization "was the victim of activities that this proposed legislation attempts to prohibit." [25] Following a careful review of his experiences in the poultry industry, including his involvement in the Arkansas broiler case, Ferry suggested that "some who protest loudest about this legislation built their business by climbing up the backs of, and exploiting, helpless producers." [26]

> Our experience over the past 5 years shows that the present legal processes are very cumbersome and long delays can be expected when subpoenas are served and challenged; while attorneys use delaying tactics when preparing cases and filing briefs; while economists delve into records and marshall facts and prepare needed information; and while time is exhausted fighting jurisdictional battles in the courts. In the meantime, the individuals or organizations on whose behalf the action was brought either have been bankrupt, forced out of business, required to retrench and their associations destroyed because of forced inactivity and loss of momentum.[27]

In Ferry's mind, S. 109 was so important to protecting the marketing rights of agricultural producers that it bore comparison to the role of the Bill of Rights in protecting the civil liberties of the individual from encroachment by government. As a parting thought, Mr. Ferry concluded: "If you wear overalls, the Department of Justice is not too concerned about your problems." [28]

The appearance of so many farm groups in support of S. 109 made a deep impression upon the senators. Among them, general agreement prevailed on the need for immediate relief and about the unresponsiveness of the FTC and the Justice Department to problems of farm businessmen. The major area of disagreement concerned the enforcement provisions. The American Farm Bureau, National Farmers Union, National Farmers Organization, California and Pacific Northwest bargaining groups supported the criminal penalties, injunctive relief, treble damages and adminstrative procedures of the Secretary of Agriculture and the USDA. Secretary Freeman and the National Grange, on the other hand, opposed the criminal penalties and treble damages. They promoted the idea of relief through the Packers and Stockyards Division and similar enforcement proceedings.

Opponent Strategy: A Change

On the surface, the objections of the antagonists to S. 109 were the same as those offered in previous hearings and in the months preceding the current

---

25. Dallas K. Ferry (former Executive Director, United States Poultry and Egg Producers Association), testimony in *ibid.*, 154.
26. *Ibid.*, 158.   27. *Ibid.*   28. *Ibid.*, 161.

Senate hearing. In general, the opposition remained concerned with what the bill "might" imply. However, a notable change in strategy was evident. In a word, the opposition was more conciliatory, and some associations even went so far as to suggest the bill might be, with amendments, acceptable.

The change in strategy could be explained by the sudden popularity of the idea symbolized by the slogan, "More bargaining power for farmers." The slogan had been popularized by farm groups that were pushing their bargaining programs, by the NFO's milk delivery stop and by the Secretary's Midwest tour.[29] The impact of this series of events sent a chill through the processing community.

Speaking for the 600-member NCA — a member of the *ad hoc* committee — Edward Dunkelberger claimed in his testimony that producers had recourse under the law to cover most, if not all, of the provisions listed in S. 109. In cold fact, however, the NCA's major objections to the bill boiled down to three points.[30] First, the canners felt the bill was "discriminatory" in that it applied only to handlers and not to bargaining associations. Secondly, they objected to the criminal penalties, treble-damage actions and injunctions in federal courts. Thirdly, the NCA interpreted the bill as revoking the right of processors to choose their own suppliers. In developing the third point, Dunkelberger referred to statements by Senator Lausche, Secretary Freeman and AFB President Shuman. To Dunkelberger, the statements that the bill did not infringe upon the freedoms of processors to choose their suppliers were not satisfying.

As if acknowledging criticism of his camp's prehearing tactics, Dunkelberger presented four points that the NCA wanted included in a revised bill. These were: (1) revision of the prohibitions in section 4 to protect the right of producers to be free of discrimination by bargaining associations; (2) elimination of the criminal penalties and treble damages; (3) protection of the handler's right to refuse to deal with a bargaining association and instead deal with producers on an individual basis; (4) additional revisions of section 5 to clarify the intent and define the prohibitions more clearly. In closing, the NCA representative indicated that a "common ground" appeared within reach and that resolution of the controversies was possible.

Most of the other *ad hoc* committee members, following the lead of the NCA, took similar positions. Charges that the legislation was one-sided, too severe in its penalties, limiting to free competition and too vague were common in the testimony offered by trade organizations such as the NBC, American Feed Manufacturers Association, National Livestock Feeders Association, Independent Livestock Marketing Association, National Independent Meat Packers Association and the National Association of Frozen Food

29. See Chapter 6.
30. Edward Dunkelberger (Attorney), testimony in *Hearings on S. 109*, 84.

Packers. Three large independent broiler farmers from Maryland also testified against the bill. Each was a member of the Delmarva Poultry Industry and American Farm Bureau, and two were members of the National Broiler Council.

Opposition in the hearings came as well from a second group, the ultra-conservative National Tax Equality Association. Speaking for the NTEA, Mr. Earl Kintner charged that S. 109 generally constituted a violation of section 5 of the FTC act.[31] In a lengthy defense of FTC and the Justice Department, Kintner argued that there was no need for a third executive agency to become an enforcer of unfair trade practice laws as proposed in the bill. Brushing aside charges that the FTC was not responsive to farmers' problems, the former FTC official maintained that the enforcement procedures should remain within the FTC and Justice Department. He also attacked the prohibitions of S. 109 as being too detailed and at the same time suggested that the discrimination prohibition was too vague. Kintner argued further that the bill would introduce abnormal rigidities into the relationship between producers, independent processors and their customers.

Despite its continued objections to the bill, the NTEA's attitude was conciliatory in comparison to previous hearings, and the organization offered its own suggestions for revisions. The general tenor of its plea was for uniform applicability of trade regulation laws.

> There are problems here, and there have been trade abuses in the marketing of agricultural products, from many quarters, which deserve the public attention they have received from this distinguished subcommittee. However, the strides which have been made here will only be forward looking if the broad public interest in preserving uniformly applicable trade regulation laws is closely observed.[32]

Among the recommendations of the NTEA were the following: (1) inclusion of the phrase ". . . individual farmers will be adversely affected unless they are free to band together *or not to band together* in cooperative organizations . . ." in the statement of legislative findings; (2) enforcement by the Attorney General; (3) deletion of the criminal sanctions. The NTEA, with particular emphasis upon the producer's right to join or not to join an association, thus recommended amendments that closely paralleled those of the NCA.

A third general group strongly protested the provisions of S. 109 through its testimony. Representing various segments of the cotton industry, three trade organizations set out to prove that cotton is still king in the Senate. Representatives of the American Cotton Shippers Association — an organization of six affiliated regional cotton associations — testified that appli-

31. Earl W. Kintner (Attorney), testimony in *ibid.*, 143.
32. *Ibid.*, 146.

cation of S. 109 to the cotton industry could hobble the ability of noncooperatives to compete fairly and effectively and at the same time would provide a means by which cotton compress cooperatives could establish a monopoly in the industry. So adamant was the association against supporting farm bargaining legislation that it saw the situation as meaning that: "On and after the passage of this act competition with cooperatives is illegal." [33]

Testifying on a similar note, Herman Eubank of the Texas Independent Ginners Association claimed that the bill "would strike at the very heart of a healthy competitive situation which exists between independent and 'co-op' gins." [34] The Texas ginners specifically objected to the "extremely severe and harsh" penalties and the fact that S. 109 would hurt the individual farmer by eliminating competition for the processing of his products.

The inference of the shippers and ginners that passage would eliminate competition was supported by Wes McAden, speaking for the American Cotton Compress and Warehouse Association. Formed in 1963, this cotton interest group was made up of cotton compress and warehousemen in the exterior markets or collection points in California, Arizona, Texas, Alabama, Louisiana, Arkansas, Tennessee and the Southeastern states. McAden, the association's executive vice-president, suggested that the long-standing practice of offering inducements to growers in competition with other handlers of cotton would be jeopardized by sections 4c and d of the prohibitions. [35] To avoid this situation, McAden offered an amendment that was intended to protect the farmer's right to bargain collectively.

> (c) The term "association of producers" means an association which acts solely as the representative of producers in bargaining collectively with handlers as to price and other sales or service costs and terms, and is not itself otherwise engaged in handling agricultural products in competition with such handlers. [36]

Ironically, this proposed amendment, if incorporated in the bill, would have been consistent with one of the initial objectives of the bill in its early form. But in proposing the amendment, McAden's intent was to limit the scope of S. 109 to the activities of bargaining for price between farmers and handlers of agricultural products. It would thus not apply to the competition between cooperatives and independent handlers involved in ginning and warehousing cotton, that is, actual handling of the product.

33. W. W. Holding, III (Member, Board of Directors, American Cotton Shippers Association), testimony in *Hearings on S. 109*, 110.
34. Herman Eubank (President, Texas Independent Ginners Association), testimony in *ibid.*, 123.
35. Wesley H. McAden (Executive Vice-President, American Cotton Compress and Warehouse Association), testimony in *ibid.*, 139. When the Cotton Compress and Warehouse Association was formed in 1963, it was mainly interested in putting the storage of cotton under current farm programs on a competitive bid basis.
36. *Ibid.*, 140.

The Irony Of S. 109

The struggle over S. 109 leading up to and surrounding the May hearing had been conducted in the same "cloak and dagger" atmosphere between producers and processors that had characterized earlier versions of the bill. Beneath the surface, however, was a situation with a touch of irony. Amid all the political skulduggery over the bill, two positions stood out clearly: The farm groups, with the exception of the AFB, preferred to promote the bill as if it were a major piece of bargaining legislation, but the opponents objected to S. 109 on the basis that it was "Wagner Act" type of legislation. In point of fact, it was neither.

The prehearing strategy of the opposing forces makes clear the situation. During the late winter and spring of 1967, the processing community objected strongly to the revised bill, whether strategically planned or not, as if it were in one of its earlier forms. They distributed copies of letters addressed to Congressman Emanuel Celler, Chairman of the House Judiciary Committee, from the FTC, Justice and Commerce departments. Written in the summer of 1966, these letters concerned the 1965 version of the bill. As a consequence of their use of the letters, the opponents' objections appeared to the informed as being oblivious to two basic revisions that the bill had undergone in September of 1966 and January of 1967. But the letters were successful in generating controversy — one tactical objective — although unsuccessful in raising enough questions to prevent the bill's being brought to hearing. In short, the letter gambit was a last-ditch effort to kill the bill.

During the time the letters were circulating, the AFB, with the aid of other farm organizations, was seeking additional congressional sponsors. The farm organizations saw their success in lining up sponsors in the House and Senate as solid evidence that they were riding a rising tide of popular farm bargaining sentiments, and they proceeded to debate the merits of S. 109 as though it were a basic piece of bargaining legislation. The enthusiasm of the farm community for some kind of bargaining legislation ultimately impressed itself upon Freeman during his shirt-sleeve conferences in the Midwest. It was after sensing the mood and vestiges of farm unrest that the Secretary had suddenly proclaimed that S. 109 was "just a little step along the way," a statement that accelerated the drive for more farm bargaining power.

Of course, a comparison of the 1967 version of S. 109 with the Wagner Act reveals some startling differences. The stated design of S. 109, as in earlier versions, was simply to pave the way for formation of bargaining associations. However, the term *bargaining* never appeared in the language of the bill. Moreover, the bill did not contain elements that were vital to a bargaining situation. The explanation for this omission was twofold.

First, the farm front did not approach the legislation with unanimity and common understanding. Operating and supply cooperatives were included in the bill's definition of "handler" and were therefore subject to the prohibitions of the 1967 bill. In addition, there was widespread feeling among some farm leaders that the bill would tend to proliferate the number of commodity bargaining associations, an undesirable outcome. This fear was a result of a basic misinterpretation that caused confusion throughout the life of S. 109. Several farm groups, including members of the AFB-NCFC-NMPF coalition, preferred to talk about bargaining *cooperatives* rather than bargaining *associations* of the AAMA and NFO stripe — without recognizing the distinct difference between the two types of organizations. The apparent failure to discriminate could have been credited to a tactical ploy to avoid legitimizing NFO bargaining activity. More likely, it was a genuine misinterpretation of structural differences and the ability of general farm interest groups to adapt to functional change. Moreover, the interest and discussion regarding cooperatives overlooked the limited original intention of S. 109 — to provide a basic, adequate legal foundation for bargaining associations and their activities, not to define specifics.

Secondly, the AFB was committed to getting legislation passed during the first session of Congress. Given his acute political instincts, Senator Aiken became irritated by the farm split in late 1966, recognizing that to pass both houses the bill would have to be in a very "basic" form.

The omission of specifics, then, was intentional. The 1967 version was simply a marketing rights bill that sought to protect farmers and their voluntary farm organizations by prohibiting unfair practices against producers solely because of their membership in any farm organization. Unfair practices were enumerated and injunctive relief and criminal enforcement provisions were provided. Passage of the bill would reaffirm congressional support for organizing activity and facilitate individual relief through the courts.

By contrast, the Wagner Act had established two firm working rules. First, it required recognition of the union by the employer after passage of a certification election. Secondly, it required the employer to "bargain in good faith" with the certified unions. In practice, employees are bound in certification elections to the union certified to represent them. The union then represents workers eligible for membership or requires them to join. In comparison, S. 109 did not propose to require processor recognition of any farmers' bargaining association or to require any processor or integrator to "bargain in good faith" with an association. Furthermore, each farmer could decide to join the association voluntarily and was not required to share in the association's costs even though he might benefit from its efforts. The differences between S. 109 and legislation similar to the Wagner Act thus were many and fundamental.

Yet the forces at work promoting and stifling congressional action on S. 109 did not uniformly recognize the dissimilarities, and the Wagner Act comparison forced re-examination of strategies. The AFB denied that S. 109 was a "little Wagner Act" and argued that the rights of purchasers were in fact doubly protected by provisions of the bill: (1) Producers' membership in a bargaining association was to be voluntary and (2) Purchasers were to be free to deal with whomever they chose. In some cases, national AFB officials risked alienating some of the more progressive state Farm Bureaus by denouncing provisions of the Wagner Act and denying similar objectives for S. 109. The officials doggedly maintained that S. 109 was designed to protect the producer's right to join in bargaining. Its goal was singular.

The developing events posed a serious problem for the AFB. While nothing was healthier to its AAMA program than to have the bargaining "bug" catch fire throughout the countryside, the practical reality of the situation was that the AFB was not prepared philosophically to accept a true and detailed bargaining measure. Furthermore, the political situation indicated that a stronger bargaining bill would not pass Congress, given the alarmed and committed opposition. Moreover, the AFB was irked by the Secretary's move to "lead" the fight for bargaining rights for the farmer. It was, however, as committed to legislating S. 109 as the opposition was to fighting it.

In an effort to extricate itself from the dilemma, the AFB decided to promote S. 109 as the "Aiken" bill. By promoting the Senator from Vermont as the leading farm legislator, the AFB attempted to overcome the impression that Freeman was at the forefront of the effort. At the same time, they hoped identification with Aiken would help them over one of the major hurdles S. 109 would face — the U.S. Senate. Following Senator Aiken's advice, the organization had encouraged other farm oranizations to support the proposal in as basic form as possible. As a result, the AFB spent as much time talking about what the bill *did not* do as it did telling what the bill would accomplish. The Farm Bureau's defensive testimony before the Senate subcommittee emphasized AFB's approach.

The opposition, led by the canners association, recognized the growing sentiment for bargaining legislation and the favorable climate for enacting the bill. If S. 109 was going to be stopped or modified, it would have to be done in the executive session of the Jordan subcommittee. To do this, a concentrated effort upon the Agriculture Committee members, and particularly those from the South, would be necessary. As if in response to the "S. 109 and free enterprise" editorial cited earlier,[37] the NCA, NBC and their cohorts mapped a strategy to modify the bill in a way that would make it acceptable to them. The new strategy called for the canner, cotton and anti-cooperative interests to come into the hearing with a carrot-and-stick approach. They objected to the bill as unnecessary and one-sided and at the same time proposed certain amendments or modifications to it.

The testimony during the hearing was therefore mixed in character. While all of the farm organizations supported the bill, some — such as the Grange — went beyond the limited objective by expressing the need for a

37. See Chapter 6.

National Agricultural Relations act, marketing boards and other institutional arrangements. The AFB decried any such implications of its bill and made a major point of the limitations written into it.

The opposition uniformly insisted that the enforcement procedures were too harsh. The NTEA, canners group and cotton interests all insisted that any prohibitions should apply equally to bargaining associations. The opposing views were poles apart, if not irreconcilable.

In the negotiations leading up to [legislation], the . . . [committees do] not rely so much upon public hearings as required by 'due process of the law' where everybody has a lawful right to be heard and the conflicting opinions are irreconcilable, as upon private and even confidential conferences with the leaders of the interests to be brought under the law, where concessions could be made and the investigations of experts could be weighted in the balance.[1]

John R. Commons

Chapter 8

Compromise and Fallout

When the hearing ended on May 11th, with a final filing date extended to May 25th, it was evident that the work of reconciling divergent views would be left to the Jordan subcommittee. The farm organizations had been successful in presenting an impressive unified position on the bill. Under pressure from this unity, and recognizing that strong congressional support now existed for the measure, the processors and integrators proposed changes to the bill even as they attempted to discredit it as unnecessary. At this juncture, Agriculture Secretary Orville Freeman became the torchbearer for the bargaining issue, giving the proponents an unexpected assist of considerable magnitude.

Freeman's Press Club Speech

In a speech at the National Press Club in Washington on May 16th, the Secretary spoke out on the most newsworthy agricultural issue of the day: farmer bargaining power. Acknowledging that a rare degree of unanimity existed among farm organizations on S. 109 and the issue of farm bargaining, Secretary Freeman ventured that this "incipient unity" in the desire for more market muscle, as he had viewed it firsthand during his travels in Iowa, Indiana and Kansas, was "unchanneled, unorganized and unfocused." [2] Yet, he

1. John R. Commons, *Myself: The Autobiography of John R. Commons* (Madison: The University of Wisconsin Press, 1964), 125. This class of negotiations was defined as "rationing transactions." Commons made this comment in reference to negotiations over Wisconsin's public utility law of 1907.

2. Orville L. Freeman (Secretary, USDA), speech, National Press Club, May 16, 1967. According to Herbert Harris, III (Legislative Counsel, American Farm Bureau Federation), the processors viewed S. 109 from a totally different perspective following the speech and it was thus of substantial assistance to the AFB people. Herbert Harris, III, personal interview, June 11, 1968.

mused that perhaps the day for farm bargaining had come and drew parallels with the experiences of labor organizers in the 1930's. In a brainstorming context, the Secretary offered ideas "that might help to create a favorable climate for farmer bargaining associations." [3] These included: (1) creating a National Farm Bargaining Board; (2) broadening the scope and authority of marketing agreement and order program and (3) establishing producer marketing boards.

In addition to these suggestions, which closely paralleled the 1966 report of the National Commission on Food Marketing, Secretary Freeman called attention to the things that farmers could do through their farmer cooperatives without additional authority.

> Some Florida citrus growers now squeeze their oranges, concentrate, can, and freeze the juice, then sell the product directly to supermarkets. There is more money in this for producers than in "raw" orange juice. Some soybean cooperatives are in the business of producing oil and other products, moving another step up the ladder of the marketing cycle.
> In short, the cooperatives, owned and operated by farmers, are "joining" the more profitable sector of the marketing cycle, assuring control of one more step in this cycle by farmers themselves, rather than off-farm interests. It is a development that I applaud and encourage.[4]

In calling farm operators' attention to potential benefits through vertical structure as well as horizontal co-ordination, Freeman indicated his awareness of concepts that no other Secretary of Agriculture had faced. What was new, according to Freeman, was the climate in rural America for legislating an economic "bill of rights" for farm operators. Through such new farm legislation, the farmer could shape his own economic destiny rather than having it shaped for him by off-farm interests.

The impact and significance of Freeman's statement was profound. Not only was a member of the Administration expressing sentiment for some type of farm bargaining legislation, he was also bringing his case dramatically before the public. The full import of this plea presented a challenge to the farm organizations and stimulated a search for a proposal that would go far beyond the Aiken bill. Freeman had focused upon the submerged issue intertwined throughout the S. 109 controversy: future farm policy.[5]

Reactions of the farm groups to the Secretary's proposal were mixed. The AFB viewed the statement with suspicion as an attempt to negate their own legislative efforts.[6] "Dairy Industry Newsletter" reported that a measure

3. Freeman, speech.
4. *Ibid.*
5. For an effective analysis of Freeman's speech, see "The Farm Power Struggle," *The Wall Street Journal*, May 24, 1967, 16.
6. Farm Bureau staff members, in confidential interviews, have attributed Freeman's action to political expediency.

encompassing the Secretary's suggestions was already in draft form.[7] The new draft was a product of certain members of the farm group alliance that carried over from the Kennedy days and the USDA but did not have the blessings of the Administration. The AFB was afraid that introduction of a stronger collective bargaining measure would lessen the chances of S. 109, which were now seen as promising in the Senate committee and on the floor, even if trouble appeared likely in the House.

To accelerate the movement of S. 109, the AFB seized upon Freeman's trial balloon to promote their own proposal to the opponents of S. 109. Simply stated, their message was, "Take our bill now or you will face a more inclusive bill later." So effective was the AFB's Washington team in carrying this "either-or" message to the trade groups, that the limited objectives of S. 109 looked more attractive to the opposition than they did prior to the Secretary's Press Club speech.

Interim Sparring

From a virtual standstill immediately following the May hearings, the activity surrounding S. 109 picked up only slowly during June. The hospitalization and convalescence of Senator Everett Jordan of North Carolina was a delaying factor, as was the customary July 4th congressional holiday during which many legislators returned to their home districts for fence mending. During this period, S. 109 was under further study by Harker Stanton, staff counsel of the Agriculture Committee, as a result of amendments proposed in the hearings. The AFB exerted considerable effort to keep the bill alive during this lull through contacts with committee staff members, trade groups and its own members. It was fully committed to achieving passage in the first session of Congress.

Following the May subcommittee hearings, the AFB mailed an "action requested" letter to its state Farm Bureaus encouraging them to put forth every effort to contact members of the full Senate Agriculture and Forestry Committee. The AFB also requested information from the state bureaus on the positions of all senators toward the bill. AFB's objective was to tally a reliable head count upon which the bill's chances of passage could be predicted. In his letter to the state groups, John Lynn indicated that the chances of passage of S. 109 in the Senate were "real good *if we go to work* to counter some of the arguments being made by the opposing forces." [8]

Feedback from the poll indicated that S. 109 had a good chance of passing if it could hurdle the full Agriculture Committee. And Aiken now gave the bill a chance of passing by a 3 to 1 margin, given proper amendments, on

---

7. A. Olivia Nicoll, "Dairy Industry Newsletter," May 24, 1967, 6.
8. John C. Lynn (Legislative Director, American Farm Bureau Federation), letter to state Farm Bureaus, n.d., 1967. From its context in relation to known dates, it was written after the Senate hearing on May 11 and before June 1.

the Senate floor.[9] The biggest problem was that S. 109 was encountering the influence of "King Cotton" head on. Early indications of the cotton opposition had been visible during the AFB's annual meeting in December of 1966. As further elaborated in the Senate subcommittee hearing, the obstruction in part involved the private war among cotton ginning and warehousing interests. Noncooperative ginners claimed that S. 109 as written would jeopardize competitive bidding practices with cooperatives. The AFB believed that it was for this reason that House Agriculture Committee Chairman Robert Poage and Senate Agriculture and Forestry Committee Chairman Allen Ellender opposed the bill.[10] Both Southern legislators, key figures in the life of S. 109, represented cotton producing states.

House action had been virtually nonexistent, except for a question of committee jurisdiction. Whereas earlier versions of S. 109 had been referred to the House Judiciary Committee, the measure introduced in the Ninetieth Congress had been referred to the Agriculture Committee. Judiciary Chairman Emanuel Celler was unhappy with this referral. Upon checking with his committee members, however, Congressman Poage decided to keep the bill in his committee. With House action being held up until the Senate had cleared the bill, all eyes were on the Senate subcommittee.

While key opponents recognized that S. 109 stood a good chance of clearing the Senate, they knew as well that passage could come only through the exercise of legislative finesse as the bill was guided through the committees. If there was any validity to the saying that politics is the art of compromise, opponents knew that they could fully expect to win revision of certain provisions. The extent of their success would be dependent upon the willingness of senators to accept their positions and the resistance of the proponents to such compromises. Complicating the picture but enhancing the bill's chances for passage was the fact that some senators and congressmen who opposed the bill didn't want to take the responsibility for bottling up the measure in committee.

Herbert Harris, III, Legislative Counsel for the AFB, was the person responsible for maneuvering S. 109 through this difficult period. In his seeking out of privately held positions, Harris discovered that a range of misconceptions about the bill existed. Some felt they had already killed it; others expressed an overwhelming fear concerning what the bill might imply.[11] Most opponents, he found, imputed much more to the bill than the AFB ever intended. Before May 16, Harris' main argument to the NCA and other opponents consisted simply of reiterating the limited intent of the farm organizations in presenting S. 109 and of assuring the opposition that AFB was committed to the voluntary, rather than compulsory, approach. After May 16,

9. Harris, interview.
10. John Datt (Legislative Director and Assistant Director, Washington Office, American Farm Bureau Federation), personal interview, June 11, 1968.
11. Harris, interview.

Freeman's speech proved the most convincing argument for S. 109. The Secretary of Agriculture's reference to "Wagner Act" legislation for agriculture and such devices as marketing boards had a strong impact upon officials of the National Canners Association.

The cotton community contined to be a tough customer in opposition. Traditionally, the industry was known for its ability to unite shippers, ginners, warehousemen and merchants into a formidable political force in furthering cotton interests. The cotton industry's chief concern with S. 109 related to the competition between cooperative and independent ginners. The prohibition contained in section 4d of the proposal relating to paying or giving anything of value was viewed as a constraint upon the independent ginners. According to Wes McAden, Executive Vice-President of the American Cotton Compress and Warehouse Association, this provision would outlaw the competitive practice of independent ginners who offer payments in lieu of patronage refunds to cotton farmers in order to solicit their business.[12] Cooperatives were considered to be archenemies of the association. As a consequence, McAden had proposed, by specifically defining a bargaining association in the May hearing, that the bill apply to the protection of bargaining associations only and not to cooperatives that were engaged in handling, storing and shipping cotton. The association continued to advocate this amendment following the hearings.

With an impasse among contesting groups imminent, the AFB met in a strategy session on June 12th to analyze the situation and to determine a course of action in dealing with opponents and the subcommittee. For the first time, all members of the AFB management committee were involved in a strategy session — Charles Shuman, Roger Fleming and Allen Lauterbach. Also included were Washington staff members John Datt, Herb Harris and John Lynn, and Gene Lemon, assistant general counsel. This top-level group faced the realities of the situation. First, the Senate staff had not yet started writing a report, but members of the Washington team and the canners had given them some material with which they could commence. Second, the group recognized that the major hurdle to passage of the bill involved the confrontation with the cotton industry alliance. Third, those in the meeting expressed displeasure with Secretary Freeman for attempting to take over leadership on the bargaining issue when it was Senator Aiken's bill.

The group's review concluded that the Texas ginners' major objection concerned the inducement prohibition.[13] The cotton associations' attempt to circumvent this provision by making S. 109 apply to bargaining associations only was known to be acceptable to the NCFC. The council favored this approach, as it had in earlier stages, because some of its member cooperatives were concerned about their ability to compete with other cooperatives and

---

12. Wesley H. McAden (Executive Vice-President, American Cotton Compress and Warehouse Association), personal interview, June 12, 1968.
13. American Farm Bureau files, notes of meeting, June 12, 1967.

because it did not feel that farmers needed protection from their own organizations. However, the bargaining-association-only approach was considered too restrictive by the AFB in light of some of its own activities, and it was not acceptable to the NMPF. The AFB felt that it was highly desirable to exclude cotton handlers without excluding the commodity. However, it considered the attempt to distinguish between marketing functions as advocated by McAden exceedingly difficult, if not embarrassing. This exercise represented a repeat of the discussion engaged in by the AFB-NCFC-NMPF coalition in 1965. In opposing the cotton exemption, the AFB knew it would have support from USDA officials who were determined to help neutralize the power of the cotton alliance.

Allen Lauterbach, chief architect of S. 109, recommended to the other AFB officials that if necessary, they should be prepared to strike section 4d. He suggested this deletion would do the least harm to the overriding purpose of the bill and suggested further that the criminal provisions, but not the treble damages, should be deleted to lessen the objections of the NCA contingent. As a substitute, he recommended that the fine for violation of the bill be increased.

The group decided to work through Senator Aiken in offering their revisions to the bill. As strategy, they decided to report to Senator Aiken that the AFB was quite open-minded and willing to accept some amendments but that they were not willing to exempt cotton. Finally, they reaffirmed their desire to seek passage of the law during the first session, before the Secretary of Agriculture could assume marketing leadership.

The Secretary's effort was considered a challenge to the role of Senator Aiken. To offset the Secretary's challenge, several farm groups initiated plans for a testimonial dinner in behalf of Senator Aiken as a means of recognizing his leadership role. They also wanted to make the Vermont Senator the hero for beating the cotton crowd.

Jordan Subcommittee Action

Recognizing the crucial importance of subcommittee action, the opponents of S. 109 used the delay caused by Jordan's illness to beef up their forces and to initiate a major rewriting of the bill. The idea for a major rewriting reportedly originated with the grain trade.[14] The idea was not entirely new, but its successful accomplishment was almost unheard of. But the sterling performance turned in by the opponents to the S. 109 proposal in accomplishing their goal testified to their ingenuity and political power. To many, they scored a first.

The ingredients necessary to achieving such a feat included an intimate

14. "Amended S. 109 now has good chance," *Broiler Industry*, 30, 8 (August, 1967), 8.

knowledge of the committee process, insights regarding individual whims and dislikes of legislators, political influence through broad-based support and financial backing, and hard-headed negotiating acumen — all of which were possessed by the opposition. To build a broader base of support, the U.S. Chamber of Commerce and the grain trade called in additional allies for help with the bill. Included in the group that now converged on S. 109 were the National Automobile Dealers Association and the American Trucking Association, as well as such old opponents as Ralston Purina, Del Monte, Cargill and the United Fruit Company. To exploit the broadened support, the opponents engaged Joseph O. Parker, Washington attorney, who played "an extremely important role in the modifications" of S. 109.[15]

Mr. Parker, regarded as one of the most knowledgeable men on agricultural trade matters in Washington, had gained renown for leading the "chicken war" fight in Europe. He and his partner, Al Densil, served a large clientele of big-money associations such as the AFMA, the American Poultry Institute, the Grain and Feed Dealers Association, the National Grange and other associations and food firms.[16] As former chief counsel of the House Agriculture Committee for nine years, Mr. Parker could draw upon his wealth of legislative expertise in handling the hotly contested proposal. He also knew firsthand the positions of parties on both sides of the bill.[17]

In a prelude to the rewriting, frequent meetings between senators, Senate staff members of the Agriculture Committee, USDA officials and farm groups and trade organizations took place. Main actors included the AFB, the cotton alliance, the grain trade and the canners contingent. The toughest nerve turned out to belong to the cotton alliance, which had found ready listeners in such ranking legislators as Senators Jordan, Ellender and Byrd and Congressmen Poage and Purcell.

The maneuvering on behalf of S. 109 was left almost exclusively in the hands of the AFB. The traditionally conservative farm group was well acquainted with other trade organizations and historically shared attitudes with them on many philosophical issues — particularly those relating to government farm programs.[18] History prior to S. 109 showed many examples of common cause, and the AFB maintained good working relationships with the National Association of Manufacturers, the American Poultry Institute, the National Canners Association and the U.S. Chamber of Commerce. Even with regard to the S. 109 proposal, the AFB had open communication channels with these trade groups and regarded them as admirable opponents. In promoting their market rights bill, AFB officials were frequently subjected

15. *Ibid.*

16. Joseph O. Parker (Attorney), personal interview, June 12, 1968.

17. According to several sources, Parker acted as counsel for both sides. He is said to have discussed S. 109 with the Committee of "17," and he was reportedly involved as well in writing amendment provisions on the processors' side.

18. Wesley McCune, *Who's Behind Our Farm Policy?* (New York: Frederick A. Praeger, Inc., 1956). See Chapter 2, "Blue Denim and Blue Serge," and p. 95.

to kidding from the trade organizations on the basis that they were asking for too much government regulation.[19] Despite history, the subjective grounds, however, dictated that the AFB face up to the realities of the political situation.

In facing these, the organization decided that there were two essentials within the bill that they had to keep intact — the prohibitions and the injunctive relief provision. Both these elements bore on matters critical at the initial organization stages of a bargaining association. So long as a bill contained these provisions, the AFB was prepared to take anything with the number S. 109 on it.

The organization accordingly was not sympathetic with the position of the American Cotton Compress and Warehouse Association in regard to deleting the inducement prohibition. On the other hand, the alternative argument of the cotton alliance that coverage of the bill should apply to bargaining associations only was also unacceptable. Yet it was realized by some officials within the organization that if the provisions were narrowed to just bargaining, the bill would help in establishing the AAMA programs because it would force farm operators, especially broiler growers in the South, to use terminology that they originally found unpalatable.

The overriding issue, however, concerned how to handle the cotton alliance in view of the amendments proposed by the USDA. While the USDA was considered an ally in helping to neutralize the influence of the powerful cotton interests, the AFB found difficulty in accepting an administrative procedure involving the Secretary of Agriculture in the bill's enforcement procedures. As some AFB people viewed it, Secretary Freeman was trying to put his wagon box on their set of running gears. The two were not compatible. This philosophical conflict with the USDA proposal made the AFB's job of securing USDA help to neutralize the cotton alliance more difficult. If cotton and tobacco warehousemen and handlers were exempted from the provisions, the AFB would lose face. If Farm Bureau officials didn't find a way to deal them out, however, it began to look as though the cotton alliance possessed enough power to stop movement on the bill by bottling it up in the subcommittee. Such were the dimensions of the dilemma faced by the AFB.

In contrast to the AFB's quandary, the NCA quietly pursued its objectives of seeking certain provisions in the bill that would make all prohibitions apply equally to farm organizations and noncooperatives. Furthermore, it sought assurances of its right to select producers from whom it purchased farm products and turned to good use AFB President Shuman's early statements assuring that AFB had originally intended to guarantee that right.

By mid-July, activity surrounding S. 109 had intensified to the point where meetings were held almost daily. Mr. Harker Stanton of the Senate

19. Lee Campbell (Executive Director, American Poultry Institute), personal interview, June 13, 1968.

staff worked with all parties to the bill and tried to develop a compromise. On one day, he would meet with one trade group and the next day another. In so doing, he isolated the positions of various groups and brought them into direct confrontation with each other over specific issues. Coincidentally, Senate Agriculture Committee members initiated personal contacts with trade groups in an effort to arrive at a compromise.

One such incident developed from a request by Senator Jordan to the NCA in which he asked the canners to submit a position paper to the subcommittee on features they desired in a compromise version of the bill.[20] Upon receiving this formal request, NCA officials had to take stock of their Washington posture and reassess their position with respect to the bill. Before framing their reply, NCA officials weighed the various factors in their favor. As a starter, they had AFB President Shuman's testimony suggesting that the farm organization did not seek a "one-sided" bill. Recalling Mr. Shuman's "Farm Bureau does not seek, and will not support" statement, the canners at last determined that it was not the intention of the AFB to infringe upon their selection rights as processors. Once a statement to that effect was in the public hearing record, NCA Legislative Director Robert Heiney claimed that the NCA "had no trouble dealing with the American Farm Bureau whatsoever." [21]

The NCA also recognized that AFB was hungry for legislation. Given this understanding, Heiney felt that he could achieve certain desirable compromises from the processor's viewpoint. Next, the canners knew that they could count on strong support from other trade groups and large corporations. Finally, the canners felt they could count on certain sympathetic members of the Agriculture Committee. Senator Jordan, a part owner in a textile firm, and other committee members tended to view S. 109 in much the same light as the processors. It was often said that Senator Jordan saw everything through a tobacco leaf. With these important factors in their favor, canner officials pursued a full-scale reappraisal of their position.

Traditionally, the policy of the NCA had been that "if there is no value in a piece of legislation, then oppose it," [22] and the canners' initial response to S. 109 was consistent with this policy. However, the AFB marketing rights bill was controversial, and continued opposition to it by the canners' group risked worsening its reputation as an organization that opposed all legislation. This risk was particularly acute in light of the NCA's persistent efforts to stymie requests by fruit and vegetable associations to extend federal marketing-order legislation to cover their commodities. To protect themselves, canner officials decided that it was in their best interests to avoid being cast in a negative posture and consequently accepted Senator Jordan's challenge to offer suggestions for compromise.[23]

20. Robert B. Heiney (Director, Government-Industry Relations, National Canners Association), personal interview, April 3, 1968.
    21. *Ibid.*   22. *Ibid.*   23. *Ibid.*

The NCA presented its position to Senator Jordan on July 13th in the form of a two-page memorandum entitled "Recommendations of the National Canners Association for Amendments to S. 109." The memorandum consisted of four parts and dealt with selection of customers and suppliers, equality of treatment for independent producers, modification of the penalties and clarification of the prohibitions. The paper keyed itself to earlier testimony presented before the subcommittee and included some specific recommendations and new language. Specifically, the NCA suggested that it would not object to provisions in the bill that would protect association members from refusals to deal or discrimination solely by reason of their membership in a bargaining association. By the same token, however, it cited statements by Mr. Shuman, Agriculture Secretary Freeman and Senator Lausche supporting the idea that handlers should not be compelled to negotiate with marketing associations or purchase through them.

Citing the vital importance of this issue, the canners proposed a new section 5 that had a striking similarity to President Shuman's statements.

> Nothing in this Act shall prevent handlers and producers from selecting their customers and suppliers on any basis other than a producer's membership in an association of producers, nor prevent handlers and producers from dealing with one another individually on a direct basis, nor require a handler to deal with an association of producers.[24]

In addition to this new section, the canners urged recognition of the right of producers to remain independent and to be free from coercion and discriminatory practices by bargaining associations. The canners thus suggested changes in the prohibitions section to make all prohibitions apply equally to associations of producers and to protect the rights of the producers not to join. Furthermore, they endorsed proposals of Senators Lausche and Williams that the criminal penalties and treble damages be eliminated. They also suggested that the bill's assurance of the private right to seek injunctive relief would encourage undue harassment of processors. As an alternative procedure, they requested that the Attorney General, rather than the Secretary of Agriculture, be authorized to bring civil actions and suggested that action through the Secretary was entirely sufficient. The canners recommended, as well, changes in the language of the prohibitions section so that it would not attempt to deal with such "broad and ambiguous" terms as boycott, interference, unfair practices and true market value.

As a final revision, the NCA requested an addition to the prohibitions to provide protections to producers who "may be dissatisfied with an earlier decision to join a bargaining association."

Having offered recommendations in four general areas, the canners urged the subcommittee to give serious consideration to the revisions and

---

24. National Canners Association, memorandum, "Recommendations of the National Canners Association for Amendments to S. 109," July 13, 1967.

argued that they were "consistent with the statements of intent by the proponents." [25] In conclusion, the processor group indicated that it would no longer oppose the legislation if the suggested revisions were adopted.

Having gone on record, the NCA had yet to convince members of the Senate Agriculture Committee of the validity of its views. Senate staff members, AFB officials and senators themselves continued their labor to bring accord among other groups. The real bottleneck continued to be the flood of amendments offered by members of the cotton alliance. In an effort to accommodate the alliance's wishes that the bill apply only to grower bargaining associations and not to vertically integrated operations, Herb Harris of the AFB drafted an addition to the prohibitions section that would limit the effect of the bill to protection for bargaining associations. The proposed wording of this addition was as follows:

(g) provided that the provisions of this Section shall not be applicable if association of producers is engaged in handling of agricultural products in competition with such handler.[26]

This change brought to five those being sought by the cotton alliance in a redrafted version of S. 109. Others were revisions of the enforcement provisions, deletion of the inducements prohibition and the injunctive-relief provision and substitution of the Attorney General for the Secretary of Agriculture in the enforcement provisions.

By mid-July, the senators returned to Washington following their customary July 4th recess. The activity surrounding S. 109 entered into one of its most crucial stages. On the basis of his frequent meetings with contestants, Harker Stanton finally reached a point at which he thought that seven of ten major parties to the bill were in substantial agreement on its provisions.[27] As a result, an executive session of the subcommittee was set for July 25th.

In meetings between July 17–19, the cotton alliance offered yet another amendment. In a meeting with John Lynn of the AFB, the cotton group suggested that a revision be made in the definitions section 3c of the bill to qualify the definition of a producer group by adding the following sentence:

The term "association of producers" means a 15a and Capper-Volstead organization which is authorized by, and seeking on behalf of, its producer members to improve the price and other terms of sale of commodities produced by its members, and not handling such products in competition with other handlers.[28]

The revision effort represented another in a series of persistent attempts by the Cotton Compress and Warehouse Association to rewrite certain provi-

25. *Ibid.*
26. American Farm Bureau files, notes, 1967.
27. Charles Weaver (Legislative Assistant to Senator George Aiken), personal interview, April 5, 1968.
28. American Farm Bureau files, notes, 1967.

sions of S. 109 so that it would apply to the simple act of buying and selling and not to other stages in the product flow such as ginning, shipping and warehousing. AFB Washington officials felt they could live with this revision.

As the pace of activities quickened with the approval of the July 25th executive session, an agreement was reached between the opponents of the bill and the AFB on taking this bargaining-function approach to the bill.[29] On Friday, July 21st, John Datt and Jack Lynn of the AFB met with representatives of the Grange, NMPF, NCFC, Farmers Union and other farm groups to advise them on the progress of the bill and what they could expect from the Jordan subcommittee. Considerable sentiment against limiting the coverage of the bill only to bargaining associations was expressed by some groups, especially the NMPF.

The makeup of the powerful Senate Agriculture subcommittee in 1967 consisted of Senators James Eastland of Mississippi, Harry Byrd of Virginia, Ernest Hollings of South Carolina, Milton Young of North Dakota, J. Caleb Boggs of Delaware and Everett Jordan of North Carolina. Its orientation was strongly Southern and heavily Democratic. When the group met in executive session on July 25 with representatives of the pressure groups involved in the bill, it took under consideration Committee Print No. 1 (see Appendix B), which had been prepared by the committee staff for examination by the subcommittee. This print consisted of a substantially redrafted version of S. 109 and included explanations of various changes made in the bill.

Important changes in the bill reflected in the print follow: (1) the phrase "free to join together *or not to join together* in cooperative organizations . . ."; (2) the purpose of establishing standards of fair practices required of handlers *and* associations of producers; (3) a revised section 3c that applied to associations that bargain collectively over price and other terms of sale only; (4) revision of the prohibitions through the addition of such words as "solely" and "maliciously" and deletion of phrases such as "true market value," "interfere with" or "restrain or threaten to interfere with" and words like "boycott"; (5) a new disclaimer section; (6) revised enforcement provisions regarding jurisdiction by the Attorney General, recovery of actual damages and deletion of treble damages and criminal penalties.

As rewritten in the print, the bill embodied nearly all of the recommendations of the NCA contingent and the cotton alliance, and had a distinct anti-farm-organization flavor. From the processors' viewpoint, the bill had "become watered down to the point where it was almost a good bill."[30] It now applied to farm organizations as well as to processors and contained a disclaimer clause proposed by the NCA. It was a legislative victory for the opposition to the bill. From the farm organizations' viewpoint, the bill had

29. McAden, interview.
30. Frank Wolfe (Legislative Assistant, National Canners Association), personal interview, April 3, 1968.

been emasculated and was discriminatory against farm organizations. A heated debate ensued in the executive session.

Even though the AFB had agreed to the inclusion of the disclaimer provision, it felt that the Jordan subcommittee, mainly under the influence of the North Carolina Senator, had been oversold on the position of the processors and had gone too far in the print. The bill had been turned into antifarm, anti-cooperative legislation. AFB officials were faced with two choices: kill the bill or go to work on it.[31]

Mr. Herb Harris, AFB's Legislative Counsel, felt that while the canners had shown their muscle by giving the bill an anti-cooperative flavor, his organization had achieved a significant feat by putting the NCA in a position where, for the first time, it had to negotiate at all. AFB accordingly viewed Committee Print No. 1 as an extreme position that provided ground from which they could work legislatively. If the AFB and its allies negotiated well, the farm organizations could end up on the producers' side of middle ground on the bill. Consequently, the AFB protested the inclusion of certain wording and provisions in the redrafted bill. Mr. Harris accused the canners of being guilty of an overkill and got them to give in on some features they were trying to include in the bill.

On the other side of the issue, Wes McAden of the Cotton Compress and Warehouse Association felt that there was substantial agreement on all the revisions in the bill except for the one change upon which he insisted: that the bill apply to selling and buying activities only. As written, the measure included the qualifying phrase in the definition of "association of producers" that limited the coverage of the bill to collective bargaining activity. Other processors wanted to have the bill's prohibitions apply specifically to marketing cooperatives as well as bargaining associations. Conversely, some backers of the bill wanted the protective aspects to cover cooperative marketing activity. As a result of these many conflicting views, McAden had been advised just prior to the July 25th morning mark-up session that he no longer had an agreement.[32]

McAden had just finished his presentation when, as if on cue, Senator Eastland of Mississippi entered the committee room and indicated that so far as he knew the cotton constituents in his state interpreted the bill as being desirable. McAden, however, regarded the Eastland statement as an arranged performance that was representative of the cotton cooperative and farm organization interests rather than of independent operators, and he informed the group that he could not live with S. 109 as written.[33] McAden's statement clearly meant the AFB was faced with the question, "Do you want a bill or don't you?" [34] At this point, cotton and tobacco were exempted from the provisions of the bill.

31. Harris, interview.   32. McAden, interview.   33. *Ibid.*
34. Harris, interview.

In agreeing to exclude the cotton and tobacco commodities from S. 109, the AFB fell back upon the rationale that these commodities operated under such complete government programs that there was no prospect for effective bargaining in the immediate future. Since tobacco was sold almost exclusively through auctions, the application of S. 109 to this commodity was viewed as being somewhat ridiculous. Secondly, AFB officials recognized that argument with the North Carolina Senator who was also the subcommittee chairman would not move the bill forward. Insofar as the Senate was concerned, the cotton group was not one to be riled.[35] The power of senators from the cotton and tobacco producing states who dominated the subcommittee had to be reckoned with. The exemption of cotton and tobacco removed a very vocal and politically powerful commodity sector from subsequent discussion on the bill. Moreover, the AFB and the USDA had challenged and lost: cotton was still king in the Senate.

At the close of the executive session, the subcommittee unanimously passed on the bill in a slightly revised form entitled Committee Print No. 2, issued on July 26th (see Appendix B), and sent it to the full Senate Agriculture and Forestry Committee. The bill was now entitled the "Agricultural Fair Practices Act of 1967" and included a restatement of the individual injunctive relief measure and a provision for action by the Secretary of Agriculture. However, the bill still contained the canners' disclaimer clause and the "to join or not to join" phrase. The continued presence of the disclaimer implied that it was a legislative finding that producers were free not to join in group action. In a letter to its legislative committee, the NCA urged its members to "advise" Senator Jordan and other committee members "that this amended version of S. 109 will not be opposed by the canning industry." [36] While the trade group did not recommend that its members cast themselves as "proponents" of the legislation, it did ask that appreciation be expressed to the subcommittee members for their actions.

The NCA also reported to its members that "it is our understanding that the principal proponent of S. 109, the American Farm Bureau Federation, is satisfied with the Senate Subcommittee's action on the bill." [37] However, AFB officials were not at all satisfied. First, they did not want the treble-damages provision deleted. Secondly, they were annoyed by the incorporation of legal terminology that would make it extremely difficult to prove that the law had been violated. Consequently, they turned again to Senator Aiken.

In response, Aiken took over leadership on the bill in the full committee and made a strenuous effort to remove some of the anti-farm-organization language from it. In his effort, the Vermont Senator consulted with Senator

---

35. *Ibid.*
36. Robert B. Heiney, memorandum to Legislative Committee, July 25, 1967.
37. National Canners Association, "Government-Industry Report," July 26, 1967.

Williams of Delaware and worked closely with Senator Jordan.[38] The NCFC-AFB-NMPF coalition again cooperated with Senator Aiken and with other friendly committee members such as Senator Holland of Florida and Senator Mondale of Minnesota.

Following the release of Print No. 2, the NCFC was forced to abandon its aloof and neutral policy on S. 109. Like the USDA, it became alarmed over the anti-cooperative tone of the bill and viewed its own gradual detachment from the subcommittee proceedings, in retrospect, as dangerous. Kenneth Naden, Executive Vice-President of the cooperative council, took heed from the old adage, "In order for evil to prevail in the world, good men do nothing," and actively sought changes in the bill along with the AFB and NMPF.[39] The greatest weakness in the farm front at this point was that unlike the opponents, none of the backers had given intensive legal analysis to the various amendments to the bill.

The NCFC charged that S. 109 had become "seriously weakened and distorted" by changes proposed by the subcommittee. It also claimed that the new version raised basic questions about the rights of farmers to conduct their cooperative businesses as assured by Congress under the Capper-Volstead Act and other legislation. Among the changes requested by the NCFC were deletion of the phrase "or not to join together"; deletion of the word "solely" in the prohibitions; substitution of the word "knowingly" for the word "maliciously" in the prohibitions and deletion of the last half of the disclaimer clause. The terms "solely" and "maliciously" were legal pitfalls that would make the burden of proof almost impossible. In promoting these changes, the NCFC worked through Senator Spessard Holland of Florida, a former cooperative attorney, and Senator Walter Mondale of Minnesota. NCFC and AFB officials successively visited the committee members in their Capitol Hill offices August 1st and 2nd. While Hampton, Marketing Director of the NCFC, visited Senators Talmadge, Holland, Eastland, Byrd and Boggs, Naden visited with Senators Mondale, Hollings, Young and Miller.[40] Both spent two hours with Senator Aiken. AFB officials, who were also working the halls, urged the council officials not to fight the bill with such vigor in fear they would kill it.[41] NCFC officials interpreted this to mean that while the AFB was suggesting changes in the bill, it was not willing to fight for them.

The NCFC and NMPF were so adamant about certain provisions that it looked as if they might withdraw their support from the bill. However, they were successful in toning down some aspects of the bill when the Senate Agri-

38. Weaver, interview.
39. Kenneth D. Naden (Executive Vice-President, National Council of Farmer Cooperatives), personal interview, June 10, 1968.
40. Robert N. Hampton (Director of Marketing and International Trade, National Council of Farmer Cooperatives), personal interview, June 14, 1968.
41. *Ibid.*

culture Committee deleted the terms "solely" and "maliciously" from the prohibitions section, and prohibition 4f in its entirety. This latter provision had sought to limit the amount of liquidated damages assessed a producer for failing to comply with a cooperative membership or marketing agreement. The NCFC-AFB-NMPF coalition was unsuccessful in its endeavors to revise the "to join or not to join" phrase in the legislative findings, and the disclaimer clause went unchanged.

On August 3rd, the full Senate Agriculture Committee passed on the amended bill without a dissenting vote. Senator Aiken, in his customary breakfast session with Senate Floor Leader Mike Mansfield of Montana, arranged to bring the bill quickly to the Senate floor, and S. 109 was reported to the Senate floor on Friday, August 4th. Shortly thereafter, it was passed unanimously with only three or four senators on the floor at the time (see Appendix B). The bill had cleared a major hurdle, although not in the form AFB had originally sought.

As the bill was sent over to the House of Representatives, Herbert Harris, chief strategist for the AFB during the May to August interim, looked upon the adventure before the full Senate committee with some pleasure. Much of the harmful language found in the first committee print had been removed through amendments. He had also maintained lines of communication with both sides that had provided the basis for further compromise. On the one hand, a façade of agricultural unity had been maintained as the bill left the Senate. At the same time, he had the consent of the opponents to carry the bill as it was amended.[42] So far as the AFB was concerned, the bill was still close to the point of facilitating the essential objectives which they desired.

From the original opponents' viewpoint, the results were also successful. The cotton and tobacco interests were happy because they had been exempted from provisions in the bill. The canners and poultry people were happy because the harsh penalties had been removed in their entirety. In addition, the bill had been made a two-way street and contained language "protecting" the farm operator's right not to join an organization. Most importantly, however, the bill contained section 5 — the disclaimer of intention to prohibit normal dealing — which the canners looked upon as a valuable "bill of rights" for processing associations.[43] In short, all of the objections of the canners, grain trade and NBC had been removed from S. 109 in the Senate. They had brought sufficient pressures to bear successfully to subvert the bill from one protecting farm interests to one establishing standards of fair practice. The agriculture subcommittee had served a crucial role in reconciling the divergent views of opposing forces.

The overall contentment that seemed to prevail between the AFB and

42. Harris, interview.
43. Heiney, interview.

the canners' contingent could be attributed to compromise. As the bill left the Senate, it reflected the viewpoints of the key parties to the bill. First, the Secretary of Agriculture's role in the enforcement provisions was included. Secondly, the canner contingent's main fears about what the bill might imply were dispelled by the inclusion of the disclaimer clause. And thirdly, the AFB-NCFC-NMPF coalition had succeeded in removing from the bill before the full Senate committee some of the features most objectionable to it. The NCFC even sent a letter of congratulations to Senator Aiken for taking steps to improve the bill. However, the contentment was only temporary.

The Administration Speaks Out

Anxious to demonstrate its willingness to do something for a restless farm population, the Administration chose this critical moment in the life of S. 109 and made its biggest pitch for a collective bargaining program. At a press conference on August 18th, President Johnson displayed his political astuteness by sidestepping a question about the effect of the NFO's milk withholding action and by delivering a prepared statement on farm bargaining. According to A. Olivia Nicoll, Johnson's statement indicated that he was giving serious consideration to "evolving some kind of a program that will give the farmers an equity, a fairness, the same basis for bargaining for the prices of his product as we have for workers in bargaining for wages they receive for their labors." [44]

Similarly, Secretary of Agriculture Freeman spoke out on the bargaining issue. In a memorandum on August 7, Bill Abbott, an assistant to the Secretary who did a lot of leg work on S. 109, reported to Freeman that the Senate had undertaken some "very fast footwork" to secure passage of the bill and to avoid USDA harassment with amendments.[45] USDA officials never saw the Senate bill that had been reported on Thursday, August 3rd and passed on Friday, August 4th. Mr. Abbott's evaluation of the bill was that it could be called "quite charitably an 'unacceptable' version." [46] Following Abbott's memorandum and recently held commodity advisory committee meetings, Freeman began laying groundwork for an alternative bill during a White House press conference on August 23rd. According to A. Olivia Nicoll, he stated that "the history, the lessons and the accomplishments of labor . . . lend themselves to some possible new kinds of direction." [47] As a specific example, Freeman noted the trend toward regional milk marketing and regional producer associations that marketed milk in 70 milk market orders.

44. A. Olivia Nicoll, "Dairy Industry Newsletter," August 30, 1967, 1.
45. William S. Abbott (Special Assistant to the Secretary, USDA), memorandum to the Secretary, August 7, 1967.
46. *Ibid.*
47. Nicoll, "Dairy Industry Newsletter," August 30, 1967, 1.

Now it is well within the range of possibility that there could be, let us say, a dozen regions that would complement normal kinds of geographical lines. Within that group then the farmers might well elect a bargaining committee or a bargaining agency, or officers in an organization for a bargaining group.

This is precisely what labor does in the labor union. Once we have done that, we go to processors, the handlers in this case, and negotiate the price, let us say for the coming year.

If that price was verified and accepted democratically by the producers, there would be an enforceable contract. Under those circumstances you would presumably be attuned to the economic facts of the market place. Those producers would have at least some power to determine their own prices.[48]

Freeman's statement carried forward the new approach by the Administration to the farm-income problem. In keeping alive the trial balloons introduced during the Press Club speech, Johnson's and Freeman's press conferences hit S. 109 in a weak moment. Although it had been already passed by one house in Congress, the Senate version of S. 109 was not well received among farm groups and the National Advisory Committee on Cooperatives chaired by Assistant Secretary John Baker.

Farm Fallout

Just as the May Press Club speech caused the processors to view S. 109 in a different light, the Administration's bargaining pitch caused the farm organizations to evaluate carefully the Senate version of S. 109. While this version looked increasingly good to the processors as time went on, the farm groups viewed its content with growing concern, once they had studied the bill and compared it to its earlier form.[49] The USDA viewed the Senate bill, particularly the disclaimer clause, as a statement of purpose by Congress instead of the original proposal to prohibit certain acts and to prescribe certain penalties.[50] The disclaimer provision was interpreted by USDA as saying that the Senate did not care what happened to farmers. If true, a significant change in posture by the Congress had taken place. Even though Senator Mondale and others were instrumental in bringing about changes that removed some of the most "glaring errors," the USDA questioned whether the bill had been improved enough.

Similarly, the Grange and NFU now viewed the bill in a somewhat dif-

48. *Ibid.,* 2.

49. The Senate action on S. 109 was almost exclusively in the hands of the AFB. The other farm groups and the USDA had been tuned out. Having not followed it closely, a time lag developed before they recognized the true content of the revised measure.

50. David Angevine (Administrator, Farmer Cooperative Service, USDA), personal interview, June 15, 1968.

ferent perspective. The Grange, which had only halfheartedly supported the bill all along, severely critized the AFB for allowing emasculation of the bill. Without the criminal penalties and treble damages, argued Harry Graham, the bill was as effective as "slapping the violators over the wrist with a wet noodle." [51] In a similar vein, the NFU indicated that it was reluctant to support the bill.[52] For one reason, the cotton and tobacco interests were now exempted. Secondly, the treble damages and criminal provisions had been dropped. Finally, the NCFC also had questioned whether it could live with the bill. If the cooperative council could not support it, then neither could the NFU as a basic supporter of cooperative activity.

Most significant however, was the fact that the NFU, after careful study by its General Counsel, former Secretary of Agriculture Charles Brannan, had formulated a bill of its own known as the National Agricultural Relations act. This proposal, which closely reflected the thinking within the Administration, was known as the "Thatcher" bill after M. W. Thatcher, General Manager of the Farmers Union Grain Terminal Association in Minneapolis, who first promoted such a measure in 1943.[53] The Farmers Union proposal went beyond the limits of S. 109. Instead of opposing S. 109 and creating an impression of farm disunity, the NFU now promoted its own bargaining bill.

Of all the position switches by farm organizations, the turnabout by the NCFC was perhaps the most significant. For while this organization had experienced internal problems in arriving at a position in support for the bill early in 1967, it had nevertheless been one of the consistent members of the AFB-NCFC-NMPF coalition. For a short time following the Senate action, it appeared that the NCFC supported the amended version. Not only had the council sent congratulatory remarks to Senator Aiken for removing some of the "undesirable" language from Subcommittee Print No. 2, but it also assumed some credit for improvements made in the bill before the full Senate Committee. In its "Washington Situation" dated August 8th, the council reported to members that the Senate had passed by unanimous consent the "bargaining rights for farmers" bill that had received the primary backing of the council and the AFB.

Upon subsequent review of the amended bill, however, several members of the NCFC became alarmed at its two-way-street implications and the inclusion of the disclaimer clause. The Mississippi Federation of Cooperatives and the Cotton Producers Association — both engaged in processing broilers — vacillated over whether or not to support the Senate bill. Some of the disturbed organizations had previously expressed their displeasure with

51. Harry Graham (Legislative Representative, National Grange), personal interview, April 4, 1968.
52. Angus McDonald (Research Director, National Farmers Union), personal interview, April 4, 1968.
53. M. W. Thatcher, "Farm Bargaining Power Will Not Come Quickly or Easily," *GTA Digest*, 28, 1 (January, 1968), 4. Mr. Thatcher retired from the GTA in 1968.

the bill through processor-oriented groups such as the American Poultry Institute and the National Canners Association. After the bill had acquired
anti-cooperative overtones, they reverted back to the NCFC to air their
views. At this point, Kenneth Naden, Executive Vice-President of the NCFC,
told them "to put up or shut up" since they couldn't vacillate on such important issues as those taken up in the S. 109 bill.[54]

The California fruit and vegetable cooperatives were also disturbed by
the amended bill. One of the leading advocates of bargaining legislation,
Ralph Bunje, led an active attack against the Senate-passed version of S. 109.
His turnabout could be explained in part by the unhappiness of certain California processing cooperatives with the provisions of the amended bill.[55] Like
the cooperatives processing broilers, the cooperative canners expressed their
displeasure through the cooperative council. In spite of these difficult internal
problems, the NCFC resolved to go on record as being against the bad features of the bill. In a letter to members on August 25th, Kenneth Naden
stressed that the NCFC's position on S. 109 was "one of support for the original bill but one of grave reservations about the amended bill passed by the
Senate." [56]

The concern expressed by the council in the letter focused on two sen-
tences, the "free to join or not to join" phrase and the last two-thirds of the
disclaimer clause. Arguing against the inclusion of these two provisions,
Naden suggested that the clause concerning freedom not to join together
would imply that the public interest is best served by a government policy of
neutrality or indifference toward group action by farmers. Such an implica-
tion would weaken and erode the climate for farm organization. Secondly,
the disclaimer statement suggesting that nothing "shall . . . prevent handlers and producers from dealing with one another individually on a direct
basis" was viewed as an entrée "for handlers to create disorganization, disunity, and cutthroat competition among individual farmers as they vied for
handlers favor." [57] Such a situation, Naden argued, would perpetuate the
great inequity in bargaining power between handlers and individual farmers
and was diametrically opposed to the purpose of all farmer bargaining activities. The NCFC announced that it would seek amendments or passage of the
original bill "to try to make it helpful rather than harmful to farmers."

The cooperative council's position on the bill notwithstanding, several
member organizations continued their vocal opposition to the amended bill.
The activity of Ralph Bunje of the California Canning Peach Association was
typical. Bunje's active involvement in S. 109, which continued through to ul-

54. Naden, interview.
55. Weaver, interview; Datt, interview. This indicates that the NCFC, like other
farm groups, had not been keeping its members informed about the contents of the bill.
56. Kenneth D. Naden, letter to presidents and managers of member organizations, August 25, 1967.
57. *Ibid.*

timate passage of the bill, departed from his statesmanlike role as leader of the West Coast bargaining associations. In that role within the NCFC, Mr. Bunje reported the findings of a bargaining association conference on the amended bill to Allen Lauterbach of the AFB.[58] His report could be traced to a legal analysis of the bill conducted for the California Canning Peach Association. The analysis concluded that the Senate version represented a substantial departure from the original bill and that it eliminated protection afforded associations of producers by watering down the penalty provisions and by extending new substantive protections to noncooperative handlers. Changes in the bill's title, enacting clause and legislative findings were all regarded as symbolic of a rewritten bill that conflicted with the congressional policy embodied in the Capper-Volstead Act and the Agricultural Marketing Act of 1929.

Of the many changes in the bill, the California association singled out two for special scrutiny. The first was the amendment to section 2 that made the individual farmer's freedom "not to join" a cooperative organization a legislative finding and declaration of policy. Bunje suggested that there was absolutely no support in the testimony to the effect that producers were subjected to undue pressures to join together in cooperative associations.[59] Secondly, the association objected generally to the prohibitions applying to producer associations, and specifically to the one dealing with the termination of agreements with handlers. Under California law, producers had the right to persuade growers to terminate their contracts with handlers and to join the association. This provision was regarded by the Californians as a basic right to the organization of producer groups. Accordingly, Bunje saw the amended S. 109 as a threat to the basic purpose of bargaining associations. He suggested to the AFB that the amended bill should receive vigorous opposition until changed and that without change, he preferred no bill at all.[60]

This course of events was taken seriously by the AFB, which was counting on further improvement in the bill before the House Agriculture Committee. All organizations except the NMPF had voiced opposition to the amended version. In addition, some state groups within the Farm Bureau family began to question its provisions. A legal interpretation conducted for the California Farm Bureau concluded that "if the intent of the original act was to permit producers themselves or their associations to effectively bring unfair charges against handlers, the substitute bill has successfully turned the attack." [61] According to this interpretation, the bill was a measure offering a "milk toast" version of protection of a member from his cooperative. Fur-

58. Ralph Bunje (General Manager, California Canning Peach Association), letter to Allen Lauterbach (General Counsel, American Farm Bureau Federation), August 31, 1967.
59. *Ibid.*
60. *Ibid.*
61. Charles A. Rummel (Attorney), memorandum to Allan Grant (President, California Farm Bureau), August 30, 1967.

thermore, the allowance of attorney's fees only to the prevailing party in a damage suit was looked upon, in a practical sense, as eliminating any actions being filed under the bill.

These events were a severe blow to the legislative progress of S. 109. What had earlier been a limited piece of farm-sponsored marketing legislation that had won the united support of all farm organizations was now a more "basic" bill that included provisions of a two-way nature and that was of questionable value to farm organizations. The insertion of the "to join or not to join" clause and the deletion of the treble-damages provision were undesirable from the AFB's viewpoint. However, it had hoped to take improving action on the bill in the House. Nevertheless, the split in the farm front and the impact of the California Farm Bureau and Bunje's legal analyses moved Allan Grant, President of the California Farm Bureau, to request discussion of the S. 109 proposal at the AFB's September board meeting. The original proponents of marketing rights legislation were about to become its major opponents.

The hottest places of hell are reserved for those who, in times of moral crisis, maintain their neutrality.	Chapter 9 # Amend or Kill

The ground swell of reaction to the Senate version generated tremendous pressures upon the AFB to salvage its original bill. The farm groups, once they understood the full implications of the bill's new provisions, became opponents of the measure. However, the original opponents, seeing the mushrooming Administration support for farm bargaining activity, became its major proponents.

The many House sponsors of the original measure provided considerable evidence of sentiment remaining for the original version. The paramount question now facing the AFB was whether the House support was sufficient to amend the bill to a more desirable form. The producers saw the choice as one either of amending the bill back to its original form or of killing it. In contrast, the processors were in favor of passing the Senate version.

Action and Reaction

Continued opposition to the amended version of S. 109 was centered in the USDA and the California bargaining contingent. Whereas the USDA used the meetings with its National Advisory Committee on Cooperatives to develop a critique of the measure, the California group actively solicited support of its position from bargaining associations in other states.

An initial confrontation between the California group and the AFB occurred when Ralph Bunje of the California Canning Peach Association, Kenneth Naden and Robert Hampton of the NCFC and Roger Fleming of the AFB reviewed the Senate passed version at a Washington luncheon. Bunje presented his view that the bill was not satisfactory in its amended form. Fleming indicated, however, that notwithstanding the cooperatives' objection, the AFB would move the bill forward. Following this meeting — with its absence of compromise — Bunje sent a letter to state bargaining groups in which he and other West Coast managers stated their opinion that the amended bill was worse than no bill at all.[1] Furthermore, the letter suggested that any substantive change from the original bill was unacceptable and should be opposed by every organized farm group.

The impact of Bunje's letter among state Farm Bureau bargaining associations was marked. Some, such as the Oregon Farm Bureau, were sparked to express considerable alarm to the AFB over the bill's provisions. Specifically, the Oregon group was concerned with the authority given to proces-

1. Ralph Bunje (General Manager, California Canning Peach Association), letter to Ohio Agricultural Marketing Association, September 6, 1967.

sors and handlers.[2] Given the bill's amended provisions, this authority was viewed as potentially troublesome for a producer association if "captive" growers, or growers who were processor-oriented, claimed that they had been "coerced" during an association membership drive. The Oregon Farm Bureau requested a thorough re-evaluation of S. 109 by the AFB.

Like the West Coast bargaining associations, the USDA conducted a thorough legal analysis of S. 109 in preparation for the House hearing. Before deciding upon an explicit stand on the bill, the USDA consulted with members of its Cooperative Advisory Committee on September 12. Assistant Secretary of Agriculture John Baker chaired this meeting and discussed certain findings of the Administration's staff. He reported that the department had concluded, based upon legal interpretations by the Office of the General Counsel and the views of Administration liaison people close to Secretary Freeman, that the Senate version of S. 109 would be detrimental to producer associations. In short, it was a "processor" bill. In explanation of this interpretation, Baker argued that: (1) the mandatory requirement that the complainant give security was a serious burden to a small cooperative's initiation of a suit; (2) the prohibition that made it illegal for a cooperative "to pay or loan money . . . *or offer any other inducement or reward to a producer . . .* for terminating an agreement with a handler" jeopardized the cooperative's patronage refund practice; (3) other language in the bill would induce handlers to harass cooperatives en masse and subject them to costly litigations. The "inducements" prohibition alone, in USDA's view, meant the bill would, in its effects, be worse than no bill at all. As a consequence of its conclusions, the USDA decided to testify in favor of amending the bill back to its original form.

The Committee of "17" farm groups also met to discuss the members' proposals to the bill and to clear them with other farm groups. Many of the organizations shared the feeling that their all-out support for the bill before the Senate subcommittee hearing precluded their taking a posture of total objection to the bill before the House committee. While most wanted to see cooperatives exempted from the bill's prohibitions, the group found their earlier testimony for the bill made it difficult to formulate a strategy in opposition. Moreover, it was difficult at this stage to argue that cooperatives would not be subject to the applications of the bill.

In a last minute maneuver, many of the groups of the "17" sent letters to their members encouraging contact with members of the House Agriculture Committee. The NCFC suggested to its members that the Senate version of the bill contained several provisions that offered "more threats than benefits to cooperative growth."[3] In an "Action Bulletin," Robert N. Hampton,

---

2. Howard Fujii (Director, Commodities and Farm Labor, Oregon Farm Bureau), letter to John C. Lynn (Legislative Director, American Farm Bureau Federation), September, 6, 1967.

3. Robert N. Hampton (Director of Marketing and International Trade, National

Director of Marketing and International Trade, encouraged NCFC members to send telegrams to congressmen emphasizing that the bill "as it now stands is on the balance adverse to farmers and cooperatives." In light of the heavy activity directed against the Senate version and the threatened overshadowing of S. 109 by a bigger bargaining proposal hinted by the Administration, the AFB felt compelled to take the case to its members.

A further complication for AFB was created when Congressman Joseph Resnick of New York, a member of the House Agriculture Committee, chose this moment to speak out. As reported in *The New York Times*, Resnick delivered a scathing attack on the Farm Bureau by charging, among other things, that the AFB owned and operated oil refineries and other giant industries; provided platforms for radical right-wing speakers; maintained a confusing and improper relationship with federal farm agencies such as the Extension service; and enrolled members for the purpose of selling them insurance.[4] While the AFB offered to open its doors to a congressional investigation of its operations in response to these charges, the publicity damage had been done. Although the attack was not aimed directly at S. 109, it was indicative of what AFB might expect from Resnick before the House Agriculture Committee.

The atmosphere of crisis and uncertainty permeated the September meeting of the AFB Board of Directors. Following the meeting, AFB President Shuman sent a letter to all state Farm Bureau presidents and secretaries acknowledging that considerable confusion and misunderstanding had developed concerning the provisions of the Senate version. To clarify AFB's position and counter misrepresentation, Shuman stated that the AFB was for "passage of the best possible bill." He encouraged state officials to develop a widespread understanding among Farm Bureau people and to enlist the support of other organizations in their states.[5] In an enclosed memorandum explaining changes in the Senate version of S. 109 point by point, the AFB indicated that it would have preferred to retain the original language but in the spirit of compromise "accepted the changes made by the Senate in order to preserve the opportunity to obtain Senate passage of the basic provisions of the bill." [6]

In sizing up AFB chances before the House Agriculture Committee, Herbert Harris viewed the Senate version in a simplistic sense as reflecting

Council of Farmer Cooperatives), "Action Bulletin" to members and Board of Directors, September 15, 1967.

4. "Farm Group Asks Inquiry of Itself," *The New York Times*, September 3, 1967.

5. Charles B. Shuman (President, American Farm Bureau Federation), letter to state Farm Bureau presidents and secretaries, September 15, 1967. Feelings generated against S. 109 were so great that many Farm Bureau members thought their organization no longer supported the bill.

6. American Farm Bureau Federation, memorandum, "S. 109, The Agricultural Fair Practices Act of 1967." This memorandum accompanied Shuman's letter of September 15, 1967.

the views of three broad groups. First, all of the USDA's recommendations were reflected in the new bill. Secondly, the bill reflected some recommendations by other farm groups. Finally the opponents to the original measure had had their say.

However, the version now before the House was drawing sharp criticism from the Grange and the USDA about provisions — such as having cooperatives defined as handlers — that they had originally insisted be put into the bill. Harris discovered the basis for this opposition during several meetings with Mr. Baker and USDA officials at which the USDA General Counsel, Mr. John Bagwell, made some "very stiff" legal arguments against the language of the Senate version.[7]

Still, the AFB calculated the prehearing lineup on S. 109 as follows: organizations that would support the bill included the NFU, NMPF, AFB and the NCFC. Organizations thought to be opposed included some members of the NCFC, and the USDA, with the latter operating covertly.

On September 21 at 10:08 A.M., House hearings on the Senate version of S. 109 convened in an atmosphere of excitement and anxiety before the full Agriculture Committee. The tension pervading the hearing room was a product of the publicity given to the Administration's endorsement of farm bargaining measures and Congressman Resnick's attacks upon the AFB. Committee Chairman Poage called the hearing to order with 28 of the committee's 34 members present, a turnout that in itself indicated that the House hearing was not an ordinary one. Whereas many of those scheduled to testify on the measure had testified already on the Senate side, some new faces were also in evidence.

Senator Aiken, chief Senate sponsor of the bill, led off the long list of witnesses by testifying that the bill was designed to "protect a producer's right to a free choice" to belong to a cooperative association.[8] While the Senator's emphasis upon the "right to a free choice" was new in relation to his previous testimony, he nevertheless insisted that the objectives had in no way been changed since the original introduction of the measure in the Eighty-ninth Congress. According to Aiken, S. 109 was a good bill. Before Aiken left the witness stand, however, Poage asked him a question that signaled a major concern that was to be present throughout the hearing: "Would you think it would be proper to enlarge the scope of this bill to include a prohibition against discrimination against a farmer because of membership in a labor union?" Anticipating that the question was aimed at concern over NFO activities, Aiken conveniently sidestepped.

No sooner had the labor-union issue surfaced than another was raised in

7. Herbert Harris, III (Legislative Counsel, American Farm Bureau Federation), personal interview, June 11, 1968.
8. George Aiken (Senator, Vermont), testimony in U.S. House of Representatives, Committee on Agriculture, *Hearings on S. 109*, 90th Cong., 1st sess., 1967, 4.

the form of a parliamentary inquiry by Representative Resnick concerning the disclosure of information by witnesses as to what associations they represented.[9] In reply to this question, obviously aimed at the pending testimony of AFB President Shuman, Poage replied that House Rules permitted such a question if it was relevant to the matter under discussion. The issue of who spoke for whom also was to receive considerable attention throughout the committee hearing.

Assistant Secretary of Agriculture John Baker, speaking for the Administration and the Department of Agriculture, backed the earlier version of the bill. He indicated, however, that the original objective of the legislation had been turned in the Senate from one of reaffirming producers' rights to join together and to operate cooperatives to one of protecting the producer in the exercise of a free choice. The adamant Baker followed his observation by suggesting that the bill seemed now designed to protect members from their own cooperatives. He charged that the new version, furthermore, overlooked the fundamental relationship between the farmer and his association that establishes the latter as an off-farm extension of the farmer's own farm operations.[10]

The USDA offered 15 amendments aimed at specific modification. These included the deletion of the "free not to join" phrase in the declaration of policy section and the modification of the "inducements" prohibition so that it did not apply to cooperatives. Baker bluntly stated that without these changes, the bill was totally unacceptable to the department. The questions put to Baker and John Bagwell, General Counsel of the USDA, dealt largely with their views of the application of S. 109 to general farm organizations as contrasted to cooperatives.

> *The Chairman.* Specifically, does it [S. 109] protect the farmer's right to belong to the National Farmers' Organization, . . . and, . . . does it protect the right of farmers to belong or not to belong to a labor union?
>
> *Mr. Baker.* Mr. Chairman . . . as I read the bill, it does not have provisions with respect to labor unions or with respect to general farm organizations. The bill relates to bargaining cooperatives or other associations that producers set up for the purpose of bargaining with the buyers of their commodities.
>
> *The Chairman.* Then I understand that you do not interpret this to protect a member's right to belong to the Farm Bureau or the Farmers Union or the Grange.

9. Joseph Resnick (Representative, New York), testimony in *ibid.*, 6. This inquiry referred to Mr. Shuman's presidency of the National Food Conference. The association was formed to discuss the economic, social and nutritional importance of food. Membership in the conference includes some of the largest food processors and retailers in the country, plus such diverse groups as the American Medical Association, Chicago Mercantile Exchange and others.

10. John Baker (Assistant Secretary, USDA), testimony in *Hearings on S. 109*, 9.

Mr. Baker. Mr. Chairman, as I understand it . . . this bill simply does not address itself to the problem of membership in general farm or-organizations.[11]

This interpretation by the Assistant Secretary of Agriculture characterized the thinking of most department officials and legislators who had handled the bill. However, it seemed oblivious to the bill's being sponsored by the AFB for the purpose of giving its bargaining endeavors a firmer legislative footing. In effect, the whole analysis of the bill by its former supporters now focused on how it might adversely affect marketing cooperatives, which Baker described as "one of the finest forms of private enterprise in this country." The original purpose of S. 109 to protect new bargaining activities undertaken by general farm interest organizations, such as the AFB's AAMA and the NFO, had been scrapped. Despite the apparent confusion over organization roles, Baker maintained under questioning that it was the purpose of the Administration and USDA to "advance and obtain more protection for the right of producers to organize and bargain collectively, to enhance their bargaining power, to raise their prices and their income on the products they sell." [12]

When pressed by Congressman Thomas Abernethy of Mississippi for a department position on the bill, Mr. Baker gave an off-the-cuff answer.

Mr. Abernethy. Don't you feel that there would be a net gain under this legislation?
Mr. Baker. No, sir. As it now is raised here, we are afraid there is a net loss.
Mr. Abernethy. Then you oppose the bill if there is a net loss?
Mr. Baker. I am urging, as persuasively as I can, that you make some amendments in the bill so that it can be a net gain for producers and their bargaining cooperatives.
Mr. Abernethy. If there is a net loss, then you wouldn't want it passed?
Mr. Baker. That is correct.[13]

Baker now found himself confronted with a series of questions from a very angry Congressman Resnick from New York. In the exchange that ensued, Resnick attacked cooperatives for not following open membership policies in the "classic cooperative" tradition and for the control that state Farm Bureaus in Ohio, Illinois and Michigan maintained over cooperative organizations.[14] Developing his attack, Resnick charged that such organizations were monopolistic and more corporate than cooperative in nature. He cited examples in which farmers were turned away from cooperatives because of the farmer's membership in other farm organizations. In defense, Baker, a former official of the National Farmers Union, brilliantly defined and defended

11. *Hearings on S. 109*, 13.
12. Baker, testimony in *ibid.*, 19–20.
13. *Hearings on S. 109*, 20.
14. Resnick, testimony in *Hearings on S. 109*, 31.

cooperative action and indicated that no evidence had been introduced in testimony to support Resnick's claims.

Congressman Resnick's apparent intent to confront AFB President Shuman personally went unfulfilled when Shuman conveniently left town to address a Farm Bureau meeting in Iowa. Instead, the AFB testimony was presented by Allen Lauterbach, the chief architect of the original bill, and by one of the bill's chief legislative strategists, Herbert Harris.

ALIGNMENT OF PRESSURE GROUPS
HOUSE HEARING ON S. 109
September 21 and 22, 1967

FOR SENATE VERSION WITH MINOR CHANGES	FOR ORIGINAL 1967 VERSION OF S. 109, BUT OPPOSED TO SENATE VERSION
Farm Groups	National Council of Farmer Cooperatives
American Farm Bureau	USDA
National Milk Producers Federation	National Grange
National Livestock Feeders Association	National Farmers Organization
	National Farmers Union
Processor Groups	Pacific Northwest bargaining associations
National Tax Equality Association	California bargaining associations
National Canner Association	Midcontinent Farmers Association
National Broiler Council	
Independent Livestock Marketing Association	
National Association of Frozen Food Packers	
Chamber of Commerce	
cotton alliance	

In presenting the AFB statement, Lauterbach indicated that his organization preferred the original language of the bill but was "committed to the passage this session of the best possible bill." [15] The AFB statement reiterated that the organization did not seek and would not support legislation to force processors to negotiate with marketing associations. The AFB offered only three amendments, two directed to language improvements. The third, however, proposed deletion of the phrase "free to join togther or not to join together" and recommended substitution with "free to join together voluntarily." This change would prevent the right "not to join" being classified as a legislative finding. Even though AFB still wanted inclusion of the treble-damages provision, the decision had been made that insistence upon the provision would jeopardize ultimate passage of the bill.

In response to questions from Poage and others, Lauterbach suggested that the bill would protect a farmer's right to join any association of producers that comes within the scope of the Capper-Volstead Act. However, when

15. Allen A. Lauterbach (General Counsel, American Farm Bureau Federation), testimony in *ibid.*, 42.

Poage asked if the protection applied to the AFB, the NFU or the National Grange, Lauterbach replied that as far as the AFB or the state Farm Bureaus were concerned, the bill would not apply.[16] Resnick then subjected the AFB representatives to grueling questions about the relation of certain state cooperatives to the state Farm Bureaus. The New York Congressman argued that cooperatives such as the Michigan Farm Services organization were not controlled by the owner-users but rather by the Michigan Farm Bureau — another corporate entity. Accordingly, Resnick argued that S. 109 should guarantee farmers the right to take the same action against "the so-called co-ops where the control no longer lies with the farmers, as it does with respect to processing organizations." [17] Harris characterized Resnick's accusations as being another "broad-gauge attack against the cooperative movement."

The finale to the AFB testimony came in a question by Congressman Zwach from Minnesota.

> *Mr. Zwach.* On February 9, I introduced H.R. 5275, which is in the form of the original bill. Now, I thought that the original bill didn't give producers too much bargaining power. Now it is my feeling S. 109 is considerably watered down. It is still your position that the original bill is the best if it can be attained?
> *Mr. Lauterbach.* Yes.[18]

The testimony by other farm groups that followed the AFB, in the main, argued for amending the Senate version of S. 109 back to its original form. To this end, representatives of the Committee of "17" left no ultimatum: it was either that or withdrawing their support for the bill. In his first S. 109 hearing appearance, L. C. Carpenter, Executive Vice-President of the Midcontinent Farmers Association, Columbia, Missouri, testified that his organization had favored the original version of S. 109 but that the bill as amended and finally passed by the Senate was "totally unacceptable and should either be amended by your committee or promptly killed." [19] Carpenter saw the inclusion of the disclaimer clause as completely changing the intent and purpose of the bill.

Carpenter's case for amending the bill back to its original form was followed by the testimony of Harry Graham of the National Grange, one of the leading spokesmen for the Committee of "17." The lengthy testimony of Mr. Graham was based upon analysis of Senate Committee Print No. 2 instead of the Senate-passed version, indicating the difficulty many groups were having in keeping abreast of the versions of S. 109. Nevertheless, the Grange representative eloquently illustrated how many industry groups used double-talk on federal order and S. 109 legislation by arguing that any action to improve

16. *Ibid.*, 44.
17. Resnick, testimony in *Hearings on S. 109*, 56.
18. *Hearings on S. 109*, 58.
19. L. C. Carpenter (Executive Vice-President, Midcontinent Farmers Association), testimony in *ibid.*, 59.

farm income would automatically eliminate producers from business, while at the same time promising that adequate income would be forthcoming to farmers through the marketplace. He made an emphatic point that the Senate and House committees were becoming the only recourse and the court of last resort to producers. According to Graham, the producer was required in no other segment of the economy to place his product upon an unpredictable market without any assurances about price or opportunities to bargain for a better price.[20]

Pointing to the inequality of bargaining power and the perishability of farm products, Graham argued that Senate changes rendered the bill unacceptable to the Grange because (1) it was not a fair bargaining practices bill; (2) it had no penalties for unethical practices; (3) it did not provide for effective prosecution; (4) it was a direct threat to present bargaining associations. Graham argued that the bill was as "antifarm as it is possible to make it"[21] and pointed out to the committee that producers would have to choose one bargaining association, as opposed to many, or suffer the consequences that labor faced prior to the Wagner Labor Relations Act. After lengthy testimony designed to give Congressman Resnick an opportunity to clarify his position on cooperatives and to allow other committee members to return from a roll-call vote, Graham concluded by suggesting that whereas a large segment of the farming community had been sold a "bill of goods" against labor legislation by the processing community, producers actually had needed legislation similar to that of labor since the 1930's.

The Farmers Union, unlike organizations that sent minor officials to testify before the committee, sent its President, Tony Dechant. He testified that the principle of cooperation is a cornerstone of his organization and that S. 109 would help determine whether the independent farmer-owner-operator could remain in business or whether the nation would move to a corporate type of farming.[22] Dechant took a very positive approach to S. 109 by offering language that would improve the bill. To illustrate the need for legislation similar to S. 109, Dechant cited extensively from the four-year-old Arkansas broiler case in which the Packers and Stockyards Division had "done their best to enforce existing law, . . . [but] have not been able to obtain relief for the broiler growers who attempted to organize a cooperative."[23] According to Dechant, the Senate Agriculture Committee amended the bill "not only [to] throw a cloud on efforts of those attempting to organize cooperatives or gain additional members, but to open the door for harassment of cooperatives."[24]

20. Harry Graham (Legislative Representative, National Grange), testimony in *ibid.*, 64.
21. *Ibid.*, 67.
22. Tony T. Dechant (President, National Farmers Union), testimony in *Hearings on S. 109*, 76.
23. *Ibid.*, 79.   24. *Ibid.*

As improving language, the NFU suggested that the bill should state explicitly that a cooperative could offer a patronage refund or a dividend as a device to gain new members and retain old ones. The NFU also offered five amendments.

The arguments offered by the Midcontinent Farmers Association, Grange, NFU and USDA prompted an exchange between Congressman Poage and Dechant.

> *The Chairman.* You have made it quite clear that you feel the original bill is much more desirable than the bill that we have before us. . . . There is no criticism of you at all or of anybody who has testified, but it doesn't make much sense to take as proponents of the legislation someone who can make as powerful an argument against the bill as the last several witnesses have made. After all, if they are the proponents of the bill, it doesn't need any opponents.
> *Mr. Dechant.* Mr. Chairman, as I said . . . we don't give up lightly on including tobacco and cotton cooperatives nor do we feel very good about giving up on the criminal provisions, but we are willing to do this because we think that the bill is necessary, but we couldn't go along with it unless there was some strong language in there encouraging and supporting cooperatives and if it didn't take out the inferences that cooperatives might be damaged under the provision.[25]

Other organizations testifying in behalf of the bill included the NMPF, NCFC, NFO and representatives of bargaining associations in the West. Representing the NMPF, Mr. M. R. Garstang, General Counsel, testified that his organization recognized that the Senate version represented a compromise but that the bill as written still retained the basic objectives. The NMPF did criticize the disclaimer provision but indicated that it was willing to go along with it. In resting the case of the milk producers organization, Garstang emphasized the need for injunctive relief and argued for continued deletion of the criminal provisions.[26]

One of the most significant bits of testimony on the amended version of S. 109 was supplied in a statement filed by Robert Hampton, Marketing Director of the NCFC. In his argument for the legislation, Hampton stressed that the original intention of S. 109 was to assist farmers attempting to form a bargaining association, not to assist those established "operating" cooperative activities that were no longer so vulnerable to duress or discrimination by noncooperative handlers. According to Hampton, the program of farmers' bargaining historically had been viewed by farm leaders as one to "*supplement*, not to replace or conflict with, useful and well established cooperatives which are already responsive to farmers' interests and needs." [27] Hampton's

25. *Hearings on S. 109*, 80.
26. M. R. Garstang (General Counsel, National Milk Producers Federation), testimony in *ibid.*, 88.
27. Robert N. Hampton, statement in *ibid.*, 89. My italics.

statement represented one of the clearest articulations of the true purpose of the original bill.

Hampton indicated that the Senate version of the bill did not describe or endorse this purpose, which was to "encourage farmers to take group action toward equalizing their negotiating strength in dealing with large and powerful food handling organizations." [28] Using the recommendations of the National Commission on Food Marketing as a reference, the cooperative council announced its continued support for the objective of the original bill. To support its claim that it was still supporting the bill, the NCFC offered more than ten amendments. Included were deletion of the last two-thirds of the disclaimer clause relating to dealings with producers on a direct basis and reinstatement of treble damages in the enforcement provisions.

Clearly the NCFC felt it had lost the battle to secure exemption for cooperatives from the definition of "handler" in the bill, and so no amendments were offered to this effect. However, the council did have doubts whether bargaining associations such as NFO were covered by the definition of handler and thus offered an amendment to Section 3a to include in the definition of "handler" any person engaged in the business or practice of "contracting or negotiating contracts or other arrangements, written or oral with *or for* producers or associations of producers." A phrase was also added to the prohibition section for the same purpose. As recommended, the prohibition section b made it unlawful to "discriminate against any producer with respect to price, quantity, quality, or other terms of purchase, acquisition, or other handling of agricultural products because of his membership in *or contract with* an association of producers." In effect, the NCFC amendment was similar to one introduced later by Congressman Latta on the House floor.

NFO had testified in support of S. 109 before the Senate Committee, but in a filed statement before the House group, Mr. Harvey Sickels argued that the bill as amended was a regulatory act applicable to bargaining associations and was poor legislation.[29] The NFO singled out the disclaimer-of-intent provision and made reference to the Ohio tomato case to make its point.

> The Act as presently worded is a bill to aid the processors of farm products who buy from the farmers . . . the processor may under the provisions of Section 5 of the Bill deal directly and individually with producers. This direct, individual dealing with a producer was a part of the reason the processor was successful in nullifying the efforts of the bargaining group in the "Tomato" case. This Act would legalize this direct approach so the processor can nullify the efforts of bargaining groups without fear of legal action. This Act is one which a processor who buys from the farmer should be happy to support. We are of the belief that no farm organization should support it.[30]

28. *Ibid.*, 88.
29. Harvey Sickels (Executive Secretary, National Farmers Organization), statement in *Hearings on S. 109*, 150.
30. *Ibid.*, 151.

The NFO, a topic of frequent discussion throughout the hearing, went on record as being "firmly" opposed to the bill.

Representatives of other bargaining associations also took negative stances with respect to the Senate version. Speaking for five Pacific Northwest bargaining associations, Mr. Walter Collett, Manager of Oregon-Washington Vegetable and Fruit Growers Association, testified that they were "diametrically opposed" to S. 109 in its Senate form. Collett admitted that he was deeply disturbed about the fact that the passengers had "switched trains," [31] an observation of the fact that the original proponents were now compelled to be opponents of the amended bill. If the needed legal climate for bargaining associations were not created, Collett argued, huge corporate farms would take over agriculture to the detriment of consumers. While the northwest bargaining associations did not look upon the original S. 109 as a panacea, Collett did emphasize their belief that it would correct "some of the business immorality" that was evident in fruit and vegetable marketing.

Ralph Bunje, by this time AFB's villain, made perhaps the strongest case for bargaining legislation. With the President of the California Canning Peach Association, Mr. Ugo Cavaini, Bunje presented lengthy testimony to the committee. The crux of Bunje's testimony was that state laws, such as the California provision after which S. 109 was modeled, did not provide adequate protection to bargaining associations. Bunje argued that "the problems were national in scope and would only be solved by national legislation." [32] If farm prices were to be raised, the Congress should give farmers the right to accomplish it through their own organizations. The prerequisite to improving farm incomes was to "create a desirable legislative climate to enable these farmers to develop bargaining associations." [33]

In a no-holds-barred attack on the Senate version, Bunje contended that all the protections afforded by the original bill had been deleted. Instead of the bill's affording producers additional protection, Bunje saw the Senate version as undercutting the protection originally accorded the association.

> The Senate bill has weakened its own objectives by effectively denying the association standing to sue under section 6 for violations of section 4 directed at its members and prospective members and by subjecting the association to limitations, the necessity of which are not supported by any evidence before the Senate committee. . . . Finally, the penalty provisions of the act, . . . were watered down . . . [and] I cannot see that there is any real inducement to comply with the act.[34]

Bunje's position was that growers would be better off without any legislation, "than with a weak bill that actually lessens their ability to bargain at arm's length with processors of fruits and vegetables." [35]

31. Walter R. Collett (Manager, Oregon-Washington Vegetable & Fruit Growers Association), testimony in *Hearings on S. 109*, 173.
32. Ralph Bunje, testimony in *ibid.*, 107.
33. *Ibid.*, 120.   34. *Ibid.*, 110.   35. *Ibid.*

These statements by farm organization leaders before the House committee made one fact abundantly clear: the first united farm front in twenty years had splintered. The crippling amendments inserted by those who worked their will on the Senate subcommittee had successfully divided and conquered the farm front. Reasons of professional jealousy and a lack of objectivity had made farm organizations, as pointed out by Congressman Poage, their own worst enemy. Not only had many proponents become major critics of the Senate version, but there was also a conspicuous absence of groups that had supported the measure since the first hearing in June of 1966. The absentees included the California Farmers-Consumers League, the Cooperative League, the National Catholic Rural Life Conference and various dairy bargaining associations.

The final breakdown indicated that the AFB, National Milk Producers Federation and the National Livestock Feeders Association supported the Senate version of S. 109 with minor amendments. By contrast, members of the Committee of "17," including the NCFC, sought to protect cooperatives and to amend the bill back to its original form. Three farm groups — the California bargaining associations, the bargaining associations of the Pacific Northwest and the NFO — were for some type of farm bargaining legislation but were unequivocally opposed to the Senate version and offered no improving recommendations.

In contrast to its performance in uncompromising opposition to S. 109 in earlier hearings, the processing community quietly went along with the Senate version of the bill before the House committee. Indeed, some former opponents gave their endorsement to the Senate measure.

Leading off the testimony in opposition before the House Agriculture Committee was the National Tax Equality Association represented by Mr. Earl Kintner. The strongly anti-cooperative group noted that its recommendations for improving the legislative text had been, in large measure, adopted by the Senate. Nevertheless, the NTEA maintained that the bill involved unnecessary duplication of existing law and argued with the legislative approach exemplified by S. 109. In brief, the group quarreled with the idea that legislation should be "tailored to one specific industry" rather than to broad trade regulation applicable to all industries.[36] The NTEA argument closely paralleled those before the May Senate subcommittee hearing that S. 109 involved "class" legislation. On specifics, Kintner argued for reinstatement of certain terminology in the prohibitions section that had appeared in Senate Print No. 2. He also requested the committee to recognize the likely creation of interagency disputes because of uncertainties of responsibility between the Attorney General or the Secretary of Agriculture for the initiation and control of litigation.

36. Earl W. Kintner (Counsel, National Tax Equality Association), testimony in *Hearings on S. 109*, 93.

During questioning from committee members, Congressman Resnick turned his attack to the FTC and to the need for legislation similar to S. 109. Focusing on the changing economic organization of agriculture, Resnick suggested that the practical effects of the broiler situation were that the "Federal Trade Commission did not raise one finger to cope with this particular situation." [37]

Mr. Resnick. Mr. Kintner, I am very surprised . . . that you feel that these inequities which are now being visited upon farmers in certain areas, poultry in particular, are within the jurisdiction of the Federal Trade Commission. . . . Now I can speak from personal experience as to what this has done to an entire industry. It has changed the broiler and poultry industry from an industry consisting of many small independent family-sized farms into an industry . . . where 70 to 80 percent of all broilers are now being produced by three or five producers. . . . Now are you saying to us we don't need this type of legislation, that there is legislation available. Where was the FTC when this was all going on?
Mr. Kintner. Well, I haven't been at the Federal Trade Commission since 1961 . . . So I cannot speak to this particular factual situation, . . . I suppose that the choice was made either by the Government agencies or by the applicants to take this course of action . . . I don't know. [38]

Congressman Zwach from Minnesota posed a similar question to the former FTC official.

Mr. Zwach. Mr. Kintner, you undoubtedly are aware that the agricultural situation in the United States is the worst it has been in 30 years. There is almost the seed for revolt here. . . . Now they are desperately looking for a way to get more muscle or strength, more bargaining power. Now, you oppose this. What constructive suggestion do you have in this area? Do you think they have adequate structure now or do you want them all in your cities?
Mr. Kintner. I would suggest that there is adequate machinery under the law, sir. If there is a shortcoming, it is probably in the failure to properly use that machinery. [39]

Testimony of a slightly different nature was forthcoming from other opponents of the bill. In a filed statement with the committee, the U.S. Chamber of Commerce still maintained that there was insufficient evidence to support the need for S. 109 but argued for retention of the Senate amendments if the bill was passed by the House. Groups representing the cotton industry presented filed statements that attempted to justify the continued exclusion of cotton from the bill. However, the hard-core testimony on S. 109 was

37. Resnick, observation in *ibid.*, 97.
38. *Hearings on S. 109*, 96.
39. *Ibid.*, 98.

presented to the committee by representatives of the Independent Livestock Marketing Association, NCA, National Association of Frozen Food Packers, NBC and several large independent producers.

Speaking for the ILMA, which represented 105 independently owned and operated auction and daily markets in the Midwest, Mr. C. E. Connor announced that the Senate-approved form of S. 109 would be acceptable to his organization as a progressive piece of legislation.[40] He expressed concern about activities of the type carried on by the NFO in 1965 against producers shipping to both cooperative and independent livestock markets. The discussion of NFO led to an exchange between Chairman Poage and Congressman Smith from Oklahoma regarding the applicability of S. 109 to general farm interest organizations.

> *The Chairman.* This question has to be put. Is the National Farmers Organization a marketing association — and is the Grange, the American Farm Bureau Federation and the Farmers Union — are they marketing associations under the terms of this bill?
> *Mr. Smith.* Well, as I understand, the organizations mentioned are not primarily marketing associations. If they were at some future date to convert themselves into some similar body, then I presume that they would be, under the law, but as it stands today I do not think that they would.[41]

The Poage-Smith dialogue indicated that the functional relations of farm organizations, and the applicability of S. 109 to this type of bargaining activity, were still hazy.

When Edward Dunkelberger took the stand to represent the NCA, whose member organizations account for packing approximately 85 per cent of the nation's production of canned fruit, vegetables, meat and fish, it became apparent that his testimony was co-ordinated with that of other trade groups. Dunkelberger indicated the nature of his commitment to the Senate-passed bill by saying:

> . . . we concluded that the [Senate] committee amendments went far enough toward meeting many — if not all — of our objections to justify the withdrawal of the canning industry's opposition to the bill. . . . What had started out as a highly controversial proposal had been so amended by the committee as to satisfy both proponents and opponents.[42]

Dunkelberger stressed that the NCA looked upon the Senate amendments as absolute prerequisites to maintaining a posture of "no opposition" to the measure. However, he did concede to one amendment offered by the AFB in

40. Charles E. Connor (Counsel, Independent Livestock Marketing Association), testimony in *Hearings on S. 109*, 126.

41. *Hearings on S. 109*, 103.

42. Edward Dunkelberger (Attorney, National Canners Association), testimony in *ibid.*, 136.

which the term "voluntary" right to join would be substituted for the right "not to join" in the legislative policy of the bill. Dunkelberger also underscored the necessity of keeping criminal penalties and treble damages out of the enforcement provisions and of keeping the disclaimer clause intact. To support the disclaimer clause, Dunkelberger quoted testimony by AFB President Shuman and indicated that unequivocal statements should be in the record to "make certain that there would be no misunderstanding in this regard." [43] In short, the canners saw the disclaimer section as a safety valve that served as insurance against S. 109 being interpreted as a compulsory bargaining bill.

The frequent arguments by the NCA against the "special interest" nature of the original bill received special attention from liberal Congressman Thomas Foley of Washington in an exchange with the NCA attorney.

> *Mr. Foley.* You would agree that the thrust of the Taft-Hartley Act legislation was against certain practices, alleging improper practices by labor unions?
> *Mr. Dunkelberger.* That is certainly correct.
> *Mr. Foley.* And it was not directed toward correcting any alleged abuses by management?
> *Mr. Dunkelberger.* That is correct.
> *Mr. Foley.* There is not any necessary reason why legislation cannot be one-sided in that sense, is there?
> *Mr. Dunkelberger.* All I can do is to come back to the fact that Taft-Hartley amended labor legislation that had been one sided.
> *Mr. Foley.* All I am saying is this: that if the Congress feels that a certain section of the economy has problems, or has practices that are undesirable, it is not inherently unconstitutional or legislatively impossible, or immoral to do something about these particular problems in that specific area.[44]

Testifying for the National Association of Frozen Food Packers, Mr. Edward Williams indicated that his association favored passage of the bill as amended by the Senate except for the role that the USDA was to play in the enforcement proceedings. Representing the processors of more than 85 per cent of the nation's production of frozen vegetables, fruits and juices, Mr. Williams indicated that his association could see no reasonable basis for the injection of the USDA into the field of trade and business activity.[45] He said his purpose in testifying before the House committee was to urge that there would be no return to the "objectionable" provisions in the earlier bill.

The National Broiler Council brought similar testimony before the committee by announcing that the Senate amendments had removed the principal

43. *Ibid.,* 138.
44. *Hearings on S. 109,* 141.
45. Edward Brown Williams (Counsel, National Association of Frozen Food Packers), testimony in *ibid.,* 147.

basis for the council's opposition to S. 109. As one of the last organizations to testify, the broiler council through its president, Mr. G. Ted Cameron, suggested that there was one major area of agreement among all groups with regard to the bill, namely, that membership in associations of producers should be voluntary.[46] The NBC also added its voice to the warning about enacting "class" legislation. The broiler industry spokesman ventured the opinion, unsupported, that the Senate amendments — rather than making the bill onesided — afforded the farmer "even more protection than under the original proposal." [47] The testimony of the NBC included appearances by four large independent grower-integrators from the Delmarva broiler-growing area. Messrs. Quillen, Wilber, Phillips and Steele had each testified before the Senate subcommittee, and all supported the Senate version of the bill. Steele, a large broiler grower from Trappe, Maryland, who was also a member of Farm Bureau, testified about his concern that the original bill "did not protect me if I chose not to belong to an association." [48] To counter the testimony of the NBC operators, the AFB filed in the hearing record written statements from six farm operators supporting the AFB position.

Only one trade organization recommended that the committee not report favorably on the bill. The Institute of American Poultry Industries argued in a filed statement that the bill was unnecessary insofar as the poultry industry was concerned and suggested that it would inject an atmosphere of distrust and controversy into daily business transactions.[49] This statement constituted the poultry group's first official position with respect to the Senate-passed bill.

From the testimony, it was readily apparent that all of the original opponents of the bill, with the exception of the poultry institute, withdrew their objections to S. 109 as passed by the Senate. The views each expressed in the House hearing were tantamount to encouraging passage of the bill. In so doing, each organization carefully guarded the amendments that had been achieved in the Senate, and only the NCA acknowledged any concessions to the amendments proposed by the various farm groups. The NCA concession was to the AFB.

As the two-day hearing was brought to a close, it appeared that S. 109 faced another crisis. Whereas most of the farm groups insisted upon amending the bill back to its original form, the processors insisted upon maintaining the amendments achieved in the Senate. The fact that some farm groups such as the NCFC and the NFO had filed only written statements was hard evidence that the farm front was badly split. Processors appeared to have maintained their upper hand.

46. G. Ted Cameron (President, National Broiler Council), testimony in *ibid.*, 153.
47. *Ibid.*, 156.
48. James Steele, testimony in *Hearings on S. 109*, 169.
49. Institute of American Poultry Industries, statement in *ibid.*, 189.

Executive Session Mark-up

Amid widespread rumors on Capitol Hill that S. 109 was dead, the House Agriculture Committee on September 26 held executive sessions on the bill immediately following the public hearing. The controversy that now raged was centered within the farm community rather than between producers and processors, as had been the case when the bill was before the Senate. The NCFC, AFB and USDA worked feverishly to rid S. 109 of language they considered to be anti-farm-organization.

The closed session of the Agriculture Committee scheduled for mark-up brought two quick attempts to kill the measure. The first, a motion by Paul C. Jones of Missouri to table further action on the bill, was defeated by a vote of 18–6.[50] This vote was followed by a motion by John McMillan of South Carolina to report out the bill as passed by the Senate. The tally on this motion showed the strength of the processors in the Agriculture Committee and also the committee members' irritation with the Senate action. The motion was defeated when Chairman Poage broke a tie for a final vote of 14–13.[51] After the defeat of these motions, the committee began to consider amendments to the Senate-passed measure. During the executive sessions, the AFB worked very closely with Mrs. May, one of the first sponsors of the House bill in the Ninetieth Congress. The NCFC, in turn, worked closely with Congressman Foley of Washington and also with Mrs. May. Both Foley and Mrs. May went to bat for the farm groups in attempts to amend the bill back to its original 1967 form.

The basic matters before the executive session were the amendments offered by the AFB, NCFC and the USDA in the House hearing. Contrasted to the three amendments offered by AFB in its testimony before the House, the NCFC advocated a total of fifteen in a memorandum distributed to House Agriculture Committee members on September 25th.[52] The NCFC amendments were grouped into two basic categories: those necessary to reaffirm long-standing congressional encouragement for cooperative efforts and those needed to give farmers a net gain in protection for them against unfair processor practices resulting from their cooperative activities. The USDA's interest was in more carefully delineating a Packers and Stockyards type of ad-

50. The motion to table the bill was supported by Congressmen Jones of Missouri, Purcell of Texas, Foley of Washington, Dow of New York, Teague of California and Price of Texas.

51. House Agriculture Committee members voting to pass the Senate version of S. 109 were Congressmen McMillan of South Carolina, Abernethy of Mississippi, Abbitt of Virginia, O'Neal of Georgia, Jones of North Carolina, Nichols of Alabama, Montgomery of Mississippi, Rarick of Louisiana, Belcher of Oklahoma, Wampler of Virginia, Mayne of Iowa, Price of Texas and Myers of Indiana.

52. National Council of Farmer Cooperatives, memorandum, "Summary of Proposed Amendments to S. 109," to Members of the House Committee on Agriculture, September 25, 1967.

ministrative proceeding under the enforcement provisions and in maintaining a record of congressional encouragement of organized farm activity.

Congressman Poage shared these concerns but wanted as well the insertion of language in the bill to prevent a labor union or similar organization's forcing farmers to accept its assistance and representation in establishing prices and marketing contract terms. In short, Poage wanted to avoid a "closed shop" in farm price bargaining. In the eyes of many farm organizations, however, language to this effect, if adopted by the committee, would have been sufficient grounds for killing the bill. Several processing industry organizations also recognized the hazard and suggested to their members that adopting such an amendment would be unwise.[53]

When the committee adjourned the executive session for the day, it had adopted two amendments. One changed the word "control" in the title of the bill to "prohibit," and the other made it clear that the Attorney General was to have discretion in the issuance of complaints. The latter provision was accomplished by striking out the words "shall immediately" and substituting the language "is authorized to" in section 6b of the bill. Still under consideration at adjournment were amendments by Chairman Poage that proposed additions to sections 4a and b of the prohibitions and a proposal by Congressman Foley that the bill be redrafted to apply only to "handlers." The committee adjourned with the committee counsel instructed to check out the language of Congressman Poage's amendments with the USDA. The executive session was not scheduled to reconvene until the following week.

After the first day in the bill's mark-up process, only some relatively minor changes had been accomplished. The NCA regarded the two approved amendments as posing no problems to its interests. In fact, NCA reported to members what it considered would be an "ideal" resolution of conflicts within the committee's closed session.

> The ideal solution to the House Committee's consideration of the bill would seem to be for it to adopt the three additional amendments, which we are identifying as Farm Bureau amendments (in part, they also have the support of the USDA and some of the other farm organizations); keep the two they have already adopted; and come up with an acceptable answer to Chairman Poage's problem.[54]

Under these conditions, the canners trade group suggested that it would even be desirable for the Congress to take final action on the measure that year.

Several farm groups utilized the interim between the September 26th and October 4th mark-up sessions on S. 109 to exchange communications with Poage. Mr. Harry Graham of the Grange indicated that he was deeply

53. National Canners Association, "Government-Industry Report," September 29, 1967. This concern suggests the extent to which many processor associations desired passage of S. 109 as amended by the Senate.
54. *Ibid.*

concerned about the future of S. 109 because the bill had been turned into an antifarmer bill and would pit farmers against farmers instead of righting an inequality that had existed between farmers and processors for many years.[55] Graham further suggested that there was little support among farm organizations for the Senate version. Rather than having the farm groups oppose legislation reported by the Agriculture Committee or forcing congressmen to decide whether to vote for legislation that was antifarm and anti-cooperative, he suggested that the committee table action on the bill and let it die a natural death. As another consideration for Poage's attention, Graham expressed concern that the "agricultural house" would be in such disarray as a result of further handling of S. 109 that it would be incapable of dealing with the 1969 renewal of the Agricultural Act of 1965.

The NCFC also took advantage of the interim to express its concern about the disclaimer clause. In a letter to Poage on September 29th, Mr. Robert Hampton informed the Texas Congressman that the cooperative council could support S. 109 only if the "anti-cooperative parts of Section 5 and other changes" made in the Senate were removed.[56] To emphasize its contentions, it quoted supporting comments from the hearing record by officials of five other farm groups.

While the farm groups were busy lobbying for the amendments they desired, Chairman Poage was involved in some soul-searching himself.[57] Although the cotton ginners in his state continued to express their opposition to S. 109, Poage was now receiving mail from cotton cooperatives in Texas expressing concern about the language in section 4b of the prohibitions involving discrimination against producers. Some of the most influential cooperative leaders in Texas were suggesting that he should let the bill die in committee.

Congressman Poage viewed this dilemma with considerable frustration. From his viewpoint, the bill caused as many problems as it solved. Nevertheless, the measure had passed unanimously in the Senate, and his committee would be in an embarassing situation if it did not act on the bill. Poage was also aware that certain senators had already experienced considerable frustration with the bill. Moreover, the Senate author of S. 109 supposedly had advised Poage that he would like to see the House kill the bill. Somewhat indignant at his attitude, Congressman Poage was sick and tired of having the Senate pass legislation, beat its breast about what it had done for the farmer and then send its dirty linen to the House to be washed.

The Texas Congressman felt it was absolutely necessary to assure farmers of their right to operate without any discrimination because of their membership or lack of membership in an organization. In attempting to work out

55. Harry Graham, personal interview, April 4, 1968.
56. Robert N. Hampton, letter to Robert Poage (Chairman, House Committee on Agriculture), September 29, 1967.
57. Robert Poage, personal interview, June 10, 1967.

language to provide this assurance, Poage submitted an amendment to his committee staff for review. The amendment would have added a new prohibition to section 4:

> It shall also be unlawful for any association of producers to discriminate or to permit any employee or agent to discriminate among its members with respect to price, quality, quantity, or other terms of purchase, acquisition, or other handling of agricultural products or for any association of producers to discriminate or permit any employee or agent to discriminate among nonmembers of such association with respect to price, quality, quantity, or other handling of agricultural products. *Provided*, that nothing in this Act shall be deemed to require any such association to deal in the products of non-members in an amount greater in value than such as are handled by it for members.[58]

In response to Poage's query regarding his proposal, staff members reported that it was "anti-cooperative," that it was one-way against farm organizations but did not apply to other handlers and that adoption of the measure would probably kill the bill.

When the Agriculture Committee again convened in executive session on October 4th, it took into consideration all of the amendments offered by the farm groups and Chairman Poage. However, the AFB amendments received the most concentrated attention. In submitting these to the committee, Mrs. May noted that they were "pro co-op" in nature.

> The first encourages participation in co-ops, the second protects contractual relationships between producers and co-operatives, and the third clarifies the cooperatives' right to encourage a producer to terminate a contract with a handler in order to negotiate a more favorable agreement.[59]

Mrs. May noted that the three amendments were supported by the USDA, the AFB and the NCFC and that they were acceptable to the NCA and other processor interests.

Three attempts were made during the session to revise the bill substantially back to its initial 1967 form. One, a motion by Congressman Foley to make the bill apply only to private handlers, was defeated on a roll-call vote by 23 to 7.[60] A second effort by Foley to strike the disclaimer clause from the bill's provisions was defeated by a vote of 25 to 6,[61] and a motion to delete the exemptions of cotton and tobacco was defeated by a voice vote.

58. U.S. House of Representatives, Committee on Agriculture, files on S. 109.
59. *Ibid.*
60. The motion to make the bill apply only to private handlers was supported by Congressmen Foley of Washington, Vigorito of Pennsylvania, Dow of New York, Brasco of New York, Teague of California, May of Washington and Zwach of Minnesota.
61. The six committee members supporting the motion to strike the disclaimer were Congressmen Foley of Washington, Vigorito of Pennsylvania, Dow of New York, Brasco of New York, Teague of California and Zwach of Minnesota.

The committee did adopt seven additional amendments to the enforcement section and an amendment to the disclaimer clause. The AFB amendments included the deletion of the controversial "not to join" clause. Revisions of the enforcement provisions were designed to allow the courts discretion to decide whether or not security should be posted by the applicant for a restraining order and provided that the measure would not modify existing state law.

Perhaps the most significant revision was a change in the wording of the disclaimer clause by the addition of the words "or contract with." As amended, the controversial clause was made to read as follows:

> Section 5. Nothing in this Act shall prevent handlers and producers from selecting their customers and suppliers for any reason other than a producer's membership in *or contract with* an association of producers, nor prevent handlers and producers from dealing with one another individually on a direct basis, nor require a handler to deal with an association of producers.

In addition to the evidence of its intent provided by the nine amendments, the committee agreed to write a formal report that would stipulate that nothing in the act would prohibit a handler from carrying out competitive marketing practices when seeking business. Rather than adopting a further amendment to section 5, legislative history was approved along this line under the sponsorship of Congressman Robert Dole of Kansas.

As a result of the two-hour executive session, the House Committee on Agriculture voted 28 to 5 to report S. 109 to the House with amendments. Voting against clearing the bill were Congressmen Jones of Missouri, Vigorito of Pennsylvania, Foley of Washington, Teague of California and Price of Texas. Further action on the bill was delayed until a formal report could be written by the committee staff and the bill and report filed with the House. A crucial decision by the committee and House leadership was also pending regarding the time and procedure for floor action. Generally, it was felt that the Chairman would soon ask the House Rules Committee for a resolution for the consideration of the bill.

Mr. Herb Harris, chief AFB strategist of the bill during the House sessions, was elated that the Agriculture Committee version reflected all of the AFB's proposed amendments and that it had passed in the face of growing opposition from the Grange and other farm groups. In a letter to state Farm Bureaus on October 5th, the AFB announced the Agriculture Committee's action on the bill and indicated that the major objectives of the original proposal had been retained.[62] AFB Legislative Director Jack Lynn encouraged the state organizations to promote maximum understanding of the measure and to be ready for an all-out legislative effort within the House in two weeks.

---

62. John C. Lynn, letter to state Farm Bureaus, October 5, 1967.

The AFB had its sights set on the next step, the House Committee on Rules. There, the bill would be examined in the context of total existing legislation and, if passed, scheduled for floor action before the full House.

The reaction of other farm organizations did not match the enthusiasm of the AFB. The NCFC suggested to its members and directors that S. 109 as amended by the House stood as the first congressional endorsement of the dubious principle that "farmers need to be protected from themselves." [63] The NCFC regarded the improving amendments as not sufficient to restore the original "Agricultural Producers Marketing Act" title to the bill. In an emotional statement to members, the cooperative council announced that the bitterest blow was retention of the disclaimer clause.

> The tortured trail of legislative maneuvering on S. 109 speaks volumes about growing political strength of processors and other non-farm interests. The original bill was fought at every step, amended, and amended again, to please almost every non-farmer objection.[64]

In the opinion of the NCFC, the "banged-up" bill was worse than the *status quo.*

The NFU somewhat ironically announced for the first time, while still supporting the S. 109 measure, a concrete legislative proposal of its own. The NFU called for the establishment of marketing or bargaining committees within a legal framework encouraging commodity-by-commodity bargaining with buyers, handlers and processors. Acting on the advice of former Agriculture Secretary Brannan, the general farm interest organization had until this time expressed support for S. 109 for purposes of "membership consumption" while confident that its chances for actual passage were nil.

Review of the amended bill by other farm-oriented groups was not so complimentary. In a lead article in the October issue of the California Canning Peach Newsletter entitled, "Processors Torpedo S. 109," Ralph Bunje stated that S. 109 had been emasculated by processors. Essentially aimed at the Senate version of the bill, the article hinted that bargaining associations would be forced to oppose the House version and that canners, processors and handlers would have to face the consequences of more stringent legislation as proposed by the President and Secretary Freeman.

> Farmers should recognize by the action of the Senate the tremendous legislative influence of the processors and handlers of Agricultural commodities. These organizations were able to prevail on the members of the Senate to take a bill designed to help farmers in their bargaining efforts and turn it into a bill designed to strengthen the bargaining power of the handlers. Small wonder that the processing trade associations

63. National Council of Farmer Cooperatives, "Washington Councilor," October 6, 1967.
64. *Ibid.,* 8.

now regard S. 109 as "their bill" and one justifying their whole-hearted support for final adoption.[65]

Congressman Teague's vote against the House measure and Bunje's continued activity on the Washington scene indicated that the California crowd was still opposed to the measure, even as amended by the House Agriculture Committee.

Intensive analysis and discussion of the amended House measure by USDA officials, and General Counsel John Bagwell in particular, resulted in the conclusion that S. 109 appeared to harm rather than help farmers and their cooperatives. The USDA and various farm groups had demonstrated before the House Agriculture Committee that their chief concern was not to create a legal clause for bargaining associations, the original purpose of the bill, as to protect cooperatives from "undesirable" language written into the bill by the Senate. In no small measure, the situation now pertaining was of the USDA's own making, since it was the USDA that had proposed classifying cooperatives as handlers in the September, 1966, hearing.

The concern shared among USDA officials in a meeting on October 11th was with the prohibitions section that made it unlawful for a cooperative to coerce any producer in the exercise of his right "to join and belong to, or to refrain from joining or belonging to" a cooperative. Similarly, the bill made it unlawful for cooperatives to discriminate against any producer with respect to price or other terms of purchase because of his membership in or contract with a cooperative. Despite the fact that no evidence had been produced to support the necessity for such provisions, the Senate had included the language. USDA officials looked upon the inclusion as providing the seeds for destruction through cooperative infighting, creation of a poor public image and the involvement of cooperatives and USDA in unwarranted litigation.

The likelihood of USDA involvement in litigation proceedings was clear from the wording of the bill. Instead of providing for administrative proceedings, as recommended by the USDA following lengthy discussions with the Justice Department, the Senate version of S. 109 provided for direct court action, an idea sponsored by AFB. Under such enforcement proceedings, cooperatives would be open to harassment by court action by handlers for alleged violation of the prohibitions section. Cooperatives would not have the benefit of administrative "screening" by the Secretary of Agriculture and would be liable to disruptive and retaliatory court action by handlers. Many cooperatives were small and could ill afford the expense of litigation. In contrast, the involvement in expensive litigation was an accepted cost of operation for large-scale business enterprises.

Importantly, USDA officials maintained that the most objectionable

65. California Canning Peach Association, newsletter, "Processors Torpedo S. 109," October, 1967, 4.

part of the Senate-passed bill remained in the amended House version. The department saw the last two-thirds of the disclaimer-of-intent clause as congressional encouragement for handlers to deal with producers directly and individually rather than through cooperatives or bargaining associations. The clause was considered an endorsement of individual rather than collective dealings between producers and those who purchased their products and a reversal of a fifty-year congressional policy. Finally, the USDA could see no justification for the exclusion of cotton and tobacco commodities from the bill. The exclusion was looked upon as a type of discrimination. Taking the prohibitions and disclaimer sections together, the USDA General Counsel concluded that there was doubt as to which side of the bargaining process the bill would help. These findings were brought to the attention of members of the Cooperative Advisory Committee in a meeting on October 16th.

Further attention was given to the bill by the Committee of "17" farm groups when it met on October 9th, following analysis of the amended House bill by individual member groups. The consensus of participants in the meeting was reflected in a legislative analysis memorandum of October 20 by Angus McDonald of the NFU. McDonald argued strenuously against certain provisions of the bill.

> The bill includes language reminiscent of hypocritical arguments against the Wagner Act and in favor of right-to-work laws. The words "to join or not to join" and the discussion in the Senate Report of normal trade relationships attempts to equate the giant lion oligarchy with the rabbit farm co-op. Using a similar metaphor, it turns the chicken out of the coop to fight it out with the fox on an equal basis.[66]

McDonald felt the bill as amended by the Senate pretended that farmers and cooperatives were equal in the marketplace and that there was no difference between the economic power of a cooperative and a group of giant corporations. In this regard, the NFU felt that the original purpose of the bill had been perverted and that the policy of Congress with regard to cooperatives had been changed by inference. Some of the language was accordingly viewed as worsening the bargaining-power situation of farmers instead of correcting the "great" disparity. The inclusion of this language "indicated an attempt to not only perpetuate the *status quo* in the market place but to enlist the support of anti-labor forces in Congress and elsewhere." [67]

The tangled situation prevailing after the House committee's action suggests that the farm organizations awoke only gradually to the implications of the Senate subcommittee's mark-up of the bill and didn't involve themselves in an intensive legal analysis and discussion of its provisions until after the House committee's action on the bill.

66. Angus McDonald (Research Director, National Farmers Union), "Legislative Analysis Memorandum #7-67," October 20, 1967.
    67. *Ibid.*

The fight against the "anti-co-op" language was led by Ralph Bunje but later spread to the other farm organizations as well. General alarm over the Senate provisions peaked toward the end of October and largely grew out of belated concern for the language in the Senate committee report and its place in the "line of legal dignity." For purposes of interpretation of a new law, the Supreme Court generally follows a prescribed analysis of the measure in the following order: (1) the statute is read and interpreted itself for its raw meaning; (2) the committee reports are analyzed to see why certain aspects were included or deleted and the reasons for the same; (3) the floor debate is examined for more precise interpretation of what the legislators intended the bill to mean; (4) the courts can as a last resort refer to the public hearing records.[68] The rank of the committee reports to which the farm organizations attached great importance was therefore second in the line of legal dignity.

In contrast to the general negative attitude of farm groups, the processor trade organizations such as the NCA reported to members that the House amendments, while favorable to "bargaining associations," weren't sufficient to justify opposition.[69] The bill at this point still contained the disclaimer clause in which the canners placed a lot of stock.

As a result of the conflicting pressures and the unhappiness of farm organizations with the bill as amended, Chairman Poage on October 17 introduced a "clean" bill known as H.R. 13541. The House Agriculture Committee met once again and reported the bill by a vote of 21 to 4. The new bill was identical to the version reported earlier by the committee except for a number change designed to permit easier handling in the House. Following its reporting of the bill, the Agriculture Committee finally submitted its report on H.R. 13541 to the whole House on October 26th. The report contained a statement and description of committee action on the bill and a minority report of opposing views by Congressmen Foley and Teague. Although the report stated that the committee amendments were designed to give producers and their associations a more favorable position than that established by the Senate version, Foley and Teague maintained in their minority report that the amended House version offered a direct and implied threat to the system of agricultural cooperatives.[70] In a report signed only by himself, Congressman Zwach of Minnesota maintained that while the bill had been substantially weakened, it nonetheless contained some good features that could be used as a base for further strengthening of farm bargaining techniques. The bill's next encounter was with the House Rules Committee.

68. I am indebted to Hyde Murray (Minority Counsel, House Committee on Agriculture) for clarifying this line of legal dignity.
69. National Canners Association, "Government-Industry Report," October 4, 1967.
70. U.S. House of Representatives, Committee on Agriculture, *Agricultural Fair Practices Act*, Report No. 824, 90th Cong., 1st sess., 1967, 8.

Congressman Sisk and the Bottle-up

The process of legislating on Capitol Hill sometimes proceeds on the basis of personalities as well as on the substance of pending legislation. When H.R. 13541 (S. 109) was referred to the Rules Committee for resolution, attention of the contestants shifted to Congressman Bernie Sisk of California. A personable legislator from the San Joaquin Valley, Mr. Sisk was recognized as an authority on agricultural legislation and was frequently consulted on agricultural matters by Congressman William Colmer, in his first term as Chairman, when farm bills came before the House Rules Committee. Given this clearing position, Sisk enjoyed the reputation of being one of the "big four" agricultural powers in the House, along with Colmer, Page Belcher of Oklahoma (the ranking minority member), and Bob Poage, Chairman of the House Committee on Agriculture.

Since the Rules Committee had the final say on the bill, Sisk's power was substantial. Only Congressmen Teague and Robert Mathias, a young Republican who lacked seniority, were California members on the Committee on Agriculture. Mathias, like other California congressmen, rode the fence on H.R. 13541 in its revised form and channeled his views through Sisk. Like Teague and Mathias, Sisk became fully aware of the importance attached to the revised bill through communications from cooperatives and bargaining associations operating in his area, as well as through those from large corporate canning interests such as the Del Monte company. The energies of Ralph Bunje, leader of the West Coast bargaining contingent in developing opposition to the bill were enormous, and the controversy raging over the fair practices bill was as acute in California as any other state in the Union.

Sisk's initial contact with S. 109 had come early in the life of the bill when the California bargaining associations, Farm Bureau and the California Farmer-Consumer Information Committee all lobbied in support of the proposal. From Sisk's viewpoint, any measure that merited the support of these strange bedfellows merited a close look.[71] The Farm Bureau was strong in Fresno County. Furthermore, the California legislator was personally acquainted with farm bargaining activity through the organization and growth of the Raisin Bargaining Association in his home district. The new producer association, which had been officially incorporated on December 9, 1966, featured Congressman Sisk as its speaker at the first annual meeting held in Fresno on December 7, 1967. As a result of these contacts, Sisk was familiar with the organization problems of bargaining associations and with the limitations of existing statutes as they applied to bargaining activity. He saw a need for protective and more extensive bargaining legislation.

As amended by the Senate and revised by the House Agriculture com-

71. B. F. Sisk (Representative, California), personal interview, June 14, 1968.

mittees, H.R. 13541 (S. 109), contained provisions that prohibited certain acts by cooperatives. Even before the bill reached the hands of the Rules Committee Chairman, the NCFC had resolved its position on the House bill. The activity of Bunje and the West Coast bargaining contingent had stirred sufficient alarm among operating cooperatives involved in packing fruits and vegetables that the NCFC was able to take a firm stand against the measure as amended. In a memorandum dated October 25th, which was later mailed to council members, the NCFC pointed to two features of the bill that it found exceedingly objectionable: the disclaimer of intent and the prohibitions applying to cooperatives.[72] The NCFC viewed the disclaimer clause as "diametrically opposed" to the ability of farmers to work through one agent in developing marketing strength; the application of prohibitions to cooperatives it considered an expression that farmers needed protection from their own cooperatives.

> Therefore, it is an open invitation to dissension and to fragmentation and to pitting one group of farmers against another. The disunity which exists among farmers and farm organizations at the present time is more than we can stand and we do not need to have any more encouraged by an Act of Congress.[73]

As a signal to the Rules Committee power structure and to the council's membership strength to marshal, the NCFC sent an "Action Bulletin" to its California members requesting defeat of the bill in the Rules Committee.

According to the council, the bill had not been sufficiently improved by the House to remove its harmful features. Consequently, the council reported it was joining other farm organizations in "requesting the Rules Committee not to grant it a rule for House floor action." [74] Three members of the Rules Committee were singled out by the NCFC for immediate contact to stop the measure: Congressmen H. Allen Smith and Sisk of California and Spark Matsunaga of Hawaii. Letters, personal contacts and telephone calls were urged in a concerted and vigorous effort to defeat the bill. A telegram from the Sunkist cooperative to another farm group in Hawaii was typical of the response to the NCFC request:

> Request help with Congressman Spark Matsunaga in preventing the granting of a rule for clearance to go to floor with H.R. 13541. Stop. This bill in its present form is anti-cooperative, anti-farmer and would do damage to the position of farmer co-ops and b. associations in representing farmers.[75]

72. National Council of Farmer Cooperatives, "Memorandum on H.R. 13541 (S. 109)," October 25, 1967.
73. *Ibid.*
74. Kenneth D. Naden (Executive Vice-President, National Council of Farmer Cooperatives), "Action Bulletin" to California members, October 27, 1967.
75. D. M. Anderson, telegram to a farm organization in Hawaii, November 1, 1967.

The California effort was supplemented by a letter to Congressman William Colmer, Chairman of the House Rules Committee, on October 31st in which Kenneth Naden announced that the cooperative council "vigorously protests the tone of withdrawal of affirmative Congressional support for farmer cooperative action as expressed particularly in Section 5 of H.R. 13541." [76] The council requested that a rule be denied to the pending bill.

The activity of the California bargaining associations and the NCFC also had impact within the processor trade organizations. Some operating cooperative managers had covertly opposed S. 109 through their trade groups at earlier points in the life of the bill. Now they questioned the position those same organizations were taking in support for a bill that applied to their cooperatives. Widely differing opinions concerning H.R. 13541 were expressed in the canning industry. As one cooperative leader expressed it, the bill could be "damaging, directly and indirectly, to farmers' opportunities to act together for more equity and orderliness in the market place." [77] The over-all effect was disquieting to the National Canners Association.

The action requests of the NCFC had their payoff when the Rules Committee met on November 16th and voted to postpone consideration of the measure. The contacts initiated by such marketing cooperatives as Sunkist, Calcan and Sun-Maid Raisins generated pressure sufficient to stymie action on the bill and also to retard the resistance of the NCA to certain proposed amendments. Nine of the committee's fifteen members voted against reporting the bill. The National Canners Association reported to its members that the two California congressmen on the committee, Sisk and Smith, were against reporting the bill and that their opposition was probably the decisive factor.[78]

In response to the unrest within the canning industry, the National Canners Association stressed to members that it had carefully avoided any reference to "cooperatives" and endeavored to make it clear that it was the "bargaining associations" who would be brought under the terms of the legislation if the processors were to be covered.[79] The canners argued that the hearings demonstrated that producers needed protection from associations organized under the Capper-Volstead Act. Furthermore, NCA acknowledged that had it not been for politics and Freeman's hints of broader legislation, the NCA would have continued to oppose the bill on the grounds that it was unnecessary. However, the political situation dictated that passage of the amended bill was the best over-all strategy.

76. Kenneth D. Naden, letter to William Colmer (Chairman, House Committee on Rules), October 31, 1967.
77. Operating cooperative manager, letter to Robert Heiney (Director, Government-Industry Relations, National Canners Association), October 30, 1967.
78. National Canners Association, "Government-Industry Report," November 16, 1967.
79. National Canners Association, "Government-Industry Report," November 20, 1967.

Victors in the successful bottling of the bill in the Rules Committee were the NCFC, the West Coast bargaining association crowd and other farm groups and governmental agencies against the bill. Ken Naden reported to members of the NCFC that the action taken by the Rules Committee was the direct result of their prompt and effective action. Had the bill not been stopped, Naden said, it would have passed the Rules Committee and perhaps the full House. He took the occasion to point out two factors demonstrated by the council's action: (1) the necessity of close cooperation between a national and a local effort in such an undertaking and (2) the effectiveness of selective action on a national scale.[80]

The postponement of H.R. 13541 (S. 109) terminated action on the fair practices bill for the first session of the Ninetieth Congress and for the year 1967. However, discussion of further bargaining legislation was very much alive. The press coverage of the NFU's bargaining proposal had been extensive, and similar coverage had been given a speech by Senator Mondale indicating that he was preparing to introduce a national bargaining bill of his own. In November, a press story suggested that President Johnson was planning to stress the need for bargaining legislation in his annual State of the Union message.[81] In addition, the most hotly debated resolution at the NMPF annual meeting, according to A. Olivia Nicoll, was a proposal to give cooperatives or federations thereof, which represent more than half of the dairy farmers in a market, the right to be certified by the Secretary of Agriculture to represent and perform marketing services, including bargaining for price and other terms of sale for handler requirements, on behalf of all the dairy farmers supplying the market.[82] This resolution, which was finally approved, was designed to amend the Marketing Agreements Act and to stave off a National Farm Relations Board as recommended by Secretary Freeman. In a further development, the Justice Department reportedly dropped its antitrust suit against the NFO in exchange for a pledge of advance notice of any future attempt to keep farm products off the market.[83] This agreement reached between the Justice Department and the NFO extended through 1972.

Obviously, no one had a monopoly on the collective bargaining idea. For the AFB, the procedural delay in handling H.R. 13541 represented the first major setback during the Ninetieth Congress. What once constituted a united farm front in common pursuit of a piece of protective legislation had disintegrated into warring factions among the farm organizations. The falling

80. Kenneth D. Naden, letter to Members of National Council of Farmer Cooperatives, November 27, 1967.

81. "Collective-Bargaining System for Farmers May Be Proposed in State of Union Speech," *The Wall Street Journal,* November 13, 1967, in files of National Canners Association.

82. A. Olivia Nicoll, "Dairy Industry Newsletter," November 22, 1967, 5.

83. National Canners Association, "Government-Industry Report," December 6, 1967.

out of farmers and their organizations, and not the lobbying activity of the processors and handlers, had brought the progress of S. 109 to a halt.

In the wake of the House postponement, Ralph Bunje suggested to AFB President Shuman that a conference should be called in California to discuss changes that would enable the bargaining associations to support the bill.[84] The two main objections of the bargaining association leader were clear: (1) he couldn't support legislation that undertook to protect members from their own associations so long as they were voluntary organizations and (2) he couldn't support legislation which stipulated that handlers could deal directly with members of an association. The initiative for resolving these issues was left in the hands of the American Farm Bureau.

84. Ralph Bunje, letter to Charles B. Shuman, December 7, 1967. In initiating this contact, it appears that Mr. Bunje felt that he, like other farm leaders, had over-reacted to the House version of S. 109. As one of the early promoters of national bargaining legislation, he therefore made initial overtures to the AFB for seeking a compromise and salvaging a "piece of something."

In its original form S. 109 would
have stimulated the development of
bargaining associations. In its present form it may do this.

A Washington Observer

Chapter 10

Horsetrading in Fresno, Horseplay on the House Floor

To the great surprise of many farm officials who thought H.R. 13541 (S. 109) was dead, a resolution of differences among opposing farm forces, which led to floor action on the bill, was brought about in the Fresno, California, offices of Congressman Bernie Sisk in early January of 1968. The confrontation that took place in Fresno resulted directly from Sisk's key role on the Rules Committee and the uniqueness of his district's constituency.

Fresno County ranks high among the 3,000 U.S. counties as one of the largest single producers of agricultural commodities. In Sisk's district alone, over 230 different commodities are grown, ranging from such perishables as vegetables and fruits to various row crops, nuts, wine and grains.[1] The 16th Congressional District is also one of the top ten cotton producing districts nationally. The spectrum of farm operators in Sisk's constituency thus included members of such well-known marketing cooperatives as Sun-Maid Raisin, California Canners and Growers and Sunkist, as well as those affiliated with bargaining associations and with Farm Bureau as well. To the presence of these basic farm organizations in the 16th, vestiges of the peripheral industries such as canners, cotton oil mills and other handlers could be added. In sum, all of the pressures manifest in the three-year S. 109 controversy were present in Congressman Sisk's San Joaquin Valley district.

The Fresno Meeting

Sisk found himself in a difficult position with respect to House action on H.R. 13541. Although he had been a cosponsor of the original 1967 House version of S. 109, he was unhappy with the bill as it came to the House from the Senate. He felt that the improving action taken by the House Committee on Agriculture was a positive step but still short of the changes needed to make the bill acceptable.[2] Farm operators in his district, responding to the efforts of Ralph Bunje and others, registered their continued displeasure with

1. B. F. Sisk (Representative, California), personal interview, June 14, 1968.
2. Tony Coelho (Legislative Assistant to Representative Sisk), personal interview, June 10, 1968.

certain provisions in the amended bill. Furthermore, Sisk felt personally that cotton did not merit exemption from the bill, as called for.[3] Given these circumstances, Sisk was content to keep the bill in the Rules Committee, short of House action.

But pressures mounted on a national front from local bargaining associations and Farm Bureaus for some type of legislation. In the 16th district, the organizing experiences of the Raisin Bargaining Association dramatized the need for legislation. Bargaining associations recognized that the pending bill, while not a panacea, was a potential help in their efforts to secure recognition. The efforts of the associations served as a strong local stimulus in the 16th district. Informal contacts with representatives of various farm organizations in his home district finally convinced Sisk that the bill was neither as bad as Bunje and other cooperative leaders thought, nor as good as the Farm Bureau people claimed. He found himself caught in the middle and began to look for a way out.

The climax to the mounting pressures came late in 1967, when Allan Grant, President of the California Farm Bureau, suggested that a meeting of the protagonists should be held in Sisk's office.[4] On January 5, 1968, representatives of various farm organizations met in Fresno at the invitation of Sisk. He had hopes of reaching an agreement that would permit him to support the bill and get it out of the Rules Committee. Attending the meeting were Allen Lauterbach and Herbert Harris of the AFB, and Grant, Richard Owens and Russell Richards of the California Farm Bureau. The California cooperatives were represented by Ralph Bunje of the California Canning Peach Association, Allen Mather of Sun-Maid Raisins, Robert McInturf of Allied Grape Growers and Richard Johnson of the California Cooperative Council. Issues were clearly drawn in the ensuing discussion with Congressman Sisk.

As spokesman for the California bargaining associations, Bunje indicated his desire to enact some type of bargaining legislation but maintained that the bill as written would not help bargaining efforts. Specifically, he wanted to delete the term "association of producers" found throughout the bill, a phrase he regarded as giving the bill a two-way-street philosophy. (The NCA had, of course, insisted on its inclusion as double insurance in case the definition of the term "handler" was revised in the legislative process to exclude cooperatives.) In addition, Bunje wanted section 5 — the disclaimer clause — deleted in its entirety.

When the discussion reached the point at which the cooperatives were asked the bare minimum they could accept as amendments to the bill, Bunje alone defended the cooperative position. Mather and McInturf, who also served as First Vice-President of the NCFC, were strangely silent and offered

3. Sisk, interview.
4. Allan Grant (President, California Farm Bureau, personal interview, December 12, 1968.

no support.[5] As a consequence, Bunje retreated from his stand of firm opposition and moved toward the idea that any bill was better than no bill at all. He did, however, insist upon the deletion of the "association of producer" phrases and the last two parts of the three-point disclaimer-of-intent provision.

The AFB people were not able to give complete assurance that their organization would support the Bunje changes,[6] although they indicated that they would not actively oppose them. Significantly, no agreement was reached regarding when or where in the process these amendments were to be made. Sisk felt the over-all effect of the two-hour meeting was productive because "it washed the dirty linen and pin-pointed the positions of each farm group. I learned a lot from that session." [7] The Congressman from Fresno had gotten a mandate to proceed with amendments to the bill.

Herb Harris of the AFB discussed the proposed amendments with the Washington office staff upon his return and secured their support to go along with the changes if necessary. However, the AFB people had reservations about Bunje's request to delete from the disclaimer the provision that nothing in the act should "require a handler to deal with an association of producers." [8]

The proposed amendments were then discussed in turn by the AFB with Senators Aiken and Jordan, and their approval was sought. Clearing the amendments with representatives of the NCA was a major task for the AFB, but it was made considerably easier by Bunje's efforts to get the California cooperative canners active on the bill.[9] As a result of the ensuing interest, Edward Dunkelberger held several meetings with Sisk and representatives of the canning cooperatives. In addition to the impetus provided by the cooperatives, the AFB received a boost from the talk about the Mondale bill, not yet introduced. It was at this time that the NCA finally accepted the AFB argument that legislation of the Mondale type could be delayed by getting S. 109 written into law. Consequently, the bill with the "Sisk" amendments was accepted by the canners, but with something less than enthusiasm.[10]

Upon his own return to the capital, Congressman Sisk personally sought the commitment of several groups to support his amendments. As expected, the AFB was somewhat hesitant in giving its commitment but finally agreed to Sisk's request. A similar commitment was obtained from the NMPF. The NCFC turned out to be the hardest organization for Sisk to con-

5. *Ibid.*

6. Herbert Harris, III (Legislative Counsel, American Farm Bureau Federation), personal interview, June 13, 1968.

7. Sisk, interview.

8. John Datt (Legislative Director and Assistant Director, Washington Office, American Farm Bureau Federation), personal interview, June 11, 1968.

9. William Anderson (Assistant Legislative Director, American Farm Bureau Federation), personal interview, April 2, 1968.

10. Harris, interview.

vince, because of its initial apprehension that allowing any amendments under an open rule would invite antifarm legislators further to emasculate the bill.[11] NCFC officials were also concerned about the influence the processors might exert through certain congressmen. The history in the Senate subcommittee had provided a lesson that amendment could result in a form completely unacceptable to farm organizations. The NCFC resistance forced Sisk to deliver an ultimatum: Either the NCFC went along with his amendments or it would have to assume responsibility for killing the bill in the Rules Committee. As an original supporter of S. 109, the NCFC did not relish the idea of being tagged with killing the bill. After carefully reconsidering the merits of the bill, NCFC supported forward movement.

In addition to his efforts with the producer groups, Sisk asked and received commitments of support from the NCA and the Del Monte Canning Company. Each "agreed reluctantly" to the amendments — despite the fact that they wanted some additional language written into the bill — when it became apparent that this was the only compromise to which all parties could agree.[12] Having cleared his pending amendments with the opposing forces to the bill, Sisk consulted with Senators Aiken and Jordan to assure their full knowledge of the action he was proposing in the House.

The results of the Fresno and follow-up meetings were significant. Shuman's testimony before the Senate subcommittee had removed the AFB as a proponent of any strong "bargaining" bill. Bunje's activity following Senate passage of the bill, however, was a source of constant discomfort to the NCA and other trade organizations.[13] The associations had persuaded other cooperative people to become active on the bill. Clearly, Bunje's personal desire to get a piece of farm legislation that would protect farm bargaining groups was intense, and he worked tirelessly. The efforts of Bunje and the associations succeeded in registering sufficient protest to the amended bill to make impossible further movement without additional changes.

The NCA could not find a way to negotiate with the bargaining groups and still preserve the features that they thought were desirable in the bill. Robert Heiney of the NCA felt that the inclusion of the disclaimer-of-intent provision by the Senate subcommittee had been a victory in changing the bill to suit his association; he recognized now that the compromises worked out in Fresno had the limited effect of "rolling back the carpet" toward the original 1967 bill.[14] As proposed, the changes were known as the "Sisk" amendments and the measure as the "Bunje" bill. Congressman Sisk did not make himself available for further consultations with farm groups after the initial commitments had been reached.

11. Coelho, interview.
12. *Ibid.*
13. Robert B. Heiney (Director, Government-Industry Relations, National Canners Association), personal interview, April 3, 1968.
14. *Ibid.*

The Mondale Bill

Senator Walter Mondale of Minnesota startled Capitol Hill and farm circles on February 15, 1968, when he introduced his bargaining bill, S. 2973, to the second session of the Ninetieth Congress. Known as the "National Agricultural Bargaining Act," the bill was cosponsored by Senators Burdick and McGovern of South Dakota, Mansfield and Metcalf of Montana, McCarthy of Minnesota, Nelson and Proxmire of Wisconsin, McGee of Wyoming and Young of North Dakota. Of these cosponsors, McCarthy, Young and Burdick had also cosponsored the original S. 109. In substance, the new bill represented a materialization of the trial balloon first floated in Secretary Freeman's Press Club speech. President Johnson's endorsement of some type of bargaining legislation in his State of the Union Message on January 17th had brought the idea closer to reality.

The Mondale measure really consisted of three bills in one. Title I provided for the creation of a five-member National Agricultural Relations Board appointed by the President, and for the establishment of bargaining committees along commodity lines. The general concept, which could be identified closely with the NFU proposal announced in October of 1967, thus called for the creation of an entirely new legal framework and procedural apparatus. Title II of the bill, strongly supported by the USDA, was framed as an amendment to the Agricultural Marketing Agreements Act of 1937. The amendment was intended to permit the establishment of minimum prices through collective bargaining between producers and purchasers, in addition to the existing hearing procedure under the Secretary of Agriculture. Title III of the bill — a potential embarrassment to the AFB — was really a reintroduction of the original S. 109, modified to provide for a Packers and Stockyards type of administrative proceeding in the enforcement provision rather than the injunctive-relief provision originally sought by the Farm Bureau.

The impact of such a "radical piece" of bargaining legislation on the agri-business community was earth-shaking. Although a similar proposal had been first suggested by M. W. Thatcher, General Manager of the Farmers Union Grain Terminal Association, before the Senate Agriculture and Forestry Committee in 1947, it had not then had even the possibility of legislative pursuit, given the continuance of World War II price support levels. Many Washington observers who viewed the Mondale proposal's chances skeptically could nevertheless recall the first reactions that had greeted the compensatory-payments idea when Charles Brannan, then Secretary of Agriculture, first suggested it in 1947. The fact that, according to Joseph O. Parker's recollection, one authority even then suggested that legislation permitting such payments was already on the books [15] did not alter the view of Brannan's idea as a radical proposal. Within a few years, however, the idea

15. Joseph O. Parker (Attorney), personal interview, June 12, 1968.

no longer seemed so, and almost every feature of the plan is now written into current agricultural programs.

As Robert B. Heiney, spokesman for the processor lobby, put it, "Everything that was in the Brannan Plan [in 1947] that was a radical piece of legislation is now on the books. A precedent has been set which suggests that we can expect legislation will be enacted with respect to bargaining." [16] The Chairman of the Senate Agriculture and Forestry Committee, Allen Ellender of Louisiana, was quick to react to the Mondale proposal by scheduling Senate hearings on the bill for April. If the Brannan Plan offered any precedent, action on the national bargaining proposal was unavoidable. In the light of the Mondale bill, the "Agricultural Fair Practices Act" that was pending before the House looked increasingly like manna from heaven to the processor groups.

House Floor Debate and Amendments

Very little action took place on H.R. 13541 (S. 109) during the first two months of 1968. Finally, Congressman Poage, Chairman of the House Committee on Agriculture, made a second request for a rule before the House Rules Committee on March 12th. Following Poage's request, the Rules Committee took up discussion on the bill for the first time since the November 15th meeting in the first session. In requesting rules action, Poage reminded committee members that the bill had been referred to them in October and noted that certain difficulties with the bill had received further consideration. He said that he would propose two amendments — the "Sisk" amendments — if the Rules Committee would authorize its consideration in the House, and he identified them as (1) removal of the language "association of producers" wherever it appeared in the measure and (2) the deletion of the phrase "nor prevent handlers and producers from dealing with one another individually on a direct basis" in section 5. To circumvent the technicality that the Rules Committee cannot make amendments, Poage indicated that he and the members of his committee would accept any amendments agreed to before the Rules Committee.[17]

Congressman Sisk, originally responsible for bottling the bill up in the Rules Committee, reported that the amendments proposed by Poage were acceptable to farm and processing groups. At this point, however, Congressman Del Latta of Ohio expressed astonishment at Poage's proposal. Latta obviously considered the amendments inconsistent with the two-way-street approach of the bill as passed by the Senate and reported by the House Agriculture Committee.[18] A conservative whose home district included strong pro-

16. Heiney, interview.
17. Anderson, interview.
18. Delbert Latta (Representative, Ohio), personal interview, June 12, 1968.

cessor interests such as Libby, Hunt, Heinz, and Campbell Soup, Latta wanted to make sure that farmers would be "protected" against possible coercion by a bargaining association as well as a handler.

The NCA reported that Poage answered Latta by stating that the removal of the "association of producers" phrase did not exempt such organizations from the measure because they were defined as "handlers" elsewhere in the bill and subject to handler provisions.[19] He said the "association of producers" language was superfluous and for all practical purposes had been added to the Senate measure for insurance purposes in case the definition of "handler" were changed. Latta persisted in his questioning and indicated that he was not entirely satisfied, and that he felt the bill was unnecessary.

With support from Congressman Page Belcher, the ranking minority member of the Agriculture Committee — and despite some opposition led by Congressman Richard Bolling — Poage's request was considered by the Rules Committee. A rule was subsequently granted H.R. 13541 (S. 109) with the stipulation that Poage and others would on the House floor engage in legislative history that would clarify the amendments. The bill was reported out of committee on March 12th with the understanding that all of the groups would accept the Sisk compromises and that only these compromises would be accepted.[20] Sisk agreed to handle the bill on the floor. The "Bunje" bill had cleared another hurdle and was scheduled to be taken up on the floor on the following Thursday morning, March 16.

By the evening of March 12, however, considerable turmoil had broken loose. Congressman "Sonny" Montgomery of Mississippi was very upset because the National Broiler Council had now decided upon opposition, based on its suspicion that the Rules Committee had sold out to the farm organizations. Montgomery was embarrassed to the point of being apologetic over the new maneuver by the NBC.[21] The NBC action resulted from information given Attorney James Rill and Frank Frazier of the National Broiler Council by a man covering the Rules Committee. From reports, Rill and Frazier suspected that the proposed Sisk amendments would exempt associations of producers from the bill and were thus unacceptable. As a consequence of the NBC action, the schedule established for floor action on the bill had to be withdrawn until the NBC was pulled back into line.

The NBC was adamant that bargaining associations should be covered by the bill and that the fact of coverage be clearly established. To accomplish both, an agreement was reached between the AFB and the NBC to allow Congressman Phil Landrum of Georgia to make legislative history on the House floor that would clarify the meaning of the bill as far as the broiler processors were concerned. As a backup measure, the NBC and NCA prepared

19. National Canners Association, "Government-Industry Report," March 13, 1968.
20. Coelho, interview.
21. *Ibid.*

and had ready an amendment to the bill that would ensure that bargaining associations were covered.[22]

The NBC was not alone in raising objections to the "Bunje" bill. The NTEA also objected to the deletion of the "association of producers" language. The effect of the muscle flexing of these two organizations demonstrated to AFB strategist Herb Harris that to achieve legislation providing protection for bargaining associations or cooperatives, it was necessary to move through the legislative arena without raising significant objections from the processing and antifarm interests.[23]

Herein was the dilemma surrounding the compromises reached in Fresno. Instead of insisting that H.R. 13541 be returned to the Agriculture Committee for amendments before it was granted a rule or insisting that it come before the House floor with a closed rule that was open to amendments from the Agriculture Committee only, the group that met in Fresno allowed the bill to come before the full House under the customary open rule.[24] Amendments could thus be offered on the floor, even though an informal agreement had been reached between Congressmen Poage, Belcher, Colmer and Sisk that only certain amendments would be allowed. In anticipation of additional amendments, a full disclosure to take place on the floor was agreed to in the Rules Committee. Even with these precautionary measures, however, the possibility remained that congressmen representing processor and antifarm interests could maneuver passage of an amendment.

The USDA played one of the most perplexing roles during this time. Having endorsed the original purposes of the bill strongly in the May hearing with an appearance by Freeman, the department now assumed an outwardly "neutral" position on the Senate-passed version in spite of internal feelings that it was an antifarm-organization bill. This passive role was foreshadowed in the House committee hearing when Assistant Secretary John Baker presented lukewarm testimony in behalf of the Administration and the department. Presumably, USDA preferred Title III of the Mondale bill, which was a slightly rewritten S. 109 as introduced in 1967. And, although most USDA officials had felt that the "Bunje" bill stood little chance of passing the Rules Committee, they saw any forward movement as potentially weakening the chances of the Mondale bill.

The position of the department was altered when AFB President Shuman and Freeman met in a brief encounter on Capitol Hill in late January of

22. R. Frank Frazier (Executive Vice-President, National Broiler Council), personal interview, April 3, 1968. This amendment was subsequently offered by Congressman Delbert Latta.

23. Harris, interview.

24. I am indebted to David Leuthold (Associate Professor of Political Science, University of Missouri) for clarifying these options. For further reference, see William J. Keefe and Morris S. Ogul, *The American Legislative Process, Congress & the States* (Englewood Cliffs, N.J.: Prentice Hall, Inc., 1964). Rules resolutions specify the time allowed and the amendments that are in order.

1968. Shuman noted that the extension appropriation was in jeopardy and suggested that AFB and USDA should work together on matters of mutual interest.[25] He informed Freeman that a way had been found to remove the objection of the California people to H.R. 13541 [S. 109], which Congressman Sisk would support, and that the help of the USDA would be appreciated in getting the bill passed. Secretary Freeman agreed to this course of action and designated Assistant Secretary John Baker and FCS Administrator David Angevine as his contact men. However, the Agriculture Secretary was the same day stricken with the flu and was unable to talk with Baker or Angevine. Thus on the next day when Shuman sent AFB Legislative Director John Lynn to the USDA for a visit with Baker and Angevine, Baker indicated that he did not believe Freeman had made any such agreement and repeated that the USDA was out to kill the AFB bill.[26]

Baker's lack of receptivity meant that the AFB had to work again on Secretary Freeman. An opportunity was presented when the Agriculture Secretary and Shuman shared the rostrum at the National Farm Institute in Des Moines on February 15–16. Shuman brought up the S. 109 issue with the Secretary and discussed the Baker incident. True to his word, Freeman agreed to keep the USDA out of the action on the bill.[27] When the measure was pending floor action in March, Tony Coelho, a legislative assistant to Sisk, tried to get a commitment on the Sisk amendments through the department's liaison people. However, "nobody, but nobody" would give the California Congressman a position.[28] Finally, Poage called Tom Hughes, Executive Legislative Assistant to Secretary Freeman, and simply demanded a position. In the absence of Secretary Freeman — who was out of Washington — Mr. Hughes said that the department was in full support of the bill. Subsequent floor debate, however, tended to refute Hughes's statement and suggested that the department was not of one mind concerning the measure.

The rescheduled floor action on H.R. 13541 commenced on Wednesday, March 25th, in an atmosphere of sensitivity. All interested groups watched the movement of the bill in expectation of last-minute changes. The processor and cotton interests maintained a close vigil on the floor proceedings in fear that efforts might be attempted to "roll the carpet back to the bill's original form." [29] The AFB watched the debate closely in hopes of seeing enactment of their bill. Whether AFB knew it or not, however, an impressive array of opposing farm groups, on the basis of a previous meeting, had decided to exert pressures to kill the bill on the House floor. Congress-

25. Charles B. Shuman (President, American Farm Bureau Federation), personal interview, September 25, 1968.
26. *Ibid.*
27. *Ibid.*
28. Coelho, interview.
29. Wesley H. McAden (Executive Vice-President, American Cotton Compress and Warehouse Association), personal interview, June 12, 1968.

man Foley and others indicated privately that they did not give the bill a chance of passing.[30]

The rescheduling of floor action coincided with the second annual National Farm Policy Conference called by the Administration. The conference was to provide Administration and Department of Agriculture officials an opportunity to listen and receive suggestions from industry and farm organization people on farm policy matters. Halfway through the meeting, on learning that the fair practices bill was being debated on the floor, Washington representatives of the NFU, NCFC, NFO, National Grange and the Midcontinent Farmers Association walked out of the policy conference en masse to the chambers of the House.[31] There, the NFU, National Grange, NFO and Midcontinent Farmers Association, with the help of the AFL-CIO, lobbied with House members and their legislative assistants in an effort to amend the bill back to its original form or kill it. Given its previous support for the bill, the NCFC was quiescent and did not lobby against the bill, although it indicated concern.

House action on the bill began when Sisk called up House Resolution 1094,[32] establishing a format for debate including a two-hour limit on general debate that would be controlled by the chairman and the ranking minority member of the House Committee on Agriculture. The bill would then be read for amendment under the five-minute rule during which any member of the House could comment on the bill and offer amendments if he so desired. The committee would then report the bill to the House with such amendments that might have been adopted, and the previous question would be moved. The bill would then be considered for final passage.

Aside from the making of extensive legislative history as had been agreed to in the Rules Committee by Congressmen Sisk, Poage and Belcher, the main discussion during the general debate directed itself to clarifying certain provisions in the bill. Congressmen Abernethy, O'Hara, Foley and Latta each raised questions, Latta again saying that he felt the bill was unnecessary. In the course of the general debate, several issues that surfaced indicated that confusion about which groups were supporting the bill still prevailed. Particularly, USDA's position on the bill seemed to be unclear to House members.

> Mr. O'Hara (Michigan). I hope, really, Mr. Speaker, that we might not complete action on this bill until we have had an opportunity to clear up and consider the provisions of the bill and get them straight in our own minds. I received varying reports. One tells me that the Department of Agriculture is for the bill, and another tells me that it is not. . . .
> Mr. Poage. Mr. Hughes, who is the Assistant Secretary told me that the

30. Kenneth D. Naden (Executive Vice-President, National Council of Farmer Cooperatives), personal interview, June 10, 1968.
31. Datt, interview.
32. U.S. *Congressional Record*, 90th Cong., 2d sess., 1968, CXIV, Part 6, H2150.

Department supported the bill and told me that I might repeat that fact on the floor of the House to the effect that the Department supported this bill if the Sisk amendments were adopted.

Mr. O'Hara. I thank the distinguished gentleman from Texas for this report. It was my information that the Department would not support the bill as presently drawn.[33]

This exchange and the confusion it reflected indicated that the Department of Agriculture's official "neutral" policy with respect to the bill had not reached everyone in USDA. While Secretary Freeman remained true to his word that the department itself would not oppose the bill, his directive was not effectively communicated to individuals and groups holding opposing views within the Department, and certain of its liaison people were active in lobbying against the bill in the House chambers.[34]

Following a lengthy legislative-history exchange, Congressman Hungate of Missouri reflected the dissenting views of certain farm groups.

Mr. Hungate. Mr. Speaker, I have information to the effect that the Midwest Farmers' Association-MFA and the National Grange as well as the NFO, would be opposed to the bill in its present form. I wonder if the chairman of the Committee on Agriculture, the distinguished gentleman from Texas [Mr. Poage] would care to comment upon that? And also what their position would be if the Sisk amendments are adopted?

Mr. Poage. In reply to the gentleman's inquiry I will say that unfortunately I cannot tell the gentleman what their position is now or what it may be if the amendments are adopted.

I have had a communication in writing advising me that the American Farm Bureau Federation favors the bill with or without the Sisk amendments. . . .[35]

The clockwork precision in handling H.R. 13541 that had been worked out in the Rules Committee was hampered by the aggressive lobby against the bill. Congressmen received phone calls in opposition to the bill from influential cooperative and bargaining association leaders in their home districts. According to one AFB official, such calls came in to congressmen from Ohio, Indiana, Missouri and California,[36] and very likely to others as well.

Other members of the House received a flurry of communications through printed word and personal contact. Congressman William Steiger of Wisconsin, a sponsor of a House version of S. 109, received a flyer from the NFU on the morning of March 25th requesting rejection of H.R. 13541.[37] He also received word that the NFO was opposed to it, and while on the

33. *Ibid.*, H2151.

34. Robert N. Hampton (Director of Marketing and International Trade, National Council of Farmer Cooperatives), personal interview, June 14, 1968.

35. U.S. *Congressional Record*, 90th Cong., 2d sess., 1968, CXIV, Part 6, H2152.

36. Harris, interview.

37. William Steiger (Representative, Wisconsin), personal interview, June 11, 1968.

floor, he was called out of the chambers to talk with representatives of farm groups requesting him to oppose the bill or offer amendments to it. Nevertheless, Steiger remained in support of the bill on the basis of encouragement he received from a "new movement" within the Farm Bureau in Fond du Lac and Washington counties in his home district.[38]

Despite the unsettling influence of the activity in opposition, the floor managers clarified their understanding of the bill as best they could. After support was announced by the ranking minority member on the House Committee on Agriculture, the House moved to take action on the bill by a vote of 270 to 39. Congressmen Poage and Belcher were then recognized to direct a one-hour discussion under the five-minute rule upon resolution of the House into a committee of the whole for consideration of H.R. 13541. When all interested congressmen had spoken, Poage asked unanimous consent that the bill be considered as read, printed in the *Record*, and open to amendment at any point.

Sisk, Latta and Foley Amendments

The amendments presented on the floor generated considerable excitement among those following the bill. Congressman Sisk first offered the amendments that had been worked out in Fresno and refined in Washington. In discussing the changes he was offering, the California legislator developed an exchange with Congressman Landrum of Georgia that had been previously arranged to clarify the definition of the term "handler" as it related to broiler processors and cooperatives. Congressman Teague of California then indicated that he would drop his previous opposition to the bill if the Sisk amendments were adopted. At this point, Congressman Latta of Ohio engaged in making some further legislative history with Congressman Sisk.

> *Mr. Latta.* It is my understanding that it is the gentleman's intent not to remove associations of producers from the coverage of this bill but merely to take the specific language out which mentions them so that we are not pointing a finger at these associations alone and also that he maintains that associations of producers are covered under the term "handlers" which appears on page 2. Is that correct?
>
> *Mr. Sisk.* The gentleman is right as I understand the definition. And, not to be redundant, it seems to be overemphasizing this idea of spotlighting a particular group. This is an attempt to remove that implication, and that is the reason why these amendments were offered.[39]

Having clarified all questions related to the amendments, the House Chairman responded to a call for the question on the Sisk proposal, and the amendments were adopted.

38. *Ibid.*
39. U.S. *Congressional Record*, 90th Cong., 2d sess., 1968, CXIV, Part 6, H2165.

The next amendment was offered by Congressman Latta of Ohio, and in introducing it, Latta indicated that his proposals were those discussed earlier in a colloquy with Poage.[40] However, when the Latta amendment was introduced, it contained more than the mere insertion of commas and the addition of the word "or," as he had earlier indicated would be the case. Each of Latta's changes seemed aimed at the definition of the term "handler" and seemed an attempt to assure that bargaining associations would be covered by the prohibitions of the bill. The intention became absolutely clear when Latta unexpectedly proposed including the words "with or on behalf of" in the phrase relating to contracting. His additions changed the definition of handler to include "any person engaged in the business or practice of . . . (3) contracting or negotiating contracts or other arrangements, written or oral *with* or *on behalf of* producers or associations of producers with respect to the production or marketing of any agricultural products."

The Latta amendment represented the careful planning of the NBC and the NCA. Its additional language was unexpected, however, and new to Sisk and Belcher. Further, it went unseen by them in the written form as presented to the Chair. Consequently, the Latta amendment was passed virtually unnoticed until later, when representatives of the bargaining associations had an opportunity to examine the bill. Bunje and Sisk had been beaten on the floor.

Potentially the most far-reaching amendments to H.R. 13541 were offered by Congressman Foley of Washington. The Washington liberal first moved that everything after the enacting clause be stricken and the original text of the bill (S. 109) substituted for it.[41] After objection from Latta, who argued that the Senate would never accept it, Poage rose to object to the Foley amendment because "it reverts to a discredited version" and because it boiled down to a question of "whether you want a part of something — or whether you want to get all of nothing."[42] Poage's position on Foley's first amendment was supported by the ranking minority leader of the Agriculture Committee, Belcher of Oklahoma, and the Foley amendment lost by a vote of 82 to 16. Having been rejected in his first amendment attempt, the Washington Congressman offered another amendment that would have removed the exemption of cotton and tobacco from the bill's prohibitions, a patent attempt to kill the bill. Foley's second try provoked immediate rebuttals from Poage and Belcher and was also rejected.

No more amendments were offered, and the House moved into consideration of final passage of the bill as amended by Sisk and Latta. By a vote of 232 to 90, H.R. 13541 was passed, and the title was amended to read "An act to prohibit unfair trade practices affecting producers of agricultural prod-

---

40. *Ibid.* Part of this discussion took place on the House floor when Congressman Poage agreed to accept amendments that would classify as a "handler" any agent that is "contracting or negotiating contracts with producers." See U.S. *Congressional Record*, 90th Cong., 2d sess., 1968, CXIV, Part 6, H2156.

41. *Ibid.*, H2166.   42. *Ibid.*

ucts, and for other purposes." The bill had survived two attempts to kill it on the House floor. As passed, however, the bill not only contained the Sisk amendments but acquired a somewhat modified form by virtue of the Latta amendment. Several of the bill's original sponsors, such as Congressman St. Germain of Rhode Island, voted against the House measure. Most of the labor vote also sided against the bill. True to the fears of some farm groups, the agreement worked out between Bunje and the California Congressman had not protected them from possible floor amendments. The processors had beaten the floor managers of the bill through the Latta amendment.

A Last Ditch Effort: Requests for a Presidential Veto

The full effect of the Latta amendment was not felt until the day after the House of Representatives passed the measure. Just when the AFB was congratulating itself for getting the measure through the House, Bunje walked into the AFB offices and indicated that the Latta amendment changed the whole character of the bill.[43] Whereas H.R. 13541 as amended by Sisk was not interpreted as covering bargaining associations, Bunje saw Latta's addition of the phrase "or on behalf of" as making bargaining associations subject to the prohibitions of a bill that was originally designed to protect them. The California bargaining association leader felt that no testimony had been presented to the National Commission on Food Marketing or the S. 109 hearings to the effect that farm operators were taking advantage of handlers.[44] Consequently, he felt application of the bill to bargaining associations was unwarranted. The immediate AFB reaction to Bunje's attitude was that he was trying to use the Latta amendment simply as justification for his continued opposition. However, subsequent analysis by other farm organizations led them to the same conclusion that Bunje had reached.

Most observers expected the bill to be referred to a Senate-House conference upon its being returned to the Senate. But in a surprising development, the Senate agreed to the House version by a voice vote on April 1st. The groundwork for the Senate move had been laid by Senator Aiken of Vermont. As Senate sponsor of the measure, he had followed it carefully through the House and had been kept informed about its progress. In a bit of legislative history on the House floor, Poage had stated that "there is no way of making a bargaining rights bill out of (S. 109), nor does it propose to set up a closed shop." [45] Poage's statement clarified to Aiken's satisfaction all but one provision to which he had objection: the Latta amendment. Nevertheless, Aiken regarded the difference between the Senate and House versions of the bill as insufficient to warrant risking a conference. As a result of his decision

43. Harris, interview.
44. Ralph Bunje (General Manager, California Canning Peach Association), personal interview, June 13, 1968.
45. U.S. *Congressional Record*, 90th Cong., 2d sess., 1968, CXIV, Part 6, H2154.

and to the surprise of farm groups still in opposition, the bill never reached the conference stage. Instead it was given its original number — S. 109 — passed and sent to President Johnson for his signature. Another burial attempt was foiled.

Subsequent analysis of the bill by the NFO, National Grange and other farm organizations led them to question whether the amended version contained more potential harm than good. In particular, NFO's analysis prompted it to report that S. 109 was the worst piece of farm legislation ever to come from Congress. NFO's major points of objection were: (1) the Latta amendment defined handlers to include producer associations and made the deletion of the "association of producers" phrases meaningless; (2) the act, which purported to protect farmers' marketing cooperatives and bargaining associations, also now regulated the farmer and his farm organizations; (3) "independent" minded producers who shared in the benefits of group action but did not want to participate in the costs could under the bill tie up producer groups in extensive court litigation. NFO saw each of these features as expensive to farm operators and as antifarm organization in intent. The message of the NFO was conveyed to the National Grange, Midcontinent Farmers Association, NFU and other organizations. These organizations in turn precipitated a major effort to secure a presidential veto.

Support of the dairy organizations was effected, in part, by a telephone call from L. C. Carpenter, Executive Vice-President of the Midcontinent Farmers Association to James Reeves, Secretary of the newly formed regional federated dairy cooperative known as Associated Dairymen.[46] The alerted dairy groups took prompt and effective action on the bill. The newly formed Milk Producers, Inc., headquartered in Texas and an activist component of Associated Dairymen, generated sufficient alarm and resistance within the NMPF that the Board of Directors, after having endorsed the bill in each of three preceding years, went on record as being opposed to the House-passed version of S. 109.[47]

The Associated Dairymen action within the NMPF was supplemented by internal action. Harold Nelson, General Manager of Associated Dairymen, read a report predicting the disastrous effects of S. 109 (reportedly the NFO analysis) at the April 5th board meeting of the Midwest organization.[48] In an "impassioned plea," the Texas lawyer convinced board members that it might be possible for private operators or dissident groups of farmers to use the provisions of the bill to interfere with price negotiations and perhaps obtain injunctions on the strength of discrimination.[49] Nelson urged that Asso-

46. L. C. Carpenter (Execuitve Vice-President, Midcontinent Farmers Association), personal interview, June 26, 1968.
47. E. M. Norton (Secretary, National Milk Producers Federation), personal interview, November 11, 1968.
48. Avery Vose (President, Associated Dairymen), letter to author, May 7, 1968.
49. James L. Reeves (Secretary, Associated Dairymen), personal interview, September 27, 1968.

ciated members request a presidential veto of the bill, and his presentation bore fruit when the board instructed him to use every means at his disposal to obtain a veto of S. 109. The board decided further that member associations should be urged to join in soliciting communications in opposition from individual farmers and farm associations. Before a meeting of Oklahoma dairy industry people the following day, Nelson urged veto action on S. 109, arguing that individual producers could tie up cooperatives on a continual basis with court litigation.[50]

The requests for a presidential veto that subsequently showered the White House came primarily from NFO members and dairy cooperatives. Action taken by members of Associated Dairymen following the board meeting prompted a tumultous request for veto of S. 109 from such Midwestern cooperatives as Land O'Lakes, the Wisconsin Council of Agricultural Cooperatives, Pure Milk Association, Gold Spot and others. Of the approximately 25 telegrams received by the President, about four-fifths were from dairy cooperatives.

In contrast, other farm organizations geared their arguments to thorough legal analysis rather than emotion. Two organizations — the NCFC and the NMPF — were in an extremely precarious position on the bill. Each had been an original supporter of the measure and had remained in support for over three years. Their rejection of the bill after having supported it for this period risked the alienation of many senators and congressmen who had worked hard on the bill. As a result, each supported presidential approval of the bill but did not actively promote it. Similarly, the National Grange was advised by Attorney Al Densil that if the bill wasn't supported by NCFC in its amended form, then the Grange should likewise drop its support for it.[51]

By far the largest number of requests for a presidential veto came from NFO officials and members. Letters and telegrams from Pennsylvania to Oklahoma and from Wisconsin to Tennessee were sent to the President and Secretary of Agriculture. Most followed a similar format, which suggested they were inspired by the national organization. In substance, the NFO letters argued that the act was a regulation of farmers and their cooperatives or associations for the protection of the handlers who bought their products. The impact of the combined efforts of dairy groups and disenchanted general farm interest organizations caused quite a commotion in the Administration. On the eve of the President's signature, a piece of farm-sponsored legislation was being opposed by farm operators and their organizations but supported by the AFB and certain processor groups.

The NBC reported to members that the story of guiding the amended

50. Leo Blakely (Professor of Agricultural Economics, Oklahoma State University), personal interview, August 19, 1968.
51. Harry Graham (Legislative Representative, National Grange), personal interview, April 4, 1968.

version of S. 109 through Congress was one of persistence in the face of great odds.

> Despite powerful opposition, the bill was successfully amended by both Agriculture Committees and then passed by the Senate and House. . . . Much credit for moving the amended bill through the Congress must go to Senators and Representatives of leading broiler-producing states.[52]

The broiler council also took the opportunity to review its two years of involvement with the bill. Whereas NBC had viewed the bill in its original form as a crippling threat to the "entire integrated broiler system," the bill as amended included: (1) the disclaimer clause, (2) injunctive proceedings and compensatory damages instead of the criminal penalties and treble damages, (3) certain guarantees for "independent" producers and processors and (4) assurance that bargaining associations were included in the term "handler" through addition of the phrase "or on behalf of." These changes were attributed to "judicious amending." [53]

The NCA also saw the positive side of S. 109 and did not take long in finding a use for it as ammunition against "special interest" legislation. In an April 9 hearing on general farm programs and farm bargaining power before the Senate Committee on Agriculture and Forestry, Robert Heiney filed a written statement in which he used S. 109 to parry further Mondale type legislation.

> In our view S. 109 as enacted should serve as further assurance that freedom of choice and action will and should be preserved in the purchase and sale of farm commodities for processing. This Association firmly believes that the introduction of private or government compulsion into the bargaining process would be contrary to the interests of growers, processors and the consuming public.[54]

Thus, the canners were quick to utilize the still unsigned bill as a forestalling argument against further bargaining legislation.

USDA officials took up discussion on the bill in response to the veto effort and House and Senate passage of the bill. As viewed by Farmer Cooperative Service officials, the Latta amendment was simply a "belt and suspender" provision that reiterated something already in the bill. FCS officials could not envision a bargaining association operating without contracts. While removal of the numerous "association of producers" phrases deleted some of the window dressing from the bill, FCS regarded bargaining associa-

52. National Broiler Council, "Bulletin," March 29, 1968.
53. *Ibid.*
54. U.S. Senate, Committee on Agriculture and Forestry, *Hearings on The Operation of Programs Established Pursuant To The Agricultural Act of 1965 And Their Continuation, And Proposed Strengthening of Farm Bargaining Power,* 90th Cong., 2d sess., 1968, 407.

tions as being still covered by the terms even without the Latta amendment.[55] To FCS, Latta's phrase was simply an attempt to nail NFO and similar organizations to the wall.

Department officials conceded that, under the bill, cooperatives could be sued by other handlers, for instance other cooperatives, for coercing producers to join in an association or for terminating a contract with a handler. They saw the disclaimer-of-intent provision as encouraging handlers to refuse to deal with farm organizations, and the "two way street" feature of the bill was looked upon as departing from the bill's earlier intent to protect producers in their right to organize producer groups. Despite this application to farm organizations, the department felt the bill did retain the protection originally sought for producers and their associations.

In weighing the possible effects of a presidential veto, department officials viewed the situation that would ensue as a trade-off between the powers of NFO and dissident cooperatives, and the American Farm Bureau. A presidential signature would permit the former groups to claim that the President diminished their potential effectiveness while paying lip service to farmers' bargaining power. A veto would certainly bring charges from AFB that President Johnson vetoed the first bill that Congress ever approved to protect farmers from handlers' intimidation and harassment. With eyes focused on the coming presidential election, the avoidance of an encounter with the AFB appeared the least costly. Furthermore, the USDA's legal analysis of the bill following the September hearing in the House had fostered the conclusion that cooperatives should not be exempted and that organizations of the NFO type should be covered by the bill. The final bill was consistent with this belief. As a consequence of the department's deliberations, Acting Secretary John A. Schnittker wrote a letter to the Bureau of the Budget on April 5th, in which he announced that the USDA was recommending approval of the bill even though it contained certain weaknesses.[56] A memorandum similar in content was prepared by USDA officials and sent to the President on April 12th.

The USDA memorandum paralleled its previous analysis by suggesting that on balance, S. 109 was a good bill. The controversial "Agricultural Fair Practices Act of 1967" awaited President Johnson's signature.

S. 109 Becomes Law

Of the many considerations that must have crossed President Johnson's mind in evaluating S. 109, the general mood of the farm community for more "market muscle" and bargaining rights must have weighed heavily. A poll

55. David Angevine (Administrator, Farmer Cooperative Service, USDA), personal interview, June 15, 1968.

56. John A. Schnittker (Acting Secretary, USDA), letter to Charles Zwick (Director, Bureau of the Budget), April 5, 1968.

A groundswell for more bargaining power had developed among farmers by the spring of 1968, and S. 109 was signed into law as farm bargaining sentiments deepened, which this *Farm Journal* cartoon illustrates.
Reprinted by special permission from *Farm Journal*, May, 1968. Copyright 1968 by Farm Journal, Inc.

taken by the *Farm Journal* in March indicated that 9 of 10 farmers favored new laws for giving farmers more power to bargain on their own without government interference.[57] Over 85 per cent of the more than 12,000 respondents wanted a fair-play "marketing rights" law, and many farm operators wanted to go further. Almost 60 per cent of the respondents agreed that when two-thirds of the producers belonging to a bargaining group voted to have processors check off their dues, that the check-off should be made from non-members as well as members. Furthermore, nearly half of the polled farmers also wanted farm bargaining groups to negotiate with handlers and to have

57. Claude W. Gifford, "Which of These Bargaining Ideas Do You Vote For?" *Farm Journal*, 92, 3 (March, 1968), 34–35.

handlers use only the products of members who belonged to the bargaining group.

Clearly, the sentiment in favor of some form of bargaining was wider than many people had thought. Farm operators wanted to work through their own organizations. The general climate was ripe for bargaining innovations in the farm sector and for arrangements not overly different from arrangements of the "closed-shop" type found in labor. Under these circumstances, the White House considered passage of the fair practices bill, even with its shortcomings, a step in the right direction.

If sufficient momentum was generated from the S. 109 experience, subsequent legislation along the Mondale lines could logically follow. Furthermore, the "No Price — No Production" slogan and the milk-dumping, hog-shooting antics of the NFO had moved the demands of farm operators squarely into the political spotlight, as *The Wall Street Journal* noted.[58] Coincidentally, the AFB and NFU had become increasingly vocal in their support for giving the farmer the right to organize for purposes of negotiating prices. In the absence of further legislative proposals by the AFB, the NFU and the Administration had taken the initiative through Senator Mondale to introduce legislation that would go beyond S. 109.

In what was almost an anticlimax, President Johnson signed into law the "Agricultural Fair Practices Act of 1967" in Honolulu, on April 16, 1968, while preparing for a strategy meeting with U.S. military and South Viet Nam leaders. No chivalry, photographs or publicity accompanied the event. Instead, S. 109 became law, almost unannounced, after the full ten days had lapsed when the bill would have automatically become law without the President's signature.

By April 18th, the AFB was congratulating itself and the President for a "major legislative achievement for Farm Bureau." According to AFB President Shuman, the "marketing rights" bill provided new impetus to voluntary bargaining-marketing programs favored by the Farm Bureau. One farm editor called it the first federal legislation in more than 45 years designed to give farm operators more power to bargain collectively on prices with users of their products.[59]

However, skeptical farm organizations still saw the measure as "innocuous" and "watered down." The NFO continued to characterize it as the worst piece of agricultural legislation passed in years. In contrast, trade associations called it "successful." "We were lucky on that one!" said Warren Gar-rard, Vice-President of Marketing, Ralston Purina Company.[60] Bedraggeled

58. John A. Prestro, "Seeds for Bargaining Down on the Farm," *The Wall Street Journal*, April 9, 1968, 20.

59. Richard Orr, "Bargaining Power Latest Slogan," April 18, 1968, in files of American Farm Bureau Federation.

60. Warren Garrard (Vice-President of Marketing, Ralston Purina Company), personal interview, May 10, 1968.

and bewildered politicans were happy to see it out of the way. Senator Aiken called the falling out of farm organizations a "display of professional jealousy" on the part of organization leaders.[61] Senator Jordan of North Carolina reportedly claimed, "I've had more trouble with that bill than any other piece of legislation since coming to Congress." [62] Even the AFB admitted that S. 109 was an exasperating experience, and Shuman wrote in his monthly column that assumptions underlying the slogan "unity in agriculture" were fallacious.[63] According to at least one Washington observer, S. 109 illustrates vividly the ability of nonfarm agri-business firms to influence legislation affecting farmers' bargaining power. Obviously, the S. 109 controversy left Capitol Hill in disarray and with mixed feelings.

Despite the lingering reservations, the Secretary of Agriculture did not take long in assigning responsibility for administering the new act. In a memorandum dated August 27th, Acting Secretary John Baker delegated the authority for carrying out the Secretary's responsibilities under the act, somewhat ironically, to the Farmer Cooperative Service of the USDA.[64] The FCS, in turn, established a separate line of responsibility by assigning Robert D. Harris, Executive Assistant to the Administrator, to handle claims of violation of the act and gave him assistance from the Office of the Inspector General to investigate complaints. The Secretary also charged the Agricultural Stabilization and Conservation Service, Consumer and Marketing Service, Packers and Stockyards Administration and Office of the General Counsel with cooperating fully in fulfilling the purposes of the act.

After a bumpy ride through Congress, the much-amended AFB-NCFC-NMPF bill became functional. Approximately four years had been consumed in meshing support and guiding the measure to final passage.

61. George Aiken (Senator, Vermont), personal interview, April 5, 1968.
62. Harris, interview. Mr. Harris related this quote to me following a meeting in the office of B. Everett Jordan (Senator, North Carolina). The basis for the Senator's comment was one of the author's numerous attempts to interview the Senator.
63. Charles B. Shuman, "Unity in Agriculture," *Nation's Agriculture*, 43 (April, 1968), 4.
64. John A. Baker (Acting Secretary, USDA), Secretary's Memorandum No. 1639, August 27, 1968.

We believe that farmers do not yet fully appreciate the importance of cooperative action in marketing their products.[1]

National Commission on Food Marketing

One of the farmers' most urgent needs is to develop political strength and sophistication through coalition with non-farm groups to attain mutually-desired objectives. Even though farmers . . . [and farm organizations] may have interests which conflict with business, labor, or other groups on certain issues, they must learn to work more effectively together when interests coincide.[2]

Robert N. Hampton

Chapter 11

An Idea Takes Hold: The Meaning and Significance of S. 109

The experience with S. 109 made it clear that farm operators are playing in a new political ball game. They have found that guiding a piece of farm legislation through the congressional arena in the 1960's is an arduous process packed with potential pitfalls. The legislative life of S. 109 demonstrated that the Farm Bloc, so powerful in the 20's and 30's, is now only one of several interest groups seeking to influence farm legislation. The Farm Bloc isn't so powerful now. Still, farm operators can make their presence felt on Capitol Hill if their farm organizations coalesce, and the initial efforts to enact basic bargaining legislation provided grounds for a display of farm unanimity that Senator Aiken, author of S. 109, has acknowledged as the high point in the life of the bill. But farm organizations are no longer the only — or indeed the dominant — groups influencing agricultural legislation. The fact that S. 109 emerged from the tortuous enactment route with merely its "essentials" surviving attests to a new alignment and power structure affecting contemporary farm legislation.

The most striking revelations in the S. 109 confrontation are: (1) the political muscle of food processors, particularly those "big" business firms acting individually or through trade associations and (2) the lack of basic accord among farm groups, notably as to a definition of bargaining and how it

---

1. National Commission on Food Marketing, *Food: From Farmer to Consumer* (Washington: U.S. Government Printing Office, 1966), 110.
2. Robert N. Hampton (Director of Marketing and International Trade, National Council of Farmer Cooperatives), speech, "The 'Climate of Opportunity' for Bargaining in Today's Markets," *Proceedings of the 11th National Bargaining Conference* (Washington: Farmer Cooperative Service, USDA, 1967), 68.

should relate to the meaning of cooperation. While the story of S. 109 demonstrates a gradual awakening of the farm population to the stark reality of a new power structure in agriculture, it also demonstrates all the pushing and pulling that might have been expected in a confrontation between agricultual producers and processors in the political arena. Perhaps no two groups in American business history are so proud of their entrepreneurship and as cautious about preserving their rights to operate in a free enterprise economy. However, many of the "processors" who contested the farm bargaining bill were not of the type farmers knew fifteen years ago. Instead, they were organisms of large-scale conglomerates — integrated and highly diversified — that sought to put off any legislation that would enable farmers to exercise effective group action.

Not only were off-farm interests capable of exerting an influence over the destiny of a piece of farm-sponsored legislation, but they were also capable of rallying support from groups possessing no active interest whatsoever in agriculture. The combined efforts of these powerful nonfarm groups outweighed the legislative efforts of farm organizations to a point where protection for farmers in bargaining was watered down, if not removed. Thus, although S. 109 began its legislative journey as a producers' marketing bill, it wound up instead as a fair practices act of mutual applicability. At the root of the S. 109 struggle was a persistent effort by the National Canners Association and its allies to forestall anything in the way of bargaining legislation. In the final analysis, the forces at work signal an economic power struggle undergirding the farming industry: Who is going to control American agriculture — processors, integrators or farm operators?

Concern over the control issue manifests itself in the quest for market power throughout the country as well as in the halls of Congress, where pressure groups interact. What appears ahead for American agriculture has perhaps been most effectively forecast by Professor V. James Rhodes, who projects four possible organizational paths that agriculture may follow.[3] These are: (1) "family farm-open márket" agriculture; (2) "family farm-collective bargaining" agriculture; (3) "corporate-integratee" agriculture; (4) "corporate-farmhand" agriculture. Whereas the first alternative would provide for a continuation of farm markets, but with fewer numbers of farm operators running larger farms (a continuation of the one direction agriculture is taking today), the second alternative suggests that farm operators must exercise effective group action to compete in a world of power blocs — big corporations, big unions and big government.

Rhodes's third and fourth organizational forms involve developments such as contracting and corporate farming. In a vertically integrated "corpo-

3. V. James Rhodes, speech, "What's Ahead for U.S. Agriculture?" 40th Annual Meeting of the National Council of Farmer Cooperatives, Washington, D.C., January 14, 1969.

rate-integratee" agriculture, as typified in the production of broilers, eggs, turkeys and some fruits and vegetables, the "farmers" would own the land and many of the physical facilities but not the variable inputs. In many cases, the livestock or seed crops, fertilizers, farm chemicals, feeds and pharmaceuticals would be supplied by the contracting corporate firm. In contrast to this model, the "corporate-farmhand" agriculture envisions farming operations being owned by large corporations headquartered in New York, Chicago, St. Louis, Kansas City and other cities. Farm production would be systematized by a computer, with work carried out by a unionized labor force and some salaried managers.

Although people associated with agriculture may long for a continuance of the "family farm-open market" agriculture, the economic world has altered. This development was highlighted in the report of the National Commission on Food Marketing, which showed a growing imbalance of producer versus buyer market power. Conventional farm markets are fading, the concentration and growth of integrated conglomerate enterprises has quickened, and farm operators are fast becoming a political minority. As a recourse to survival, farm operators have turned to group action to offset this imbalance in market power.

Gearing up for the "family farm-collective bargaining" agriculture of the future has not been easy. Farm operators have had to learn that many slogans of the past and concepts that promoted them are meaningless. As a part of the transition to a more highly organized agriculture, they have had to forego their fundamentalist notions of free and independent individual action in marketing their products. They have also had to learn that small losses of individual freedom through voluntary group action are compensated for by the stronger influence and greater freedom as a group that comes from joining other farm operators. The failure of many farmers, and farm organizations, to recognize that the benefits of group action have a higher value than individual economic freedom has served as an impediment to this transition. However, the alternative paths in the economic organizations of agriculture — the "corporate-integratee" and "corporate-farmhand" agricultures — offer less opportunity for farm operators to exercise their decision-making powers and to participate in the benefits that can result from assuming market risks. Farmers cannot unite effectively until they recognize the full dimensions of the new structure of political action and the size of their stake in the outcome.

If the future of the "family farm-open market" agriculture is assumed tenuous at best, it appears that farm operators will have to set up a "big" agriculture through their own organization structure, or they will be economically absorbed by the power blocs. In what manner farmers should organize (that is, through what organization structure) and how cooperatives and general farm groups should relate to each other in the bargaining process are two of the crucial questions facing the farm community. Clearly, the mechanics and proper relationships in the farm bargaining process and the institutional devices farm organizations will choose in order to relate to processors will be among the "gut" issues of future legislation. The significance of S. 109 in this perspective is simply that several farm organizations decided that they were not going to "take it sitting down" but were actively seeking farm legislation that would help them retool for the coming era of "family farm-collective bargaining" agriculture.

The legislative life of the American Farm Bureau's bargaining bill demonstrates how seriously the question of farm bargaining is taken by various segments of the agri-business community. As a policy measure that could potentially supplant or supplement existing farm programs, the continued support of group action by farm operators contained broad ramifications for the economic organization of agriculture. Farm organizations, to a point, support it, but processors and integrators are not favorably disposed to farm bargaining — at least not without a good, stiff fight. In particular, the processors and integrators utilized all of their resources to lobby against S. 109. Furthermore, they excelled their farm-organization counterparts in keeping their members informed about the bill's progress and in using in-depth legal analysis to bolster their testimony before congressional committees. Their effort can best be described as an impressive and professional performance.

The influence of processors and integrators upon the legislative life of S. 109 can be measured in the positions assumed by the USDA and the Administration at various stages. Theoretically, governmental agencies attempt to reflect the best interests of society in their deliberations.[4] However, they also interact with pressure groups and other governmental agencies and are influenced by them. One government official has recently described his agency as a "crucible where all the pressures can be brought" to mold public policy and programs.[5] Obviously, pressure groups lobby with these agencies, and the agencies lobby among themselves, to influence the outcome of administrative rulings and legislative proposals. If we assume that governmental agencies react, in part, to pressures resulting from their interaction with pressure groups, using USDA's performance as an indicator of the influence on the outcome of S. 109 exerted by the processing community and farm organizations is logical. Generally, one clue to the importance any agency or lobby group attaches to a particular piece of legislation is provided by the level of

4. Governmental agencies, like other bureaucracies, devote considerable time as well to organizational maintenance and protection of their own well-being. I do not suggest either that all agencies are knowledgeable and receptive to the pleas of interest groups. Obviously, the FTC and Justice Department in the S. 109 story were not receptive to problems encountered by farm operators.

5. Rodney E. Leonard (Administrator, Consumer and Marketing Service, USDA), speech, American Marketing Association Workshop, Washington, D.C., November 20, 1968.

executive sent to testify in behalf of the group. An examination of USDA positions from this perspective yields some interesting insights.

The position of the processors and integrators, with respect to the original version of S. 109 (which was in the form of an amendment to the Capper-Volstead Act), was one of outright rejection. Unable to resolve conflicting internal positions on the controversial bargaining issue and on whether to support a Farm Bureau bill, the USDA sent a deputy administrator to testify at the first Senate hearing in June of 1966. However, the farm organizations made a sufficient case for new legislation, in principle, to carry the bill forward. Thus, when Senator Aiken introduced his substitute, which stood on its own base, in September of that year, and the Food Commission recommended bargaining legislation, David Angevine, Administrator of the Farmer Cooperative Service, was sent to testify in behalf of the USDA and offered several amendments. All farm organizations appeared in general support of the proposal.

The processors and integrators continued to offer strenuous opposition to the measure as reintroduced in the first session of the Ninetieth Congress, even though it now applied to cooperative businesses as well as proprietary and corporate handlers. In contrast to earlier hearings, the Senate's third hearing on S. 109, held in May of 1967, saw one of the most impressive displays of farm unification in recent history. The Administration had entered the picture in recognition of growing farm unrest as exemplified by the NFO milk action and the farm operators' general interest in securing more bargaining power. Having successfully aligned all governmental agencies to either neutral positions or support for the bill, the Administration and USDA were represented by the top of the pecking order in the person of Secretary of Agriculture Orville Freeman. During this hearing, the processors continued to offer strenuous, if more conciliatory, opposition.

Following action by the Jordan subcommittee in which the processors and integrators scored a tactical victory by subverting the bill into an anti-farm-organization measure, the briefly unified farm front blew apart. As S. 109 approached its first House hearing in September of 1967, the Administration and the USDA detected the growing displeasure of farm organizations with the much-amended bill, and the fact that many of the processors were now its proponents. Consequently, the department sent a second-level administrator, Assistant Secretary John Baker, to urge amendment of the bill back to its pre-Jordan subcommittee form in a relatively low-key House hearing. Coincidentally, the department's attention shifted to broader bargaining legislation and the original 1967 version of S. 109 as embodied in the Mondale bill.

Having obtained Secretary Freeman's word that the USDA would not oppose the measure as it came before the full House, the AFB finally obtained passage of S. 109 before both houses in March and April of 1968. The first Senate hearings on the Mondale bill, held in April of that year, indicated that the processors and integrators were in firm opposition to any further "bargaining" legislation along this line. Moreover, the testimony offered by the farm organizations — cooperatives and general farm interest organizations alike — displayed their still-unsettled position with respect to the broader bargaining question. As a result of this dying thrust the USDA and Administration cooled off on the bargaining issue. By the summer of 1968, some department officials were suggesting that bargaining was not an answer and were playing down the bargaining theme.[6]

The strength of the processors' retort to the producers' cry for more bargaining legislation was successful in altering the content of S. 109 and in causing the USDA to drop the bargaining question. The bill had traversed four critical periods in which substantive changes were brought about in its provisions. During these four critical periods, S. 109 was changed successfully from a bold farm bargaining amendment that came under the umbrella of antitrust protection embodied in the Capper-Volstead Act —

To a protective bargaining bill that carried stiff enforcement penalties,

To a two-way-street proposal that was applicable to marketing cooperatives as well as other handlers,

To a watered-down bill that was more processor than producer oriented and contained limited enforcement provisions and a disclaimer,

To a mild bargaining measure that suggested congressional support for the right of farm operators to organize for group action but restricted bargaining associations as well as cooperative and noncooperative handlers.

The "pecking order," illustrated by the successive appearances of USDA in relation to S. 109, reflects a vacillation from limited to strong support, and then a cooling-off in response to the prospects of legislating the Mondale bill and to the pressures of processors and farm groups. In particular, the lobbies of the canner, "big" grain and cotton alliances, widely regarded as among the most effective in Washington, wield considerable influence in farm legislative matters. In short, the economic power struggle taking place throughout the countryside has already manifested itself in political circles in Washington and was very much in evidence throughout the S. 109 controversy, with the balance of power clearly left in the hands of the processors.

Although S. 109 fell short of its original objectives, it did get a piece of something: reaffirmation by Congress of the producers' right to organize for collective action and the taking of a first step in establishing farm bargaining legislation. Uniquely, what happened to S. 109 finds a historical parallel with the Clayton act, some 50 years its predecessor. Instead of enhancing free

6. Orville L. Freeman (Secretary, USDA) in his speech to the National Grange in the fall of 1967 first signalled this change. Subsequent speeches by USDA officials through the summer of 1968 became increasingly pessimistic about bargaining prospects.

competition by making a large corporation cut prices in all of its markets when it did so in one locality in order to kill off a small competitor — a recommendation of the eminent economist J. B. Clark that was popularly supported by legislators — the Clayton bill was amended by powerful company lobbyists by inserting the words "except in good faith to meet competition." This amendment compelled small businessmen either to fall back into line and follow the price leaders or to face extinction.[7] S. 109 had as its amendment sequel the addition of the words "or on behalf of," which made the act, originally designed to protect them, explicitly applicable to bargaining associations.

At best, S. 109 offers a foundation statute for the bargaining activities carried out by general farm interest organizations. At worst, the phrase "or on behalf of" may provide handlers and dissident members with an excuse to harass bargaining associations. Since cooperatives have been defined as "handlers" by the terms of the bill, S. 109 may also invite general farm interest organizations outwardly to bargain against cooperatives just as they would any independent or corporate handler. This possibility was the seed of destruction that divided and conquered the farm front. The language and the fact of its inclusion is bitterly resented by cooperative business leaders, who feel that, in any case, the new statute may ultimately proliferate the number of commodity bargaining associations.

In the final analysis, S. 109 will just barely come out somewhere on the plus side of the "best-worst" extremes. Its final form must be considered a tribute to the power of the processor lobby. In terms of future legislation concerning who is going to control American agriculture, the S. 109 experience should serve as a lesson not soon lost by farm organizations.

A Lesson In Unity

The second major revelation in the S. 109 controversy was the unsettled posture of farm organizations concerning the broader bargaining question. It was also the most complex. Although farm groups initially appeared united in support of S. 109, they had not resolved themselves to act with respect to the objectives or approach to bargaining inherent in the bill. This disequilibrium was, in part, a result of uncertainty about the functional roles of farm organizations as farm operators retool for a new era in farm marketing. However, it is from the uncertainty that some of the most instructive lessons, some positive and some negative, can be derived from the legislative life of S. 109.

The temporarily unified farm front proved that farm organizations can work together in coalitions and alliances for the common goals of farm operators. Just as trade pressure groups coalesce in their common business inter-

7. John R. Commons, *Institutional Economics: Its Place In Political Economy*, Vol. II (Madison: The University of Wisconsin Press, 1961), 895.

ests, farm organizations are realizing that they cannot achieve desired legislation by acting alone. Despite the fact that farm unity on S. 109 disintegrated at one point in the life of the bill, it was perhaps the sole reason for congressional enactment of the first round of farm bargaining legislation. Even so, the initiative to unity came from outside in the person of Senator George Aiken, after the bill had made little progress because of a lack of broadly based farm support.

The coalescing efforts by pressure groups active during the life of S. 109 were exemplified on both sides of the bill. Food and fiber handlers active in opposing the bill offer one of the best examples. Even among the more effective lobbies in Washington, the cotton alliance stands out as one of the best organized and most influential. Perhaps no other industry has an equal knack for aligning all its segments — from ginners to merchants — behind a cause. An amalgamation of pressure groups that obviously wields considerable influence through the Southern legislators who dominate the agricultural committees, the cotton alliance demonstrated its influence by successfully exempting cotton and tobacco from S. 109. The farm cooperatives were unable to accomplish the feat for themselves. Even with its strong influence, however, the cotton alliance found it useful to build fences with other processor and integrator lobbies in opposition to S. 109.

Leadership of the opposition *ad hoc* committee rested with the National Canners Association. Beginning with a dual effort between the canners and the National Broiler Council, the *ad hoc* committee expanded to include such diverse groups as the American Feed Manufacturers Association, American Poultry Institute, Independent Meat Packers Association and members of the cotton alliance. These industry organizations were able, in turn, to spark opposition from the National Automobile Dealers Association, the National Trucking Association and other nonagricultural pressure groups. Similarly, several large conglomerates including canning companies, dairy manufacturers, chemical companies and feed firms lobbied against the bill on their own behalf. In short, the singleness of purpose of these coalescing forces was capable of massing sufficient influence on the Senate subcommittee to overcome the lobby of the American Farm Bureau and the united farm front.

The significance of the initial farm front on S. 109 was that farm organizations took a hard look at trends in farm income and the economic organization of agriculture and decided there was more to fight for than to fight about. Instead of attempting to further their individual pet philosophies and interests by giving a peculiar twist to a piece of legislation, they united behind S. 109 to the astonishment of many political observers and farm critics. Throughout the life of the bill the farm front was comprised of basically four groupings: (1) the coalition of the American Farm Bureau-National Council of Farmer Cooperatives-National Milk Producers Federation; (2) the bargaining association coalition comprised of California, Pacific Northwest and

Midwest bargaining groups; (3) the Committee of "17" general farm interest and commodity organizations (particularly the National Farmers Union, National Grange, National Farmers Organization and the Midcontinent Farmers Association); (4) the USDA's National Advisory Committee on Cooperatives.

The internal problems of the American Farm Bureau and the National Council of Farmer Cooperatives notwithstanding, the farm front was united in its purpose to secure more bargaining power for farm operators. The farmers' strongest allies in seeking bargaining legislation were labor unions, church groups and, oddly enough, consumer organizations. Significantly, the Administration, bolstered by the report of the National Commission on Food Marketing, also lent its support and leadership to establishing proper institutional arrangements for carrying out farm bargaining efforts. In this search, Secretary Freeman testified in behalf of the Farm Bureau bill as comprising one component of a farm bargaining legislative package. Together, the combined efforts of the farm organizations, the Secretary of Agriculture, the USDA, and assorted supporting groups provided a formidable proponent force unequaled in recent farm legislative history.

The Achilles' heel of S. 109 was the application of the unlawful practices section to marketing and supply cooperatives. No testimony was offered to the effect that cooperatives were discriminating against producers. Instigated by the National Grange and the Farmer Cooperative Service and accepted by the American Farm Bureau, cooperatives were incorporated into the definition of the term *handler*, whereas they had been excluded previously by a special exemption. Apparently, the proponents did not fully realize the import of the change.

Its significance became clear later, when the Jordan subcommittee further amended the bill in executive mark-up sessions to (1) emphasize farm operators' right not to join an association of producers, (2) disclaim any interference with the rights of handlers to deal with producers on a direct basis and (3) jeopardize the legitimacy of the cooperatives' patronage refund practice. The outcome suggests that a good farm bill cannot successfully be enacted by legislating something against farm allies. As a major proponent group representing farm interests before the Jordan subcommittee, the AFB did not take corrective action.

The costs of farm disunity in the S. 109 contest were high. Not only was the end product watered down, but also the aftermath took its toll among politicians and lobbyists. Although it is difficult to attribute the events explicitly to S. 109, there is little doubt that some relationship exists. Among the politicians who likely felt the effects of the controversial farm bill was Senator Frank Lausche of Ohio, an original cosponsor of the measure, who failed in his bid for re-election in 1968. Congressman Joseph Resnick, Farm Bureau Enemy Number One following his outspoken attacks on the organization, failed in his bid for congressional re-election in New York and in his primary election bid as the Democratic candidate for the Senate in the fall of 1968.[8]

While many politicians were stung in this hotly contested struggle between producers and processors, at least one was benefited. Congressman Bernie Sisk of California, the legislator responsible for achieving compromises among farm groups in Fresno, was appointed to the House Agriculture Committee in January of 1969. The appointment signalled recognition of Sisk as an authoritative spokesman on farm legislative matters and his own personal interest in getting involved in farm legislation at the agriculture committee level.

The toll among lobbyists was heavy. Harry Graham, the articulate Legislative Representative for the National Grange who verbally castigated the Amrican Farm Bureau before agricultural committees of both houses, was dismissed when a new president assumed leadership of that general farm interest organization. Mike Norton, a sixteen-year veteran Secretary of the National Milk Producers Federation, "resigned" from his post following the commodity organization's annual meeting in St. Louis in November of 1968. His departure was in part precipitated by static from the activist Milk Producers, Inc., concerning the S. 109 proposal. The repercussions from S. 109 also caused casualties within the Farm Bureau family. C. H. DeVaney, President of the Texas Farm Bureau, was deposed in November of 1967 by cotton producers, riled by the independent ginners, and by free enterprisers for not opposing S. 109 as vigorously as they wanted. Similar repercussions were felt in the Iowa Farm Bureau.

Perhaps the biggest casualty of all, however, is the farmer himself and his farm organizations. Agriculture did not change its reputation as being a political "hot potato" in the S. 109 struggle. To the contrary, the falling out of farm organizations following the Senate subcommittee action, no matter how well founded, only served to reaffirm the suspicions of politicians that professional jealousy will lead to sure-fire defeat for a farm-sponsored bill. For the politician, it is much easier to look the other way and let nonfarm interests assume control of the farming industry.

While each of the lessons derived from S. 109 is of importance to farm operators and their organizations, the most important is that general farm interest organizations are not dead. They have not yet been supplanted by line commodity organizations. Moreover, by working together, general farm interest organizations played an instrumental role in enacting S. 109 and can play an important role in future legislative efforts. Success in this endeavor depends upon their ability to patch up old wounds, to coalesce with other farm organizations and nonfarm groups and to communicate effectively with their members.

8. Resnick continued his attack on the AFB through an article "The Right-wing in Overalls," *The Progressive*, 32 (March, 1968), 24. He has since died in October, 1969.

In the aftermath of S. 109, I believe two erroneous conclusions have been drawn. The first is that farm unity cannot be attained. Charles B. Shuman, President of the AFB, has suggested, based upon the S. 109 experience, that farm groups cannot be unified in purpose and that resolving conflicts within the farm family internally makes for a weak farm front.[9] Had the American Farm Bureau not been so willing to take anything with S. 109 written on it, and had more care been exercised in presenting testimony — much of which was thrown back in the Farm Bureau's face in the disclaimer clause — a much stronger bill might have been enacted, and the embarrassing farm disintegration could have been avoided. The luxury of having farm groups bickering with each other can no longer be afforded. Disagreements should be settled within the farm family rather than washing dirty linen in public and allowing legislators to work out compromises between farm groups before congressional committees. One might ask what will happen if farm operators do not unite through a "family farm-collective bargaining" agriculture? The handwriting is on the wall concerning the power struggle in agriculture. The outcome is dependent upon the answer to the question, Who is going to take the initiative — producers or processors?

The second erroneous conclusion would appear to support the first. Several Washington observers have ironically concluded that since such dissonance and professional jealousy had been created among the general farm interest organizations during the S. 109 fallout, the cooperatives would have to carry the ball in the next round of bargaining legislation. However, this conclusion is inconsistent with the needs felt by some general farm groups and with the internal problems the farm front experienced in the first round of bargaining legislation. Not only have two general farm interest organizations already introduced further farm bargaining bills, but it will be left to their joint efforts to resolve differences and unselfishly align other farm and nonfarm groups to achieve legislative victory in round two of the fight for more farm marketing legislation.

Farm Organization Structure: New Roles in Changing Times

The central issue within the farm community throughout the four-year life of S. 109 was how bargaining related to the meaning of cooperation. Collective bargaining is group negotiation over the price of farm products. Every farm group wanted a piece of the action and appropriated to itself a role as the farm operators' bargaining agent. To a great extent, the emergence of the NFO on the farm scene precipitated the interest. The challenge of nationwide bargaining to existing farm groups played upon the legislative life of S. 109 and was the source of discord within the farm community. The underlying issues were of a structural and functional nature.

9. Charles B. Shuman (President, American Farm Bureau Federation), "Unity in Agriculture," *Nation's Agriculture*, 43 (April, 1968), 4.

Farm operators have characteristically organized through two types of organizations in representing the economic interests of their farm firms: general farm interest organizations and cooperatives. Each type has a distinctive structural form and functional role. Through farmer-owned and -controlled cooperative businesses, farm operators have pooled price risks and their products in marketing and their buying power in purchasing supplies. In many cases, they have taken the product clear through the marketing channel to the consumer's doorstep or retailer's shelf with brand names such as Sunkist oranges, Land O'Lakes butter and turkeys, Co-op petroleum products and Ocean Spray cranberries. Simultaneously, farm operators have organized through professional interest organizations that have operated in the legislative arena on state and national levels to protect farm interests and to secure

EMPLOYMENT IN SELECTED PROFESSIONAL OCCUPATIONS AND MEMBERSHIP IN RELATED ORGANIZATIONS

Occupation	Employment*	Related Organization(s)†	Membership†
Teachers			
Elementary and Secondary	1,850,000	National Education Association‡	813,000
		American Federation of Teachers§	100,000
College	200,000	American Association of University Professors	62,000
Engineers	1,000,000	American Institute of Electrical and Electronic Engineers‖	156,500
		American Society of Mechanical Engineers‖	59,500
		American Society of Civil Engineers‖	49,000
		American Institute of Aeronautics and Astronautics‖	36,000
		American Institute of Chemical Engineers‖	22,000
Registered Engineers	250,000	National Society of Professional Engineers‖	60,000
Registered Nurses	550,000	American Nursing Association	170,000
Clergymen	300,000	No relevant organization	
Physicians	275,000	American Medical Association	176,000
Lawyers	275,000	American Bar Association	115,000
Dentists	100,000	American Dental Association	100,000
Certified Public Accountants	80,000	American Institute of Certified Public Accountants	48,000

NOTES: * U.S. Department of Labor, Bureau of Labor Statistics, *Occupational Outlook Handbook, 1966–67 Edition,* Bulletin No. 1450, pp. 23, 72.
† Frederick G. Ruffner, Jr., R. C. Thomas, Ann Underwood, and H. C. Young (eds.), *Encyclopedia of Association,* Vol. 1 (Detroit: Gale Research Company, 1964).
‡ NEA membership includes elementary and secondary schoolteachers, college and university professors, administrators, principals, counselors, and others interested in education. Bulk of membership composed of elementary and secondary teachers and administrators.
§ U.S. Department of Labor, Bureau of Labor Statistics, *Directory of National and International Labor Unions in the United States, 1965,* Bulletin No. 1493, p. 32.
‖ Membership includes students.
Source: E. F. Beale and E. D. Wickersham, The Practice of Collective Bargaining (Homewood, Ill.: R. D. Irwin, 1963), p. 86.

desirable farm programs. Within the framework of these structural forms and functional roles, we can expect farm operators to adapt their organizations to changing environmental and marketing conditions.

In years past, when rural residents were more numerous and city populations were relatively small, farm operators wielded an effective political influence on Capitol Hill. The general farm interest organizations had their heyday in national politics in the Farm Bloc era of the 1920's and 1930's. Similarly, cooperatives exercised a competitive influence on local markets and, in a competitive yardstick sense, provided greater returns to patrons. Each form of organization had a rebalancing effect in the producer versus buyer relationship. However, times have changed. Farm operators now must contend with regional and national markets, organized labor, giant feed firms, national processors, large chain stores and big government. As pointed out by the National Commission on Food Marketing, the scales are in need of rebalancing. Farm operators are sizing up this situation and retooling for a new era in agriculture. S. 109 may be looked upon as a part of this transition.

It is the thesis of this writer that the political power lost by farm operators through diminishing farm numbers will reappear in the form of economic power. The effective exercise of this economic power is dependent upon how well farm operators organize for the "family farm-collective bargaining" agriculture of the future and how well they co-ordinate their organized activity. Existing farm organizations will take on new dimensions in their structure and program of activities. While cooperatives will federate through regional and national associations along commodity lines, farm operators will adapt their general farm interest organizations to take on the added responsibility of farm bargaining. The co-ordination of these organizations — the cooperative systems approach to improving farm incomes — will ultimately determine how much producer power can be wielded at the bargaining table.

The fact that farm operators have used more than one organization structure in representing their economic interests has often been obscure and has never been clearly understood. Consequently, some confusion exists about recurring "farmer movements" and legislation relating to farm organization efforts. Essentially, the confusion stems from the assumptions that *all* types of farm organizations are cooperatives and that within this broad category, there are different forms such as bargaining cooperatives and operating cooperatives. This confusion was implicit in the thinking of politicians as they weighed the merits of S. 109, in the assessment of government officials who sought ways to amend it and in the discussions of certain general farm interest organizations who tried to write off the ramifications of defining cooperatives as a handler.

The variety of organizations used by a farm operator can be attributed to his multidimensional role as manager, laborer, financier and owner of his farm enterprise. Farm operators process and market their products through cooperatives, and represent their professional interests through general farm interest organizations. Parallels can be found in other occupational groups such as wage earners, teachers and bankers. As the process of bargaining replaces the role of open assembly markets in determining the value of farm products, farm operators will probably have more in common with laborers than they care to admit. They have been frequently challenged of late: "Labor can do it — why can't you?" [10]

Through cooperative marketing and purchasing organizations, farm operators can become basic in securing their needed supplies and aggressive in marketing their farm output. Through general farm interest organizations, farm operators have not only a forum for discussion and an outlet for their professional business interests, but also representation in the price formulational process of farm bargaining and in the legislative process of political lobbying. In the cooperative relationship, they are committed to efficient handling and merchandising of farm products through farmer owned and controlled facilities; in their general organization membership, they are committed to representation of professional interests with the least possible commitment to facilities. Whereas cooperatives may present a more conservative outlook on the basis of what the market will bear, general farm interest organizations have been typically used as instruments through which producers express their discontent and as instruments for use of the "bluff" technique, that is, pie-in-the-sky price requests, in the bargaining process. The first is an off-farm extension of the component farm firms, and the second is an aggregate of farm operators as persons. Given the uniqueness of voluntary organizations, each structural form is necessary for the successful exercise of producer power.

If this duality in farm organization structure and its implications for farm bargaining are not clearly perceived, it is probably for good reason. There are many distractions. The use of state and federal marketing orders and agreements has tended to proliferate the number of commodity bargaining associations — erroneously called bargaining cooperatives — that draw their member support from their overblown price requests in public hearings. In a few cases, bargaining associations have eventually acquired reserve processing facilities to handle market surpluses, in which case they may be more properly classified as underdeveloped operating cooperatives. The Eastern Milk Producers, California Canning Peach and Raisin Bargaining associations are examples of commodity bargaining associations. Their continued existence is dependent upon institutional arrangements that are local in nature — such as state and federal marketing orders — and upon locational monopolies in the production of specialized crops. However, this latter category is more often an exception than a rule. Production of most crops

10. Orville L. Freeman, speech, "In Union There is Strength: 'Labor Can Do It, Why Can't You'," Centennial Convention of the National Grange, Syracuse, New York, November 18, 1967; "Labor Can Do It . . . Why Can't You?" *Farm Journal*, 91 (October, 1967), 33.

and livestock is widely dispersed and marketed in national rather than local markets. Hence, the cry has gone out for more market muscle to countervail the power of large-scale buyers through federated organizations and regional and eventually national marketing orders.

The rather peculiar structural forms that many general farm organizations have acquired is also distracting. It can be argued that many have developed other interests and so deviated from performing as professional interest organizations — where producers have a protest outlet and forum for discussion — that a void was left which the National Farmers Organization attempted to fill. American agricultural history shows clearly that new farm organizations will be created to fill gaps left when existing farm organizations do not modify their structures and objectives to meet changed conditions. In many cases, the erosion of original purposes can be attributed to the fact that some general farm groups were incorporated under state cooperative laws instead of "not for pecuniary profit" organization laws and could not resist the temptation to diversity in purpose. In a maneuver, first worked out by Donald Kirkpatrick in Illinois, general farm interest organizations became involved in extracurricular "cooperatives" through the establishment of legally separate organizations whose control and stock rested with the parent organization instead of the member patrons.[11] Business was conducted only with those who maintained membership in the general farm interest organization.

Farm operators confronting such a complex organization structure cannot help but experience some difficulty in distinguishing between the general and the associated "cooperative" business activities. When Congressman Resnick questioned this relationship in light of traditional working rules that characterize cooperative operations, he struck a tender nerve. Just as the classic study by Emelianoff concluded that the legal unit of incorporated voluntary associations conceals their plurality and cloaks their aggregative economic nature, the preoccupation of many general farm interest organizations with their sideline business activities has clouded their outlook with conservatism and has limited their effectiveness as professional interest organizations.[12] The problem is especially acute, as experienced internally by the American Farm Bureau in promoting S. 109, when the general farm interest organizations attempt to assume a role in farm bargaining.

A third reason for the confusion regarding farm organization structures centers on a trend in some sectors, previously noted, toward a "corporate-integratee" agriculture. Broiler growers who are growing out company-owned birds with company-owned feeds, equipment and pharmaceuticals have no need for a cooperative business. While the Farm Bureau has been putting considerable energies into organizing such growers, the inherent loss of deci-

11. Mancur Olson, Jr., *The Logic of Collective Action* (Cambridge, Mass.: Harvard University Press, 1965), 153–55.
12. Ivan V. Emelianoff, *Economic Theory of Cooperation* (Ann Arbor, Mich.: Edwards Brothers, Inc., 1948), 249.

sion-making powers by such people places them in a category not far removed from wage earners. The growers' organizational instrument for negotiating contract terms in such cases could be a labor union as well as an AAMA or NFO. Clearly, these are not bargaining "cooperatives," although present thinking in the USDA's Farmer Cooperative Service would describe them as such. As the character of the farm operators' decision-making abilities is diversified through the use of production and risk-sharing contracts, just as it is through the widening spread in farm size, heterogeneity increases and voluntary organization efforts become more difficult.

A final distraction in clarifying the types of organizations through which farm operators represent their economic interests concerns the status of existing legal statutes. The term "association of producers" found in the Capper-Volstead Act is very broad and nondefinitive. While the act was purposely set up to cover cooperative marketing activity, many officials of general farm interest organizations also consider their groups to be "associations of producers" under the law. The testimony on S. 109 unraveled the difficulties involved with this interpretation. Although many attempts have been made historically to bargain collectively — most associated with short-lived "farmer movements" — no national legislation predating S. 109 refers specifically to this process. In the absence of such measures, many state legislatures in the 1960's have enacted protective bargaining bills. Furthermore, as farm political power has diminished and national farm organizations have become engaged in farm bargaining activities — typified by the efforts of the American Farm Bureau and the National Farmers Organization — the hue and cry for farm bargaining legislation has increased. Not only were marketing cooperatives unwilling to accept general farm interest organizations under the umbrella of the Capper-Volstead Act, but also general farm interest and commodity bargaining organizations began to question whether they rightfully belonged there.

This lack of clarity in the content and interpretation of existing laws has been compounded by a tendency for some farm groups to shy away from the term "bargaining." Many associate the term with "unionism," historically difficult for independent-minded farm operators to digest. This view has been long perpetuated by some general farm interest organizations. To break with this tradition of suspicion, the American Farm Bureau has spoken of "marketing" rather than "bargaining" activity and initially sold its new functional role as a one-step, one-membership answer to farm operators' income problems. The American Agricultural Marketing Association was given its name for this reason. As time has gone by and bargaining power has been eagerly sought by farm operators, the Farm Bureau has shifted the emphasis to "marketing-bargaining" activity. In another year or two, we can expect them to talk simply about "bargaining." In sum, the structural issues surrounding farm organizations have been fogged by four major distractions. The major question is: How will these be faced up to in the immediate future?

But distractions aside, farm operators are being compelled to re-examine their organizations in light of changes in the economic organization of agriculture, with little time to do so. As demonstrated in the poultry industry, once contracting by large corporations begins, it accelerates rapidly. Either farm operators realign their organizations to accomplish their economic objectives or they will succumb in the onslaught. Inherent in this realignment is an acceptance of farm bargaining as a working part of the pricing mechanism, rather than a rejection of it as a threat to existing farm organizations and traditional markets. Farm bargaining can be expected to become a major function of the general farm interest organizations along with their legislative activities. The two may well become closely interrelated. As shown in the legislative life of S. 109, the milk delivery stop carried out by the NFO not only dramatized the farmer's plight, but also gave an unexpected assist to the Farm Bureau bill. What remains to be created in terms of future legislation is an institutional arrangement that will bring producers, processors and chain-store buyers around the bargaining table.

Farm Bargaining: Horizons in Perspective

What turned out to be a tactical victory for the National Canners Association and other opponents of S. 109 may have been a strategic defeat. Despite President Shuman's testimony that the American Farm Bureau did not seek and would not support legislation that would compel processors to deal with an association of producers, members of the organization were not to be denied at their December, 1968, annual meeting in Kansas City — the organization's 50th anniversary. By an overwhelming vote, delegates passed a resolution calling for new legislation that would include: standards for recognition of bargaining associations by buyers; provisions that failure of a buyer to negotiate with a recognized bargaining group would constitute an unfair trade practice; strengthening and improving marketing rights and the definition of agricultural fair practices; broadening the rights of bargaining associations under antitrust laws.

Not only did this resolution represent a significant departure from past AFB philosophy, but also it pointed out some of the most important aspects of farm bargaining for which present statutes, including S. 109, are either unclear or insufficient. This resolution was followed up by a draft, one of several alternatives, that the AFB Board of Directors selected to push at its March, 1969, meeting. Introduced in the Congress by Catherine May of Washington on April 3rd, the new bill was written as an amendment to the Agricultural Fair Practices Act of 1967 (see Appendix D).[13] The bill contained a defini-

13. U.S. *Congressional Record*, 91st Cong., 1st sess., 1969, CXV, Part 2, H2501. The bill introduced by Catherine May (Representative, Washington) was numbered H.R. 9950 and was entitled Agricultural Marketing and Bargaining Act of 1969. Since introduction, the bill has picked up eight additional sponsors including Congressmen

tion of the term "agricultural bargaining association," an addition to the prohibitions of S. 109 that would make failure to negotiate with a bargaining association an unfair trade practice, and it contained several additions to the
disclaimer clause, notably that "nothing in the act shall be construed to forbid
the affiliation of an association of producers." In contrast to the Kansas City
AFB resolution, the bill was relatively mild but nevertheless represented the
opening bell for round two in farm bargaining legislation.

The AFB action represents another signal of the transition that one of
America's leading general farm interest organizations is undergoing as it re-
structures to provide greater economic returns to farm operators. Before seeking new legislation, however, farm leaders have to settle three fundamental
issues: (1) resolution of the structural and functional roles of different farm
organizations; (2) determination of the proper institutional arrangement
under which farm bargaining can be exercised; (3) formulation of a bargaining proposal that includes a statutory definition of a bargaining association
and provides for flexibility under antitrust laws, bargaining in good faith and
other provisions necessary for effective bargaining.

As a first step, farm leaders will be forced to recognize that farm operators require two organization arms — cooperative business and professional
interest organizations — to represent effectively the economic interests of
their farm firms. Farm bargaining power can be developed only by building
up strong, self-governing organizations. It is dependent on organized
strength. Co-ordinated, farm organizations will provide farm operators with
needed market power equal with that of big business. Unco-ordinated, they
will remain divisive and more concerned with organization maintenance than
purposeful action.

While farm operators have a tremendous potential for increasing farm
bargaining power through these organizational instruments, they have not
made very good use of them. Many farm operators, particularly those engaged in livestock production, are still unorganized. Too many farm organizations have also been attempting to justify their existence on social and political grounds instead of the economic function they should be performing.
Many farm organizations are still attempting to wear two hats as both general
farm interest and cooperative organizations, with typical results of an unim-
pressive performance in each area. Internal problems over S. 109 encountered by the American Farm Bureau, National Council of Farmer Cooperatives and the National Milk Producers Federation through a conflict between
their operating and bargaining contingents attest to the dilemma.

Historically, the impasse of conflicting interests within many so-called
general farm organizations has led to periodic "farmer movements." The recent formation of the National Farmers Organization provides a ready exam-

Zwach of Minnesota, Rarick of Louisiana, Morton of Maryland and Alexander of Arkansas. Cosponsors of the Senate version are Senators Aiken of Vermont, Allen of Alabama, Curtis of Nebraska and Holland of Florida.

ple. Similarly, the House Committee on Agriculture experienced difficulty in determining whether general farm interest organizations, such as the National Farmers Organization and the American Farm Bureau, were covered by the protection provided in the S. 109 proposal. Generally, legislators concluded they were not because S. 109 was designed to protect cooperatives. This interpretation conflicted with the original intent of the bill to protect activities of the general farm groups and suggests that needed educational work must be undertaken to eliminate these basic misunderstandings. With equal dedication, farm operators must make a determined effort to increase the effectiveness of their organizations.

There are signs of internal change within organizations serving agriculture. Current philosophy within the American Farm Bureau tends toward a limited commitment of facilities, that is, to leaving the investment in brick and mortar to marketing cooperatives. This commitment is consistent with the challenge placed before the American Farm Bureau in 1967, when William A. Haffert, Jr., suggested that the farmer should "stop being a nice guy and should bargain as effectively as his industrial labor counterpart." [14] It is also consistent with the prediction that the American Farm Bureau's bargaining efforts will make or break the organization within five years. In a complementary fashion, the current trend among dairy and grain marketing cooperatives to form regional and national federations along commodity lines is setting the pace in this area of organized farm activity. No single organization can do the job for the farm entrepreneur. However, the "integratee" who does not supply any of the variable inputs in his farming operation and does not have title to the raw product that is marketed has no need for a cooperative business organization. He does have need for an association or union to represent him in dealings with the integrator. In this limited case, a producer has need for only one type of farm organization. Clearly, each type of farm organization is currently underdeveloped, and the strengthening of both forms will be a prerequisite to coping with the challenges of economic change.

The second fundamental issue that must be settled concerns the proper institutional arrangement desired by farm operators to carry out farm bargaining. Up to this point, farm leaders have been unsettled with respect to the objectives and approach to bargaining. More often than not, the subject has been viewed in terms of a threat to existing farm organization structure, rather than as a new feature of the pricing mechanism that is replacing the once-prevalent open market agriculture. Unquestionably, new legislation is required to encourage the new pricing process on a broader basis and to provide general farm interest organizations with a legal basis, in fact, for undertaking a major role in the bargaining process. While a consensus has not been

---

14. William A. Haffert, Jr. (Editor, *Broiler Industry*), speech, "The Challenge: Can AAMA Make The Grade?" 49th Annual Meeting of the American Farm Bureau Federation, Chicago, Illinois, December 14, 1967.

reached on this approach, we can draw some inferences from the legislative life of S. 109, some current proposals and recent congressional testimony.

Four approaches to the problem have been offered at this point: (1) creation of a National Agricultural Relations Board and supporting marketing committees; (2) expansion of the Agricultural Marketing Agreements Act to include collective bargaining; (3) accreditation of a bargaining association by the Secretary of Agriculture followed by a notice to handlers, buyers and processors that they must bargain in good faith with the association; (4) the AFB's direct bargaining association-individual handler approach. The first alternative is a proposal by the National Farmers Union and represents the work of former Secretary of Agriculture Charles F. Brannan.[15] Introduced as Title I of the Mondale bill, the measure proposed the creation of a five-man National Agricultural Relations Board, appointed by the President, and the establishment of producer marketing committees whose membership would be initially selected by the Board upon recommendations submitted to it by the Agricultural Stabilization and Conservation Service County Committees (ASCS). A referendum would be held in which producers would vote to engage or not to engage in bargaining and to elect a producers' committee from the list of approved names.

After producers had elected to bargain by a simple majority and approved a committee to represent them, prospective purchasers of any commodity would select a negotiating committee that would meet to decide on price and other terms of trade. This scheme would involve a rather complex network of committee systems (see page 225). Its major weakness is its heavily political orientation, from the National Agricultural Relations Board down to the ASCS-sponsored committees. In short, it appears designed to wipe out the roles of existing cooperatives and general farm interest organizations in favor of a politically oriented committee system. It is doubtful whether any existing farm organization could support such a proposal, given its intent to institutionalize the existing ASCS committee system, rather than to provide producers with greater bargaining power.[16]

The second alternative consists of expanding federal market order activity to include bargaining. As proposed in Title II of the Mondale bill, federal order activity would be extended to all commodities instead of only those produced on a more local basis. In addition, the proposal would enable negotiations to take place under the umbrella of the federal orders (see page 226). Handlers would be required to bargain in good faith with a selected produc-

15. See Tony T. Dechant (President, National Farmers Union), testimony in U.S. Senate, Committee on Agriculture and Forestry, *Hearings on the Operation of Programs Established Pursuant To The Agricultural Act of 1965 And Their Continuation, And Proposed Strengthening of Farm Bargaining Power*, 90th Cong., 2d sess., 1968, 5.

16. Mr. Brannan and other officials of the National Farmers Union reportedly admit that this plan would have devastating effects on existing farm organizations. Initial response to the Mondale bill in *Hearings on the Operation of Programs . . . Farm Bargaining Power*.

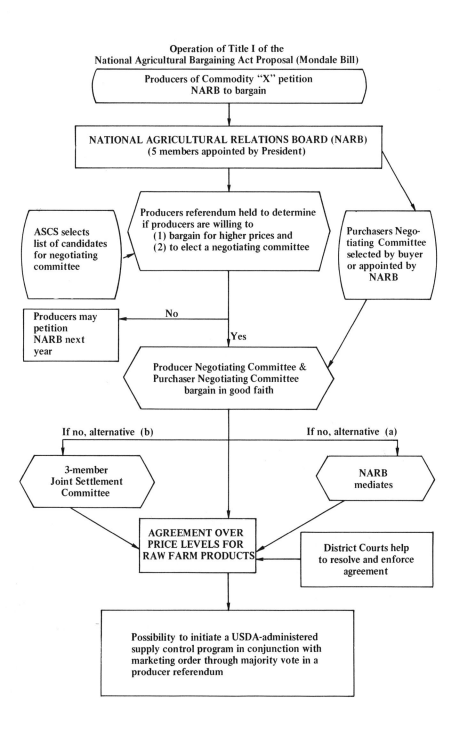

Operation of Title I of the
National Agricultural Bargaining Act Proposal (Mondale Bill)

Producers of Commodity "X" petition
NARB to bargain

NATIONAL AGRICULTURAL RELATIONS BOARD (NARB)
(5 members appointed by President)

ASCS selects
list of candidates
for negotiating
committee

Producers referendum held to determine
if producers are willing to
(1) bargain for higher prices and
(2) to elect a negotiating committee

Purchasers Nego-
tiating Committee
selected by buyer
or appointed by
NARB

Producers may
petition
NARB next
year

No

Yes

Producer Negotiating Committee &
Purchaser Negotiating Committee
bargain in good faith

If no, alternative (b)

If no, alternative (a)

3-member
Joint Settlement
Committee

NARB
mediates

AGREEMENT OVER
PRICE LEVELS FOR
RAW FARM PRODUCTS

District Courts help
to resolve and enforce
agreement

Possibility to initiate a USDA-administered
supply control program in conjunction with
marketing order through majority vote in a
producer referendum

**Operation of Title II of the
National Agricultural Bargaining Act Proposal
(Mondale Bill)**

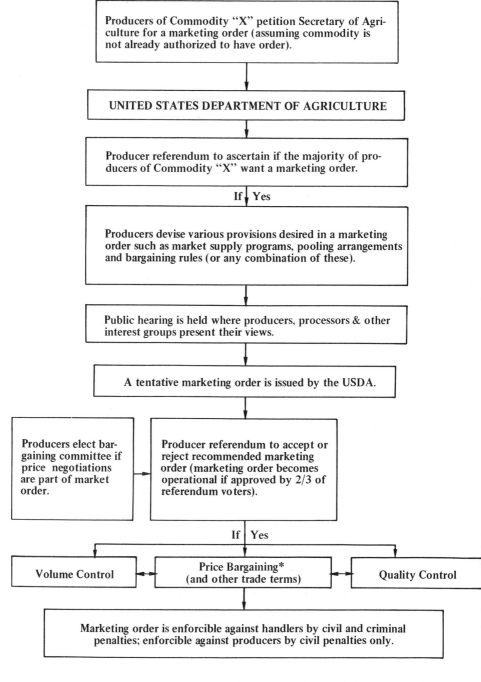

Producers of Commodity "X" petition Secretary of Agriculture for a marketing order (assuming commodity is not already authorized to have order).

UNITED STATES DEPARTMENT OF AGRICULTURE

Producer referendum to ascertain if the majority of producers of Commodity "X" want a marketing order.

If Yes

Producers devise various provisions desired in a marketing order such as market supply programs, pooling arrangements and bargaining rules (or any combination of these).

Public hearing is held where producers, processors & other interest groups present their views.

A tentative marketing order is issued by the USDA.

Producers elect bargaining committee if price negotiations are part of market order.

Producer referendum to accept or reject recommended marketing order (marketing order becomes operational if approved by 2/3 of referendum voters).

If Yes

Volume Control

Price Bargaining*
(and other trade terms)

Quality Control

Marketing order is enforcible against handlers by civil and criminal penalties; enforcible against producers by civil penalties only.

* Agreements must be reached between producer negotiating committee and handlers representing 50 per cent of the volume, before minimum price and other terms become binding.

ers' bargaining committee. Perhaps the most noteworthy feature of this proposal — one that has been long sought by the National Milk Producers Federation — is that producers could negotiate with more than one handler at a time. This approach has support in the USDA and among some commodity groups and will probably receive considerable play before Congress. In particular, dairy cooperatives and fruit and vegetable bargaining groups will be inclined to support it. The major weaknesses of the proposal are that it may tend to proliferate the number of bargaining associations, already large in number, and that minimum prices negotiated would ultimately have to be approved by the Secretary of Agriculture. Again, free play by voluntary farm organizations — general farm interest organizations and cooperatives — is not recognized and is somewhat constrained. A cross-commodity approach to farm pricing is not involved.

The approach to the problem through accreditation of a bargaining association by the Secretary of Agriculture — with subsequent notice to handlers that they must bargain in good faith — represents a plan offered by Ralph Bunje of the California Canning Peach Association.[17] The key to this proposal is that the Secretary would, after investigation of the quantity controlled, contracts, organization bylaws and financial structure of an association, accredit only a bona fide farmer-controlled bargaining association. The procedure is aimed at eliminating "bargaining" groups that ride the federal orders but that do not actually perform bargaining activities. In short, it is one method of limiting the number of bargaining associations to only those that represent a sufficient tonnage and number of producers to make them effective price leaders for producers they purport to represent. The proposal is viewed as fitting into the National Agricultural Relations Board framework as a replacement for the ASCS-approved producer committees.

In contrast to the foregoing approaches to farm bargaining, the new Farm Bureau bill appears directed toward taking things one step at a time. Rather than focusing on an institutional arrangement to bring parties together, the AFB is committed to dealing with processors and chains directly on an individual basis.

Significantly, none of the proposals includes recognition of the dual organization structure that farm operators typically use in representing their economic interests. Instead each directs itself to the "one" organization approach. As clearly demonstrated in the S. 109 struggle, failure to recognize this fundamental economic fact of life can only lead to dissension within and among farm organizations at a time when they can ill afford it. Cooperatives want a piece of the action. So do general farm interest organizations. Moreover, some governmental agencies such as the ASCS and federal order programs have their continued existence to protect, an interest evidenced in the

17. Ralph Bunje (General Manager, California Canning Peach Association), testimony in *ibid.*

Mondale bill. Before round two in farm bargaining legislation can commence in serious fashion, farm organizations must agree on just how big a role government should play in new farm programs and just how farm organizations should relate to each other in the bargaining process.

A reading on the current attitudes of many farm organizations suggests they desire to see government play a lesser role in determining farm prices and incomes. Many cooperative leaders foresee a bigger role for their organizations and a shift of responsibility in market regulation to their shoulders. At least two major general farm interest organizations foresee themselves playing a bigger role in farm bargaining. In deliberating the solutions to these fundamental issues, some lessons from other countries in which farm bargaining has been ongoing since the end of World War II would appear instructive. In particular, the lessons to be learned from Norwegian and Swedish action on the matter should serve as input to any constructive institutional arrangement.[18] In each instance, negotiations over price level now involve the general farm interest organizations and the co-ordinated cooperative systems in one capacity or another (see page 229).

The third fundamental issue that must be resolved by farm groups concerns the contents of a formulated bargaining proposal that all can support. Having formulated such a measure, farm groups must then seek the support of nonfarm allies in securing passage of the bill. S. 109 revealed that further bargaining legislation will not be greeted with enthusiasm by processors, packers, feed firms and other handlers. After all, any manufacturer wants to obtain his raw product at the lowest possible cost, and noncooperative handlers in agriculture are no different. Given the balance of political power exhibited in the life of S. 109, it behooves farm operators and their organizations to unite and seek support from as many nonfarm allies as possible. Anything less will result in no more than a token bargaining bill. Obviously, the bill must be written with thoughts of achieving support from nonfarm sources.

While the American Farm Bureau's 1969 policy resolution did not embody any specific proposal for institutional arrangements to carry out farm bargaining, it did define the ingredients. The resolution touched upon nearly every issue that was questioned in the discussions surrounding S. 109, and it provided support for an Agricultural Marketing and Bargaining act of 1969 to define and clarify the rights and limitations of bargaining associations.[19]

One of the first tasks in formulating this bill will be to write a statutory

18. Randall E. Torgerson, "Are There Lessons We Can Learn from Swedish Farmers?" *Hoards Dairymen*, 110 (January 10, 1965), 13; Randall Everett Torgerson, "The Cooperative Systems Approach to Improving Farm Incomes" (unpublished Ph.D. dissertation, Dept. of Agricultural Economics, University of Wisconsin, microfilm © 1968), 154.

19. American Farm Bureau Federation, *Farm Bureau Policies for 1969* (Chicago: American Farm Bureau Federation, 1969), 11.

**Scandinavian Farmers Relate Their Marketing
Cooperatives to General Farm Interest Organizations
in a "Cooperative Systems" Model for Purposes of Bargaining**

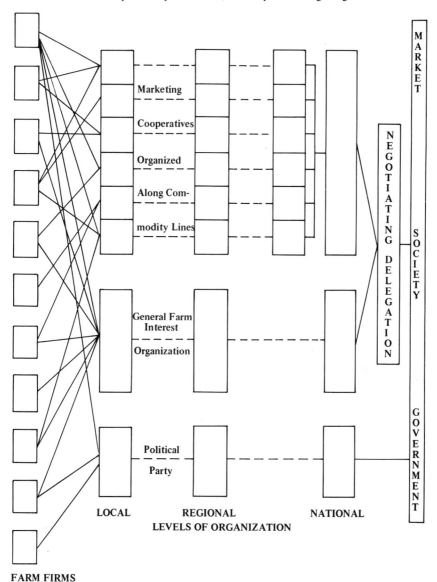

FARM FIRMS

Source: Randall E. Torgerson, "The Cooperative Systems Approach to
Improving Farm Incomes" (unpublished Ph.D. dissertation, Dept. of
Agricultural Economics, University of Wisconsin, 1968), 120.

definition of a bargaining association. For the American Farm Bureau and other general farm interest organizations, the problem is very thorny, since inevitably they will bump into other dimensions of their programs. Nevertheless, bargaining associations need a legal base to stand on even at the cost to general farm interest organizations of dispensing with other "cooperative" activities. As a working definition for purposes of discussion, a bargaining association might be comsidered an organization of farm operators that negotiates for price and other terms of trade as a representative for its members but does not handle or take title to the product or assume other major financial risks or responsibilities. It may be a single-commodity organization or one that bargains for farm operators on a cross-commodity basis, that is, general farm interest organizations.

A new bargaining bill must also specify recognition of bargaining associations by buyers of agricultural products and provide that they bargain in good faith. More than any other provision, this will draw rapid fire from processors and other handlers who deal with farm operators. As indicated by S. 109, processors and integrators will emotionally dramatize farm bargaining as leading to inefficiency and ultimate denial of their right to deal with producers on a direct basis. As Frank Frazier, one spokesman for poultry integrators, has argued: "As we look at low farm prices today, let's go beyond a sympathetic concern for the sociological problems they create and avoid legislating a course of action for more commodities that would shift control over the allocation of resources from the market place to big bargaining associations and the federal government." [20] No punches will be pulled by big business in opposing farm operators.

Despite charges to the contrary, most farm organizations are committed to a voluntary approach to farm bargaining and not to a closed shop. This commitment is the greatest weakness and also the greatest strength of farm organization efforts. In seeking bargaining rights, producers are neither compelling buyers to reach an agreement with them nor requiring producers to join an organization, although nonjoiners who participate in the benefits of group action should be expected to share in the costs of it. Given the voluntary nature of farm organizations, it is necessary that buyers be brought to the bargaining table through a legislative provision that provides standards of recognition of producer associations.

The difficulty in achieving the recognition of this provision will be surpassed only by that of broadening the rights of bargaining associations under antitrust law.[21] This undertaking will require every bit of legislative finesse

20. R. Frank Frazier (Executive Vice-President, National Broiler Council), "Compulsory Bargaining — The Road Ahead?" *Feedstuffs*, 39 (December 9, 1967), 9.
21. John E. Noakes, "Agricultural Cooperatives," *Antitrust Law Journal*, 33 (1967), 7; L. Gene Lemon (Assistant General Counsel, American Farm Bureau Federation), "Antitrust and Agricultural Cooperatives: Collective Bargaining in the Sale of Agricultural Products," *North Dakota Law Review*, 44, 4 (Summer, 1968), 505.

and ingenuity that farm groups can muster. As noted in the report of the National Commission on Food Marketing, some form of government sanction will be required by farm operators in the foreseeable future.[22] However, needing and receiving, especially as they relate to the political arena, are two different things. Just as man doesn't change an imperfect setting until there is enough incentive for him to change, Congress may not act upon a measure unless pressures are forthcoming from congressional districts and the Administration to initiate such changes.[23] Even after a bill such as S. 109 is started down the road of congressional committees, it is subject to the legislative process and a series of compromises between differing points of view.

It may be surmised that general farm interest organizations do not presently have any specific legal foundation upon which to base their activities. Establishment of a legal base under the antitrust umbrella, as originally introduced by the American Farm Bureau in 1964, will require a special act of Congress. Similarly, the question of affiliation of cooperatives with each other, whether through a federated system or merger or acquisition, needs further clarification. In particular, a new mandate is probably needed to enable cooperatives to federate through regional and national federations to effect greater market power for farm operators. In undertaking current legislative efforts, general farm interest organizations and cooperatives should note that they share a common need for securing new legislation.

Farm operators must face some hard realities and immense obstacles in seeking new legislation. As a political minority, they can no longer afford the luxury of having many organizations performing ineffectively. Farm operators must scuttle those organizations that are only consuming time and are living off of past grandeur, although one sociologist has suggested that we lack good means of providing organizations in this country with a decent burial.[24] Farm organizations must also view their organization structures and functions as complementary instead of competitive. Instead of asking, "What do we have to show for the assistance we have given cooperatives?", leaders of general farm interest organizations must continue to lend every support to fostering and improving cooperative marketing activity. Only through a combination of both organization structures can farm operators survive as viable entrepreneurs. At the same time, cooperative leaders must also take a careful look at their policy of not participating in political activities, and a strengthening of their lobbying efforts also seems desirable. While neither type of farm organization can afford to adhere to partisan political alignment, each

22. National Commission on Food Marketing, *Food: From Farmer to Consumer*, 102.

23. This is not to suggest that legislators do not exercise creativity or that the Congress does not engage in long-range planning. However, certain humanitarian and economic needs are not forthcoming unless the deprived mobilize their forces to call public attention to it.

24. My good friend Donald E. Johnson (Professor of Rural Sociology, University of Wisconsin) is responsible for this view.

must achieve a position of neutral flexbility and strength that can be enjoyed as a minority power.

In terms of obstacles, farm operators face not only a politically and economically strong big business lobby, but also certain antifarm organization groups — typified by the National Tax Equality Association — that ruffle their feathers every time the words "cooperative" or "farm bargaining" are mentioned. Furthermore, many trade lobbies in Washington are doing a better job of "educating" their legislators than are farm groups. Many legislators openly express the idea that American agriculture and family farmers are on their last legs. Several suggest a movement to 100 corporations controlling agriculture.[25] In light of these developments, American consumers must take stock of the tremendous potential for price fixing and ask themselves whether they are interested in maintaining the farm operator's position through strengthened farm organizations and public support or whether they want agriculture to come under the control of several "bigs."

The greatest challenge in achieving further bargaining legislation is for farm groups to unite with each other and with nonfarm groups to attain desired objectives. S. 109 proved that farm operators can still pack a wallop when their farm organizations are united. S. 109 also proved that farmers do have allies in labor, consumers and rural-oriented church organizations. The support of these off-farm interests may well determine the success of future farm legislative efforts and coincidentally the future economic organization of American agriculture. As farm operators strive for producer power at the bargaining table, the question that looms on the horizon is not whether they are moving, but whether they are moving fast enough.

25. Several legislators, including Senator Aiken and Congressmen Poage and Latta, conveyed this prognostication to me.

Appendixes

California

CHAPTER 606

*An act to add Chapter 4a (commencing with Section 1223) to Division 6 of
the Agricultural Code, relating to co-operative bargaining associations.*

[Approved by Governor May 27, 1961. Filed with Secretary of State
May 30, 1961.]

The people of the State of California do enact as follows:

SECTION 1. Chapter 4a (commencing with Section 1223) is added to
Division 6 of the Agricultural Code, to read:

CHAPTER 4a. CO-OPERATIVE BARGAINING ASSOCIATIONS

1223. As used in this chapter a "co-operative bargaining association" is
a farmer association organized and functioning under Chapter 4 (commencing with Section 1190) of Division 6 of this code, for the purpose of group
bargaining between its producer members and the first handler or processor,
with respect to the sale of any agricultural commodity except milk, cotton or
cotton seed.

1224. It is the public policy of the State of California to establish and
support the right of any farmer to join voluntarily and belong to co-operative
bargaining associations.

1225. It is an unfair trade practice, and unlawful, for any processor,
handler, distributor, or agent thereof, or for any other person to do any of the
following:

(a) Interfere with, restrain, coerce or boycott producers in the exercise
of the rights guranteed pursuant to Section 1224.

(b) Discriminate against producers with respect to price or other terms
of purchase of raw agricultural commodities, by reason of the producer's
membership in or contract with co-operative bargaining associations.

(c) Pay or loan money, or give any other thing of value to a producer
as an inducement or reward for refusing to or ceasing to belong to a co-operative bargaining association.

(d) Maliciously or knowingly give false reports about the finances.
management or activities of a co-operative bargaining association.

1226. The willful violation of any provisions of this chapter is a misdemeanor punishable by a fine of not less than fifty dollars ($50) nor more than five hundred dollars ($500) for each and every such violation.

(b) In addition to the penalty provided for above, any person who violates any provision of this chapter shall be liable civilly for a penalty in an amount not to exceed a sum of five hundred dollars ($500) for each and every violation thereof.

1227. For the purpose of enforcing the provisions of this chapter the director is authorized to receive complaints from producers against any processor, handler, distributor or any agent thereof, or any other person, with respect to violations of the unfair trade practices specified in Section 1225. Upon verification of the complaint the director shall, or upon his own motion may, make any and all necessary investigations, examinations or inspections of any transaction involving a suspected violation of any provision of this chapter.

1228. The director may bring an action to enjoin the violation or threatened violation of any provision of this chapter in the superior court of the county in which such violation occurred or is about to occur. Actions against different defendants may be consolidated, in the discretion of the court, if the alleged violations are of the same provision, have occurred in the same or an adjoining county, relate to the same agricultural commodity, occurred in the same production season, and such consolidation can be done without prejudice to a substantial right of any defendant. Any proceedings brought pursuant to this section shall be governed in all other respects by the provisions of Chapter 3 (commencing with Section 525) Title 7 of Part 2 of the Code of Civil Procedure.

1229. The director shall have and may exercise any or all of the powers conferred by Article 2 (commencing with Section 11180), Chapter 2, Part 1, Division 3, Title 2 of the Government Code upon the head of a department of the State with respect to hearings and investigations under this chapter.

Ohio

(Amended Senate Bill No. 60)

AN ACT

To enact sections 1729.181 and 1729.99 of the Revised Code, to establish marketing rights for agricultural associations and their members.

Be it enacted by the General Assembly of the State of Ohio:

SECTION 1. That sections 1729.181 and 1729.99 of the Revised Code be enacted to read as follows:

Sec. 1729.181. (A) No processor, handler, distributor, dealer, or agent thereof who purchases or contracts to purchase milk, fruits, vegetables, sweet corn, or other canning crops from producers of such raw agricultural products shall:

(1) Use duress against, coerce, or boycott producers of raw agricultural products in the exercise of their rights to join and belong to co-operative agricultural marketing associations;

(2) Discriminate against producers of raw agricultural products with respect to price, quantity, or quality, or other terms of purchase of raw agricultural products, solely by reason of the producer's membership in or marketing contract with co-operative agricultural marketing associations.

(B) For the purpose of enforcing section 1729.181 of the Revised Code, the director of agriculture may receive sworn complaints from affected producers of raw agricultural products or the co-operative agricultural marketing association of which such producers are members, or with whom they have a marketing contract, with respect to violations or threatened violations of such section. The director may make all necessary investigations, examinations, or inspections of any violation or threatened violation specified in the sworn complaint filed with him under this division.

(C) The director may, after receiving a sworn complaint and the holding of an informal hearing on the charges made in such complaint, bring an action to enjoin the violation of any of the provisions of section 1729.181 of the Revised Code as set forth in such complaint in the court of common pleas of the county in which such violation occurred. A summons in such action against any defendant shall be issued to the sheriff of any county within this state in which such defendant resides or may be served as in other civil actions. Actions against different defendants may be consolidated, in the discretion of the court, if the alleged violations are of the same provision, have occurred in the same or an adjoining county, relate to the same agricultural product, occurred in the same production season, and such consolidation can be made without prejudice to a substantial right of any defendant.

Nothing in this section shall be interpreted in any way to affect the rights of a producer of raw agricultural products, who has not signed a contract with a co-operative agricultural marketing association, to bargain for his crop individually with any processor. A processor may, but shall not be required to, bargain for any of his raw agricultural product requirements with any co-operative agricultural marketing association or associations. The inability of a processor or his refusal to meet the terms and conditions of any co-operative agricultural marketing association proposed contract shall not be interpreted as a boycott or discrimination against the co-operative agricultural marketing association or its members.

Sec. 1729.99 Whoever violates section 1729.181 of the Revised Code shall be fined not less than fifty nor more than five hundred dollars for each offense.

ROGER CLOUD,
Speaker of the House of Representatives.

JOHN W. BROWN,
President of the Senate.

Passed June 29, 1965.
Approved July 6, 1965.
JAMES A. RHODES,
Governor.

The sectional numbers herein are in conformity with the Revised Code.
OHIO LEGISLATIVE SERVICE COMMISSION
LAUREN A. GLOSSER, *Director.*

Filed in the office of the Secretary of State at Columbus, Ohio, on the 7th day of July, A. D. 1965.

Oregon

PRODUCERS' COOPERATIVE BARGAINING ASSOCIATIONS
646.515 Definitions for ORS 646.515 to 646.545. As used in ORS 646.515 to 646.545, unless the context requires otherwise:

(1) "Agricultural commodity" or "commodities" means any and all agricultural, horticultural, viticultural and vegetable products produced in this state, either in their natural state or as processed by a producer for the purpose of marketing such product, including bees and honey, but not including timber, timber products, grain and grain products or seed products.

(2) "Cooperative bargaining association" means an association of producers formed or operated pursuant to ORS chapter 62 with the purpose of group bargaining with respect to the sale of any agricultural commodity or commodities.

(3) (a) "Dealer" means, except as provided in paragraph (b) of this subsection, any person or his agent who purchases or contracts to purchase an agricultural commodity from a producer or his agent, for the purpose of packing, processing or marketing such commodity.

(b) "Dealer" shall not include any organization operating as an agricultural cooperative corporation.

(4) "Producer" means a person engaged in the business of producing agricultural commodities.
[1963 c.514 §1]

646.520 [Repealed by 1953 c.391 §2]

646.525 Cooperative bargaining associations authorized. Producers shall have the right to join voluntarily and belong to cooperative bargaining associations.

[1963 c.514 §2]

646.530 [Repealed by 1953 c.391 §2]

646.535. Unfair trade practices prohibited. No dealer shall maliciously and knowingly engage in the following unfair trade practices:

(1) Interfere with, restrain, coerce or boycott a producer in the exercise of the rights guaranteed pursuant to ORS 646.525; or

(2) Discriminate against a producer with respect to price or other terms of purchase of raw agricultural commodities, by reason of the producer's membership in or contract with cooperative bargaining associations; or

(3) Pay or loan money, or give any other thing of value to a producer as an inducement or reward for refusing to or ceasing to belong to a cooperative bargaining association.

[1963 c.514 §3]

646.540 [Repealed by 1953 c.391 §2]

646.545 Remedy for unfair trade practices; jurisdiction. (1) In addition to any other remedies provided by law, any producer injured by a violation of ORS 646.535 may maintain an action for damages sustained by such producer.

(2) The prevailing party in any action brought pursuant to subsection (1) of this section shall be allowed, in addition to the costs and disbursements otherwise prescribed by law, a reasonable sum for attorney's fees for the prosecution or defense of such action.

(3) Notwithstanding the provisions of ORS 46.060 to 46.080, the district court shall not have jurisdiction in any action damages for violation of ORS 646.535.

[1963 c.514 §§4, 5]

Appendix B

Forms of S. 109 — 1964–1968

88TH CONGRESS
2D SESSION **H. R. 11146**

IN THE HOUSE OF REPRESENTATIVES

MAY 5, 1964

Mr. SECREST introduced the following bill; which was referred to the Committee on the Judiciary

---

A BILL

To amend the Capper-Volstead Act, with respect to the control of unfair practices affecting associations of producers of agricultural products and members thereof.

1   *Be it enacted by the Senate and House of Representa-*

2   *tives of the United States of America in Congress assembled,*

3   That the Act to authorize associations of producers of agri-

4   cultural products, approved February 18, 1922 (42 Stat.

5   388; 7 U.S.C. 291-2), is amended by the addition of the

6   following new sections:

7   "SEC. 3. UNLAWFUL PRACTICES.—It shall be unlawful

8   for any processor, handler, distributor, dealer, or agent there-

9   of, doing business in interstate or foreign commerce, who

10   purchases or contracts to purchase an agricultural commodity

1

2

1 from a producer engaged in the production of agricultural

2 products, knowingly to do any of the following:

3   "(a) Interfere with, restrain, coerce, or boycott any

4   agricultural producer in the exercise of his rights to

5   join and belong to an association of producers of agricul-

6   tural products;

7   "(b) Discriminate against any agricultural pro-

8   ducer with respect to price, quantity, quality, or other

9   terms of purchase of raw agricultural commodities by

10   reason of his membership in, or contract with, such

11   association;

12   "(c) Coerce or intimidate any association member

13   or other person to breach, cancel, or otherwise terminate

14   a membership agreement or marketing contract with

15   such association;

16   "(d) Pay or loan money, or give any other thing of

17   value, to a producer as an inducement or reward for

18   refusing to or ceasing to belong to such association;

19   "(e) Make false reports about the finances, manage-

20   ment, or activities of such associations, or interfere in

21   any way with the efforts of such associations in carrying

22   out the legitimate objects thereof.

23 "SEC. 4. CRIMINAL PENALTY—DAMAGES.— (a) Any

24 person who violates, or combines or conspires with any other

25 person to violate, any provision of section 3 of this Act is

3

1 guilty of a misdemeanor, and, on conviction thereof, shall be

2 punished by a fine not exceeding $1,000, or imprisonment

3 not exceeding one year, or both, in the discretion of the

4 court.

5 "(b) Any person injured in his business or property by

6 reason of any violation of, or combination or conspiracy to

7 violate, any provision of section 3 of this Act may sue

8 therefor in the district court of the United States for the

9 district in which the defendant resides or is found or has an

10 agent, without respect to the amount in controversy, and

11 shall recover threefold the damages sustained, and the cost

12 of the suit, including a reasonable attorney's fee.

13 "(c) The foregoing provisions shall not be construed to

14 deprive the proper State courts of jurisdiction in actions for

15 damages thereunder.

16 "SEC. 5. AFFILIATION OF ASSOCIATIONS.—Nothing

17 contained in this Act shall be construed to forbid the affilia-

18 tion of an association, as described in section 1 of this Act,

19 with other associations having similar objectives, or with bona

20 fide agricultural or horticultural organizations whose primary

21 objectives are to promote, protect, and represent the business

22 and economic interests of farmers and ranchers."

89TH CONGRESS
1ST SESSION

S. 109

IN THE SENATE OF THE UNITED STATES

JANUARY 6, 1965

Mr. AIKEN (for himself, Mr. LAUSCHE, Mr. MCCARTHY, and Mr. YOUNG of North Dakota) introduced the following bill; which was read twice and referred to the Committee on Agriculture and Forestry

A BILL

To amend the Act authorizing association of producers of agricultural products, approved February 18, 1922.

1   *Be it enacted by the Senate and House of Representa-*

2 *tives of the United States of America in Congress assembled,*

3 That the Act entitled "An Act to authorize association of

4 producers of agricultural products", approved February 18,

5 1922 (42 Stat. 388; 7 U.S.C. 291–2), is amended by add-

6 ing the following new sections at the end thereof:

7   "SEC. 3. It shall be unlawful for any processor, handler,

8 distributor, dealer, or agent thereof, doing business in inter-

9 state or foreign commerce, who purchases or contracts to pur-

10 chase an agricultural commodity from a producer engaged in

VII—O

2

1 the production of agricultural products, knowingly to do any

2 of the following—

3   "(a) Interfere with, restrain, coerce, or boycott any

4   agricultural producer in the exercise of his rights to

5   join and belong to an association of producers of agri-

6   cultural products;

7   "(b) Discriminate against any agricultural pro-

8   ducer with respect to price, quantity, quality, or other

9   terms of purchase of raw agricultural commodities be-

10   cause of his membership in, or contact with, such

11   association;

12   "(c) Coerce, or intimidate any association member

13   or other person to breach, cancel, or otherwise terminate

14   a membership agreement or marketing contract with,

15   such association;

16   "(d) Pay or loan money, or give any other thing

17   of value, to a producer as an inducement or reward for

18   refusing to or ceasing to belong to such association;

19   "(e) Make false reports about the finances, man-

20   agement, or activities of such associations, or interfere

21   in any way with the efforts of such associations in carry-

22   ing out the legitimate objects thereof.

23 "SEC. 4. (a) Any person who violates, or combines or

24 conspires with any other person to violate, any provision of

25 section 3 of this Act is guilty of a misdemeanor, and, on con-

3

1 viction thereof, shall be punished by a fine not exceeding

2 $1,000, or imprisonment not exceeding one year, or both,

3 in the discretion of the court.

4   "(b) Any person injured in his business or property by

5 reason of any violation of, or combination or conspiracy to

6 violate, any provision of section 3 of this Act may sue there-

7 for in the district court of the United States for the district

8 in which defendant resides or is found or has an agent, with-

9 out respect to the amount in controversy, and shall recover

10 threefold the damages sustained, and the cost of the suit,

11 including a reasonable attorney's fee.

12   "(c) The foregoing provisions shall not be construed

13 to deprive the proper State courts of jurisdiction in actions

14 for damages thereunder.

15   "SEC. 5. Nothing contained in this Act shall be con-

16 strued to forbid the affiliation of an association, as described

17 in the first section of this Act, with other associations having

18 similar objectives, or with bona fide agricultural or horticul-

19 tural organizations whose primary objectives are to promote,

20 protect, and represent the business and economic interests of

21 farmers and ranchers."

89TH CONGRESS
2D SESSION

S. 109

IN THE SENATE OF THE UNITED STATES

SEPTEMBER 21, 1966

Referred to the Committee on Agriculture and Forestry and ordered to be printed

AMENDMENTS

Intended to be proposed by Mr. AIKEN to S. 109, a bill to amend the Act authorizing association of producers of agricultural products, approved February 18, 1922, viz: Strike out all after the enacting clause and insert the following:

1 "That this Act shall be known as the Agricultural Producers

2 Marketing Act of 1966.

3   "LEGISLATIVE FINDINGS AND DECLARATION OF POLICY

4   "SEC. 2. Agricultural products are produced in the

5 United States by many individual farmers and ranchers scat-

6 tered throughout the various States of the Nation. Such

7 products in fresh or processed form move in large part in the

8 channels of interstate and foreign commerce, and such prod-

9 ucts which do not move in these channels directly burden or

Amdt. No. 933

2

1 affect interstate commerce. The efficient production and mar-

2 keting of agricultural products by farmers and ranchers is of

3 vital concern to their welfare and to the general economy of

4 the Nation. Because agricultural products are produced by

5 numerous individual farmers, the marketing and bargaining

6 position of individual farmers will be adversely affected un-

7 less they are free to band together in cooperative organiza-

8 tions as authorized by law. Interference with this right is

9 contrary to the public interest and adversely affects the free

10 and orderly flow of goods in interstate and foreign commerce.

11   "It is, therefore, declared to be the policy of Congress

12 and the purpose of this Act to establish standards of fair

13 practices required of handlers in their dealings with producers

14 of agricultural products and their cooperative associations.

15   "Sec. 3. When used in this Act—

16   "(a) The term 'handler' means any person, other than

17 an association of producers, engaged in the business or prac-

18 tice of (1) acquiring agricultural products from producers

19 or associations of producers for processing or sale; (2) grad-

20 ing, packaging, handling, storing, or processing agricultural

21 products received from producers or associations of producers;

22 (3) contracting or negotiating contracts or other arrange-

23 ments, written or oral, with producers or associations of pro-

24 ducers with respect to the production or marketing of any

25 agricultural product; or (4) acting as an agent or broker

3

1 for a handler in the performance of any function or act spec-
2 ified in clause (1), (2), or (3) of this paragraph.

3 "(b) The term 'producer' means a farmer, rancher, or
4 any other person who produces raw agricultural products.

5 "(c) The term 'association of producers' means any
6 farmer-owned and controlled cooperative marketing, bar-
7 gaining, shipping, or processing organization as defined in
8 section 15(a) of the Agricultural Marketing Act of 1929,
9 as amended (49 Stat. 317; 12 U.S.C. 1141j(a)), or in
10 section 1 of the Act entitled 'An Act to authorize associa-
11 tion of producers of agricultural products', approved Febru-
12 ary 18, 1922 (42 Stat. 388; 7 U.S.C. 291).

13 "(d) The term 'person' includes individuals, partner-
14 ships, corporations, and associations.

15 "SEC. 4. It shall be unlawful for any handler knowingly
16 to engage or permit any employee or agent to engage in the
17 following practices:

18 "(a) To interfere with or restrain, or threaten to inter-
19 fere with or restrain, by boycott, coercion, or any unfair or
20 deceptive act or practice, any producer in the exercise of his
21 rights to join and belong to an association of producers; or

22 "(b) To discriminate or threaten to discriminate against
23 any producer with respect to price, quantity, quality, or other
24 terms of purchase of agricultural commodities because of

4

1 his membership in or contract with an association of pro-

2 ducers; or

3 "(c) To coerce or intimidate any producer or other

4 person to breach, cancel, or otherwise terminate a member-

5 ship agreement or marketing contract with an association

6 of producers; or

7 "(d) To pay or loan money, give any thing of value in

8 excess of the true market value of any agricultural commodity

9 which is being purchased, or offer any other inducement or

10 reward to a producer for refusing to or ceasing to belong to

11 an association of producers; or

12 "(e) To make false reports about the finances, man-

13 agement, or activities of associations of producers or interfere

14 by any unfair or deceptive act or practice with the efforts of

15 such associations in carrying out the legitimate objects

16 thereof; or

17 "(f) To conspire, combine, agree, or arrange with any

18 other person to do, or aid or abet the doing of, any act made

19 unlawful by this Act.

20 "SEC. 5. (a) Whenever any handler has engaged or

21 there are reasonable grounds to believe that any handler is

22 about to engage in any act or practice prohibited by section

23 4, a civil action for preventive relief, including an application

24 for a permanent or temporary injunction, restraining order,

25 or other order, may be instituted by the person aggrieved.

5

1 In any action commenced pursuant hereto, the court, in its

2 discretion, may allow the prevailing party a reasonable at-

3 torney's fee as part of the costs.

4   "(b) Whenever the Secretary of Agriculture has rea-

5 sonable cause to believe that any handler or group of handlers

6 has engaged in any act or practice prohibited by section 4,

7 he may bring civil action in the appropriate district court of

8 the United States by filing with it a complaint (1) setting

9 forth facts pertaining to such pattern or practice, and (2)

10 requesting such preventive relief, including an application for

11 a permanent or temporary injunction, restraining order, or

12 other order against the handler, or handlers, responsible for

13 such acts or practices.

14   "(c) Any person injured in his business or property

15 by reason of any violation of, or combination or conspiracy

16 to violate, any provision of section 4 of this Act may sue

17 therefor in the district court of the United States for the

18 district in which defendant resides or is found or has an

19 agent, without respect to the amount in controversy, and

20 shall recover threefold the damages sustained, and the cost

21 of the suit, including a reasonable attorney's fee.

22   "(d) Any person who violates, or combines or con-

23 spires with any other person to violate, any provision of

24 section 4 of this Act is guilty of a misdemeanor, and, on

25 conviction thereof, shall be punished by a fine not exceed-

6

1 ing $1,000, or imprisonment not exceeding one year, or
2 both, in the discretion of the court.

3 "(e) The district courts of the United States shall have
4 jurisdiction of proceedings instituted pursuant to this sec-
5 tion and shall exercise the same without regard to whether
6 the aggrieved party shall have exhausted any administrative
7 or other remedies that may be provided by law.

8 "(f) The foregoing provisions shall not be construed
9 to deprive the proper State courts of jurisdiction in actions
10 for damages thereunder.

11 "SEC. 6. If any provision of this Act or the application
12 thereof to any person or circumstances is held invalid, the
13 validity of the remainder of the Act and of the application
14 of such provision to other persons and circumstances shall
15 not be affected thereby."

Amend the title so as to read: "A bill to control
unfair trade practices affecting producers of agricultural
products and associations of such producers, and for other
purposes."

90TH CONGRESS
1ST SESSION

S. 109

IN THE SENATE OF THE UNITED STATES

JANUARY 11, 1967

Mr. AIKEN (for himself, Mr. LAUSCHE, and Mr. YOUNG of North Dakota) introduced the following bill; which was read twice and referred to the Committee on Agriculture and Forestry

---

A BILL

To control unfair trade practices affecting producers of agricultural products and associations of such producers, and for other purposes.

1   *Be it enacted by the Senate and House of Representa-*

2 *tives of the United States of America in Congress assembled,*

3 That this Act shall be known as the Agricultural Producers

4 Marketing Act of 1967.

5   LEGISLATIVE FINDINGS AND DECLARATION OF POLICY

6   SEC. 2. Agricultural products are produced in the

7 United States by many individual farmers and ranchers scat-

8 tered throughout the various States of the Nation. Such

9 products in fresh or processed form move in large part in

10 the channels of interstate and foreign commerce, and such

    II—O

★(Star Print)

2

1 products which do not move in these channels directly bur-

2 den or affect interstate commerce. The efficient production

3 and marketing of agricultural products by farmers and ranch-

4 ers is of vital concern to their welfare and to the general

5 economy of the Nation. Because agricultural products are

6 produced by numerous individual farmers, the marketing and

7 bargaining position of individual farmers will be adversely

8 affected unless they are free to band together in cooperative

9 organizations as authorized by law. Interference with this

10 right is contrary to the public interest and adversely affects

11 the free and orderly flow of goods in interstate and foreign

12 commerce.

13   It is, therefore, declared to be the policy of Congress and

14 the purpose of this Act to establish standards of fair practices

15 required of handlers in their dealings with producers of agri-

16 cultural products and their cooperative associations.

17   SEC. 3. When used in this Act—

18   (a) The term "handler" means any person engaged in

19 the business or practice of (1) acquiring agricultural prod-

20 ucts from producers or associations of producers for process-

21 ing or sale; (2) grading, packaging, handling, storing, or

22 processing agricultural products received from producers or

23 associations of producers; (3) contracting or negotiating

24 contracts or other arrangements, written or oral, with pro-

25 ducers or associations of producers with respect to the pro-

3

1 duction or marketing of any agricultural product; or (4)

2 acting as an agent or broker for a handler in the perform-

3 ance of any function or act specified in clause (1), (2), or

4 (3) of this paragraph.

5   (b) The term "producer" means a person engaged in

6 the production of agricultural products as a farmer, planter,

7 rancher, dairyman, fruit, vegetable, or nut grower.

8   (c) The term "association of producers" means any

9 marketing, bargaining, shipping or processing organization

10 as defined in section 15 (a) of the Agricultural Marketing

11 Act of 1929, as amended (49 Stat. 317; 12 U.S.C.

12 1141j (a)), or in section 1 of the Act, entitled "an Act to

13 authorize association of producers of agricultural products,"

14 approved February 18, 1922 (42 Stat. 388; 7 U.S.C. 291).

15   (d) The term "person" includes individuals, partner-

16 ships, corporations, and associations.

17   SEC. 4. It shall be unlawful for any handler knowingly

18 to engage or permit any employee or agent to engage in the

19 following practices:

20   (a) To interfere with or restrain, or threaten to inter-

21 fere with or restrain, by boycott, coercion, or any unfair or

22 deceptive act or practice, any producer in the exercise of his

23 right to join and belong to an association of producers; or

24   (b) To discriminate or threaten to discriminate against

25 any producer with respect to price, quantity, quality, or

4

1 other terms of purchase or acquisition of agricultural com-
2 modities because of his membership in or contract with an
3 association of producers; or

4   (c) To coerce or intimidate any producer or other
5 person to breach, cancel, or otherwise terminate a member-
6 ship agreement or marketing contract with an association
7 of producers; or

8   (d) To pay or loan money, give any thing of value
9 in excess of the true market value of any agricultural com-
10 modity which is being purchased, or offer any other induce-
11 ment or reward to a producer for refusing to or ceasing to
12 belong to an association of producers; or

13   (e) To make false reports about the finances, manage-
14 ment, or activities of associations of producers or interfere
15 by any unfair or deceptive act or practice with the efforts
16 of such associations in carrying out the legitimate objects
17 thereof; or

18   (f) To conspire, combine, agree, or arrange with any
19 other person to do, or aid or abet the doing of, any act
20 made unlawful by this Act.

21   SEC. 5. (a) Whenever any handler has engaged or
22 there are reasonable grounds to believe that any handler is
23 about the engage in any act or practice prohibited by section
24 4, a civil action for preventive relief, including an application
25 for a permanent or temporary injunction, restraining order,

5

1 or other order, may be instituted by the person aggrieved. In

2 any action commenced pursuant hereto, the court, in its

3 discretion, may allow the prevailing party a reasonable

4 attorney's fee as part of the costs.

5 (b) Whenever the Secretary of Agriculture has reason-

6 able cause to believe that any handler or group of handlers

7 has engaged in any act or practice prohibited by section 4,

8 he may bring civil action in the appropriate district court of

9 the United States by filing with it a complaint (1) setting

10 forth facts pertaining to such pattern or practice, and (2)

11 requesting such preventive relief, including an application

12 for a permanent or temporary injunction, restraining order,

13 or other order against the handler, or handlers, responsible

14 for such acts or practices.

15 (c) Any person injured in his business or property by

16 reason of any violation of, or combination or conspiracy to

17 violate, any provision of section 4 of this Act may sue there-

18 for in the district court of the United States for the district

19 in which defendant resides or is found or has an agent, with-

20 out respect to the amount in controversy, and shall recover

21 threefold the damages sustained, and the cost of the suit,

22 including a reasonable attorney's fee.

23 (d) Any person who violates, or combines or conspires

24 with any other person to violate, any provision of section

25 4 of this Act is guilty of a misdemeanor, and, on conviction

6

1 thereof, shall be punished by a fine not exceeding $1,000,

2 or imprisonment not exceeding one year, or both, in the dis-

3 cretion of the court.

4   (e) The district courts of the United States shall have

5 jurisdiction of proceedings instituted pursuant to this section

6 and shall exercise the same without regard to whether the

7 aggrieved party shall have exhausted any administrative or

8 other remedies that may be provided by law.

9   (f) The foregoing provisions shall not be construed to

10 deprive the proper State courts of jurisdiction in actions for

11 damages thereunder.

12   SEC. 6. If any provision of this Act or the application

13 thereof to any person or circumstances is held invalid, the

14 validity of the remainder of the Act and of the application

15 of such provision to other persons and circumstances shall not

16 be affected thereby.

[COMMITTEE PRINT NO. 1]

JULY 25, 1967

TO ILLUSTRATE PROPOSALS MADE BY VARIOUS WITNESSES

EXPLANATION

This Committee Print has been prepared by the Committee staff to illustrate proposals by various witnesses and present the issues raised by those proposals to the subcommittee for its decision. It is limited to proposals which appeared to have substantial support or which were of a technical nature. The Committee staff has prepared in a separate document a list of all specific proposals received by the Committee prior to July 7.

90TH CONGRESS
1ST SESSION

S. 109

IN THE SENATE OF THE UNITED STATES

JANUARY 11, 1967

Mr. AIKEN (for himself, Mr. LAUSCHE, Mr. BAYH, Mr. BURDICK, Mr. CHURCH, Mr. HART, Mr. HICKENLOOPER, Mr. McCARTHY, Mr. TYDINGS, and Mr. YOUNG of North Dakota) introduced the following bill; which was read twice and referred to the Committee on Agriculture and Forestry

[Omit the part struck through and insert the part printed in italic]

A BILL

To control unfair trade practices affecting producers of agricultural products and associations of such producers, and for other purposes.

1   *Be it enacted by the Senate and House of Representa-*

2 *tives of the United States of America in Congress assembled,*

    J. 81–715——1

2

1   That this Act shall be known as the Agricultural Producers
2   Marketing Act of 1967.

3   LEGISLATIVE FINDINGS AND DECLARATION OF POLICY

4   SEC. 2. Agricultural products are produced in the
5   United States by many individual farmers and ranchers scat-
6   tered throughout the various States of the Nation. Such
7   products in fresh or processed form move in large part in
8   the channels of interstate and foreign commerce, and such
9   products which do not move in these channels directly bur-
10 den or affect interstate commerce. The efficient production
11 and marketing of agricultural products by farmers and ranch-
12 ers is of vital concern to their welfare and to the general
13 economy of the Nation. Because agricultural products are
14 produced by numerous individual farmers, the marketing and
15 bargaining position of individual farmers will be adversely
16 affected unless they are free to ~~band together~~ *join together or*
17 *not to join together* in cooperative organizations as authorized
18 by law. Interference with ~~this right~~ *these rights* is contrary
19 to the public interest and adversely affects the free and orderly
20 flow of goods in interstate and foreign commerce.

21   It is, therefore, declared to be the policy of Congress and
22 the purpose of this Act to establish standards of fair practices
23 required of handlers ~~in their dealings with producers of agri-~~

3

1 ~~cultural products and their cooperative associations~~ *and asso-*

2 *ciations of producers in their dealings in agricultural products.*

> Explanation: The use of the word "join" rather than "band" was suggested by Senator Lausche. Other witnesses proposed that the right not to join be protected, and that bargaining associations, which might not come within the definition of "handler", be prohibited from predatory practices.

3   Sec. 3. When used in this Act—

4   (a) The term "handler" means any person engaged in

5   the business or practice of (1) acquiring agricultural prod-

6   ucts from producers or associations of producers for process-

7   ing or sale; (2) grading, packaging, handling, storing, or

8   processing agricultural products received from producers or

9   associations of producers; (3) contracting or negotiating

10 contracts or other arrangements, written or oral, with pro-

11 ducers or associations of producers with respect to the pro-

12 duction or marketing of any agricultural product; or (4)

13 acting as an agent or broker for a handler in the perform-

14 ance of any function or act specified in clause (1), (2), or

15 (3) of this paragraph.

16 (b) The term "producer" means a person engaged in

17 the production of agricultural products as a farmer, planter,

18 rancher, dairyman, fruit, vegetable, or nut grower.

19 (c) ~~The term "association of producers" means any~~

20 ~~marketing, bargaining, shipping or processing organization~~

4

1 ~~as defined in section 15 (a) of the Agricultural Marketing~~

2 ~~Act of 1929, as amended (49 Stat. 317; 12 U.S.C.~~

3 ~~1141j(a)), or in section 1 of the Act, entitled "an Act to~~

4 ~~authorize association of producers of agricultural products,"~~

5 ~~approved February 18, 1922 (42 Stat. 388; 7 U.S.C. 291).~~

6 *The term "association of producers" means any associa-*

7 *tion as defined in section 15(a) of the Agricultural Market-*

8 *ing Act of 1929, as amended (49 Stat. 317; 12 U.S.C.*

9 *1141j(a)), or in section 1 of the Act entitled "An Act to*

10 *authorize association of producers of agricultural products,"*

11 *approved February 18, 1922 (42 Stat. 388; 7 U.S.C. 291),*

12 *which is authorized and seeking on behalf of its producer*

13 *members to bargain collectively with handlers as to price and*

14 *other terms of sale, and is not engaged in handling agricul-*

15 *tural products in competition with such handlers.*

> **Explanation:** Many witnesses, particularly cotton ginners and warehousemen, were apprehensive that normal competitive practices designed to obtain customers might be construed to be prohibited inducements or discriminations under the bill. By excluding associations which are competing as handlers from the definition of "association of producers" it is intended to allay these fears.

16 (d) The term "person" includes individuals, partner-

17 ships, corporations, and associations.

18 SEC. 4. It shall be unlawful for any handler *or associa-*

19 *tion of producers* knowingly to engage or permit any em-

20 ployee or agent to engage in the following practices:

21 (a) ~~To interfere with or restrain, or threaten to inter-~~

22 ~~fere with or restrain, by boycott, coercion, or any unfair or~~

5

1 deceptive act or practice, any producer in the exercise of his

2 right to join and belong to an association of producers; or *To*

3 *coerce any producer in the exercise of his right to join and*

4 *belong or to refrain from joining or belonging to an associa-*

5 *tion of producers, or to refuse to deal with any producer solely*

6 *because of the exercise of his right to join and belong to such*

7 *an association; or*

Explanation: Many witnesses suggested that the terms "interfere with or restrain, or threaten to interfere with or restrain" and
"unfair or deceptive act or practice" were not sufficiently definite, and
the amendment omits these terms.

A memorandum from the Office of the Legislative Counsel, and
various witnesses pointed out that "boycott" described collective action, and that the bill's prohibition would be strengthened by substitution of the term "refuse to deal", which describes unilateral
action by one handler as well as collective action. The amendment
makes this substitution.

Witnesses also suggested that there might be many appropriate
reasons for refusing to deal with a producer, such as inefficiency,
credit, and inferior production. Use of the word "solely" is designed
to restrict the prohibition to refusal to deal for inappropriate reasons.

The amendment would prohibit a cooperative from coercing a
producer to join it. Many witnesses suggested that the producer
should be free to make up his own mind without coercion from either
handler or cooperative. A cooperative would, however, be free to
refuse to deal with a nonmember.

8 (b) To discriminate or threaten to discriminate against

9 any producer with respect to price, quantity, quality, or

10 other terms of purchase, *sale,* or acquisition, *or other handling*

11 of agricultural commodities *solely* because of his membership

12 in or contract with an association of producers; or

Explanation: Witnesses objected to "threaten to discriminate"
as indefinite, difficult to prove or disprove.

Insertion of the words "sale" and "other handling" would extend
this section to the furnishing of seeds, feed, plants, or fertilizer, contract production requirements, storage, and other handling which

6

might not be included in "purchase" or "acquisition". This would make it clear that the prohibition applied to a handler who furnished chicks, seeds, or seedlings and kept title to them during the growing period.

The word "solely" makes it clear that differentiation on the basis of grade, efficiency, and other factors not related to association membership would not be prohibited.

An association would still be free to treat its members differently from nonmembers.

Some witnesses objected to "or contract with" because an exclusive agency contract might by its terms prevent the handler from dealing directly with the producer; and the amendment omits those words.

1   (c) To coerce or intimidate any producer or other

2 person to *enter into, maintain,* breach, cancel, or ~~otherwise~~

3 terminate a membership agreement or marketing contract

4 with an association of producers *or a contract with a handler;*

5 or

Explanation: The above amendments would prohibit coercion to cause a producer to (1) enter into or maintain a contract with a cooperative, or (2) enter into, maintain, breach, cancel, or terminate a contract with a handler. Many witnesses suggested that the producer should be protected from coercive practices of the type that a cooperative might engage in, as well as those a proprietary handler might engage in.

6   (d) To pay or loan money, give any thing of value

7 ~~in excess of the true market value of any agricultural com-~~

8 ~~modity which is being purchased,~~ or offer any other induce-

9 ment or reward to a producer *solely* for refusing to or ceasing

10 to belong to an association of producers, *or solely for termi-*

11 *nating an agreement with a handler;* or

Explanation: "True market value" was objected to as difficult to establish, as distinguished from price. "Solely" is inserted to make it clear that the sole purpose of the inducement must be to discourage membership in a cooperative or an agreement with a handler. Thus, where a cotton gin or warehouse or other handler might offer inducements to a producer, such as rebates, loans, or trucking, to do business with the handler instead of with the cooperative, the induce-

7

ment would not be "solely" for the purpose of discouraging membership in the cooperative.

The subsection was extended to prohibit inducements to terminate agreements with handlers in order to provide handlers with protection from predatory practices by cooperatives in a manner similar to that by which cooperatives would be protected from handlers.

1   (e) To make false reports *maliciously* about the finances,

2   management, or activities of associations of producers *or*

3   *handlers* ~~or interfere by any unfair or deceptive act or prac-~~

4   ~~tice with the efforts of such associations in carrying out the~~

5   ~~legitimate objects thereof;~~ or

    Explanation: The amendments would restrict this provision to "maliciously" false reports; extend it to false reports against handlers; and eliminate language which many witnesses objected to as creating an indefinite offense.

6   *(f) To require any producer, as a condition of his*

7   *joining and belonging to an association of producers, to be*

8   *subject to unreasonable liquidated damages or penalties for*

9   *failing to comply with the terms of a membership agreement*

10   *or marketing contract with such association; or*

    Explanation: This prohibits imposition of "unreasonable" liquidated damages on a producer's failure to comply with a cooperative membership or marketing agreement.

11   ~~(f)~~ *(g)* To conspire, combine, agree, or arrange with

12   any other person to do, or aid or abet the doing of, any act

13   made unlawful by this Act.

14   *SEC. 5. Nothing in this Act shall prevent handlers and*

15   *producers from selecting their customers and suppliers for*

16   *any reason other than a producer's membership in an associa-*

17   *tion of producers, nor prevent handlers and producers from*

8

1 *dealing with one another individually on a direct basis, nor*

2 *require a handler to deal with an association of producers.*

   Explanation: A number of witnesses desired a clear statement
   that handlers and producers be able to deal with each other directly,
   and that the bill does not make dealing with a cooperative
   compulsory.

3 SEC. ~~5.~~ *6.* ~~(a) Whenever any handler has engaged or~~

4 ~~there are reasonable grounds to believe that any handler is~~

5 ~~about the engage in any act or practice prohibited by section~~

6 ~~4, a civil action for preventive relief, including an application~~

7 ~~for a permanent or temporary injunction, restraining order,~~

8 ~~or other order, may be instituted by the person aggrieved. In~~

9 ~~any action commenced pursuant hereto, the court, in its~~

10 ~~discretion, may allow the prevailing party a reasonable~~

11 ~~attorney's fee as part of the costs.~~

   Explanation: Some witnesses objected to providing for an injunction upon the application of the aggrieved party on the ground
   that a temporary injunction during the processing season, or even an
   application therefor, might tie up the processor and cause him to
   lose the processing of an entire crop. The Farm Bureau and other
   witnesses have asserted that the need for relief by injunction is necessary to protect the producer, so that prohibited practices do not
   result in the loss of the crop to the producer. They assert that a prime
   need for the bill results from the fact that existing procedures are
   too slow and may result in the issuance of a cease and desist order
   only after the marketing season has passed. If this section is restored,
   consideration should be given as to whether it should be expanded
   to provide for injunctions against cooperatives, as has been proposed
   in the following subsection.

12 ~~(b)~~ *(a)* Whenever the ~~Secretary of Agriculture~~ *Attor-*

13 *ney General* has reasonable cause to believe that any

14 handler ~~or group of handlers,~~ *group of handlers, or associa-*

15 *tion of producers* has engaged, in any act or practice pro-

16 hibited by section 4, he may bring civil action in the appro-

9

1 priate district court of the United States by filing with it

2 a complaint (1) setting forth facts pertaining to such ~~pattern~~

3 *act* or practice, and (2) requesting such preventive relief,

4 including an application for a permanent or temporary injunc-

5 tion, restraining order, or other order against the handler,

6 ~~or handlers,~~ *handlers, or association of producers* responsible

7 for such acts or practices.

> The above would make the Attorney General, rather than the Secretary of Agriculture, the official to seek an injunction; extend the provision to provide for injunctions against cooperatives; and substitute "act" for "pattern" so that it correctly refers back to "act" in the introductory language.

8 ~~(e)~~ *(b)* Any person injured in his business or property

9 by reason of any violation of, or combination or conspiracy

10 to violate, any provision of section 4 of this Act may sue

11 therefor in the *appropriate* district court of the United States

12 ~~for the district in which defendant resides or is found or has~~

13 ~~an agent,~~ without respect to the amount in controversy, and

14 shall recover ~~threefold~~ the damages sustained~~, and the cost~~

15 ~~of the suit, including a reasonable attorney's fee.~~ *In any*

16 *action commenced pursuant to this subsection, the court may*

17 *allow the prevailing party a reasonable attorney's fee as a*

18 *part of the costs. Any action to enforce any cause of action*

19 *under this subsection shall be forever barred unless com-*

20 *menced within two year after the cause of action accrued.*

> Explanation: The above would provide for (A) compensatory damages instead of treble damages, (B) the award of attorney's fees to the prevailing party, whether plaintiff or defendant, rather than plaintiff only, (C) venue in the "appropriate" district, rather than the

10

district in which the defendant resides or is found or has an agent, and (D) a two-year statute of limitation on actions for damages. The venue provision now in the bill is the same as that contained in 15 U.S.C. 15 dealing with offenses against the antitrust laws. Under the proposed amendment "appropriate" venue would be governed by 28 U.S.C. 1391 (b) and (c), which provide for venue in the district where all defendants reside, except as otherwise provided by law. A corporation may be sued in any judicial district in which it is incorporated or licensed to do business or is doing business.

1   ~~(d) Any person who violates, or combines or conspires~~

2   ~~with any other person to violate, any provision of section~~

3   ~~4 of this Act is guilty of a misdemeanor, and, on conviction~~

4   ~~thereof, shall be punished by a fine not exceeding $1,000,~~

5   ~~or imprisonment not exceeding one year, or both, in the dis-~~

6   ~~cretion of the court.~~

Explanation: Senator Williams of Delaware and others proposed deletion of provisions for criminal penalties.

7   ~~(e)~~ *(c)* The district courts of the United States shall

8   have jurisdiction of proceedings instituted pursuant to this

9   section and shall exercise the same without regard to whether

10   the aggrieved party shall have exhausted any administrative

11   or other remedies that may be provided by law.

12   ~~(f) The foregoing provisions shall not be construed to~~

13   ~~deprive the proper State courts of jurisdiction in actions for~~

14   ~~damages thereunder.~~

Explanation: Some witnesses suggested that the above disclaimer was unnecessary and might be construed as authorizing double collection of damages.

11

1   Sᴇᴄ. 6̶. 7. If any provision of this Act or the application

2   thereof to any person or circumstances is held invalid, the

3   validity of the remainder of the Act and of the application

4   of such provision to other persons and circumstances shall not

5   be affected thereby.

[COMMITTEE PRINT NO. 2]

JULY 26, 1967

(Showing Amendments Recommended by the Subcommittee on Agricultural Research and General Legislation)

90TH CONGRESS
1ST SESSION

S. 109

IN THE SENATE OF THE UNITED STATES

JANUARY 11, 1967

Mr. AIKEN (for himself, Mr. LAUSCHE, Mr. BAYH, Mr. BURDICK, Mr. CHURCH, Mr. HART, Mr. HICKENLOOPER, Mr. McCARTHY, Mr. TYDINGS, and Mr. YOUNG of North Dakota) introduced the following bill; which was read twice and referred to the Committee on Agriculture and Forestry

[Omit the part struck through and insert the part printed in italic]

A BILL

To control unfair trade practices affecting producers of agricultural products and associations of such producers, and for other purposes.

1   *Be it enacted by the Senate and House of Representa-*

2   *tives of the United States of America in Congress assembled,*

3   That this Act shall be known as the Agricultural Producers

4   Marketing *Fair Practices* Act of 1967.

Explanation: The subcommittee felt this to be more descriptive of the Act.

J. 81–842——1

2

1   LEGISLATIVE FINDINGS AND DECLARATION OF POLICY

2   SEC. 2. Agricultural products are produced in the

3   United States by many individual farmers and ranchers scat-

4   tered throughout the various States of the Nation. Such

5   products in fresh or processed form move in large part in

6   the channels of interstate and foreign commerce, and such

7   products which do not move in these channels directly bur-

8   den or affect interstate commerce. The efficient production

9   and marketing of agricultural products by farmers and ranch-

10   ers is of vital concern to their welfare and to the general

11   economy of the Nation. Because agricultural products are

12   produced by numerous individual farmers, the marketing and

13   bargaining position of individual farmers will be adversely

14   affected unless they are free to ~~band together~~ *join together or*

15   *not to join together* in cooperative organizations as authorized

16   by law. Interference with ~~this right~~ *these rights* is contrary

17   to the public interest and adversely affects the free and orderly

18   flow of goods in interstate and foreign commerce.

19   It is, therefore, declared to be the policy of Congress and

20   the purpose of this Act to establish standards of fair practices

21   required of handlers ~~in their dealings with producers of agri-~~

22   ~~cultural products and their cooperative associations~~ *and asso-*

23   *ciations of producers in their dealings in agricultural products.*

   Explanation: The use of the word "join" rather than "band"
was suggested by Senator Lausche. Other witnesses proposed that
the right not to join be protected, and that bargaining associations,

3

which might not come within the definition of "handler", be prohibited from predatory practices.

1   SEC. 3. When used in this Act—

2   (a) The term "handler" means any person engaged in

3   the business or practice of (1) acquiring agricultural prod-

4   ucts from producers or associations of producers for process-

5   ing or sale; (2) grading, packaging, handling, storing, or

6   processing agricultural products received from producers or

7   associations of producers; (3) contracting or negotiating

8   contracts or other arrangements, written or oral, with pro-

9   ducers or associations of producers with respect to the pro-

10   duction or marketing of any agricultural product; or (4)

11   acting as an agent or broker for a handler in the perform-

12   ance of any function or act specified in clause (1), (2), or

13   (3) of this paragraph.

14   (b) The term "producer" means a person engaged in

15   the production of agricultural products as a farmer, planter,

16   rancher, dairyman, fruit, vegetable, or nut grower.

17   (c) The term "association of producers" means any

18   ~~marketing, bargaining, shipping or processing organization~~

19   *association of producers of agricultural products engaged in*

20   *marketing, bargaining, shipping, or processing* as defined in

21   section 15 (a) of the Agricultural Marketing Act of 1929, as

22   amended (49 Stat. 317; 12 U.S.C. 1141j (a)), or in

23   section 1 of the Act, entitled "an Act to authorize association

4

1 of producers of agricultural products," approved February 18,

2 1922 (42 Stat. 388; 7 U.S.C. 291).

3   (d) The term "person" includes individuals, partner-

4 ships, corporations, and associations.

5   *(e) The term "agricultural products" shall not include*

6 *cotton or tobacco or their products.*

> **Explanation:** The change proposed in subsection (c), the addition
> of subsection (e), and the substitution of "products" for commodities
> in section 4(b) are designed to exclude cotton and tobacco and their
> products from the Act. The competitive relationship between cooper-
> atives and other handlers of cotton and the method of marketing
> tobacco are so different from other commodities that the subcom-
> mittee felt there was neither a need for, nor a feasible and fair way
> of, including those commodities in the bill.

7   SEC. 4. It shall be unlawful for any handler *or associa-*

8 *tion of producers* knowingly to engage or permit any em-

9 ployee or agent to engage in the following practices:

10   (a) ~~To interfere with or restrain, or threaten to inter-~~

11 ~~fere with or restrain, by boycott, coercion, or any unfair or~~

12 ~~deceptive act or practice, any producer in the exercise of his~~

13 ~~right to join and belong to an association of producers; or~~ *To*

14 *coerce any producer in the exercise of his right to join and*

15 *belong or to refrain from joining or belonging to an associa-*

16 *tion of producers, or to refuse to deal with any producer solely*

17 *because of the exercise of his right to join and belong to such*

18 *an association; or*

> **Explanation:** Many witnesses suggested that the terms "inter-
> fere with or restrain, or threaten to interfere with or restrain" and
> "unfair or deceptive act or practice" were not sufficiently definite, and
> the amendment omits these terms.
> A memorandum from the Office of the Legislative Counsel, and
> various witnesses pointed out that "boycott" described collective ac-

5

tion, and that the bill's prohibition would be strengthened by substitution of the term "refuse to deal", which describes unilateral action by one handler as well as collective action. The amendment makes this substitution.

Witnesses also suggested that there might be many appropriate reasons for refusing to deal with a producer, such as inefficiency, credit, and inferior production, or because the producer was unwilling to raise the specific variety of product desired by the handler. Use of the word "solely" is designed to restrict the prohibition to refusal to deal for inappropriate reasons.

The amendment would prohibit a cooperative from coercing a producer to join it. Many witnesses suggested that the producer should be free to make up his own mind without coercion from either handler or cooperative. A cooperative would, however, be free to refuse to deal with a nonmember.

1   (b) To discriminate or threaten to discriminate against

2   any producer with respect to price, quantity, quality, or

3   other terms of purchase, *sale,* or acquisition, *or other handling*

4   of agricultural commodities *products solely* because of his

5   membership in or contract with an association of producers;

6   or

Explanation: Witnesses objected to "threaten to discriminate" as indefinite, difficult to prove or disprove.

Insertion of the words "sale" and "other handling" would extend this section to the furnishing of seeds, feed, plants, or fertilizer, contract production requirements, storage, and other handling which might not be included in "purchase" or "acquisition". This would make it clear that the prohibition applied to a handler who furnished chicks, seeds, or seedlings and kept title to them during the growing period.

The word "solely" makes it clear that differentiation on the basis of grade, efficiency, and other factors not related to association membership would not be prohibited.

An association would still be free to treat its members differently from nonmembers.

Some witnesses objected to "or contract with" because an exclusive agency contract might by its terms prevent the handler from dealing directly with the producer; and the amendment omits those words.

7   (c) To coerce or intimidate any producer or other

8   person to *enter into, maintain,* breach, cancel, or otherwise

J. 81–842——2

6

1   terminate a membership agreement or marketing contract

2   with an association of producers *or a contract with a handler*;

3   or

> **Explanation:** The above amendments would prohibit coercion to cause a producer to (1) enter into or maintain a contract with a cooperative, or (2) enter into, maintain, breach, cancel, or terminate a contract with a handler. Many witnesses suggested that the producer should be protected from coercive practices of the type that a cooperative might engage in, as well as those a proprietary handler might engage in.

4   (d) To pay or loan money, give any thing of value

5   ~~in excess of the true market value of any agricultural com-~~

6   ~~modity which is being purchased~~, or offer any other induce-

7   ment or reward to a producer *solely* for refusing to or ceasing

8   to belong to an association of producers, *or solely for termi-*

9   *nating an agreement with a handler*; or

> **Explanation:** "True market value" was objected to as difficult to establish, as distinguished from price. "Solely" is inserted to make it clear that the sole purpose of the inducement must be to discourage membership in a cooperative or an agreement with a handler. Thus, where a handler might offer inducements to a producer, such as rebates, loans, or trucking, to do business with the handler instead of with the cooperative, the inducement would not be "solely" for the purpose of discouraging membership in the cooperative.
>
> The subsection was extended to prohibit inducements to terminate agreements with handlers in order to provide handlers with protection from predatory practices by cooperatives in a manner similar to that by which cooperatives would be protected from handlers.

10   (e) To make false reports *maliciously* about the finances,

11   management, or activities of associations of producers *or*

12   *handlers* ~~or interfere by any unfair or deceptive act or prac-~~

13   ~~tice with the efforts of such associations in carrying out the~~

14   ~~legitimate objects thereof~~; or

> **Explanation:** The amendments would restrict this provision to "maliciously" false reports; extend it to false reports against

7

handlers; and eliminate language which many witnesses objected to
as creating an indefinite offense.

1   *(f) To require any producer, as a condition of his*

2   *joining and belonging to an association of producers, to be*

3   *subject to unreasonable liquidated damages or penalties for*

4   *failing to comply with the terms of a membership agreement*

5   *or marketing contract with such association; or*

> Explanation: This prohibits imposition of "unreasonable" liqui-
> dated damages on a producer's failure to comply with a cooperative
> membership or marketing agreement.

6   ~~(f)~~ *(g)* To conspire, combine, agree, or arrange with

7   any other person to do, or aid or abet the doing of, any act

8   made unlawful by this Act.

9   *SEC. 5. Nothing in this Act shall prevent handlers and*

10   *producers from selecting their customers and suppliers for*

11   *any reason other than a producer's membership in an associa-*

12   *tion of producers, nor prevent handlers and producers from*

13   *dealing with one another individually on a direct basis, nor*

14   *require a handler to deal with an association of producers.*

> Explanation: A number of witnesses desired a clear statement
> that handlers and producers be able to deal with each other directly,
> and that the bill does not make dealing with a cooperative
> compulsory.

15   SEC. ~~5~~ *6.* (a) Whenever any handler *or association of*

16   *producers* has engaged or there are reasonable grounds to

17   believe that any handler *or association of producers* is about

18   ~~the~~ *to* engage in any act or practice prohibited by section 4,

19   a civil action for preventive relief, including an application

8

1 for a permanent or temporary injunction, restraining order,

2 or other order, may be instituted by the person aggrieved. In

3 any action commenced pursuant hereto, the court, in its

4 discretion, may allow the prevailing party a reasonable

5 attorney's fee as part of the costs. *No restraining order or*

6 *preliminary injunction shall issue except upon the giving of*

7 *security by the applicant, in such sum as the court deems*

8 *proper, for the payment of such costs and damages as may*

9 *be incurred or suffered by any party who is found to have*

10 *been wrongfully enjoined or restrained.*

> **Explanation:** This would permit an aggrieved party to apply for an injunction against an association of producers, as well as a handler, to restrain violations of section 4. The applicant would be required to provide security for the payment of damages caused by a wrongful restraining order or temporary injunction. The provision for such security is taken from rule 65(c) of the Rules of Procedure for the United States District Courts.

11 (b) Whenever the Secretary of Agriculture has rea-

12 sonable cause to believe that any handler ~~or group of han-~~

13 ~~dlers,~~ *group of handlers, or association of producers* has

14 engaged, in any act or practice prohibited by section 4, he

15 may *request the Attorney General to* bring civil action *in his*

16 *behalf* in the appropriate district court of the United States

17 by filing with it a complaint (1) setting forth facts pertain-

18 ing to such ~~pattern~~ *act* or practice, and (2) requesting such

19 preventive relief, including an application for a permanent

20 or temporary injunction, restraining order, or other order

21 against the handler, ~~or handlers,~~ *handlers, or association of*

9

1   *producers* responsible for such acts or practices. *Upon receipt*

2   *of such request, the Attorney General shall immediately file*

3   *such complaint.*

> The above would extend the provision to provide for injunctions against cooperatives; require the Attorney General to file a complaint immediately upon the request of the Secretary of Agriculture; and substitute "act" for "pattern" so that it correctly refers back to "act" in the introductory language.

4   (c) Any person injured in his business or property

5   by reason of any violation of, or combination or conspiracy

6   to violate, any provision of section 4 of this Act may sue

7   therefor in the *appropriate* district court of the United States

8   ~~for the district in which defendant resides or is found or has~~

9   ~~an agent~~, without respect to the amount in controversy, and

10 shall recover ~~threefold~~ the damages sustained~~, and the cost~~

11 ~~of the suit, including a reasonable attorney's~~ fee. *In any*

12 *action commenced pursuant to this subsection, the court may*

13 *allow the prevailing party a reasonable attorney's fee as a*

14 *part of the costs. Any action to enforce any cause of action*

15 *under this subsection shall be forever barred unless com-*

16 *menced within two year after the cause of action accrued.*

> Explanation: The above would provide for (A) compensatory damages instead of treble damages, (B) the award of attorney's fees to the prevailing party, whether plaintiff or defendant, rather than plaintiff only, (C) venue in the "appropriate" district, rather than the district in which the defendant resides or is found or has an agent, and (D) a two-year statute of limitation on actions for damages. The venue provision now in the bill is the same as that contained in 15 U.S.C. 15 dealing with offenses against the antitrust laws. Under the proposed amendment "appropriate" venue would be governed by 28 U.S.C. 1391 (b) and (c), which provide for venue in the district where all defendants reside, except as otherwise provided by law. A corporation may be sued in any judicial district in which it is incorporated or licensed to do business or is doing business.

10

1   (d) Any person who violates, or combines or conspires

2   with any other person to violate, any provision of section

3   4 of this Act is guilty of a misdemeanor, and, on conviction

4   thereof, shall be punished by a fine not exceeding $1,000,

5   or imprisonment not exceeding one year, or both, in the dis-

6   cretion of the court.

Explanation: Senator Williams of Delaware and others proposed deletion of provisions for criminal penalties.

7   (e) *(d)* The district courts of the United States shall

8   have jurisdiction of proceedings instituted pursuant to this

9   section and shall exercise the same without regard to whether

10   the aggrieved party shall have exhausted any administrative

11   or other remedies that may be provided by law.

12   (f) The foregoing provisions shall not be construed to

13   deprive the proper State courts of jurisdiction in actions for

14   damages thereunder.

Explanation: Some witnesses suggested that the above disclaimer was unnecessary and might be construed as authorizing double collection of damages.

15   SEC. 6. 7. If any provision of this Act or the application

16   thereof to any person or circumstances is held invalid, the

17   validity of the remainder of the Act and of the application

18   of such provision to other persons and circumstances shall not

19   be affected thereby.

Calendar No. 459

90TH CONGRESS
1ST SESSION

S. 109

[Report No. 474]

IN THE SENATE OF THE UNITED STATES

JANUARY 11, 1967

Mr. AIKEN (for himself, Mr. LAUSCHE, Mr. BAYH, Mr. BURDICK, Mr. CHURCH, Mr. HART, Mr. HICKENLOOPER, Mr. McCARTHY, Mr. TYDINGS, and Mr. YOUNG of North Dakota) introduced the following bill; which was read twice and referred to the Committee on Agriculture and Forestry

AUGUST 3, 1967

Reported by Mr. AIKEN, with an amendment

[Strike out all after the enacting clause and insert the part printed in italic]

A BILL

To control unfair trade practices affecting producers of agricultural products and associations of such producers, and for other purposes.

1   *Be it enacted by the Senate and House of Representa-*

2   *tives of the United States of America in Congress assembled,*

3   ~~That this Act shall be known as the Agricultural Producers~~

4   ~~Marketing Act of 1967.~~

5   ~~LEGISLATIVE FINDINGS AND DECLARATION OF POLICY~~

6   ~~SEC. 2. Agricultural products are produced in the~~

7   ~~United States by many individual farmers and ranchers scat-~~

II

2

1 tered throughout the various States of the Nation. Such

2 products in fresh or processed form move in large part in

3 the channels of interstate and foreign commerce, and such

4 products which do not move in these channels directly bur-

5 den or affect interstate commerce. The efficient production

6 and marketing of agricultural products by farmers and ranch-

7 ers is of vital concern to their welfare and to the general

8 economy of the Nation. Because agricultural products are

9 produced by numerous individual farmers, the marketing and

10 bargaining position of individual farmers will be adversely

11 affected unless they are free to band together in cooperative

12 organizations as authorized by law. Interference with this

13 right is contrary to the public interest and adversely affects

14 the free and orderly flow of goods in interstate and foreign

15 commerce.

16 It is, therefore, declared to be the policy of Congress and

17 the purpose of this Act to establish standards of fair practices

18 required of handlers in their dealings with producers of agri-

19 cultural products and their cooperative associations.

20 SEC. 3. When used in this Act—

21 (a) The term "handler" means any person engaged in

22 the business or practice of (1) acquiring agricultural prod-

23 ucts from producers or associations of producers for process-

24 ing or sale; (2) grading, packaging, handling, storing, or

25 processing agricultural products received from producers or

3

1 associations of producers; (3) contracting or negotiating

2 contracts or other arrangements, written or oral, with pro-

3 ducers or associations of producers with respect to the pro-

4 duction or marketing of any agricultural product; or (4)

5 acting as an agent or broker for a handler in the perform-

6 ance of any function or act specified in clause (1), (2), or

7 (3) of this paragraph.

8   (b) The term "producer" means a person engaged in

9 the production of agricultural products as a farmer, planter,

10 rancher, dairyman, fruit, vegetable, or nut grower.

11   (c) The term "association of producers" means any

12 marketing, bargaining, shipping or processing organization

13 as defined in section 15 (a) of the Agricultural Marketing

14 Act of 1929, as amended (49 Stat. 317; 12 U.S.C.

15 1141j (a)), or in section 1 of the Act, entitled "an Act to

16 authorize association of producers of agricultural products,"

17 approved February 18, 1922 (42 Stat. 388; 7 U.S.C. 291).

18   (d) The term "person" includes individuals, partner-

19 ships, corporations, and associations.

20   SEC. 4. It shall be unlawful for any handler knowingly

21 to engage or permit any employee or agent to engage in the

22 following practices:

23   (a) To interfere with or restrain, or threaten to inter-

24 fere with or restrain, by boycott, coercion, or any unfair or

4

1   deceptive act or practice, any producer in the exercise of his

2   right to join and belong to an association of producers; or

3   (b) To discriminate or threaten to discriminate against

4   any producer with respect to price, quantity, quality, or

5   other terms of purchase or acquisition of agricultural com-

6   modities because of his membership in or contract with an

7   association of producers; or

8   (c) To coerce or intimidate any producer or other

9   person to breach, cancel, or otherwise terminate a member-

10   ship agreement or marketing contract with an association

11   of producers; or

12   (d) To pay or loan money, give any thing of value

13   in excess of the true market value of any agricultural com-

14   modity which is being purchased, or offer any other induce-

15   ment or reward to a producer for refusing to or ceasing to

16   belong to an association of producers; or

17   (e) To make false reports about the finances, manage-

18   ment, or activities of associations of producers or interfere

19   by any unfair or deceptive act or practice with the efforts

20   of such associations in carrying out the legitimate objects

21   thereof; or

22   (f) To conspire, combine, agree, or arrange with any

23   other person to do, or aid or abet the doing of, any act

24   made unlawful by this Act.

25   SEC. 5. (a) Whenever any handler has engaged or

5

1   ~~there are reasonable grounds to believe that any handler is~~

2   ~~about the engage in any act or practice prohibited by section~~

3   ~~4, a civil action for preventive relief, including an application~~

4   ~~for a permanent or temporary injunction, restraining order,~~

5   ~~or other order, may be instituted by the person aggrieved. In~~

6   ~~any action commenced pursuant hereto, the court, in its~~

7   ~~discretion, may allow the prevailing party a reasonable~~

8   ~~attorney's fee as part of the costs.~~

9   ~~(b) Whenever the Secretary of Agriculture has reason-~~

10   ~~able cause to believe that any handler or group of handlers~~

11   ~~has engaged in any act or practice prohibited by section 4,~~

12   ~~he may bring civil action in the appropriate district court of~~

13   ~~the United States by filing with it a complaint (1) setting~~

14   ~~forth facts pertaining to such pattern or practice, and (2)~~

15   ~~requesting such preventive relief, including an application~~

16   ~~for a permanent or temporary injunction, restraining order,~~

17   ~~or other order against the handler, or handlers, responsible~~

18   ~~for such acts or practices.~~

19   ~~(c) Any person injured in his business or property by~~

20   ~~reason of any violation of, or combination or conspiracy to~~

21   ~~violate, any provision of section 4 of this Act may sue there-~~

22   ~~for in the district court of the United States for the district~~

23   ~~in which defendant resides or is found or has an agent, with-~~

24   ~~out respect to the amount in controversy, and shall recover~~

6

1 ~~threefold the damages sustained, and the cost of the suit,~~

2 ~~including a reasonable attorney's fee.~~

3 ~~(d) Any person who violates, or combines or conspires~~

4 ~~with any other person to violate, any provision of section~~

5 ~~4 of this Act is guilty of a misdemeanor, and, on conviction~~

6 ~~thereof, shall be punished by a fine not exceeding $1,000,~~

7 ~~or imprisonment not exceeding one year, or both, in the dis-~~

8 ~~cretion of the court.~~

9 ~~(e) The district courts of the United States shall have~~

10 ~~jurisdiction of proceedings instituted pursuant to this section~~

11 ~~and shall exercise the same without regard to whether the~~

12 ~~aggrieved party shall have exhausted any administrative or~~

13 ~~other remedies that may be provided by law.~~

14 ~~(f) The foregoing provisions shall not be construed to~~

15 ~~deprive the proper State courts of jurisdiction in actions for~~

16 ~~damages thereunder.~~

17 ~~Sec. 6. If any provision of this Act or the application~~

18 ~~thereof to any person or circumstances is held invalid, the~~

19 ~~validity of the remainder of the Act and of the application~~

20 ~~of such provision to other persons and circumstances shall not~~

21 ~~be affected thereby.~~

22 *That this Act shall be known as the Agricultural Fair Prac-*

23 *tices Act of 1967.*

24 *LEGISLATIVE FINDINGS AND DECLARATION OF POLICY*

25 *Sec. 2. Agricultural products are produced in the United*

26 *States by many individual farmers and ranchers scattered*

7

1 *throughout the various States of the Nation. Such products in*

2 *fresh or processed form move in large part in the channels of*

3 *interstate and foreign commerce, and such products which*

4 *do not move in these channels directly burden or affect inter-*

5 *state commerce. The efficient production and marketing of ag-*

6 *ricultural products by farmers and ranchers is of vital*

7 *concern to their welfare and to the general economy of the*

8 *Nation. Because agricultural products are produced by nu-*

9 *merous individual farmers, the marketing and bargaining*

10 *position of individual farmers will be adversely affected unless*

11 *they are free to join together or not to join together in coop-*

12 *erative organizations as authorized by law. Interference with*

13 *these rights is contrary to the public interest and adversely*

14 *affects the free and orderly flow of goods in interstate and*

15 *foreign commerce.*

16 *It is, therefore, declared to be the policy of Congress and*

17 *the purpose of this Act to establish standards of fair practices*

18 *required of handlers and associations of producers in their*

19 *dealings in agricultural products.*

20 *DEFINITIONS*

21 *SEC. 3. When used in this Act—*

22 *(a) The term "handler" means any person engaged in*

23 *the business or practice of (1) acquiring agricultural prod-*

24 *ucts from producers or associations of producers for process-*

25 *ing or sale; (2) grading, packaging, handling, storing, or*

8

1   *processing agricultural products received from producers or*

2   *associations of producers; (3) contracting or negotiating*

3   *contracts or other arrangements, written or oral, with pro-*

4   *ducers or associations of producers with respect to the pro-*

5   *duction or marketing of any agricultural product; or (4)*

6   *acting as an agent or broker for a handler in the perform-*

7   *ance of any function or act specified in clause (1), (2), or*

8   *(3) of this paragraph.*

9   *(b) The term "producer" means a person engaged in*

10 *the production of agricultural products as a farmer, planter,*

11 *rancher, dairyman, fruit, vegetable, or nut grower.*

12   *(c) The term "association of producers" means any*

13 *association of producers of agricultural products engaged in*

14 *marketing, bargaining, shipping, or processing as defined in*

15 *section 15(a) of the Agricultural Marketing Act of 1929, as*

16 *amended (49 Stat. 317; 12 U.S.C. 1141j (a)), or in*

17 *section 1 of the Act, entitled "an Act to authorize association*

18 *of producers of agricultural products," approved February*

19 *18, 1922 (42 Stat. 388; 7 U.S.C. 291).*

20   *(d) The term "person" includes individuals, partner-*

21 *ships, corporations, and associations.*

22   *(e) The term "agricultural products" shall not include*

23 *cotton or tobacco or their products.*

9

PROHIBITED PRACTICES

2   *SEC. 4. It shall be unlawful for any handler or associa-*

3   *tion of producers knowingly to engage or permit any em-*

4   *ployee or agent to engage in the following practices:*

5   *(a) To coerce any producer in the exercise of his right*

6   *to join and belong to or to refrain from joining or belonging to*

7   *an association of producers, or to refuse to deal with any*

8   *producer because of the exercise of his right to join and belong*

9   *to such an association; or*

10   *(b) To discriminate against any producer with respect*

11 *to price, quantity, quality, or other terms of purchase, acqui-*

12 *sition, or other handling of agricultural products because of*

13 *his membership in an association of producers; or*

14   *(c) To coerce or intimidate any producer or other per-*

15 *son to enter into, maintain, breach, cancel, or terminate a*

16 *membership agreement or marketing contract with an asso-*

17 *ciation of producers or a contract with a handler; or*

18   *(d) To pay or loan money, give any thing of value, or*

19 *offer any other inducement or reward to a producer for re-*

20 *fusing to or ceasing to belong to an association of producers,*

21 *or for terminating an agreement with a handler; or*

22   *(e) To make false reports about the finances, manage-*

23 *ment, or activities of associations of producers or handlers; or*

10

1   *(f) To conspire, combine, agree, or arrange with any*

2   *other person to do, or aid or abet the doing of, any act*

3   *made unlawful by this Act.*

4   DISCLAIMER OF INTENTION TO PROHIBIT NORMAL

5   *DEALING*

6   *SEC. 5. Nothing in this Act shall prevent handlers and*

7   *producers from selecting their customers and suppliers for*

8   *any reason other than a producer's membership in an associa-*

9   *tion of producers, nor prevent handlers and producers from*

10   *dealing with one another individually on a direct basis, nor*

11   *require a handler to deal with an association of producers.*

12   *ENFORCEMENT*

13   *SEC. 6. (a) Whenever any handler or association of*

14   *producers has engaged or there are reasonable grounds to*

15   *believe that any handler or association of producers is about*

16   *to engage in any act or practice prohibited by section 4, a*

17   *civil action for preventive relief, including an application*

18   *for a permanent or temporary injunction, restraining order,*

19   *or other order, may be instituted by the person aggrieved.*

20   *In any action commenced pursuant hereto, the court, in its*

21   *discretion, may allow the prevailing party a reasonable*

22   *attorney's fee as part of the costs. No restraining order or*

23   *preliminary injunction shall issue except upon the giving of*

24   *security by the applicant, in such sum as the court deems*

25   *proper, for the payment of such costs and damages as may*

11

1   *be incurred or suffered by any party who is found to have*

2   *been wrongfully enjoined or restrained.*

3   *(b) Whenever the Secretary of Agriculture has rea-*

4   *sonable cause to believe that any handler, group of handlers,*

5   *or association of producers has engaged in any act or prac-*

6   *tice prohibited by section 4, he may request the Attorney*

7   *General to bring civil action in his behalf in the appropriate*

8   *district court of the United States by filing with it a com-*

9   *plaint (1) setting forth facts pertaining to such act or prac-*

10   *tice, and (2) requesting such preventive relief, including an*

11   *application for a permanent or temporary injunction, re-*

12   *straining order, or other order against the handler, handlers,*

13   *or association of producers responsible for such acts or prac-*

14   *tices. Upon receipt of such request, the Attorney General*

15   *shall immediately file such complaint.*

16   *(c) Any person injured in his business or property*

17   *by reason of any violation of, or combination or conspiracy*

18   *to violate, any provision of section 4 of this Act may sue*

19   *therefor in the appropriate district court of the United States*

20   *without respect to the amount in controversy, and shall re-*

21   *cover damages sustained. In any action commenced pur-*

22   *suant to this subsection, the court may allow the prevailing*

23   *party a reasonable attorney's fee as a part of the costs. Any*

24   *action to enforce any cause of action under this subsection*

12

1 *shall be forever barred unless commenced within two years*

2 *after the cause of action accrued.*

3 *(d) The district courts of the United States shall*

4 *have jurisdiction of proceedings instituted pursuant to this*

5 *section and shall exercise the same without regard to whether*

6 *the aggrieved party shall have exhausted any administrative*

7 *or other remedies that may be provided by law.*

8 *(e) The foregoing provisions shall not be construed to*

9 *deprive the proper State courts of jurisdiction.*

10 *SEPARABILITY*

11 *SEC. 7. If any provision of this Act or the application*

12 *thereof to any person or circumstances is held invalid, the*

13 *validity of the remainder of the Act and of the application*

14 *of such provision to other persons and circumstances shall not*

15 *be affected thereby.*

90TH CONGRESS
1ST SESSION

S. 109

IN THE HOUSE OF REPRESENTATIVES

AUGUST 7, 1967
Referred to the Committee on Agriculture

AN ACT

To control unfair trade practices affecting producers of agricultural products and associations of such producers, and for other purposes.

1   *Be it enacted by the Senate and House of Representa-*

2   *tives of the United States of America in Congress assembled,*

3   That this Act shall be known as the Agricultural Fair Prac-

4   tices Act of 1967.

5   LEGISLATIVE FINDINGS AND DECLARATION OF POLICY

6   SEC. 2. Agricultural products are produced in the United

7   States by many individual farmers and ranchers scattered

8   throughout the various States of the Nation. Such products in

9   fresh or processed form move in large part in the channels of

10   interstate and foreign commerce, and such products which

I

2

1 do not move in these channels directly burden or affect inter-

2 state commerce. The efficient production and marketing of

3 agricultural products by farmers and ranchers is of vital

4 concern to their welfare and to the general economy of the

5 Nation. Because agricultural products are produced by

6 numerous individual farmers, the marketing and bargaining

7 position of individual farmers will be adversely affected unless

8 they are free to join together or not to join together in coop-

9 erative organizations as authorized by law. Interference with

10 these rights is contrary to the public interest and adversely

11 affects the free and orderly flow of goods in interstate and

12 foreign commerce.

13 It is, therefore, declared to be the policy of Congress and

14 the purpose of this Act to establish standards of fair practices

15 required of handlers and associations of producers in their

16 dealings in agricultural products.

17   DEFINITIONS

18 SEC. 3. When used in this Act—

19 (a) The term "handler" means any person engaged in

20 the business or practice of (1) acquiring agricultural prod-

21 ucts from producers or associations of producers for process-

22 ing or sale; (2) grading, packaging, handling, storing, or

23 processing agricultural products received from producers or

24 associations of producers; (3) contracting or negotiating

25 contracts or other arrangements, written or oral, with pro-

3

1 ducers or associations of producers with respect to the pro-

2 duction or marketing of any agricultural product; or (4)

3 acting as an agent or broker for a handler in the perform-

4 ance of any function or act specified in clause (1), (2), or

5 (3) of this paragraph.

6 (b) The term "producer" means a person engaged in

7 the production of agricultural products as a farmer, planter,

8 rancher, dairyman, fruit, vegetable, or nut grower.

9 (c) The term "association of producers" means any

10 association of producers of agricultural products engaged in

11 marketing, bargaining, shipping, or processing as defined in

12 section 15 (a) of the Agricultural Marketing Act of 1929, as

13 amended (49 Stat. 317; 12 U.S.C. 1141j(a)), or in

14 section 1 of the Act, entitled "an Act to authorize association

15 of producers of agricultural products," approved February

16 18, 1922 (42 Stat. 388; 7 U.S.C. 291).

17 (d) The term "person" includes individuals, partner-

18 ships, corporations, and associations.

19 (e) The term "agricultural products" shall not include

20 cotton or tobacco or their products.

21 PROHIBITED PRACTICES

22 SEC. 4. It shall be unlawful for any handler or associa-

23 tion of producers knowingly to engage or permit any em-

24 ployee or agent to engage in the following practices:

25 (a) To coerce any producer in the exercise of his right

4

1 to join and belong to or to refrain from joining or belonging
2 to an association of producers, or to refuse to deal with any
3 producer because of the exercise of his right to join and be-
4 long to such an association; or

5 (b) To discriminate against any producer with respect
6 to price, quantity, quality, or other terms of purchase, acqui-
7 sition, or other handling of agricultural products because of
8 his membership in an association of producers; or

9 (c) To coerce or intimidate any producer or other per-
10 son to enter into, maintain, breach, cancel, or terminate a
11 membership agreement or marketing contract with an asso-
12 ciation of producers or a contract with a handler; or

13 (d) To pay or loan money, give any thing of value, or
14 offer any other inducement or reward to a producer for re-
15 fusing to or ceasing to belong to an association of producers,
16 or for terminating an agreement with a handler; or

17 (e) To make false reports about the finances, manage-
18 ment, or activities of associations of producers or handlers; or

19 (f) To conspire, combine, agree, or arrange with any
20 other person to do, or aid or abet the doing of, any act
21 made unlawful by this Act.

5

1   DISCLAIMER OF INTENTION TO PROHIBIT NORMAL

2   DEALING

3   SEC. 5. Nothing in this Act shall prevent handlers and

4   producers from selecting their customers and suppliers for

5   any reason other than a producer's membership in an associa-

6   tion of producers, nor prevent handlers and producers from

7   dealing with one another individually on a direct basis, nor

8   require a handler to deal with an association of producers.

9   ENFORCEMENT

10   SEC. 6. (a) Whenever any handler or association of

11   producers has engaged or there are reasonable grounds to

12   believe that any handler or association of producers is about

13   to engage in any act or practice prohibited by section 4, a

14   civil action for preventive relief, including an application

15   for a permanent or temporary injunction, restraining order,

16   or other order, may be instituted by the person aggrieved.

17   In any action commenced pursuant hereto, the court, in its

18   discretion, may allow the prevailing party a reasonable

19   attorney's fee as part of the costs. No restraining order or

20   preliminary injunction shall issue except upon the giving of

21   security by the applicant, in such sum as the court deems

6

1 proper, for the payment of such costs and damages as may

2 be incurred or suffered by any party who is found to have

3 been wrongfully enjoined or restrained.

4   (b) Whenever the Secretary of Agriculture has rea-

5 sonable cause to believe that any handler, group of handlers,

6 or association of producers has engaged in any act or prac-

7 tice prohibited by section 4, he may request the Attorney

8 General to bring civil action in his behalf in the appropriate

9 district court of the United States by filing with it a com-

10 plaint (1) setting forth facts pertaining to such act or prac-

11 tice, and (2) requesting such preventive relief, including an

12 application for a permanent or temporary injunction, re-

13 straining order, or other order against the handler, handlers,

14 or association of producers responsible for such acts or prac-

15 tices. Upon receipt of such request, the Attorney General

16 shall immediately file such complaint.

17   (c) Any person injured in his business or property

18 by reason of any violation of, or combination or conspiracy

19 to violate, any provision of section 4 of this Act may sue

20 therefor in the appropriate district court of the United States

21 without respect to the amount in controversy, and shall re-

22 cover damages sustained. In any action commenced pur-

23 suant to this subsection, the court may allow the prevailing

24 party a reasonable attorney's fee as a part of the costs. Any

25 action to enforce any cause of action under this subsection

7

1 shall be forever barred unless commenced within two years

2 after the cause of action accrued.

3   (d) The district courts of the United States shall

4 have jurisdiction of proceedings instituted pursuant to this

5 section and shall exercise the same without regard to whether

6 the aggrieved party shall have exhausted any administrative

7 or other remedies that may be provided by law.

8   (e) The foregoing provisions shall not be construed to

9 deprive the proper State courts of jurisdiction.

10   SEPARABILITY

11   SEC. 7. If any provision of this Act or the application

12 thereof to any person or circumstances is held invalid, the

13 validity of the remainder of the Act and of the application

14 of such provision to other persons and circumstances shall not

15 be affected thereby.

      Passed the Senate August 4, 1967.

      Attest: FRANCIS R. VALEO,

                                     Secretary.

90TH CONGRESS
1ST SESSION

H. R. 13541

IN THE HOUSE OF REPRESENTATIVES

OCTOBER 17, 1967

Mr. POAGE introduced the following bill; which was referred to the Committee on Agriculture

A BILL

To prohibit unfair trade practices affecting producers of agricultural products and associations of such producers, and for other purposes.

1   *Be it enacted by the Senate and House of Representa-*

2   *tives of the United States of America in Congress assembled,*

3   That this Act shall be known as the Agricultural Fair Prac-

4   tices Act of 1967.

5   LEGISLATIVE FINDINGS AND DECLARATION OF POLICY

6   SEC. 2. Agricultural products are produced in the United

7   States by many individual farmers and ranchers scattered

8   throughout the various States of the Nation. Such products in

9   fresh or processed form move in large part in the channels of

10   interstate and foreign commerce, and such products which

I

1 do not move in these channels directly burden or affect inter-
2 state commerce. The efficient production and marketing of
3 agricultural products by farmers and ranchers is of vital
4 concern to their welfare and to the general economy of the
5 Nation. Because agricultural products are produced by
6 numerous individual farmers, the marketing and bargaining
7 position of individual farmers will be adversely affected unless
8 they are free to join together voluntarily in cooperative or-
9 ganizations as authorized by law. Interference with this right
10 is contrary to the public interest and adversely affects the
11 free and orderly flow of goods in interstate and foreign
12 commerce.

13   It is, therefore, declared to be the policy of Congress and
14 the purpose of this Act to establish standards of fair practices
15 required of handlers and associations of producers in their
16 dealings in agricultural products.

17   DEFINITIONS

18   SEC. 3. When used in this Act—

19   (a) The term "handler" means any person engaged in
20 the business or practice of (1) acquiring agricultural prod-
21 ucts from producers or associations of producers for process-
22 ing or sale; (2) grading, packaging, handling, storing, or
23 processing agricultural products received from producers or
24 associations of producers; (3) contracting or negotiating
25 contracts or other arrangements, written or oral, with pro-
26 ducers or associations of producers with respect to the pro-

1 duction or marketing of any agricultural product; or (4)

2 acting as an agent or broker for a handler in the perform-

3 ance of any function or act specified in clause (1), (2), or

4 (3) of this paragraph.

5   (b) The term "producer" means a person engaged in

6 the production of agricultural products as a farmer, planter,

7 rancher, dairyman, fruit, vegetable, or nut grower.

8   (c) The term "association of producers" means any

9 association of producers of agricultural products engaged in

10 marketing, bargaining, shipping, or processing as defined in

11 section 15(a) of the Agricultural Marketing Act of 1929, as

12 amended (49 Stat. 317; 12 U.S.C. 1141j(a)), or in

13 section 1 of the Act entitled "An Act to authorize association

14 of producers of agricultural products," approved February

15 18, 1922 (42 Stat. 388; 7 U.S.C. 291).

16   (d) The term "person" includes individuals, partner-

17 ships, corporations, and associations.

18   (e) The term "agricultural products" shall not include

19 cotton or tobacco or their products.

20   PROHIBITED PRACTICES

21   SEC. 4. It shall be unlawful for any handler or associa-

22 tion of producers knowingly to engage or permit any em-

23 ployee or agent to engage in the following practices:

24   (a) To coerce any producer in the exercise of his right

25 to join and belong to or to refrain from joining or belonging

26 to an association of producers, or to refuse to deal with any

4

1 producer because of the exercise of his right to join and be-

2 long to such an association; or

3 (b) To discriminate against any producer with respect

4 to price, quantity, quality, or other terms of purchase, acqui-

5 sition, or other handling of agricultural products because of

6 his membership in or contract with an association of pro-

7 ducers; or

8 (c) To coerce or intimidate any producer or other per-

9 son to enter into, maintain, breach, cancel, or terminate a

10 membership agreement or marketing contract with an asso-

11 ciation of producers or a contract with a handler; or

12 (d) To pay or loan money, give any thing of value, or

13 offer any other inducement or reward to a producer for re-

14 fusing to or ceasing to belong to an association of producers;

15 or

16 (e) To make false reports about the finances, manage-

17 ment, or activities of associations of producers or handlers; or

18 (f) To conspire, combine, agree, or arrange with any

19 other person to do, or aid or abet the doing of, any act

20 made unlawful by this Act.

21 DISCLAIMER OF INTENTION TO PROHIBIT NORMAL

22 DEALING

23 SEC. 5. Nothing in this Act shall prevent handlers and

24 producers from selecting their customers and suppliers for

25 any reason other than a producer's membership in or con-

5

1 tract with an association of producers, nor prevent handlers

2 and producers from dealing with one another individually

3 on a direct basis, nor require a handler to deal with an asso-

4 ciation of producers.

5 ENFORCEMENT

6 SEC. 6. (a) Whenever any handler or association of

7 producers has engaged or there are reasonable grounds to

8 believe that any handler or association of producers is about

9 to engage in any act or practice prohibited by section 4, a

10 civil action for preventive relief, including an application

11 for a permanent or temporary injunction, restraining order,

12 or other order, may be instituted by the person aggrieved.

13 In any action commenced pursuant hereto, the court, in its

14 discretion, may allow the prevailing party a reasonable

15 attorney's fee as part of the costs. The court may provide

16 that no restraining order or preliminary injunction shall

17 issue except upon the giving of security by the applicant,

18 in such sum as the court deems proper, for the payment

19 of such costs and damages as may be incurred or suffered

20 by any party who is found to have been wrongfully enjoined

21 or restrained.

22 (b) Whenever the Secretary of Agriculture has rea-

23 sonable cause to believe that any handler, group of handlers,

24 or association of producers has engaged in any act or prac-

25 tice prohibited by section 4, he may request the Attorney

6

1 General to bring civil action in his behalf in the appropriate
2 district court of the United States by filing with it a com-
3 plaint (1) setting forth facts pertaining to such act or prac-
4 tice, and (2) requesting such preventive relief, including an
5 application for a permanent or temporary injunction, re-
6 straining order, or other order against the handler, handlers,
7 or association of producers responsible for such acts or prac-
8 tices. Upon receipt of such request, the Attorney General
9 is authorized to file such complaint.

10 (c) Any person injured in his business or property
11 by reason of any violation of, or combination or conspiracy
12 to violate, any provision of section 4 of this Act may sue
13 therefor in the appropriate district court of the United States
14 without respect to the amount in controversy, and shall
15 recover damages sustained. In any action commenced pur-
16 suant to this subsection, the court may allow the prevailing
17 party a reasonable attorney's fee as a part of the costs. Any
18 action to enforce any cause of action under this subsection
19 shall be forever barred unless commenced within two years
20 after the cause of action accrued.

21 (d) The district courts of the United States shall
22 have jurisdiction of proceedings instituted pursuant to this
23 section and shall exercise the same without regard to whether
24 the aggrieved party shall have exhausted any administrative
25 or other remedies that may be provided by law.

7

1 The provisions of this Act shall not be construed to
2 change or modify existing State law nor to deprive the
3 proper State courts of jurisdiction.

4   SEPARABILITY

5 SEC. 7. If any provision of this Act or the application
6 thereof to any person or circumstances is held invalid, the
7 validity of the remainder of the Act and of the application
8 of such provision to other persons and circumstances shall
9 not be affected thereby.

Public Law 90-288
90th Congress, S. 109
April 16, 1968

An Act

To prohibit unfair trade practices affecting producers of agricultural products,
and for other purposes.

*Be it enacted by the Senate and House of Representatives of the
United States of America in Congress assembled,* That this Act shall
be known as the Agricultural Fair Practices Act of 1967.

Agricultural
Fair Practices
Act of 1967.

LEGISLATIVE FINDINGS AND DECLARATION OF POLICY

SEC. 2. Agricultural products are produced in the United States by
many individual farmers and ranchers scattered throughout the various States of the Nation. Such products in fresh or processed form
move in large part in the channels of interstate and foreign commerce,
and such products which do not move in these channels directly
burden or affect interstate commerce. The efficient production and
marketing of agricultural products by farmers and ranchers is of
vital concern to their welfare and to the general economy of the
Nation. Because agricultural products are produced by numerous
individual farmers, the marketing and bargaining position of individual farmers will be adversely affected unless they are free to join
together voluntarily in cooperative organizations as authorized by
law. Interference with this right is contrary to the public interest
and adversely affects the free and orderly flow of goods in interstate
and foreign commerce.

It is, therefore, declared to be the policy of Congress and the purpose
of this Act to establish standards of fair practices required of handlers
in their dealings in agricultural products.

82 STAT. 93
82 STAT. 94

DEFINITIONS

SEC. 3. When used in this Act—
(a) The term "handler" means any person engaged in the business
or practice of (1) acquiring agricultural products from producers or
associations of producers for processing or sale; or (2) grading,
packaging, handling, storing, or processing agricultural products
received from producers or associations of producers; or (3) contracting or negotiating contracts or other arrangements, written or oral,
with or on behalf of producers or associations of producers with respect
to the production or marketing of any agricultural product; or (4)
acting as an agent or broker for a handler in the performance of any
function or act specified in clause (1), (2), or (3) of this paragraph.
(b) The term "producer" means a person engaged in the production
of agricultural products as a farmer, planter, rancher, dairyman, fruit,
vegetable, or nut grower.
(c) The term "association of producers" means any association of
producers of agricultural products engaged in marketing, bargaining, shipping, or processing as defined in section 15(a) of the Agricultural Marketing Act of 1929, as amended (49 Stat. 317; 12 U.S.C.
1141j(a)), or in section 1 of the Act entitled "An Act to authorize
association of producers of agricultural products", approved February
18, 1922 (42 Stat. 388; 7 U.S.C. 291).
(d) The term "person" includes individuals, partnerships, corporations, and associations.
(e) The term "agricultural products" shall not include cotton or
tobacco or their products.

Pub. Law 90-288   - 2 -   April 16, 1968

PROHIBITED PRACTICES

SEC. 4. It shall be unlawful for any handler knowingly to engage or permit any employee or agent to engage in the following practices:

(a) To coerce any producer in the exercise of his right to join and belong to or to refrain from joining or belonging to an association of producers, or to refuse to deal with any producer because of the exercise of his right to join and belong to such an association; or

(b) To discriminate against any producer with respect to price, quantity, quality, or other terms of purchase, acquisition, or other handling of agricultural products because of his membership in or contract with an association of producers; or

(c) To coerce or intimidate any producer to enter into, maintain, breach, cancel, or terminate a membership agreement or marketing contract with an association of producers or a contract with a handler; or

(d) To pay or loan money, give any thing of value, or offer any other inducement or reward to a producer for refusing to or ceasing to belong to an association of producers; or

(e) To make false reports about the finances, management, or activities of associations of producers or handlers; or

(f) To conspire, combine, agree, or arrange with any other person to do, or aid or abet the doing of, any act made unlawful by this Act.

82 STAT. 94
82 STAT. 95

DISCLAIMER OF INTENTION TO PROHIBIT NORMAL DEALING

SEC. 5. Nothing in this Act shall prevent handlers and producers from selecting their customers and suppliers for any reason other than a producer's membership in or contract with an association of producers, nor require a handler to deal with an association of producers.

ENFORCEMENT

SEC. 6. (a) Whenever any handler has engaged or there are reasonable grounds to believe that any handler is about to engage in any act or practice prohibited by section 4, a civil action for preventive relief, including an application for a permanent or temporary injunction, restraining order, or other order, may be instituted by the person aggrieved. In any action commenced pursuant hereto, the court, in its discretion, may allow the prevailing party a reasonable attorney's fee as part of the costs. The court may provide that no restraining order or preliminary injunction shall issue except upon the giving of security by the applicant, in such sum as the court deems proper, for the payment of such costs and damages as may be incurred or suffered by any party who is found to have been wrongfully enjoined or restrained.

(b) Whenever the Secretary of Agriculture has reasonable cause to believe that any handler, or group of handlers, has engaged in any act or practice prohibited by section 4, he may request the Attorney General to bring civil action in his behalf in the appropriate district court of the United States by filing with it a complaint (1) setting forth facts pertaining to such act or practice, and (2) requesting such preventive relief, including an application for a permanent or temporary injunction, restraining order, or other order against the handler, or handlers, responsible for such acts or practices. Upon receipt of such request, the Attorney General is authorized to file such complaint.

(c) Any person injured in his business or property by reason of any violation of, or combination or conspiracy to violate, any provision of section 4 of this Act may sue therefor in the appropriate district court of the United States without respect to the amount in controversy, and shall recover damages sustained. In any action commenced pur-

April 16, 1968   - 3 -   Pub. Law 90-288

82 STAT. 95

suant to this subsection, the court may allow the prevailing party a reasonable attorney's fee as a part of the costs. Any action to enforce any cause of action under this subsection shall be forever barred unless commenced within two years after the cause of action accrued.

(d) The district courts of the United States shall have jurisdiction *Jurisdiction.* of proceedings instituted pursuant to this section and shall exercise the same without regard to whether the aggrieved party shall have exhausted any administrative or other remedies that may be provided by law.

The provisions of this Act shall not be construed to change or modify existing State law nor to deprive the proper State courts of jurisdiction.

SEPARABILITY

SEC. 7. If any provision of this Act or the application thereof to any person or circumstances is held invalid, the validity of the remainder of the Act and of the application of such provision to other persons and circumstances shall not be affected thereby.

Approved April 16, 1968, 9:40 a.m., Honolulu, Hawaii.

LEGISLATIVE HISTORY:

HOUSE REPORT No. 824 accompanying H. R. 13541 (Comm. on Agriculture).
SENATE REPORT No. 474 (Comm. on Agriculture & Forestry).
CONGRESSIONAL RECORD:
    Vol. 113 (1967): Aug. 4, considered and passed Senate.
    Vol. 114 (1968): Mar. 25, considered and passed House, amended,
        in lieu of H. R. 13541.
        Apr. 1, Senate concurred in House amendment.

Appendix C

**Substitute Versions
of S. 109
Proposed by
National Council of Farmer
Cooperatives
and National
Milk Producers Federation**

National Council of Farmer Cooperatives Proposal — 1965

H.R. 898

A BILL

To control unfair practices affecting associations of producers of agricultural products and members thereof engaged in bargaining

---

Be it enacted by the Senate and House of Representatives of the United States of America in Congress assembled:

SECTION 1: That persons, such as farmers, fruit growers, ranchers, dairymen, and others engaged in the production of agricultural products may act together in associations, corporate or otherwise, with or without capital stock, for the exclusive purpose of bargaining for desirable terms of sale in interstate and foreign markets for the raw products of the persons so engaged. Such associations may conduct joint promotion activities and may conduct their marketing through a common sales agency; and such associations and their members may make the necessary contracts and agreements to effect such purposes; provided, however, that such associations are operated for the mutual benefit of the members thereof as producers and conform to all of the following requirements:

(1) That no member of the association is allowed more than one vote because of the amount of stock or membership capital he may own therein; or that the Association does not pay dividends on stock or membership capital in excess of eight percent per annum; and

(2) That the association shall not deal in the products of nonmembers to an amount in greater value than such as are handled by it for members; and

(3) That the association takes title to products of its members for which it acts as bargaining agent for such products.

SECTION 2: Unlawful Practices. It shall be unlawful for any processor, handler, distributor, dealer, or agent thereof, doing business in interstate or foreign commerce who purchases or contracts to purchase an agricultural commodity from a producer engaged in production of agricultural products, who belongs to or seeks to belong to any association defined in SECTION 1, knowingly to do any of the following:

REMAINDER OF H.R. 898 REMAINS SAME

National Council of Farmer Cooperatives Proposal — 1966

DRAFT April 25, 1966

H. R. ─────────

IN THE HOUSE OF REPRESENTATIVES

A BILL

To control unfair trade practices affecting producers of fruits and vegetables and associations of such producers and for other purposes.

Be it enacted by the Senate and House of Representatives of the United States of America in Congress assembled, That this Act shall be known as the Fruit and Vegetable Producers Fair Trade Act of 1966.

Legislative Findings and Declaration of Policy

Sec. 2. Fruits and vegetables produced in the United States constitute a highly important part of the food supply of the nation. Such fruits and vegetables are produced by many individual farmers scattered throughout the various states of the nation. The fruits and vegetables so produced are consumed throughout the nation either in fresh form or in the form of processed fruits and vegetables or products thereof. Fruits and vegetables in fresh or processed form or in the form of food products move in large part in the channels of interstate and foreign commerce and such fruits and vegetables which do not move in such channels directly burden or affect interstate commerce in fruits and vegetables. It is, therefore, found that all fruits and vegetables produced in the United States are in the current of interstate or foreign commerce or directly burden, obstruct, or affect interstate or foreign commerce in fruits and vegetables. The efficient production and marketing of fruits and vegetables by farmers is of vital concern to the welfare of such farmers and to those concerned with distributing, using, and processing fruits and vegetables as well as the general economy of the nation. Because fruits and vegetables are produced by numerous individual farmers the marketing and bargaining position of individual farmers will be adversely affected unless they are free to band together in cooperative organizations as authorized by law. Interference with such rights to cooperative action by farmers and unfair trade practices relative thereto which may be engaged in by handlers of fruits and vegetables produced by such farmers is contrary to the public interest.

It is, therefore, declared to be the policy of Congress and the purpose of this Act, through the exercise of the powers provided herein, to establish certain standards of fair dealing to be required of handlers in their dealings with producers of fruits and vegetables, of cooperative associations of such producers and others.

Definitions

Sec. 3. When used in this Act —

(a) The term "person" includes individuals, partnerships, corporations, and associations;

(b) The term "Secretary" means the Secretary of Agriculture;

(c) The term "fruits and vegetables" includes all horticultural and agricultural commodities usually included in the term "fruits and vegetables" regardless of the type of market (fresh, canned, frozen, dried or otherwise processed) for which ultimately destined;

(d) The term "commerce" means commerce in fruits or vegetables, or the products thereof, between any State, any territory, or the District of Columbia, and any place outside thereof; or between points within the same State, territory, or the District of Columbia, but through any place outside thereof; or within any State or territory or the District of Columbia. The term "commerce" includes all acts, activities, dealings and transactions directly or indirectly relating to the placement and flow of fruits or vegetables, or their products, in the channels of trade or commerce.

(e) The term "handler" means any person, other than a cooperative association, engaged in the business or practice of (1) acquiring fruits or vegetables from producers or associations of producers for processing or sale; (2) grading, packaging, handling, storing or processing fruits and vegetables received from producers or associations of producers; (3) contracting or negotiating contracts or other arrangements, written or oral, with producers or associations of producers for any purpose specified in subparagraphs (1) or (2); or (4) acting as an agent or broker for a handler in the performance of any function or act specified in subparagraphs (1), (2), or (3) of this paragraph.

(f) The term "producer" means a person who produces fruits or vegetables for disposition for use in commerce.

(g) The term "association of producers" means any farmer-owned and controlled cooperative fruit or vegetable marketing, bargaining, shipping or processing organization, as defined in section 15a of the Agricultural Marketing Act of 1929, as amended, 49 Stat. 317, 12 U.S.C. 1141j(a).

Prohibited Acts

Sec. 4. With respect to any negotiations, contracts (oral or written), or dealings directly or indirectly relating to or affecting business relationships between *handlers* and *producers or associations of producers* it shall be unlawful for any person:

(a) To interfere with, restrain, coerce, or boycott any producer in the exercise of his rights to join and belong to an association of producers; or

(b) To coerce or intimidate any member of an association of producers or other person to breach, cancel, or otherwise terminate a membership agreement or marketing contract with such association; or

(c) To pay or loan money, give any thing of value, or offer any other inducement or reward to a producer for refusing to or ceasing to belong to an association of producers; or

(d) To make false reports about the finances, management, or activities of associations of producers or interfere in any way with the efforts of such associations in carrying out the legitimate objects thereof; or

(e) To engage in or use any unfair, unjustly discriminatory, or deceptive practice or device in commerce; or

(f) To make or give, in commerce, any undue or reasonable preference or advantage to any particular person or locality in any respect whatsoever or subject in commerce any particular person or locality to any undue or unreasonable prejudice or disadvantage in any respect whatsoever; or

(g) To conspire, combine, agree, or arrange with any other person to do, or aid or abet the doing of, any act made unlawful by subdivisions (a), (b), (c), (d), (e), or (f).

Complaints, Hearings and Orders

Sec. 5. (a) Whenever the Secretary has reason to believe that any handler has violated or is violating any provisions of this Act, he shall cause a complaint in writing to be served upon the handler, stating his charges in that respect, and requiring the handler to attend and testify at a hearing at a time and place designated therein; and at such time and place there shall be afforded the handler a reasonable opportunity to be informed as to the evidence introduced against him (including the right of cross-examination), and to be heard in person or by counsel and through witnesses, under such regulations as the Secretary may prescribe. Any person for good cause shown may, on application, be allowed by the Secretary to intervene in such proceedings, and appear in person or by counsel. At any time prior to the close of the hearing the Secretary may amend the complaint; but in case of any amendment adding new charges the hearing shall, on the request of the handler, be adjourned for a period not exceeding fifteen days.

(b) If, after such hearing, the Secretary finds that the handler has violated or is violating any provisions of this Act covered by the charges, he shall make a report in writing in which he shall state his findings as to the facts, and shall issue and cause to be served on the handler an order requiring such handler to cease and desist from continuing such violation. The testimony taken at the hearing shall be reduced in writing and filed in the records of the Department of Agriculture.

(c) Until the record in such hearing has been filed in a court of appeals of the United States, as provided in section 6, the Secretary at any time, upon such notice and in such manner as he deems proper, but only after reasonable opportunity to the handler to be heard, may amend or set aside the report or order, in whole or in part.

(d) Complaints, orders, and other processes of the Secretary under this section may be served in the same manner as provided in section 5 of the Act entitled "An Act to create a Federal Trade Commission, to define its powers and duties, and for other purposes," approved September 26, 1914.

Appeals

Sec. 6. Any handler aggrieved by a final order of the Secretary issued pursuant to section 5 may, within sixty days after entry of such order, file a petition to review such order in the United States court of appeals for the judicial circuit in which the handler filing the petition for review resides or has its principal office, or in the Unted States Court of Appeals for the District of Columbia. Upon the filing and service of a petition to review, the court of appeals shall have jurisdiction of the proceeding. For the purposes of this Act, the provisions of Chapter 19A (Hobbs Act) of Title 5, United States Code, shall be applicable to appeals pursuant to this section.

Criminal Penalties

Sec. 7. Any handler, or any officer, director, agent, or employee of a handler, who fails to obey any order of the Secretary issued under the provisions of section 5, or such order as modified —

(1) After the expiration of the time allowed for filing a petition in the court of appeals to set aside or modify such order, if no such petition has been filed within such time; or

(2) After the expiration of the time allowed for applying for a writ of certiorari, if such order, or such order as modified, has been sustained by the court of appeals and no such writ has been applied for within such time; or

(3) After such order, or such order as modified, has been sustained by the courts as provided in section 6: shall on conviction be fined not less than $500 nor more than $10,000, or imprisoned for not less than six months nor more than five years, or both. Each day during which such failure continues shall be deemed a separate offense.

Civil Enforcement

Sec. 8. In addition to and not exclusive of, any other remedies provided by this Act or otherwise provided by law, the several district courts of the United States are vested with jurisdiction specifically to enforce and to prevent and restrain any person from violating any provision of this Act or any regulation issued pursuant thereto.

Accounts and Records of Business; Punishment for Failure to Keep

Sec. 9. Every handler shall keep such accounts, records, and memoranda as fully and correctly disclose all transactions involved in his business, including the true ownership of such business by stockholding or otherwise. Whenever the Secretary finds that the accounts, records, and memoranda of any such person do not fully and correctly disclose all transactions involved in his business, the Secretary may prescribe the manner and form in which such accounts, records, and memoranda shall be kept, and thereafter any such person who fails to keep such accounts, records, and memoranda in the manner and form prescribed or approved by the Secretary shall upon conviction be fined not more than $5,000, or imprisoned not more than three years, or both.

Federal Trade Commission Powers Adopted for Enforcement of Act

Sec. 10. For the efficient execution of the provisions of this Act, and in order to provide information for the use of Congress, the provisions (including penalties) of sections 46 and 48–50 of Title 15, are made applicable to the jurisdiction, powers, and duties of the Secretary in enforcing the provisions of this Act and to any person subject to the provisions of this Act, whether or not a corporation. The Secretary, in person or by such agents as he may designate, may prosecute any inquiry necessary to his duties under this Act in any part of the United States.

Responsibility of Principal for Act or Omission of Agent

Sec. 11. When construing and enforcing the provisions of this Act, the act, omission, or failure of any agent, officer, or other person acting for or employed by any handler, within the scope of his employment or office, shall in every case also be deemed the act, omission, or failure of such handler, as well as that of such agent, officer, or other person.

Attorney General to Institute Court Proceedings for Enforcement

Sec. 12. The Secretary may report any violation of this Act to the Attorney General of the United States, who shall cause appropriate proceedings to be commenced and prosecuted in the proper courts of the United States without delay.

Laws Unaffected

Sec. 13. Nothing contained in this Act, except as otherwise provided herein, shall be construed —

(a) To prevent or interfere with the enforcement of, or the procedure under, the provisions of the Act entitled "An Act to protect trade and commerce against unlawful restraints and monopolies," approved July 2, 1890, the Act entitled "An Act to supplement existing laws against unlawful restraints and monopolies, and for other purposes," approved October 15, 1914, the Interstate Commerce Act as amended, the Act entitled "An Act to promote export trade, and for other purposes," approved April 10, 1918, or sections 73 to 77, inclusive, of the Act of August 27, 1894, entitled "An Act to reduce taxation, to provide revenue for the Government, and for other purposes," as amended by the Act entitled "An Act to amend sections seventy-three and seventy-six of the Act of August twenty-seventh, eighteen hundred and ninety-four, entitled "An Act to reduce taxation, to provide revenue for the Government, and for other purposes," approved February 12, 1913, or

(b) To alter, modify, or repeal such Acts or any part or parts thereof, or

(c) To prevent or interfere with any investigation, proceeding, a prosecution begun and pending on the effective date of this Act.

Rules and Regulations; Appropriations

Sec. 14. The Secretary may make such rules, regulations, and orders as may be necessary to carry out the provisions of this Act and may cooperate with any department or agency of the Goverment, any State, Territory, District, or possession, or department, agency, or political subdivision thereof, or any person; and shall have the power to appoint, remove, and fix the compensation of such officers and employees, not in conflict with existing law, and make such expenditures for rent outside the District of Columbia, printing, telegrams, telephones, law books, books of reference, periodicals, furniture, stationery, office equipment, travel, and other supplies and expenses as shall be necessary to the administration of this chapter in the District of Columbia and elsewhere, and as may be appropriated for by Congress, and there is authorized to be appropriated, out of any money in the Treasury not otherwise appropriated, such sums as may be necessary for such purpose.

Separability of Provisions

Sec. 15. If any provision of this Act or the application thereof to any person or circumstances is held invalid, the validity of the remainder of the Act and of the application of such provision to other persons and circumstances shall not be affected thereby.

National Milk Producers Federation Proposal

DRAFT 6/6/66

A BILL

To prohibit interference with the right of agricultural producers to belong to cooperative associations and for other purposes.

Be it enacted by the Senate and House of Representatives of the United States of America in Congress assembled, That this Act may be cited as the Cooperative Marketing Interference Act.

Sec. 2. For the purposes of this Act:

(a) "person" means an individual, firm, corporation, or other business entity, and includes any officer, employee, or agent thereof;

(b) "cooperative association" means a cooperative association of producers which is engaged in the cooperative marketing of agricultural commodities for producers, either in raw or processed form, and includes a federation or marketing agency in common which is engaged in the cooperative marketing of agricultural commodities;

(c) "producer" means any person engaged in the production of an agricultural commodity or entitled to a share of the production of an agricultural commodity;

(d) "agricultural commodity" means any agricultural or horticultural commodity, including nuts, fruits, and vegetables, and includes also livestock, poultry, eggs, milk, and butterfat;

(e) "commerce" means interstate or foreign commerce and includes commerce between any state or the District of Columbia and any place outside thereof, or within the District of Columbia or any territory or possession of the United States;

(f) "in commerce" means engaging in commerce and includes the acquiring, processing, transporting, or handling of agricultural commodities or the products thereof in commerce, or after the same have been moved in commerce, or prior to the movement of such commodities or the products thereof in commerce; and

(g) "affecting commerce" means in commerce, or burdening or obstructing commerce or the free flow of commerce, or tending to burden or obstruct commerce or the free flow of commerce.

Sec. 3. It shall be unlawful, and an unfair practice in commerce under the Federal Trade Commission Act, for any person acquiring any agricultural commodity in commerce, or so as to affect such commerce, from producers or cooperative associations, to do any of the following:

(a) by coercion, intimidation, discrimination, or threats, to interfere with the right of any producer to join or maintain membership in a cooperative association, or by any such means to induce or attempt to induce any producer to terminate his membership in any cooperative association;

(b) to pay or loan money or give any other thing of value to a producer as an inducement or reward not to join or maintain membership in a cooperative association;

(c) to discriminate or threaten to discriminate against any producer in any manner for the purpose of inducing such producer not to join or maintain membership in a cooperative association; or

(d) to interfere or attempt to interfere with the organization or operation of any cooperative association or to make or circulate any false report about the finances, management, or activities of any cooperative association.

Sec. 4. This Act shall be enforced by the Federal Trade Commission, and all remedies, procedures, and authority available for enforcement of the Federal Trade Commission Act shall be available for the enforcement of this Act. In addition, the Federal Trade Commission may proceed in any United States court having jurisdiction over the defendant to enjoin a violation or threatened violation of this Act, and upon proper showing a temporary injunction or restraining order may be granted without bond.

Sec. 5. Any producer or cooperative association injured or damaged by reason of a violation of this Act may sue therefor in any United States court having jurisdiction over the defendant without respect to the amount in controversy.

Sec. 6. If any provision of this Act or the applicability thereof to any person or circumstance is held invalid, the validity of the remainder of this Act and the applicability thereof to other persons and circumstances shall not be affected thereby.

Appendix D

**The Agricultural Marketing and
Bargaining Act of 1969**

91st CONGRESS
1st SESSION

H. R. 9950

IN THE HOUSE OF REPRESENTATIVES

APRIL 3, 1969

Mrs. MAY introduced the following bill; which was referred to the Committee on Agriculture

---

A BILL

To strengthen voluntary agricultural organizations, to provide for the orderly marketing of agricultural products, and for other purposes.

1   *Be it enacted by the Senate and House of Representa-*

2 *tives of the United States of America in Congress assembled,*

3 That this Act may be cited as the Agricultural Marketing

4 and Bargaining Act of 1969.

5   LEGISLATIVE FINDINGS AND DECLARATION OF POLICY

6   SEC. 2. Congress has recognized and has moved to pro-

7 tect the right of farmers and ranchers to market and bargain

8 cooperatively. It has been held that interference with this

9 right is contrary to the public interest and adversely affects

10 the free and orderly flow of goods in interstate and foreign

I

1 commerce. It is essential that handlers of agricultural prod-

2 ucts recognize this right if we are to avoid the disputes and

3 inefficiencies in agriculture which can cause irreparable harm

4 to farmers and ranchers and to the general economy of the

5 Nation. Proper relationship between handler and agricul-

6 tural bargaining association should be encouraged in order

7 to promote friendly adjustment of marketing problems and

8 to achieve efficient delivery of reasonably priced, high qual-

9 ity food to the general public.

10 It is therefore declared to be the policy of Congress

11 and the purpose of this Act to encourage cooperative market-

12 ing and bargaining with respect to farm products by estab-

13 lishing standards of fair practices with respect to the rela-

14 tionship of handlers and agricultural bargaining associations.

15 SEC. 3. The Agricultural Fair Practices Act of 1967

16 (82 Stat. 93 et seq; 7 U.S.C. 2301) is amended—

17 (a) By adding the following new subsection to section 3:

18 "(f) The term 'agricultural bargaining association'

19 means an association of producers which has as its principal

20 function, as agent of producers, the negotiation with handlers

21 of prices and other terms of contracts with respect to the

22 production, sale, or marketing of agricultural products."

23 (b) In section 4 by redesignating subsection "(f)" as

24 subsection "(g)" and inserting the following new sub-

25 section:

3

1   "(f) To refuse to negotiate prices and other terms of

2   contracts at reasonable times and places with agricultural

3   bargaining associations which represent producers of agri-

4   cultural products from whom the handler usually obtains

5   agricultural products, or who may reasonably and efficiently

6   supply agricultural products to, or produce agricultural

7   products for, such handler when proof of representation is

8   provided the handler by the agricultural bargaining associa-

9   tion in the form of a written authorization signed by the

10   producer."

11   (c) By changing section 5 to read as follows:

12   "SEC. 5. Nothing in this Act shall—

13   "(a) prevent handlers and producers from selecting

14   their suppliers and customers for any reason other than

15   a producer's membership in or contract with an associa-

16   tion of producers,

17   "(b) compel producers to join or belong to an asso-

18   ciation of producers,

19   "(c) compel handlers and associations of producers

20   to conclude an agreement with respect to any negotia-

21   tions, or

22   "(d) be construed to forbid the affiliation of an

23   association of producers, as defined in section 3 of this

24   Act, with other associations having similar objectives, or

25   with bona fide agricultural or horticultural organizations

4

1   whose primary objectives are to promote, protect, and

2   represent the business and economic interests of farmers

3   and ranchers."

Index

Agricultural Fair Practices Act of 1967, 19, 144, 201, 203; early draft, 33; introduction as H.R.11146, 41; reintroduction as S.109, 49; Aiken substitute, 79; Senate version, 145; House Committee on Agriculture version (H.R.13541), 178; floor debate, 189–97 *passim*; final passage, 198

Agricultural Marketing Agreements Act of 1937, 108, 188, 224

Aiken, Senator George, 41, 49, 53, 57, 65, 75, 76, 79, 92, 94, 99, 129, 136, 144, 197, 186, 187, 204, 205, 209, 212, 222n13, 232n25; cross-examination of witnesses by, 59, 67, 69, 89; testimony of, 58, 84, 90, 114, 115, 146, 156

American Agricultural Marketing Association, 2, 25, 30, 32, 47, 56, 71, 96–97, 220; organization of, 26. *See also* American Farm Bureau Federation

American Farm Bureau Federation, 2, 19, 20, 21, 25, 26, 28, 31, 35, 36, 39, 43, 51, 53, 55, 90, 102, 155n5, 182, 192, 194, 197, 201, 203, 213, 219, 221–22, 223; amendments offered by, 173–74; legislative strategy of, 53, 57, 74–75, 96, 102, 109–10, 129, 135–36, 138, 144, 170; management committee, 29; philosophy of, 35, 75; policy resolutions by, 29, 221, 228. *See also* American Agricultural Marketing Association; Coalition, American Farm Bureau Federation-National Council of Farmer Cooperatives-National Milk Producers Federation

Angevine, David, 83, 84, 116, 192, 209

Arkansas broiler case, 7–12, 57, 67, 68, 99, 120, 123, 161, 166. *See also* Discriminatory practices by processors

Arkansas Poultry Federation, 8, 10

Bagwell, John, 55, 156, 176

Baker, John, 56, 83, 154, 191, 192, 204, 209; testimony of, 157–58

Blacklist, 8, 11, 12, 87

Boycott, 3, 12

Brannan, Charles, 92, 149, 175, 188, 224

Breimyer, Harold F., 56n13, 58n22, 82–83

Broiler Industry, 58, 94, 105

Bunje, Ralph, 13, 13n30, 14n31, 44–45, 150, 153, 175, 178, 179, 180, 183, 183n84, 184, 185, 187, 196, 197, 227; testimony of, 69, 72, 88, 117–18, 164. *See also* California Canning Peach Association

California Canning Peach Association, 13, 15, 27, 69, 117, 151, 164, 175, 227. *See also* Bunje, Ralph

California Farm Bureau, 14, 16, 151, 152, 185

California raisin case, 12–17

Campbell Soup Company, 27, 30, 32, 77, 101, 123

Cannery Growers, Inc., 3, 4, 6, 25, 27, 30

Capper-Volstead Act of 1922, 30–31, 34, 36, 37, 43, 44, 108, 116, 181, 220; proposed amendment of, 20, 33, 38, 39, 41, 42, 44–49, 53, 66, 74, 75, 77, 209, 210

Carpenter, L. C., 160, 198

Cease-and-desist order: in Ohio tomato case, 4; in Arkansas broiler case, 12

Clayton Act of 1914, 76, 87, 108, 210–11

Coalition, American Farm Bureau Federation-National Council of Farmer Cooperatives-National Milk Producers Federation, 39, 44, 48, 58, 66, 77, 85, 87, 93, 97, 97n10, 102, 128, 145, 146, 204, 212; formation of, 36. *See also* American Farm Bureau Federation; National Council of Farmer Cooperatives; National Milk Producers Federation

Committee of "17", 98, 109, 119, 154, 160, 165, 177, 213

Commons, John R., 23n8, 131, 131n1

Cooperatives, 26, 26n14, 36, 70–71, 118, 127, 132, 145, 158, 176, 178, 181, 201, 211, 213, 217–18; proposed exemption

of, 53, 61, 80, 81–84, 85, 86, 87, 91, 156, 176, 201; role of, 216
Cooperative League of the USA, 23, 65, 66, 83
Corporate farming, 161, 206–7
Cotton alliance, 89–90, 101, 125–26, 134, 135, 138, 141, 166, 192, 210, 212
Criminal penalties, concern for, 81, 81n25, 89, 91, 115, 136, 140, 146, 164, 168, 200

Datt, John, 29, 32, 34, 40, 50, 91, 92, 97, 102, 109, 110, 135, 142
Dechant, Tony, 161–62
Discriminatory practices by processors, 3, 8, 9, 10, 11, 13, 45, 90, 123, 177. See also Arkansas broiler case; Ohio tomato case
Dunkelberger, Edward, 31, 186; testimony of, 62–63, 88–89, 124, 167–68
DuVall, Leland, 8, 8n18, 9

Economic organization of agriculture: changes in, 1, 105–6, 121, 132, 208, 212, 221, 232; question of future control of, 105, 206, 211, 214, 217

Farm Bloc, 205, 217
Farm market power: quest for, 117, 201–2, 206, 219; farm unrest, 1, 106, 166
Federal Trade Commission, 2, 3, 4, 5, 18, 25, 28, 49, 66, 75, 112, 120, 125, 166; unresponsiveness of, 120, 123
Federal Trade Commission Act, 36, 125; inadequacy of, 61, 166
Ferry, Dallas K., 12n27, 67, 123
Fleming, Roger, 29, 40, 78, 135, 153
Foley, Representative Thomas, 168, 170, 171, 173, 174, 178, 193, 196
Frazier, Frank, 101, 190, 230
Freeman, Orville, 35, 55, 57, 97, 114, 131, 140, 147, 175, 181, 182, 191, 192, 194, 209, 210n6, 213; Press Club speech by, 131–32, 135, 188; shirt-sleeve conferences with, 111–12, 131; testimony of, 116–17

General farm interest organizations, 20–22, 70–72, 80n23, 207, 211, 214, 215, 216, 217, 222, 223, 230
Graham, Harry, 98, 149, 171–72, 214; testimony of, 68, 87, 119–20, 160–61
Grain trade, 136, 137, 210

Haffert, William, Jr., 58, 94, 105, 223
Hale, Ellis, 7n14, 9, 11, 57, 67, 123

Hale vs. Tyson, Arkansas Valley Industries, and Ralston Purina, 7n14, 12, 18n42,119
Hampton, Robert N., 48, 54, 92, 118, 145, 153, 154, 162–63, 172, 205
Harris, Herbert, III, 29, 32, 48, 92, 98, 110, 134, 135, 141, 143, 146, 174, 185, 186, 191
Hartley, Harold, 26, 29, 109
Healy, Patrick, 48, 83; testimony of, 66, 72, 85–86, 118
H. J. Heinz Company, 31, 32

Injunctive relief, 54, 57, 61, 76, 77, 139, 144
Johnson, President Lyndon B., 19, 147, 182, 188, 198, 201, 203
Jordan, Senator Everett, 66, 87, 102, 109, 110, 133, 137, 139, 186, 187, 204

Kennedy farm program, 20, 35
Kintner, Earl W., 63, 125, 165–66

Labor-Management Relations Act of 1947, 88
Labor-union analogy with farm action, 30, 68, 76, 86, 111, 119, 121–22, 147, 148, 161, 218, 220, 223; related legislative needs, 76, 168, 171, 177, 203
Latta, Representative Delbert, 40, 47, 48, 189, 190, 193, 195, 196, 232n25
Lausche, Senator Frank, 41, 49, 73, 94, 140, 213; testimony of, 58, 115–16
Lauterbach, Allen A., 4n5, 26, 27, 29, 32, 38n9, 48, 49, 70, 109, 135, 136, 151, 185; Houston talk, 32; testimony of, 61, 61n29, 71, 159–60
Lynn, John C., 32, 47, 74, 85, 87, 95, 96, 102, 133, 135, 141, 142, 174, 192

McAden, Wesley, 126, 135, 143
McCarthy, Senator Eugene, 49, 73, 188
McDonald, Angus, 83, 88, 120–21, 177
MacIntyre, Everett, 76, 77
Marketing orders, state and federal, 12, 28, 42, 54, 55, 132, 139, 147, 218, 219, 227
Mather, Allen F., 14n32, 17, 46, 47, 185
May, Representative Catherine, 94, 96, 99, 170, 173, 221, 221n13
Michigan Farm Bureau, 99, 160
Mondale, Senator Walter, 23n5, 119, 145, 148, 182, 188, 203, 209; proposed bargaining bill by, 119, 186, 188, 189, 191, 200, 210, 224
Murphy, William B., 60, 63

Naden, Kenneth D., 19, 36, 48, 50, 54, 55, 71, 82, 86, 92, 145, 150, 153, 181, 182; testimony of, 66

National Advisory Committee on Cooperatives, 56, 56n12, 97, 109, 153, 154, 177, 213

National Broiler Council, 56, 65, 79, 95, 101, 168–69, 190, 196, 199, 212; "Broilercade" organized by, 102

National Canners Association, 35, 42, 62, 88, 95, 100, 112, 124, 139, 167, 171, 178, 181, 185, 186, 187, 190, 196, 200, 206, 212, 221; recommended changes by, 140–42

National Commission on Food Marketing, 49, 74, 85, 97, 122, 163, 197, 205, 207, 213, 217, 231

National Council of Farmer Cooperatives, 22, 36, 37, 44, 48, 49, 50, 72, 91, 93, 145, 149, 162, 169, 170, 172, 175, 180, 186–87, 193, 199, 213, 222; proposed amendments by, 170; proposed substitute bill by, 50, 54, 66, 75; resolutions by, 37, 38. See also Coalition, American Farm Bureau Federation-National Council of Farmer Cooperatives-National Milk Producers Federation

National Grange, 20, 68, 87, 149, 193, 194, 198, 199, 213, 214

National Farmers Organization, 2, 20, 21–22, 25, 27, 39, 42, 44, 45, 46, 55, 64, 70, 82, 103, 104, 111, 121, 128, 147, 157, 163, 167, 169, 182, 193, 194, 198–99, 201, 203, 215, 219, 220, 221, 222; veto effort of, 199

National Farmers Union, 20, 22, 49, 65, 83, 120, 149, 161, 175, 177, 182, 188, 193, 203, 224

National Labor Relations Act of 1935, 54, 95, 105, 111, 119, 121, 128, 161, 177; "little Wagner act" for agriculture, 74, 101, 128

National Milk Producers Federation, 22, 36, 38, 48, 55, 66, 118, 151, 162, 165, 182, 186, 198, 199, 214, 222, 227; bargaining objectives sought by, 55; proposed substitute bill by, 66, 75. See also Coalition, American Farm Bureau Federation-National Council of Farmer Cooperatives-National Milk Producers Federation

National Tax Equality Association, 63, 89, 125, 165, 191, 232

Northwest Poultry Growers Association, 7, 8, 10, 11

Norton, E. M., 36, 38n10, 50, 72n52, 78, 214

Ohio Agricultural Marketing Association, 6, 27

Ohio Farm Bureau, 6, 25, 28, 30, 31, 40, 48, 53

Ohio tomato case, 3–6, 26, 36, 61, 75, 76, 163. See also Discriminatory practices by processors

Packers and Stockyards Administration, 7n14, 9, 10, 11, 12, 18, 120, 204; Packers and Stockyards Act, 36, 54, 55, 66; proposed amendment of, 67, 170, 188. See also United States Department of Agriculture

Parker, Joseph O., 137, 188

Poage, Representative Robert, 26, 111, 134, 137, 162, 165, 170, 172, 178, 179, 189, 191, 192, 193, 194, 195, 196, 196n40, 197, 232n25; cross-examination of witness by, 167

Pressure groups, 20, 159, 208; lobbyists for, 23

Processors' ad hoc committee, 100–101, 102, 124, 212; legislative strategy of, 129

Raisin Bargaining Association, 12, 15–17, 18, 179, 185

Resnik, Representative Joseph, 155, 157, 158, 160, 166, 213, 214n8, 219

Schnittker, John A., 77, 78, 201

Secrest, Representative Robert, 41, 47, 49, 74, 76, 81

Sherman Act of 1890, 57, 63, 76, 122

Shuman, Charles B., 25, 28, 36, 47, 53, 57, 70, 97, 135, 155, 157n9, 183, 191, 192, 203, 204, 215; disclaimer statement by, 61, 95, 124, 139, 140, 150, 163, 168, 174, 177, 180, 186, 187, 221; Princeton, New Jersey, talk, 28, 28n20; talk to National Canners Association Board, 42; testimony of, 59–60, 95, 117

Sisk, Representative B. F., 112, 179, 180, 181, 184, 186, 189, 191, 192, 195, 214

Staley, Oren Lee, 121

Stanfield, Douglas R., 27, 28, 32, 40, 50, 51, 53

Stanton, Harker, 78, 92, 138

State bargaining bills, 30–32, 74; of California, 12, 15, 16, 18, 30, 31, 32, 36, 92; of Ohio, 6, 18, 31, 32; of Oregon, 30, 31, 32

Summer, Robert, 4, 61*n*28
Swank, C. William, 5, 6
Swanton, Milo, 45–46

United States Department of Agriculture, 9, 23, 36, 54, 55, 59, 79, 84, 85, 108, 114–15, 120, 133, 147, 176, 188, 191, 193, 200, 208, 210, 227; Agricultural Stabilization and Conservation Service, 20, 224; amendments offered by, 114–15, 116, 157, 170; Consumer and Marketing Service, 84–85, 204; Farmer Cooperative Service, 59, 83, 85, 200, 204, 213, 220; legal analysis of bill by, 154, 176–77, 201. *See also* Packers and Stockyards Administration
United States House of Representatives: floor action on bill, 193–97; Committee on Agriculture, 99; executive session, 170–74, 178; hearings on bill by, 156–69; Committee on the Judiciary, 40, 41, 47, 49, 99, 127, 134; Committee on Rules, 174, 175, 179, 180–82, 185, 189
United States Senate: floor action on bill, 146; Committee on Agriculture and Forestry, June, 1966, hearing, 58–70; September, 1966, hearing, 84–90; May, 1967, hearing, 114–26; executive mark-up session, 136–46

Williams, Robert D., 14, 14*n*34

Young, Senator Milton, 49, 73, 84, 94, 145, 188; cross-examination of witness by, 68

Zwach, Representative John M., 99, 160, 178, 221*n*13